SECULAR NATIONS UNDER NEW GODS

Christianity's Subversion by Technology and Politics

The ongoing political muscle flexing of diverse Christian communities in North America raises some deeply troubling questions regarding the collective role they play in contemporary Western society. *Secular Nations under New Gods* proceeds based on a dialogue between Jacques Ellul's viewpoint on the task of Christians in the world and his interpretation of the roles of technique and the nation-state in individual and collective human life. Author Willem H. Vanderburg adds new insight into humanity as a symbolic species by arguing that we cope with our finitude by living through the myths of society and building new secular forms of moralities and religions. If everything is political and amenable to discipline-based scientific and technical approaches, Vanderburg argues, we are perhaps treating these human creations the way earlier societies did their gods: as being omnipotent, without limits. *Secular Nations* predicts that until organized Christianity becomes critically aware of sharing these commitments with Western society, it will remain entrapped in the service of false gods and will continue to turn a message of freedom and love into one of morality and prescriptive religion.

WILLEM H. VANDERBURG is the founding director of the Centre for Technology and Social Development and is now professor emeritus at the University of Toronto.

WILLEM H. VANDERBURG

Secular Nations under New Gods

Christianity's Subversion by Technology and Politics

UNIVERSITY OF TORONTO PRESS
Toronto Buffalo London

Toronto Buffalo London
utorontopress.com

ISBN 978-1-4875-0397-0 (cloth)
ISBN 978-1-4875-2303-9 (paper)

Library and Archives Canada Cataloguing in Publication

Vanderburg, Willem H., author
Secular nations under new gods : Christianity's subversion by technology and politics / Willem H. Vanderburg.

Includes bibliographical references and index.
ISBN 978-1-4875-0397-0 (cloth). – ISBN 978-1-4875-2303-9 (paper)

1. Technology – Religious aspects – Christianity. 2. Religion and politics. 3. Religion and sociology. 4. Secularism. I. Title.

BR115.T42V36 2018 261.5′6 C2018-903751-2

This book has been published with the help of a grant from the Federation for the Humanities and Social Sciences, through the Awards to Scholarly Publications Program, using funds provided by the Social Sciences and Humanities Research Council of Canada.

University of Toronto Press acknowledges the financial assistance to its publishing program of the Canada Council for the Arts and the Ontario Arts Council, an agency of the Government of Ontario.

Canada Council for the Arts
Conseil des Arts du Canada

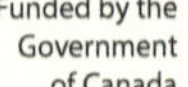

Contents

Preface

Before I can help you decide whether or not this book is for you, I need to briefly step back because its topic is one against which our life in North America has largely been poisoned. In my teenage years I entered an engineering faculty to study technology. This gradually made me realize that I was entering into a problematic relationship with a world dominated by all manner of technological gadgets, large systems that provided most of the necessities of life, and an urban habitat that may be regarded as a technical life-milieu of our own making that we had inserted into our natural life-milieu. By this I mean that my engineering mindset and its related approaches that were becoming my own were making it very difficult, if not impossible, for all of us to be ourselves, and that all our efforts to "move forward" were no longer under the control of our aspirations. I could not dismiss a growing sense that I was learning to use a tool without simultaneously learning when to put it down when another one was required for the job. Worse, neither my faculty nor the university had any answers or showed any interest in this dilemma. They were supported in all this by a society that appeared to live with its technology as if it had no limits – or at least no limits that we needed to be concerned about. Consequently, the outcome would be the same as if we had hired a contractor who was so lacking in experience that he believed his hammer was the right tool for all the different repairs that needed to be made to our home. Our society appeared to be in the grip of a kind of frenzy to increase its economic fertility, accompanied by a willingness to surrender a great deal of ourselves, to the point that we would never be able to achieve our aspirations because we were constantly adjusting them in a downward fashion.

When I admitted these kinds of reservations to others, it was not uncommon to be greeted by disbelief as to how I could possibly be so pessimistic. A few people even became hostile, accusing me of technology bashing and of wanting to go back to the dark ages. At the time I could not understand their reactions; it appeared to me that I was only asking common-sense questions as to what technology could and could not accomplish and how to respond to this situation.

To get a better grip on these dilemmas I plunged into the social sciences as soon as I had completed my doctorate in engineering. They provided me with a deeper understanding of our economic, social, political, and environmental situation, including what appeared to work well for us and what did not. At the same time, there was something unreal about it all: the works I read in the social sciences made little or no reference to science and technology, as if human life and the world at that time could be understood with minimal reference to them, while to me it appeared that our lives and our world have become unthinkable without them. The practical implication of all this was that I was completely frustrated in becoming a better engineer who knew exactly how my "tool" was affecting everything in a positive or negative manner or whether it left things relatively unaffected. From cultural anthropology and some other disciplines I did learn that the accusation of technology bashing was essentially equivalent to a taboo against touching something sacred in a traditional society. Moreover, although we had generally become increasingly aware of how everything was related to, and evolved in relation to, everything else as a consequence of the power of our technical means, all earlier societies had lived with certain entities in this interrelatedness as if they were autonomous, without limits, and thus all powerful, so as to shield them from any external influences. These entities were symbolized and lived with as a sacred or as myths in the traditional pre-industrial societies. It slowly began to dawn on me that our failure to deal with technology in a common-sense manner was the result of our having a secular religious attitude towards it, thus treating it in exactly the same way as earlier societies had dealt with their gods – gods who needed to be brought around to aiding human life by the means of a morality and a religion through which these gods were served.

The more I learned and the more I used it to take stock of who we were and where we were going, the more I was uncomfortably reminded of past societies who saw their agricultural fertility threatened by a lack of rain and who engaged in all kinds of magical and religious rituals to have their gods co-operate to grant them this rain. We used to scoff at these stories when we heard them in our Sunday school classes because we could not make any sense of them. Surely, these people would have been better off if they had developed some technology to deal with droughts directly, which could provide water for agriculture in other ways. Nevertheless, the more I learned about our own civilization, the more I could not shake the idea that such stories essentially described our problematic relationships with science, technology, the state, and politics by treating them as if they had no limits.

With a great deal of hindsight and decades of struggle, it now appears surprisingly obvious how to demonstrate the validity of the above intuitions regarding our so-called secular civilization. As will be shown in greater detail later, almost every aspect of our contemporary ways of life is organized, adapted, and improved on the basis of discipline-based approaches to scientific knowing, technical doing, and political organizing. These approaches essentially deal with human life and the world one category of phenomena at a time, since the specialists of each discipline deal with only one such category to the exclusion of all others from each domain of their disciplines. Consequently, these discipline-based approaches to human knowing, doing, and organizing have proved themselves to be spectacularly successful for dealing with situations characterized by the influence of one category of phenomena, so dwarfing the influences of all other categories that they can be neglected. These approaches are entirely unsuited to all the other situations characterized by multiple categories of phenomena making non-negligible contributions. As a result, such situations cannot be examined one category of phenomena at a time without a significant loss of understanding, which will distort the situation if we act on it by means of these discipline-based approaches.

Our problematic relationships with our most significant undertakings have thus come into focus. The kinds of situations to which discipline-based approaches are eminently suited are almost entirely found within those parts of our world that are organized like classical or information machines and everything built up with them, including the complex socio-technical systems by which we accomplish almost everything. In contrast, the kinds of situations to which discipline-based approaches cannot be applied without significant distortions and aberrations are mostly found in everything living. Any biological life is highly enfolded because the "design" of any organism is enfolded into each cell as well as expressing the architecture of all life via the DNA pool. Consequently, the architecture of life is not amenable to being divided into distinct and separate parts that can be defined on their own terms, measured, and mathematically represented, to be added to our overall understanding of that life. Its complexity is such that an overall comprehension cannot be arrived at by adding the understanding of all parts one at a time. In attempts to understand ourselves as a symbolic species, matters are even more complex because the lives of the members of a community are also dialectically enfolded by the way they are suspended in its language and culture. All this can explain how our civilization succeeds so brilliantly in some endeavours and fails so spectacularly in others. The latter may be summed up as endangering the liveability and viability of our societies as well as the life-sustaining capacities of the biosphere.

In sum, if what we truly desire is a happier, more liveable, meaningful, and purposeful life, our endless stimulation of our scientific, technical, and organizational "fertility" is without sense or purpose. Once we recognize the limitations of our discipline-based approaches, it will not be very difficult to find alternative ones in order to transcend these limits and thus complement the discipline-based approaches. We will then be able to use the discipline-based approaches where they are appropriate and use others where they are not. It is no different from having different tools in a toolbox, each eminently suited to a particular purpose that is circumscribed by limits that are overcome by other tools. Consequently, what really stands in our way is not the limitations of our endeavours as such but our secular religious attitudes towards our discipline-based approaches with which we build up our science, technology, and organizations of all kinds. It has nothing to do with philosophy or metaphysics. Take a look around you and try to identify a university doing research on finding the limits of discipline-based approaches in order to transcend them with complementary alternatives. You will not be able to find one, nor will you find such efforts in any other institutions. Once again, we live with these discipline-based approaches as if they have no limits – or at least none we need to be concerned about. We are thus no different from all the other civilizations that have preceded us whose member societies treated certain entities in their experience as godlike, that is, as being omnipotent, autonomous, and without limits, to the point that the only way to influence them was by means of religious approaches.

It has become strategically important to understand why all traditional societies, without any exceptions, symbolized some entities in the experiences of their members as godlike and thus without limits, and why this persists in our present civilization in the form of secular religious attitudes towards those human works furthest removed from anything moral or religious. Although the sociology of religion has provided us with some answers, recent developments have made it possible to go much further. Our discipline-based approaches to human knowing, doing, and organizing have largely displaced their cultural counterparts. This has had a powerful de-symbolizing effect on the symbolic cultures of our contemporary societies. It has resulted in a diminished capacity of the symbolic cultures to sustain human life. The traditional and the new media compensate for this lack by submerging everyone in a bath of images that collectively accomplish much of what customs and traditions did in earlier societies – but not by words and with a lesser existential depth. These developments have made us more aware of the complexity of our links with what we refer to as reality than have the explanations of our simplistic scientism with its objective and detached observers capable of uncovering the "facts" without any decisive internal or external influences, and so on. From the perspective of the social sciences, this capability is simply impossible. It compelled me to carefully examine our being a symbolic species, with the humanity of its members completely dependent on listening to human words in order to suspend them in a language and a culture.

The difficulty faced by any such language or culture is that it symbolizes everything in human life and the world by relating it to everything else, thus opening ourselves up to a potential chaos that could result from relativism, nihilism, and anomie. Every language and culture has dominated this threat by creating absolute points of reference based on the body of experience of a community. This experience is absolutized by essentially interpolating and extrapolating all experiences of a person into a life, and these lives of the members of a community into a way of life with a history. At the same time, the unknown is thus symbolized as more of what a community knows and lives, and this symbolization corresponds to what in disciplines such as cultural anthropology have been referred to as a sacred and myths.

All this reminded me of a parallel explanation in the opening chapters of the book of Genesis in the Jewish and Christian Bibles. The only threat to humanity, against which it was warned by God, was constituted by eating the fruit of the tree of the knowledge of good and evil. In Hebrew this latter expression can also mean "everything," with the result that what is symbolized here is also the living of human life by symbolically appropriating everything and thus refusing to live as a creature, by putting oneself in God's place. Good and evil thus have no moral or religious content, and these chapters of Genesis mount an attack against all morality, religion, and magic.

This interpretation is consistent with the entire so-called creation account and everything that follows in the Jewish and Christian Bibles. It opens by telling us that light, interpreted as "time" by early Jewish commentators, is created, and thus begins a powerful polemic against the culture that made time into a god. In the periods of creation that follow, we are told that everything that surrounds us in this universe is also created and thus not a god. The stars, the crocodile, the hippopotamus, the serpent, or anything created cannot become sacred other than through religious attitudes towards it. Hence, the creation account is also a powerful polemic against all cultures that, following the break with God, found it necessary to treat one or more created entities as being sacred, autonomous, and limitless. Consequently, faithful Jews and Christians ought to behave in ways that show that there cannot be anything sacred in this creation, while understanding from insights gained from cultural anthropology, the sociology of religion, and history that the relativity of everything in human life and in this creation imposes the necessity of struggling against the constant threat of relativism, nihilism, and anomie. Some of us cannot escape serving two masters: the living God in whom we believe and the false gods that make human life in a time, place, and culture possible. The entire Jewish and Christian Bibles speak to this dilemma.

If, at this point, you my reader are tempted to close this book because of what in North America passes for Christianity, I could hardly blame you. What the churches have collectively revealed about it is so contradictory, confusing, and judgmental, and so detached from our daily lives, that it may be difficult to imagine the possibility that it should all have been very different given this attack on morality and religion in the opening pages of the Jewish and Christian Bibles. Neither Judaism nor Christianity was supposed to fill the moral and religious needs that human life had following the break between God and a humanity that now desired to know and decide everything for itself. Hence, if my reader can bear with me for a few more paragraphs, I will briefly attempt to provide a preview of what is set out in this work as an alternate interpretation of the task of Judaism and Christianity to the benefit of all humanity, which is as strategically important today as it was in earlier days.

This task was clearly understood by a faithful remnant in Israel that was usually opposed and often even persecuted by the religious and political establishments. The role of Christianity in Western civilization, from which our global civilization was born, rarely gave any evidence that there was no possibility whatsoever of anything being sacred or godlike; and this being the case, there was a total impossibility of any absolute points of reference that could anchor a morality or a religion. In other words, Christians rarely lived in total freedom in a perfectly secular universe, with God being its creator. Given the deeply religious and moral world in which they lived, they rarely lived as if, following the break between God and humanity, this architecture of the creation became unliveable without religious enslavement. Humanity was not God, and thus every society was faced with the threat of anomie, which the Greeks understood as the impossibility of human relationships resulting from lawlessness. Anomie would result from relativism and nihilism unless absolute reference points could be created in a world in which everything was related to, and evolved in relation to, everything else, thus making everything relative. A society therefore had to spiritually name itself by means of the creation of a sacred and myths that permeated daily life by means of a morality and religion.

The early Christians found themselves in a unique situation, where they had to interpret their faith and life in relation to their Jewish roots, the Christian gospel, and the pagan cultures in which they lived. It gave them a unique iconoclastic orientation, which appears not to have lasted beyond an influx of converts from more affluent and educated strata of the societies of the Roman Empire. With this influx came a growing influence of Greek philosophy on Christianity at the expense of its Jewish roots. Nevertheless, for a time, because of the way the early Christians lived by refusing anything sacred and religious, their presence in the Roman Empire shook everything for which it stood. Eventually Rome recognized that there was no other solution but to make Christianity the official religion of its empire – but when Christians accepted this, Christianity was lost. It simply became another religion and morality serving the sacred and the myths that societies needed to provide life with absolute meaning, direction, and purpose. Christianity thus became dedicated to absolutizing those entities in human experience that were so important and essential that without them this life would simply be unimaginable and unliveable: How would people live, how would they do anything, and what would their world be like without these entities? It was as if these entities had created human life and the world to be who and what they were. They were the greatest good a community could know, were therefore sacralized as such, and were related to by means of gods and idols appeased by a religion and a morality. In this way the institutionalized Christian church became the sacred of the medieval societies of Western Europe. It completely ignored the orientation of its gospel, which taught that the only religion acceptable to God was to serve the weakest and most vulnerable members of society, as is evident from the letter of James and the parables of the kingdom of heaven, for example.

We have become so accustomed to the idea that we live in secular mass societies that we have not bothered to investigate whether there continue to be sacred entities in our midst. Had the Jewish and Christian communities understood the opening chapters of Genesis (and especially their reinforcement by Qohelet) with the hindsight of the history of the Jewish people, the course of events in North America during the last few centuries might have been entirely different – and this most likely would have been the case in Europe as well. The Jewish and Christian presence would have been one that refused anything sacred, omnipotent, or limitless. However, this does not mean that these communities would have "bashed" science, technology, the state, and politics any more than the early Christians bothered to "bash" the gods of the Roman Empire. Their behaviour was a great deal more disturbing than that, and it unsettled the societies of their time. As a result, today's Jews and Christians would have recognized that the discipline-based approaches to scientific knowing are very effective within their limits, but that beyond these limits they treat everything as being non-living. Consequently, it would have become obvious that this approach to scientific knowing could be extremely destructive beyond its limits of validity. The same is true for technology. The discipline-based approaches to human doing are very powerful within their limits and equally destructive outside of them, where they have created almost all the crises by which we are surrounded today. It is no different than the previously referred to contractor who hammers away at everything. Our banging away at everything with our discipline-based approaches is also making a big mess within everything living. In sum, our secular religious attitudes to science and technology have robbed us of our ability to behave sensibly in a truly secular creation.

It would appear that Jews and Christians need to reinterpret what they understand by religion and morality, while at the same time we all need to rethink our sociological and historical conceptions of religion, which had their roots in the interpretations of Karl Marx, Max Weber, and others. Had Judaism and Christianity lived by the first three promises of the Decalogue, these communities would have demonstrated how we can maintain our freedom in relation to our most powerful works and avoid becoming enslaved to them. It is but one aspect of the way in which Christianity addresses every aspect of our lives, making its reduction to an enslaving morality and religion the antithesis of itself. All this takes us right back to God's setting aside the Jewish people for this task. Following their liberation from slavery, he gave them permission to live without gods, without idols, and thus without morality and religion, and took the necessary steps to make this possible. Instead, the Decalogue itself was quickly turned into a morality and a religion.

God had made new life possible by restoring a relationship between himself and his people to the extent that they would permit it. With the incarnation, this link became permanent and could never be eliminated; the architecture of the creation in terms of the fundamental relationships between God, humanity, and the creation was changed for all time.

This "structural" dimension of Christianity was entirely eliminated when it was engulfed by the upheavals that accompanied industrialization, urbanization, and so-called secularization. As we will show later in greater detail, Christianity became split into two streams. One stream was so bewildered by the turmoil and the tremendous suffering unleashed by these developments that it clung to the "vertical" dimension of Christianity at the expense of the "horizontal" dimension, thus separating the two great commandments that jointly summed up everything. There was an emphasis on our relationship with God through Bible-reading, prayer, and devotional activities at the expense of everything else. Its significance can readily be explained by using a biblical metaphor in which Jews and Christians are to bear the Light of the revelation as a lamp illuminating their way in a world of darkness. The lamp they carry represents the Light in so far as they have understood it. Consequently, conservative Christians made their lamps almost into ends in themselves, and by concentrating on their lamps their eyes grew accustomed to them as opposed to the dark world that they no longer actively illuminated. They promptly lost their way and became irrelevant in terms of their roles as Light, yeast, or salt for the world, to use other biblical metaphors.

In contrast, the liberal stream was so concerned about the turmoil and the suffering it had caused during the early phase of industrialization, urbanization, and so-called secularization, that it found it necessary to emphasize the second great commandment dealing with the "horizontal" dimension associated with relationships among people. Their lamps were thus affected in another way, one that initially helped them understand the world, but they quickly did the equivalent of putting their lamps down in order to free both hands to be more effectively of help in the world. Soon they moved out of range of their lamps and also lost their way in the world.

Simply put, the conservative stream of Christianity opened itself up to becoming assimilated by the way of their society, which they essentially complemented by filling a supposed void with a Christian morality and religion. The liberal stream of Christianity opened itself up to the way of its society by contributing what it perceived was the social good so urgently needed in the turmoil and suffering all around it, in the context of which people once again had to learn to be their brothers' and sisters' keepers. In neither stream were the lamps used to illuminate the way of God in the world, and over time their ways became essentially indistinguishable from the cultural way of their society. This resulted in everyone serving two masters: the secular sacred and myths of a society, and God. Both streams, each in its own way, lived as if they could have both good and evil and thus have it all. This serving of two masters continues to characterize our situation today. Only if Jews and Christians walk with their lamps to light their ways in a dark world are they able to be in the world but not of the world, and only thus can they transform the world by being what yeast is to dough and salt is to food. Today this kind of integral Christianity is almost entirely missing in North America. For this reason my analysis concludes that the Christian presence in North America is a false one. It also means that the creation of new secular sacreds and myths to shield contemporary societies from relativism, nihilism, and anomie has gone unchallenged by the presence of people who ought to have been completely indifferent to anything sacred or religious, and who by their presence ought to have called everything into question.

If my reader is still with me, I invite you to embark on a journey that has left none of my received ideas standing. I trust it may do the same for you because beyond them you will most likely encounter something infinitely more beautiful and liveable. This journey represents a dialogue between a number of passages from the Jewish and Christian Bibles and the new awareness of ourselves as a symbolic species under the enormous pressure of de-symbolization – an awareness that has lifted the veil on our claims of being secular. We, as members of a symbolic species, interact with the Jewish and Christian Bibles in ways that are necessarily reciprocal in character. With our human words we inevitably project something on these texts, but, by the Spirit, these texts may create something new in us that is greater than what our human words can contain. Moreover, because we read these texts as a revelation from a transcendent God, they represent something radically other than the way of our culture. There is always, however, a strong possibility of what Devereux examined as counter-transference reactions, through which we reduce the anxiety and tension that results from coming in contact with something that threatens all our received ideas and our lives. At the same time, this reciprocal interaction can also help us to become more aware of what we are projecting on the text as we read it in the language and culture in which we are suspended. Such a reading thus confronts the two masters we inevitably serve. The complexity of this relationship will be developed further in this work.

In sketching the scope and aim of this work, I cannot suppress the sentiment of being back in graduate school and having just proposed a near impossible thesis project to my supervisor. In case my reader shares this feeling, I should explain that the present work seeks to elaborate what may be regarded as a kind of "intellectual base map" of what is happening to individual and collective human life in an increasingly global civilization at the beginning of the twenty-first century. This map was previously developed by "re-symbolizing" the findings of discipline-based approaches through a dialectical reinterpretation of the meaning and significance of each finding relative to all the others. This was done in dialogue with broader interdisciplinary studies that had attempted to create alternative base maps of how everything in human life is related to, and evolves in relation to, everything else. Such maps were implicit in all the great classical works such as those of Karl Marx, Max Weber, Arnold Toynbee, and, most recently, Jacques Ellul. The present work seeks to enrich this intellectual base map by filling in the critically important role played by our secular religious attitudes towards our most powerful and successful creations and how, especially in North America, Christianity has become enslaved to them. This work thus continues a kind of intellectual ecumenism aimed at overcoming the fragmentation of our knowing and doing by discipline-based approaches.

I began the development of this base map as a post-doctoral fellow in France under Jacques Ellul. It contained societies and civilizations as the cultural entities of human history prior to the emergence of discipline-based approaches. When it was completed, we agreed that it was entirely implicit in Ellul's own work. Its publication was followed by four volumes that jointly examined the evolving relationship between technique and culture. *Technique* refers to the system of discipline-based approaches for knowing, doing, economic growing, and political organizing, and *culture* refers to the alternative approaches by which we make sense of and live in the world by symbolizing everything in human experience via a language and everything associated with its acquisition. With my engineering background, I was able to establish detailed "sub-maps" of the inner workings of technique, since it may be argued that the engineering discipline is to technique what the discipline of physics is to science.

The intellectual base map elaborated in this volume also builds on Jacques Ellul's interpretation of Christianity as a non-religion and a non-morality, which he illuminated by examining the relevant parts of the Jewish and Christian Bibles. These studies were an integral part of his reading the Bible with students and colleagues who had approached him with existential questions that were triggered by events in their lives and by following his courses or reading his publications. During the time that I was able to attend these discussions, the groups were carefully balanced between Protestant, Catholic, Jewish, and agnostic participants. I found these discussions so helpful and so unlike anything I had heard in churches that I urged Jacques Ellul to publish the presentations he made to these groups for the purpose of drawing together our discussions. He was reluctant to do so until we met for the last time about a year before his death, when he knew he would be unable to do it himself, and he gave me permission to proceed. This resulted in a two-volume intellectual base map of his understanding of Christianity, which has also profoundly influenced the present work. His interpretation of Christianity as a non-religion and a non-morality would shock many people, but it is partly rooted in the works of Søren Kierkegaard and Karl Barth, and the very possibility was acknowledged by some agnostic thinkers, including Karl Marx. Of course, this interpretation pulls the rug out from under much of institutionalized and politicized Christianity in North America, making it highly controversial with so much at stake.

To reach out to as many readers as possible, I did what I could to make this volume understandable to people who have not read the above seven volumes and who may not be familiar with the work of Jacques Ellul. Doing so involved some difficult strategic choices as to what parts of the intellectual base map to include and which sub-maps could simply be referenced for readers interested in the interrelatedness of some of its "parts." It was, without doubt, the most complex interdisciplinary task that I have tackled thus far. Hence, I was delighted when two of my anonymous reviewers explicitly stated that I had made this volume readable by itself. However, my strategic choices had two unavoidable consequences. Since the references I chose were designed to support readers seeking to inquire into important segments of the "map" that had to be left relatively undetailed, these references have been largely limited to the above seven volumes, the work of Jacques Ellul, and the scholarship this produced. It turns out that much of the scholarship based on the work of Jacques Ellul is not very helpful for reasons that become apparent from Frédéric Rognon's interviews with some sixty scholars who were influenced by Ellul. Simply put, much of this body of scholarship neither elaborates nor evolves the intellectual base map, especially for the developments that occurred after Ellul's death. Generally speaking, this also applies to the biblical scholarship carried out in particular denominational contexts.

It is via the sub-maps to which the references primarily refer that this work is connected to the broader literature.[1] The sub-maps generally require a re-symbolization that encounters a variety of intellectual obstacles because the architecture of the findings of discipline-based approaches is fundamentally different from that of their alternatives, as Benson Snyder's distinction between numeracy and literacy helps to explain. Moreover, numeracy is separated from experience and culture, while literacy is embedded in them, which has led to distinctions in the literature such as that between "intuitive physics" and "school physics." These kinds of reinterpretations were thus much more integral to the works referred to in the references than to the present volume and the reader should consult the works cited for specific entry points into the broader literature.

The second unavoidable consequence of my strategic decision to make this volume as readable as possible on its own was the difficulty of including specific page numbers in these references. They point to descriptions of sub-maps and patterns of connections. Consequently, when these descriptions are entirely contained within one chapter, I indicated this; but in most cases the context of the entire reference is indispensable.

I trust that this work continues the spirit of my French mentor, Jacques Ellul, who was always much more interested in dialogue with students who understood his work but disagreed with him, than with those who understood it but took it no further, as if it answered all questions. I have always told my students that what I fear most as a teacher is to discover something I have overlooked or misinterpreted that could call my entire intellectual life into question. The possibility of wasting your life and that of your students in this way ought to make us do all we can to remain "intellectual extroverts," constantly interested in dialogue. In sum, the strategic choices I made in relation to this work and its references were done to support *informed* dialogue.

My greatest debt is obviously to Jacques Ellul, who is among the few intellectuals using their lamps to understand human life (including his own) and our world while at the same time questioning the possibility of this understanding being imposed on the very texts that fuel his lamp. This includes the counter-transference reactions that are unavoidable when our secular sacred collides with and is challenged by what is holy (what is set apart by God for his work of reconciliation and the making of all things new). Since his lamp is not the Light itself, my responsibility and that of my reader is to make their own discernment of his and my interpretations. Another model for living with and thinking with the Light as a lamp for understanding our life and our world is that of Søren Kierkegaard, who I understand less well. Apart from these two Christian thinkers, I am not aware of any other models of this approach, but this may be my own limitation.

I am also deeply indebted to the translations of the Jewish and Christian Bibles into French by André Chouraqui. I know of no English equivalent. He translated the Hebrew, and the Greek rooted in it, as closely as the French language permits. There are several other such attempts in the French language: they are partial translations but equally helpful for this work. I know from experience how difficult translation work is, but I am disturbed by our modern English translations of the Jewish and Christian Bibles, which all too often completely veil the meaning of the text with readable and eloquent contemporary English prose. For example, most translations of Revelation 21:8 speak of people being thrown into the burning lake (the second death). However, the Greek words are in the neuter and thus designate the evil they have committed, rather than the people themselves, that is being thrown into the lake of fire. These kinds of errors have greatly contributed to the interpretation of Christianity as a morality and a religion. This problem can be further illustrated by examining the extent to which words added in the translation that do not appear in the Hebrew text are the result of the kind of counter-transference reactions of a time, place, and culture that will be discussed in this work. Our modern translations show a disturbing lack of respect for these texts that the Jews and Jewish Christians so painstakingly put together, edited, and presented to the people – who discerned them as a Word from God.

This attitude stands in complete opposition to the confidence that Jesus displayed in these texts. This disrespect is also practised by a great many Christians today, whose reading of the English translation is so literal and simplistic that they would not even read a letter from a friend in this way. Worse, they do not hesitate to lift particular texts out of their context in order to use them to create a particular effect of piety, or as "spiritual bullets" aimed at destroying the arguments of those with whom they disagree. It is time to remind ourselves of some Rabbinic humour, which held that every text has seventy explanations plus the one that only God knows. Hence, our best attempts at understanding any text will always fall short of its true and full meaning. One day I will know how much of this book was wheat and how much of it was tares, to use a biblical metaphor.[2]

I would like to thank my anonymous reviewers for their helpful suggestions and for making me realize the need to make explicit my strategic choices for this work and its references. My special thanks go to Rita Vanderburg, who once again copy-edited this manuscript prior to sending it to the publisher. I am also grateful to Hannah and Justin Wong, who word-processed my dictated manuscript and to Hannah, who prepared the index. It is always a humbling experience to then turn over the manuscript to a professional copy-editor. I am deeply grateful to Angela Wingfield for further clarifying the text and making changes where it triggered misunderstandings that I ought to have prevented. These final touches have undoubtedly lightened the task of my readers. Finally, I wish to thank the volunteers of PAL-Reading Services, especially for recording André Chouraqui's translations, which were indispensable for this work.

Bill Vanderburgh
Peterborough, Ontario

SECULAR NATIONS UNDER NEW GODS

Christianity's Subversion by Technology and Politics

Introduction

A Secular Way of Life in Search of Spirituality?

In North America we all live more or less as if we are members of secular mass societies to which we seek to add our own individual "spirituality." For example, those of us who have our roots in Western European societies may turn to Judaism or Christianity for our morality and religion, of a more or less conservative or liberal kind depending on our interpretations of our Bibles. Those of us who have our roots in other civilizations may attempt much the same thing by means of other religious traditions such as Islam, Buddhism, and Hinduism. Still others of us attempt to add a more neutral spirituality or live out of deep political convictions.

During an earlier time in human history, such a plurality of moral, religious, and political traditions would have been both rare and unstable because of religious intolerance. As a matter of fact, a significant number of us had ancestors who fled this kind of intolerance to find religious freedom in North America. The reason our current situation is relatively rare socially and historically can perhaps be found in our having something religious in common that goes much deeper in terms of the influence it has on our persons and our own lives, namely, the secular religious attitudes we share towards science, technology, the state, politics, and history. Whether or not this is the case can be tested by conducting the following inquiries.

For decades I have explored these secular religious attitudes by asking professional audiences as well as my students in engineering, sociology, and environmental studies to make a list of subjects that we will never be able to know scientifically, no matter how many gifted researchers we assign to the task and back with all the necessary resources. After a long pause interspersed with a few silly answers, I was usually obliged to take things further by inquiring whether this implied that science is our secular god who is omnipotent in the domain of human knowing, much like the traditional gods were in their jurisdictions. Since these kinds of encounters happened mostly in Toronto, which is one of the most multicultural cities in the world, many members of the audience still knew enough about their traditional cultural inheritance to become profoundly uncomfortable by this suggestion. Science is not supposed to have any limits; if it did, our universities as well as many other institutions would have failed to do their jobs. They rely entirely on our scientific approaches to knowing, which would be impossible if these had any limits. In such a case, these institutions would have to devote considerable effort and resources to the discovery of such limits as a first step to developing alternative approaches that would be capable of transcending these limits. Since this is not happening, we live with science as if it had no limits, much as earlier societies lived with their traditional gods.

The discussion was continued by next asking what technology will never be able to deliver for us, and consequently what alternative means need to be developed. The responses were usually very similar to those received to the question about the limits of science. The audience was then asked how they would like to do business with a contractor, to make some repairs on their home, who had so little experience that he believed his hammer could do almost everything. Of course, by this time some members in the audience recognized that the same situation occurs as with science because technology has also been organized by means of disciplines. We will later show that the crises faced by our civilization can almost always be attributed to the limitations imposed by these discipline-based approaches to technology.

Finally, the audience was asked for examples of situations and difficulties that cannot and never will be amenable to political solutions. Once again, it was clear that most people found it very difficult to come up with any examples. Does this mean that we live as if the state were omnipotent? Do we live with this institution as a secular god served by a secular political religion?

It is more than a little unsettling that we appear to have so little awareness of the limitations of our scientific, technological, and political undertakings while we believe that we live in secular mass societies. It has plunged all our lives into profound moral and religious contradictions, to the point that we may well ask ourselves who we really are and what we are doing.

Where Are We and What Have We Done?

The questions "Where are we?" and "What have we done?" are not intended to be an open door to any kind of metaphysics. On the contrary, they are an invitation for readers to join me in exploring what may be truly happening to our lives, our communities, and our planet beyond our widely shared impressions. What I have in mind may perhaps be analogous to what has been referred to as a life review, in which people near death relive their lives. This experience has little in common with simply remembering life's events. Those who, for whatever reasons, did not pass into death and were able to tell others about such experiences, appear to agree that this recollection of the events of their lives went much further than their mere memories. For example, in their dealings with others, they became aware of how they had truly affected these people, and, in many cases, this would have been unbearably disturbing were it not for an enveloping sensation of its taking place in the context of a loving and reassuring light. According to what we currently understand of the way we symbolize our experiences as moments of our lives and how these lives in turn are symbolized in the context of a time, place, and culture, it is possible to think of this in terms of the neural and synaptic connections that make up the organization of people's brain-minds and are being weakened in the face of death along with all the other biological functions that are shutting down. If this were indeed the case, it would mean that all metaconscious knowledge implied in the organization of people's brain-minds, including the deepest forms usually referred to as myths in cultural anthropology, was dropping out of people's lives and thus making room for something else before the moment of death. These myths may thus be thought of as veiling the experiences of their lives in order to make them liveable and bearable.

When we regard this situation from the perspective of collective human life, we can take the example of humanity having declared its contemporary ways of life as being unsustainable by the biosphere. It amounts to an acknowledgment that we are slowly but surely destroying what sustains all life on this planet. We appear to veil this situation by living as if this were not the case. What is happening in engineering and management schools is all too typical. There is plenty of talk about sustainable practices, but the fundamental structure of the curriculum has not changed for more than half a century. Similarly, our economic practices have not undergone a profound mutation, as if we collectively recognized the need for a kind of "intellectual conversion" to produce a new intelligence by which we could make sense of and live in the world – an intelligence that is capable of understanding how we have backed ourselves into this corner and which points us towards radically other ways of life. Equally significantly, we are well aware of a growing incidence of anxiety and depression in the members of each new generation, which could be correlated with a parallel inability of contemporary ways of life to sustain the lives of the people who live by them, as a consequence of not providing the necessary meaning, direction, and purpose for their lives. We have either a mistaken awareness of the liveability and sustainability of our civilization or an awareness of ourselves and the world that is enslaved to what threatens all life and our planet. Surely what ought to have emerged is an awareness of how we have collectively backed ourselves into a corner and that we must take responsibility for it by changing course.

If we are serious about embarking on an investigation of what is happening to our lives, our communities, and our planet, and not getting trapped into some kind of metaphysics, ideology, or secular political religion, perhaps the best way to proceed is by using a comparative approach as to where we are as a civilization and where we are going in relation to where humanity was going and what it was doing by means of earlier cultures. Cultures should be understood as possibly the most important creations of our symbolic species because they allow the members of a group or society to make sense of and live in the world in a way that affects individual and collective human life on the deepest levels of freedom or alienation. Such a comparative approach can then set the stage for an inquiry into how all this might change if there were a God, and if that God introduced something into contemporary cultures that was not merely another of their own creations but something entirely other. As such, we will attempt to compare people of a time, place, and culture with people of a time, place, and universal technical order, and both of them to a "people of the Word" living in either situation. It will thus become evident that, as a consequence of de-symbolization primarily driven by our growing dependence on discipline-based approaches to knowing and doing as well as to economic growing and political organizing, we are endangering everything that has made us human until now: as a symbolic species making sense of and living in the world by means of symbolization, experience, and cultures. Doing so used to make it possible to live in a creation in which everything was related to and evolved in relation to everything else and did so collectively within a dependence on a Creator.

Seeing and Listening

Following a five-volume study of our civilization, including the link between its spectacular successes and equally important failures,[1] I would sum up our situation as follows: We are essentially re-engineering everything by means of our contemporary ways of life, which rely on technical approaches for improving everything, where we used to rely on cultural approaches for doing so. Our successes are a consequence of technical approaches, while our failures are a consequence of our dwindling dependence on cultural approaches. We are now fitting ourselves more and more into a technical order, while in the past we would fit everything into a cultural order. The technical order is the "architecture" of our modern world, while the cultural orders were once the "architectures" of the worlds of traditional societies. Our participation in contemporary ways of life is based on a knowing and a doing that have been entirely reorganized by means of scientific and technical disciplines, whereas this knowing and doing in the past was based on symbolization, experience, and culture.

These changes are affecting everything, including our languages. In the past, human languages had the architecture that corresponded to the cultural orders by which people made sense of and lived in the world. Today language is trapped between the technical order with an incompatible architecture and the fragmented remains of a highly de-symbolized cultural order in our personal lives with family, friends, and acquaintances. It has been argued that a new kind of "plastic" words is spreading into our languages,[2] but this will almost certainly turn out to be a symptom of what is happening to us on a much deeper level. Our languages have been relegated to the service of images, while in the past images served human languages.[3]

Human life within a technical order mostly depends on seeing. It dominates what we apprehend by hearing, language, and culture, which is the reverse of what is typical for human life in a cultural order. People living in contemporary societies receive little guidance and support from their highly de-symbolized cultures. They have come to rely more on images of what others are doing and correspondingly less on talking to them about their lives. They scan what everyone else is doing and saying for clues to how they should behave in order to fit in and "go with the flow." The result is a statistical morality that is largely displacing its tradition-based equivalent, and public opinion is being substituted for private opinion (which requires reading, thinking, and critical discussion). These developments fundamentally depend on the traditional media and increasingly on the internet-based ones. These immerse people in a bath of images that collectively perform the equivalent functions of customs, traditions, and cultures in the past.[4] These images show them what they must know to get on with their lives: what they must wear, eat, drink, drive, consume, and know about their world, what insurances the informed people have, what the smart people ask their doctors, what the experts think of everything and anything, and a great deal more about how others cope with daily life.

The contacts with others are similarly affected. The usual ways of meeting others are largely supplanted by immersion in the Facebooks and Twitters of the internet. A great deal of emphasis is placed on what we can visually learn about others, and what we can orally learn by speaking to them face to face is becoming less frequent and, by implication, less important. From an abundance of potential contacts, selections are made on the basis of visual impressions accompanied by self-advertising. Dialogues may begin with the people "behind" these impressions, but these are mediated by the internet, which filters out a great deal of what would be available from face-to-face encounters. Moreover, they are initially driven by the image-dominant prejudgments of others, which may affect one's interpretation of what is learned about the other person's life that is behind it all. What we learn visually about the other may well turn out to be completely different when these first impressions are placed in the full context of their lives, to which we have access only by talking to one another.

These elementary observations are indicative of the differences between human life in a technical order and human life in a cultural order. The architecture of the technical order corresponds to how we apprehend the world by means of seeing. Visually, the world presents itself to us as made up of many constituents, each existing in its own space and time. No contradiction is possible: something is either a tree or a cloud, farmland or a river, and so on. Each constituent can be separated from all the others, and this abstraction does not lead to any loss in understanding. Similarly, each constituent can be defined on its own terms independently from any other constituent. It can be measured, quantified, and mathematically represented. Finally, the complexity of this world is thus a simple one; it can be arrived at by adding one constituent at a time, and the sequence of doing so is immaterial. In sum, the architecture of the world we apprehend by seeing may be expressed in terms of the principles of non-contradiction, separability, closed definitions, mathematical representation, and a simple complexity.[5] The implication of this architecture is that the visual order can be "assembled" from its constituent elements, much as a machine can be assembled from pre-existing separate parts.

Now imagine making holographic images of what people are looking at. The architecture of these images would be entirely different. No matter how small a portion of the image we select, the entire image can be retrieved from it. There is only a loss of resolution as the portion selected is diminished in size. In other words, the whole is enfolded into each part, and each part is an expression of the whole. In a somewhat analogous fashion, traditional cultures took what was apprehended by means of language as the primary order, which gave a meaning and value to the order that was visually perceived. Nevertheless, their coexistence was an uneasy one because human life in a symbolic universe has a dialectically enfolded order, while the visually perceived reality "behind" it has an order with diametrically opposite characteristics. The symbolization of human life in the world has five dimensions of experience corresponding to the five senses, with additional dimensions of experience corresponding to what people perceive of what is happening in their bodies and brain-minds. Among all these dimensions of experience, the visual one does not quite fit into the others and could even challenge them. For example, what people perceive is instantly available at a glance. This is not the case with language and culture. A listener must wait for the speaker to complete a series of words before the meaning can be grasped. When danger looms, the warning to "look out!" may suffice to have visual perception take over. In other situations this is not the case. This helps us to understand why, in many traditional cultures, numbers had first and foremost a symbolic significance and only secondarily a function related to measuring and quantifying. In contrast, the visual representations of the gods were often used to have this visual religious experience dominate all the rest.[6] Since all human knowing and doing is relative as opposed to being absolute, the most effective way to further our understanding of what is happening in our lives and our world is to study humanity living in a technical order relative to humanity living in a cultural order, and vice versa. Such a comparative approach remains incomplete because the unfolding of humanity's symbolic potential results in people's being of a time, place, and culture if no significant de-symbolization intervenes. De-symbolization occurs when our ability to relate everything to everything else – and, over time, when the way in which everything adapts to everything else – is constrained and limited in some way.

People of a Time, Place, and Culture

The unfolding of the potential of a symbolic species begins with the biological potential. An embryo grows by stem cells containing this potential in the form of the DNA. They become heart cells, lung cells, liver cells, and every kind of cell necessary to build the tissues, organs, and everything else required to form a human body. The potential of our species is thus enfolded into each "part," and each one of these parts is an expression of that potential. It is then unfolded by the brain that is growing its genetically provided and limited organization by symbolizing every experience through neural and synaptic additions and modifications, thereby transforming it into the organization of the brain-mind. It symbolizes a person's social self and life. These are always working in the background of any lived experience, thereby transforming it into a moment of a person's life. In this way, growing up is synonymous with learning to make sense of and live in the world, and with unfolding one's symbolic potential by acquiring the culture of a community. It is an entry into a symbolic universe that is artificial, that is, a culturally created world, which is very different from those lived in by animals with non-symbolic cultures.

The architectures of the cultural orders of the symbolic universes created by the groups, societies, and civilizations of our symbolic species have the characteristics of a dialectically enfolded whole. Since the unfolding of the limited organization of the brain into the organization of the brain-mind of a member of our symbolic species has been described in great detail elsewhere,[7] I will limit myself to a few highlights of how it grows as a result of living a life.

Following the formation of the cortex, babies appear to be able to hear the heartbeat and breathing rhythms of their mothers. It may also be possible that some external sounds contribute to the growth of the brain-mind. Following birth, babies are able to make little sense of their surroundings and thus relate to them in only the most elementary ways. For example, they are able to follow something moving with their eyes, but they have to learn to focus on it. Similarly, they have as yet no awareness of their physical selves. All this and more is learned by unfolding this limited ability to make sense of and live in the world into what is made possible by means of the culture of their community.

Initially, a baby's "world" is limited to his or her physical surroundings. By the differentiation of babies' experiences and the integration of them into their lives, the organizations of their brain-minds begin to constitute a metalanguage, in the context of which certain words can make sense and become vocal signs. With the onset of language, a double referencing system develops in which these local signs continue to be differentiated via the metalanguage but also gradually become directly differentiated from all other elements of what is becoming the child's language. This development manifests itself by toddlers being able to transcend their immediate surroundings by learning to experience a kind of language foreground that no longer needs to have anything in common with the background of the situation in which the communication takes place. In other words, toddlers may begin to have a sense of what their mothers mean, for example, when their mothers respond to their fussing by saying that soon they will be home and then they will get something to eat.

At first, the unfolding of the symbolic potential of human babies is entirely metaconscious and shows itself only in a growing ability to make sense of and relate to others and their surroundings. With the onset of language, this unfolding becomes much more accessible to others. For example, when the attention of toddlers is attracted by whatever moves above them in the sky, they may first differentiate this from what is stationary such as tall trees or buildings. The corresponding experiences will help build a metalanguage in the context of which the pointing by others and their use of the word *bird* begin to make sense. The word becomes a vocal sign, and one day they may excitedly point to a small plane and say, "Big bird." When others insist that it is not a bird but a plane, toddlers may take another careful look at it. Gradually the complexity of what moves above them in the sky will unfold into birds and everything else; then birds, planes, and everything else; still later, birds, planes, kites, and everything else; and so on. What the toddlers learn is relative. They learn something of what moves relative to what is stationary; something about birds relative to planes, and something about planes relative to birds; then something about birds relative to kites, something about planes relative to kites, and vice versa. In this way an ever greater complexity unfolds itself from a simpler complexity.

These kinds of developments are created everywhere in the lives of toddlers and children. For example, they may first experience cats and dogs as essentially alike from a distance. When they play with them, however, these animals quickly turn out to be very different from one another. This may attract attention to their features so that the children are able to recognize them at a distance and be better prepared for interacting with them. They may also be assisted by the way others talk about what the animals are doing. Thus, what initially may have been undifferentiated experiences of playing with cats-dogs will break up into the experiences of cats and those of dogs, since they have been found to be essentially different in ways that matter for children's lives. Once again, the children have learned about dogs relative to cats and about cats relative to dogs. This differentiation is nested in all the other differentiations out of which it came.

In this manner a relatively simple complexity of relationships with others and the world unfolds into an ever greater complexity as this differentiation grows and is integrated into their lives. They gradually enter into the symbolic universe of the culture of their community. The way they differentiate its constituent elements increasingly converges with that of the other members of their community. The cultural orders of the symbolic universes of traditional groups and societies thus constitute a very different kind of architecture whose principles are the diametrical opposite of non-contradiction, separability, closed definitions, mathematical representation, and a simple complexity. A language, as well as the symbolic universe it maps, has an architecture that is characterized by every constituent element's being dialectically enfolded into all the others. Simply put, the meaning of a word is directly differentiated from those that most resemble it and, via these, from all the others. To sum up, a particular situation that children have learned to respond to and live with in a certain way can, on the basis of subsequent experiences, become symbolically differentiated as two or more kinds of situations whose differences are crucial. The unfolding of their symbolic potential thus grows the complexity of the kinds of relationships that children can make sense of and deal with in their lives. Two words or phrases that appear to have essentially similar meanings up to a certain point may thus unfold into two or more distinct words or phrases, as what they symbolize turn out to have differences that children have discovered to be significant. The meaning of each word or phrase thus enfolds something of the meanings of all the others that children have learned to differentiate at this point in their lives. Everything they hear and speak becomes part of the symbolic elements of the language of their community. Learning a language is, therefore, inseparable from acquiring a culture and entering into its symbolic universe.

In traditional groups and societies the visual dimension of experience was mostly subject to the oral one, with the result that the image served the word and not the other way around. The meaning as well as the value of everything was established by differentiating it from everything else and by integrating all this into a life. This meaning and value symbolized its place and significance in a person's life. Life was lived in a way that was individually unique and culturally typical and thus had a subjective as well as a culturally objective dimension.

As human languages develop by the previously noted double referencing system, a symbolic universe is not limited to what is presented to the senses. In contrast, animal cultures are limited in this way. The symbolic universes entered into by human languages contain a great many constituents that are entirely artificial, that is, cultural as opposed to natural in character. For example, the symbolic universes of traditional societies contained institutions, a morality, and the gods of a religion. The technical order of what we call reality contains artificial elements: corporations with a limited liability, patents, currencies, nation-states, and a great deal else. Traditional societies always inserted a symbolic universe between everything that presented itself to the senses of its members and an ultimately unknowable world and universe that lay beyond it and from which an endless flow of new discoveries and relationships entered into it.

Every symbolic culture was thus obliged to deal with the threat of the unknown. No culture could avoid addressing it head on. After all, the unfolding of the potential of a symbolic species resulted in individual and collective human life being lived relative to the dialectically enfolded symbolic universe of a culture. Since the meaning and value of everything within that symbolic universe was essentially what all the other meanings and values were not, everything was related to everything else in a way that left it open to the possibility of this life coming into the grip of relativism, nihilism, and anomie. Given that the members of any human society have always differed on a great many things, it would not be long before some would intuit a certain arbitrariness in the way their culture made sense of and ordered life in the world. An ultimate reference point and orientation was required, but this could come from within a culture or from beyond it. Without any exceptions (including the attempts to create Jewish, Christian, or Muslim societies), cultures have always dealt with the threat of relativism, nihilism, and anomie by symbolizing the unknown as more of what their members already knew and lived. In other words, everything that remained to be discovered and lived would simply turn out to be "interpolation" and "extrapolations" of what was known and lived. Metaconsciously, this corresponds to the organization of people's brain-minds symbolizing the gaps between the moments of their lives as more of these lives to be lived in the future. It may be compared to our fitting a curve through experimental data, which greatly strengthens our confidence in the experiment because this is how we expect the world to behave according to our prior experience. In the same way, the organization of people's brain-minds symbolized the unknown by interpolating and extrapolating their experiences into moments of their lives, and these moments into complete lives in complete worlds. The threat of the unknown is thus eliminated, and people can confidently proceed with their lives without ever having to play the thought experiments of some philosophers who had attempted to radically doubt their own existence and that of the world in which they lived. The symbolization of the unknown forms the deepest metaconscious knowledge implied in the organization of people's brain-minds. This mostly corresponds to what in disciplines such as cultural anthropology, the sociology of religion, and depth psychology are called myths, with the central myth being commonly referred to as the sacred.[8]

Before these myths begin to form in teenage children, the threat of the unknown is initially countered with a playful attitude to the world. For example, when toddlers go for a walk with their parents in a new neighbourhood, they may confidently run ahead, knowing that at any time they can turn around and count on their parents to help them out of any difficulties. If they get too far ahead and their parents are delayed by talking to someone they have met on the street, these children may burst into tears when they turn around and do not see their parents. At this point the unknown neighbourhood may become a threat. Toddlers happily explore the world when they are enveloped in the loving care of their parents and others. In other words, when they have learned to differentiate birds and planes from everything else in the sky, the "everything else" represents an unknown of undifferentiated stimuli that cannot as yet take a place in their lives. They do not yet have the ability to establish a meaningful relationship with this unknown and thus integrate it into their lives. It is simply dealt with as a harmless "noise" of as yet undifferentiated stimuli.

It may be supposed that the early development of babies follows the same kinds of patterns that become evident with the onset of language.[9] We cannot really speak of the experiences of babies shortly after birth; they live in a body-world since the two are as yet undifferentiated. There is no physical self and no "world" out there. They live as if the two were one. Initially, experiences may be little more than associations of things they are able experience at the same time: a feeling of being held, the effort of sucking, and a growing sense of well-being. Such an association may be differentiated from that of experiences where they have not yet been picked up, where they are hungry and feel wet, or where they are lying in the crib busy following movements they are not yet able to focus on. As these kinds of metaconscious associations become increasingly differentiated from one another, babies may begin to form a metaconscious context within which other things can have some meaning, thereby making particular associations more complex. For example, being picked up to be fed may become associated with a visual blur that consistently moves within a much larger but stationary visual blur. In turn, this may encourage attempts at focusing since there appears to be something significant to focus on.

Lying in the crib and playing with one's limbs will lead to other associations. Some of these will involve two tactile sensations, as when the baby touches his own body, while others will involve only a single one when he touches his crib or his rattle. In this way, the body-world will gradually unfold into a metaconscious awareness of a self and a world differentiated from it. The corresponding developments in the organizations of the brain-mind can then begin to sustain new ways of expressing oneself. The movements of the limbs become a little more deliberate and can be used to touch things. Eventually the earlier associations that entirely lacked any metaconscious awareness of a physical self will disappear and be "forgotten" when they unfold into embryonic experiences with some awareness of a physical self. The more such kinds of experiences become differentiated, the sooner a growing awareness of a physical self will develop a social component, when body movements become a kind of body language for responding to others. A growing differentiation of the behaviour of others towards babies will build the kind of metaconscious knowledge that encourages babies to experiment with attempts to respond to people; this in turn will gradually lead to non-verbal communication and the eventual development of a social self.

During all these kinds of developments, babies and toddlers grow a great deal of metaconscious knowledge that is implicit in an expanding organization of their brain-minds.[10] They intuitively respond to this as they attempt all manner of new things. The growing metaconscious knowledge of a physical self is followed by that of a social self and eventually that of a cultural self. All these developments are put to use in expanding the relationships that children can make sense of and participate in. Nothing is learned in an absolute sense; babies can only learn what something is in their own lives, that is, relative to everything else in their lives. There can be no question of a lived ontology or a defining world-view, but only a metaconscious commitment to the myths that orient the life of a community. The symbolic potential of our species would not have developed outside of a human community with a language and a symbolic culture. In this context, every experience helps to grow a diversity of metaconscious knowledge implied in the organization of people's brain-minds, yielding intuitions that can stimulate further growth and development. This takes place within the "everything else" that is made up of as yet undifferentiated stimuli that cannot enter into the lives of babies and children because they are still unable to establish a relationship with it. Initially, the threat of the unknown is curtailed by their being able to enter into relationships only when these can take on a meaning and value in their lives; when at any point they are overwhelmed, a loving and nurturing care can reassure them.

There is a corresponding level of differentiation and integration in their physical, social, and cultural embodiment in the symbolic universe of their culture: the network of relationships they can make sense of, participate in, and thus use to build their lives; the objects of these relationships that jointly constitute their "world"; and the undifferentiated stimuli that they are yet unable to make sense of and establish a relationship with. Gradually, the development of the deepest metaconscious knowledge that we have referred to as myths protects people from being overwhelmed by the unknown and from giving way to relativism, nihilism, and anomie.

The unfolding of the potential of a symbolic species has nothing in common with a kind of genetic determinism or cultural determinism. The potential unfolds in the context of the complex web of relationships within which it occurs; it also depends on and is influenced by that web. For example, this unfolding will be influenced increasingly by the modifications of the DNA pool by genetically modified organisms (GMOs), by all manner of pollutants including human-made hormones and estrogens, and by the contamination of matter with nanoparticles. In addition, there is a growing confusion between lived activities or functions and their machine-based equivalents such as information, knowledge, expertise, language, memory, communication, "visiting," and just about everything else.

In conclusion, I will highlight a few additional details of the transition from the use of vocal signs by toddlers to the use of a symbolic language by children.[11] I have noted that a double referencing system is required before vocal signs can evolve into symbols. As long as the words and phrases used by adults act as vocal signs in the lives of babies and children, these will fully participate in the symbolization of the experiences of these babies and toddlers and thus contribute to the growth of the organizations of their brain-minds and their lives. When the behaviour of babies begins to imply a metaconscious recognition that some words and phrases are vocal indices, their relationships with the experiences at hand will become untenable because indices have no direct bearing on the situation at hand. An index transcends the situation by pointing to something else, thus potentially dividing the experience into two unrelated parts. The only way to avoid this is to place the vocal index into the foreground of the experience and everything else into the background. In other words, vocal indices require an entirely new kind of development than that highlighted above. It involves entirely new experiences whose foregrounds are not directly related to their backgrounds. Gradually the required metaconscious transformations develop within the organizations of the brain-minds of toddlers, and these new experiences will have to be directly differentiated from one another because the meaning of each one is in the foreground that is no longer enfolded into the background, as was the case for all the earlier experiences. The development of vocal indices thus requires an entirely new level of metaconscious differentiation and integration. A vocal index continues to be differentiated from all previous experiences, but these continue to function as a metalanguage in the context of which the index gained its first meaning as a vocal sign. However, by joining a new cluster of experiences whose foregrounds are what is spoken and heard, the vocal index will be directly differentiated from all other indices via the experiences in which they are embedded. Increasingly, all experiences with the language foreground will become directly differentiated from one another and jointly differentiated from all other experiences, with the result that words and phrases can take on new meanings based on this differentiation. The more these metaconscious developments proceed, the more a vocal index is transformed into a symbolic concept.

The acquisition of a symbolic language manifests itself in two ways. It appears to be concentrated in a portion of the brain-mind that becomes increasingly associated with language. It also gives rise to new kinds of memories associated with this development. These semantic memories are distinguished from the episodic memories of direct experiences. The latter memories are associated with the processes of differentiation and integration that help to build the portion of the organization of the brain-mind described earlier. For example, we can only have a semantic memory of a corporation as a legal fiction (i.e., it exists only as a legal creation), but we can have episodic memories of its manifestations in the form of factories, offices, and advertising. The two memories are also distinct, as shown by the fact that a brain injury can cause a person to lose one kind of memory but retain the other. These new developments result in a growing metaconscious knowledge of a symbolic language, which in turn allows the organization of the brain-mind of a child to sustain ever more complex language behaviour. In most toddlers and children all of this happens so gradually that it is almost unnoticeable. In deaf-blind children these developments encounter so many difficulties that they frequently take much longer, although for some this metaconscious knowledge of a symbolic language can break through quite suddenly, as was the case in the life of Helen Keller.[12] She suddenly intuited that language was a gateway to an entirely different life in a very different world, and her transformation was spectacular. It involved a relatively rapid mutation of a social self into a cultural self that was able to transcend immediate experience and enter into the symbolic universe of her community. Such a transition does not merely come from a discovery from the "outside." The metaconscious unfolding of the symbolic potential has to be sufficiently advanced before children can begin to make their own the culture of the community in which they are growing up.

From the above highlights it is clear that the acquisition of a symbolic culture has nothing in common with taxonomic activities. The implications of Wittgenstein's study of language point to the impossibility of creating a list of the characteristics shared by all members of a category (such as tables or games) that could be given to a hypothetical Martian in order to be able to identify them.[13] What is metaconsciously being differentiated and integrated into the lives of children who are learning to identify tables and games are the experiences that are symbolized by their lives working in the background. These experiences thus represent first and foremost the *lived* relationships with tables or games that have been differentiated from all relationships with other people, animals, plants, or objects. Consequently, what tables have in common is not a set of features but their convenient relationship between a lived activity and whatever is required for that activity by bringing these objects within easy reach of a person's hands. Similarly, the characteristics of games are secondary to the fact that they allow people to distract themselves from all regular activities by entering as closely as possible into a rule-based micro-world.[14]

The acquisition of a language is almost certainly the most complex task faced by children, and yet it can be learned by almost all of them. It points to the fact that the languages of all symbolic cultures have the potential of being grafted into the metalanguage created by the kinds of developments of babies and toddlers briefly highlighted earlier. What all these languages have in common is a compatibility with these developments that makes them accessible to almost every child. It is almost certainly the result of a long co-development of languages and the organizations of human brain-minds.

People of a Time, Place, and Universal Technical Order

The double referencing system associated with traditional cultures and symbolic universes is also necessary for human life in contemporary societies, but it is entirely insufficient. The reasons go back some two hundred years – when the cultures of the industrializing societies began to produce a growing range of constituents that, with a great deal of hindsight, turned out to be global and universal in character, that is, no longer belonging to a time, place, and culture. Anything universal or global amounts to a kind of "one size fits all" and is thus incompatible with what is local and cultural. These constituents necessitated a separation from experience and culture, as well as a universal order that was very different from the cultural orders of traditional societies. They jointly built a universal science and technology, global markets, transnational institutions (such as the modern corporation), universal means (increasingly used by all institutions but especially the state), a worldwide web, and a great deal more.[15] Making sense of and living with these constituents gradually led to the development of a triple referencing system that enormously limited the unfolding of the symbolic potential of each successive generation. It amounted to a re-engineering of ourselves as a symbolic species and a gradual exit from the symbolic universes that humanity had interposed between what presented itself to the senses and what was unknown beyond what people knew and lived. The symbolic universes of traditional societies have been almost replaced by what we refer to as "reality." It is the reality of a universal technical order. Some highlights of these developments are essential for what will follow later.[16]

Our present situation is deeply rooted in our highly unique scientific and technical division of labour based on the creation of disciplines. Previously they had been organized by means of symbolization and experience embedded in a culture. The discipline-based approach to human knowing divided everything into different categories of phenomena, as if these were the building blocks of every situation examined by science. Each category was then parcelled out to a corresponding discipline, where its phenomena were placed in its domain. Physics became the study of physical phenomena, chemistry was to deal with chemical phenomena, biology was to examine biological phenomena, and so on. This approach was later extended from the natural to the social-cultural world. Economics began to examine economic phenomena, sociology dealt with social phenomena, and so on. Human knowing began to grow by studying everything one category of phenomena at a time. From time to time hybrid disciplines needed to be created such as physical chemistry, sociobiology, and cultural anthropology, but these proceeded in exactly the same manner.

Science became the approach to human knowing, organized by means of disciplines. Its intellectual division of labour excels when applied to situations dominated by one category of phenomena to the point that all the other categories of phenomena can be neglected, or to situations constituted by a single category of phenomena, or to situations in which all categories of phenomena but the one to be studied are essentially static.[17] This straightforward observation could have predicted which disciplines would be successful and develop into model disciplines and which would be regarded as "less scientific." Physics, in its examination of situations dominated by physical phenomena such as the big bang, or those existing on a subatomic level, rapidly became the model discipline. The disciplines of the social sciences were not so fortunate. They dealt with situations in which many different categories of phenomena made non-negligible contributions. For example, in the nineteenth century, economic or social phenomena were studied against the background of all the other categories of phenomena that helped to constitute human life in a symbolic universe. Such an approach corresponds to the way in which we deal with everything in our daily lives. What we are paying attention to forms the foreground while everything remains available in the background, which includes our entire lives as well as our hopes and anticipations for the future.

In contrast, the members of the category of phenomena examined by a particular discipline are abstracted from any symbolic universe. They are placed in the domain of that discipline, which excludes all other categories of phenomena. It represents the separation of human knowing from experience and culture.[18]

By way of an example, consider physics. As babies and children grow up, they learn a great deal about physical phenomena, but this is entirely embedded in their experiences: learning to crawl, walk, run, play ball, ride a bicycle, climb a tree, and almost every other daily life activity since they almost all include physical phenomena. However, when teenagers begin to learn the discipline of physics in high school, all this knowledge of physical phenomena embedded in experience is swept aside. They now enter the domain of physics whose constituents can be mathematically defined and represented, measured and quantified, and added to a growing complexity one item at a time. There can be no compatibility between the architectures of the symbolic universes of earlier societies and the architectures of the domains of scientific disciplines. The gateway into the former was by means of language, while the gateway into the latter is by means of images called free body diagrams as well as by mathematical equations. In the literature, the knowledge of physical phenomena embedded in experience and culture has been referred to as *intuitive physics*, while the knowledge of physical phenomena in the domain of physics has been referred to as *school physics*.[19]

When students reach the frontiers of physics as they complete a doctoral thesis in this field, their knowledge of the domain of physics remains entirely void of all other categories of phenomena because these have been excluded from it. Contrary to what students are told in high school to the effect that physics is a scientific study of physical phenomena in the world, it is really the study of these phenomena separated from all other categories of phenomena – which requires their removal from the world to be placed into the domain of physics. Consequently, it is often next to impossible to verify this knowledge experimentally other than in a laboratory designed to mimic this domain by keeping the influences of all other categories of phenomena at bay. Even so, the influences of the observer and of the entire experimental context cannot be neglected because they are an integral part of an experimental design. In sum, physics is the scientific study of physical phenomena in a domain that can be applied to the real world only when the situation at hand makes it possible to neglect all other categories of phenomena without any loss of understanding. Hence, the scientific knowledge of physical phenomena represents a highly de-symbolized form of human knowing. It has severed the relationships with all other categories of phenomena and thus with the world in which we live.

Organizing human doing on the basis of disciplines again amounts to dealing with anything one category of phenomena at a time.[20] It thus has the same kinds of limitations discussed in relation to the discipline-based approach to knowing. The discipline-based approach to doing is ideally suited to dealing with entities whose architecture can be expressed in terms of the principles of non-contradiction, separability, closed definitions, measurement, quantification, mathematical representation, and a simple complexity. Such an entity is built up from separate and distinct subdomains that exchange inputs and outputs with other subdomains in such a way that within each one of them a particular member of a category of phenomena repeatedly transforms the received inputs into the outputs passed on to another subdomain. This is done in such a way that the transformation process cannot easily be affected by what happens in all the other subdomains. It is the kind of architecture found in any technological device, process, or system.

For example, in an electronic circuit a signal is received by one of its components, to be transformed by a particular electrical or magnetic phenomenon into an output that is sent to the next component, and this continues until the final desired result has been obtained. Whatever happens in all the other subdomains cannot function in the background. The autonomy of any subdomain relative to all others must be ensured. Consequently, repetition replaces adaptation and evolution. For example, if a numerical procedure in a computer depended on the information stored in its memory, the machine would be utterly useless. This is equally true for any other technology including classical machines, chemical plants, buildings, or internal combustion engines. In the case of the latter, the space above the piston successively functions as four different subdomains, each characterized by a single phenomenon performing a particular operation: the intake of air; the compression of this air; the ejection of fuel and its combustion; and the exhaust of the combustion products. Similarly, a building can be conceived and designed as built up from subdomains because its components have a primary function open to a discipline-based analysis.

This discipline-based approach to doing is incapable of dealing with anything that does not have the above kind of simple complexity. This is the case for all life. We have noted how the DNA of any organism is enfolded into each and every cell. We have also seen that the unfolding of the symbolic potential of babies and children results in the culture of their community being symbolically enfolded into the organization of their brain-minds. They are thus both individual and society because the former is a unique expression of the latter. Since all the relationships that people have with their surroundings are internalized and symbolized, their lives enfold something of these surroundings. This is the case whether these surroundings are primarily social, natural, or physical.

Despite the limitations of discipline-based approaches to doing, contemporary societies make an unlimited and uncritical use of them. That this is the case can readily be confirmed by consulting the academic programs offered by professional faculties or schools. There are no programs seeking to define the limitations of their disciplines in order to transcend them by developing alternative approaches to human doing.[21]

It is by means of discipline-based approaches that we seek to improve almost everything and anything, including the running of a factory, an office, a university, a hospital, and a government ministry. It is clear that discipline-based approaches cannot directly be applied to such a task. There are too many phenomena that are intermingled, enfolded, and making non-negligible contributions to the whole. Before anything resembling a subdomain can even be accessed, a triple abstraction must be made by the experts who apply the disciplines in which they have a recognized competence.

Take the running of a factory as an example. To begin with, the world in which it operates must be reduced to the inputs that the factory receives from it and the outputs that the factory returns to that world. Next, the process that transforms these inputs into outputs involves many different categories of phenomena, with the result that it must be broken down into a diversity of aspects, each of which must be delegated to the domain of an appropriate discipline. Finally, the decision criteria for guiding the improvement process and for choosing between alternative options cannot be based on anything that lies beyond the disciplines being used. There can thus be no question of doing what is best for human life, society, and the biosphere. Improvements must be made in terms of what happens within a subdomain, which is thus limited to obtaining the most desired intermediary outputs that can be produced from the inputs. No human values can be used other than output-input ratios such as efficiency, productivity, and return on investment.

Consequently, adapting and evolving the ways of life of contemporary societies by means of discipline-based approaches has been turned into a kind of engineering megaproject.[22] The limitations of doing so derive from the inability of discipline-based approaches to effectively deal with anything that is integral to the way in which everything is related to everything else and evolves in relation to everything else, so that the likelihood of anything repeating itself in the same way is nearly impossible. Everything must be reified and commoditized by a triple abstraction in order to be treated and organized exactly in the way that engineers organize and optimize the inner workings of any technological device, process, or system. By implication, we may regard most engineering disciplines as the gold standard of discipline-based approaches to human doing, just as physics became the model discipline for human knowing.

These engineering megaprojects of contemporary societies are turning human history into a "moving forward." Doing so by increasing everywhere the desired outputs from requisite inputs has nothing in common with the improvement of human lives, societies, or the biosphere. On the contrary, every reified and commoditized aspect is made as "good" as it can be on its own terms rather than on the contribution it makes to everything else. This "good" is related to increasing the efficiency and performance of whatever it does without any consideration for its connection to, and dependence on, its evolving in relation to everything else. By having anything produce as much as possible of whatever it contributes to its surroundings and via them to the world, its efficiency and power are increased. However, this is done by disordering the way in which everything is related to and evolves in relation to everything else. In a world that is biologically and culturally enfolded and that may also be materially enfolded (according to some physicists),[23] this spells a reification of everything and the disordering of all relationships. Our global technical order is constructed by interconnecting everything that has been made more efficient and is performing according to the necessary exchanges of inputs and outputs. These include matter, energy, and everything built up with them, as well as labour, capital, and discipline-based knowing and doing. Consequently, anything that can be opened up to the technical order by means of reification and commoditization will be technically developed, but everything that cannot be made compatible with it will become impaired and remain under-developed.[24] This new form of development now directs human history, and this is bound to continue until our civilization recognizes the limitations of discipline-based approaches. In the meantime, the word *development* has joined a growing vocabulary that used to have a meaning associated with a symbolic universe and a cultural order – a meaning that has been lost in the context of a technical order.

This kind of development has its roots in industrialization, which necessitated one of the greatest reversals in human history.[25] Simply put, it is essential to recognize that human life is bound together by a biology-based connectedness, a technology-based connectedness, and a culture-based connectedness. We are all unique expressions of the DNA pool, which is now beginning to be re-engineered by biotechnology. All our activities can neither create nor destroy the energy on which they depend; they connect us to the biosphere either directly or via chains of other human activities, thus revealing the dependence of our society on the biosphere. The way of life of a society that integrates all these activities thus determines the organization of a network of flows of matter as well as a network of flows of energy, and these networks overlap when we deal with anything built up with these flows. Such a way of life respects the limits expressed by the first and second laws of thermodynamics, but it is not determined by them. It expresses a cultural order that results from symbolizing everything in relation to everything else, thus establishing its place in and significance for this way of life.[26]

For most of human history, the culture-based connectedness of human life generally coincided with bonds of kinship, social ties, and obligations of all kinds. This social organization translated into corresponding networks of flows of matter and energy and of everything built up with them. Industrialization changed all that.[27] The introduction of the technical division of labour transformed human work into an image of the machine, thereby bringing into the cultural order of the society the beginnings of a technical order based on repetition rather than adaptation and evolution. Each production step essentially constituted a subdomain that was connected by the inputs being received from another subdomain and by the outputs being transferred to still another one. This organization of production essentially became a calculus of inputs and outputs of matter, energy, everything built up with this matter, as well as labour and capital. The meaning and value of each of these production steps for human life and society became entirely secondary. The result was that the organization of production became a direct expression of the thermodynamic limits because any leakages of intermediary outputs were considered to be costly and wasteful. A technology-based connectedness was thus established. Since this order of production had an architecture that was diametrically opposite to that of the cultural order, its relationships with the latter had to be mediated by an economic order that initially incorporated the embryonic technical order of production.[28] Industrializing societies were thus split into a distinct and separate economy and the remainder of society. The former was characterized by the technology-based connectedness dominating the culture-based connectedness according to an economic order, while in the remainder of society the cultural order dominated. The economic order corresponded to what was "real" in terms of the five principles described previously, while the cultural order was established by means of symbolization associated with a dialectical enfolding of everything into everything else.[29]

It was entirely self-evident for the members of these industrializing societies that every year there were more machines; every year these machines became larger and faster; every year there were more factories full of these machines; the total output of these factories was constantly increasing; and there was nothing on the horizon of people's experiences suggesting that these trends could not continue forever. When such experiences were interpolated and extrapolated by the organizations of the brain-minds of the people of that time, the deepest metaconscious knowledge took the form of the myths of progress, work, and happiness, with the central myth of capital presiding over it all.[30] With hindsight, we can explain this explicitly. Thanks to a steadily growing economic output, soon the material needs of everyone could be satisfied. Poverty would be eliminated along with all the social scourges that accompanied it, with the result that material progress would lead to social progress. With the most intractable social problems out of the way, the focus would shift to spiritual progress. Any limits to this progress became unthinkable. Consequently, what could be achieved by everyone working hard at material progress was equally unlimited. The prospects for human happiness also appeared limitless. To ensure this progress, work, and happiness, a society had to endlessly renew and accumulate its capital to make the necessary investments. All this was so self-evident that any other way of life became unliveable and unthinkable. For example, Karl Marx interpreted all of human history in terms of what was thinkable in the nineteenth century.[31] There would be five successive economic bases on which five different superstructures would be erected. Any other historical path was unthinkable until the anomalies of the First World War, the Great Depression, and the Second World War shattered the nineteenth-century myths. As these myths gradually rose into consciousness, they gave rise to a mythology that dominated the mass media and advertising. Alcohol, toothpaste, cars, and many other consumer goods were portrayed as producing all manner of social and spiritual miracles that jointly testified to the unsurpassed achievements of the American way of life.

According to the myths of the industrializing societies of the nineteenth century, all previous societies and civilizations had made a strategic mistake by believing that the good life on this earth would come through human beings incarnating the morality and religion created by their culture.[32] Through the creation of myths, every cultural order has always established its gods that must be served above all else.[33] In the nineteenth century, this was turned around: pursue economic growth, and all other things will be granted. It undermined the moral and religious traditions of the first generation of industrial societies, turning them inside out and upside down.[34] Adam Smith began to proclaim the virtues of self-interested behaviour: as long as wage earners maximized the utility they derived from their wages, and the entrepreneurs maximized the returns on their investments, the best possible world for most people would miraculously appear.[35] It was contrary to every moral, religious, philosophical, and political tradition invented by humanity up to that point. It helped to constitute a mythology that remains alive and well today: be good stewards of the economy, and it will grant everything else; and if by any chance social, legal, or political problems come your way, the miraculous powers of capital will overcome them. From a religious perspective, this mythology created three forms of the American way of life: those practised by Jews, Protestants, and Catholics. These three religious traditions now serve the gods of this mythology.[36]

The assimilation of these three religious traditions in Western civilization has been in the making for some time. As the industrializing societies became torn into an economic order (into which a technological order was embedded) and the remainder of the cultural order (into which these orders were born), these three traditions were also torn into two relatively distinct fragments, commonly referred to as *liberal* and *conservative*. The former attempted to rescue from these traditions whatever was socially useful in terms of how to deal with one's neighbour. This was not difficult to understand in the context of the profound upheavals of the time, made worse by the de-symbolization of the symbolic cultures of the industrializing societies. It represented an attempt at finding a new and meaningful Christian orientation for society. The conservative fragment was both a reaction to this development and an attempt to rescue what it regarded as most fundamental in this turbulent age, namely, the relationship with God and (implicitly) an acceptance of the status quo as ordained by him. This adaptation of and subservience to the new myths (what in these traditions were referred to as false gods) was greatly facilitated as they became either an escape from or a conformity to the world, when they should have been neither.[37]

As is always the case, the myths of the industrializing societies of the nineteenth and early twentieth centuries sowed the seeds of their own destruction. The interpolation and extrapolation of the experiences of the people of that time failed to take into account the other component of industrialization: as people changed technology, technology also changed people through its vast influence on human lives, societies, and local ecosystems.[38] It transformed "human nature" in a manner that helped to prepare for the possibility of a consumer society in which people needed whatever technology could produce. As a result, material progress would be matched by people's insatiable needs. This development ensured that the basic needs of the poor would not become satisfied and that the social scourges of poverty would not be eliminated. Equally fundamental were the problems posed by the growing technological and economic orders within the cultural orders that had birthed them.

Gradually it became apparent that the cultural approach to making sense of and living in the world by means of symbolization was not well suited for the building of these new orders. The introduction of the technical division of labour and the accompanying mechanization significantly increased the throughput in the technology-based connectedness, and it became paramount to find the "one best way" to effectively have each and every production step transform its inputs into an intermediary output in order to keep cost prices well below market prices to ensure the renewal and accumulation of capital.[39] It was also essential to match such inputs and outputs with the adjacent production steps. To do so required taking into account a context that was limited to that of the local technology-based connectedness, while a cultural approach would have focused on the local culture-based connectedness dealing with the meaning and value of everything in relation to everything else and thus to human lives, societies, and ecosystems.[40] It was no longer a matter of living one's life but of pursuing specific goals. The implications were far reaching, as was clearly recognized by Max Weber.[41] Imposing a goal on the ways in which everything is related to everything else and evolves in relation to everything else mentally limits as well as transforms this interconnectedness. This happened as a consequence of singling out only those relationships that mattered for achieving the goal, and paying only peripheral attention to those relationships that could marginally affect it, and ignoring all the other relationships because taking them into account would not be rational with respect to the imposed goal. Doing so in the context of daily life showed a kind of weak rationality given the complex interconnectedness of everything, but when it came to the technology-based connectedness, this rationality could easily be imposed in a strong and rigid manner. As a consequence, the cultural approach gradually mutated into the rational approach of imposing goals on the interconnectedness of human life in the world. Putting all this into practice led to a disorganization of the kind of interconnectedness that would have been taken into account by means of symbolization.

Developing the technological and economic orders by pursuing goals directly related to improving the local dynamic equilibrium of the technology-based connectedness by ongoing mechanization and industrialization encountered other obstacles that were immediately evident in the chemical and electrical industries; what could be symbolized or observed in relation to a goal did not correlate very well with what happened in chemical or electrical transformations. These obstacles were overcome by logical knowing and doing that separated themselves from experience and culture to become organized in terms of disciplines.[42] Rational approaches thus mutated into the technical approaches that led to the phenomenon of technique, as examined by Jacques Ellul.[43]

The far-reaching consequences appear not to have been fully recognized until the so-called information and computer revolution.[44] Initially, the scope of the role of the computer was believed to be rather limited. This assessment was justified by the findings of industry that the expected productivity increases were not materializing. With the discovery that all business processes had to be re-engineered into a kind of intellectual assembly line and that the results had to be integrated across the entire enterprise, the vast implications of the introduction of the technical division of labour, mechanization, and industrialization came into focus.[45] The entire corporation was now being re-engineered in the image of the computer, thereby making it a model of how to extend and perfect the technique-based connectedness of the technical order.[46] Many prior developments had made this possible. Human life had already been interpreted in cybernetic terms as depending on negative feedback control. Such controls could be represented in terms of information flows once these had been redefined in physical terms by information theory. Knowledge was interpreted in terms of artificial intelligence, not by having it imitate human functions but by reducing these functions to what could be captured through rules, algorithms, and programs. Classical machines could now be regarded as one kind of peripheral device. Numerical control had paved the way for their reinterpretation. Human beings were now dealt with as another kind of peripheral device, as they were compelled to act in strict conformity with and as a local expression of the technical order of a corporation. There was no longer any need for cultural values – value chains measured and quantified what could be sold to the customer.

This model of the corporation functioning as the technique-based connectedness of a technical order could readily be extended to other large organizations. Enterprise integration became the technical approach par excellence, and today there is no large institution that can function without it. When all such endeavours are connected by the internet, societies become organized and reorganized to resemble one vast integrated enterprise in which human beings act more and more like peripheral devices re-engineered in the image of the computer. It must not be imagined that, outside of their participation in these re-engineered organizations, human beings are left to recover their humanity as best they can. They take their screen-based devices with them as well as adding other such devices, leaving little room for non-technically mediated, face-to-face relationships with family members, friends, and acquaintances.

What had begun as the reversal between the culture-based connectedness and the technology-based connectedness of the first generation of industrial societies gained strength as the latter mutated into the technique-based connectedness. It has reached the point that today we have no difficulty in regarding everything as a resource of the technical order. There are human and natural resources or human, social, and natural "capital." There is very little difference in the ways that contemporary societies treat human resources and natural resources, as our human resource departments clearly demonstrate.[47]

Moreover, the technique-based connectedness is constantly expanding. Some are dreaming of re-engineering our buildings to make them "intelligent." Others wish to extend this to transportation, beginning with autonomous vehicles and "smart" roads. Still others hope to integrate all such endeavours to create "intelligent" cities. The hinterland of our cities is being re-engineered into large-scale agrobusiness with high levels of automation and computerization. We are trapped in a cult of efficiency that makes it self-evident that our problems can be dealt with by the application of discipline-based approaches, which operate within a triple abstraction centred on efficiency. The warnings issued by Jacques Ellul some fifty years ago have gone unheeded, with the result that everything he predicted has come true for lack of decisive human intervention.[48]

Everything being created through discipline-based approaches cannot contribute to an unfolding of the complexity of the dialectically enfolded elements that have taken on a meaning and a value in individual and collective human life. Instead of these kinds of elements, we now have facts that are integrated into a reality that has displaced the symbolic universes of the past. As noted, the specialists that helped to build the technical order are suspended in a triple abstraction that makes it impossible for them to know the meaning and value of what they do. The resulting complete de-symbolization of human knowing and doing is masked by a cult of the fact. These facts have nothing to do with what is true for human life and society because they are of the order of what is "real," that is, what is *exact* relative to the theories and models of the domain of a discipline. Traditionally, facts established through symbolization were dialectically enfolded into a symbolic universe and were related to what was true for human life within it. Today, facts are established in the context of the domain of a discipline as being exact in their conformity with it. Since our contemporary civilization can no longer envisage any limits to discipline-based science, the facts produced by it have gone from simply being exact in relation to the domain of a particular discipline to becoming universal, unlimited, and objective in order to parallel the unlimited character of the approaches by which they are established. They are no longer relative to a particular time, place, and culture as contributions to human history.

Much the same applies to our discipline-based approaches to doing. They produce the absolutely efficient elements in the sense that they are measured on their own terms as opposed to the contribution they make to all life in the world. They are the fruits of our cult of efficiency.

All this provides us with an intuition of what may constitute our deepest metaconscious knowledge or myths. Living with any of our creations as if they have no limits is surely equivalent to the way in which traditional societies lived with their gods – the creations of their cultures that were considered omnipotent and having no limits. In other words, our losing sight of the limits of disciplined-based approaches and the economic growth they produce is no different from the way in which humanity lived with its gods in the past. It cost humanity very dearly, and we can expect nothing different from our secular gods. Just because ours are not found on the mountains or in the heavens does not mean that we have become secular and of age. We have created our own all-powerful entities. This creation blocks the road to preventive approaches, which use symbolization and culture to transcend the limits of discipline-based science and technique, and use science and technique to transcend the limits of symbolization and culture.[49]

Thomas Kuhn attempted to relativize discipline-based science by turning it into a unique human activity. This showed that, although we unquestionably know much more today than at any other time, it does not mean that we know things better.[50] He showed that facts owe their status to the theories that organize the domains of a discipline. When such a domain is reorganized during a scientific revolution, some elements may retain their status as facts, but others may lose that status, and still others may gain it. Consequently, facts are relative to a time, a place, a discipline, and a highly de-symbolized culture that helped to create the discipline. In other words, facts cannot compel us to be "realistic," that is, to slavishly follow them without any decisive human intervention. Such interventions are capable of changing the facts. Nevertheless, the cult of the fact is everywhere in our civilization.

Jacques Ellul attempted to relativize technique by symbolizing it in terms of its meaning and value for human lives, societies, and the biosphere.[51] Nevertheless, the cult of efficiency makes it unthinkable that the optimization of everything and anything would simply aggravate our current problems much more than it might alleviate a few of them. This cult of efficiency is the exact parallel to our living with discipline-based approaches as if they were all-powerful and without limits.

In the same vein, the economic growth achieved with discipline-based approaches to human knowing and doing is also treated as being limitless. It too has become a cult of growth that is good in itself and thus no longer subject to critical scrutiny as to what mere growth can really deliver for us. These cults are complemented and supported by the cult of the "state-nation." Everything has become political, which means that we accept and live as if the state were all in all, because any limits to politics have disappeared. It also means that we live as if the technical means at the disposal of the state could do everything. Otherwise we would spend a great deal more time devising non-political solutions based on a careful analysis of what politics and the state cannot accomplish. In the meantime we accept that the state has a role to play in everything and that its role is essentially limitless. This turned communism, National Socialism, and democracy into the secular religions of the twentieth century. I will return to this subject.

Living in a reality that is regarded as factual, efficient, and political is impossible for a symbolic species, whose members need to make some sense of their lives and their world in order to individually and collectively establish their bearings and to fend off the ever-present danger of relativism, nihilism, and anomie. This continues to be the case despite high levels of de-symbolization and the re-engineering of our symbolic species by "technique changing people." Here the traditional mass media, now complemented by the new media, play a decisive role as the necessary complement to our highly de-symbolized cultures.[52] Since they are an integral part of our technical order, they do not sustain individual and collective human life in the way that cultures did in the past. The media replace custom, tradition, morality, and most of our opinions with what we derive from a bath of images into which the media immerse us. We have taken on a kind of statistical morality because a traditional morality can no longer be provided by our highly de-symbolized cultures. We regard what everyone else is doing, and treat what we discover, as normal, and the reality of these images thus becomes normative. We all know that not a single moral or religious tradition has ever suggested that what everyone does defines what is right. On the contrary, morality and religion have always been based on what a cultural community accepts as the only possible discernment of good and evil. In the same vein, the media permit us to take on a public opinion on everything and anything when we no longer have time to symbolize, experience, and live the reality of a technical order by reading about it, discussing it with others, and arriving at a private opinion following a critical reflection on it. Similarly, these images show us that, thanks to democracy, we remain in control as opposed to increasingly being one of the peripheral devices required by the technique-based connectedness of the technical order. We watch everyone everywhere exercising this control at the ballot box, where people choose the policies and the government that will guide the state to harness the limitless powers of science, technique, and economic growth for this purpose.

Including the scientific and technical specialists who help build the new technical order, we are all on the receiving end of the collective enterprise of re-engineering everything and placing it in the technique-based connectedness of this order. The only thing that counts are the facts produced by discipline-based approaches and our acting on them by means of other discipline-based approaches. Only this is real.

Symbolizing this massive re-engineering project in order to discover what is true for our lives in order to distance ourselves from the technical order and create a more liveable symbolic universe has become regarded as too philosophical to be practical, or even downright unrealistic. What little symbolization continues to take place has been relegated to sustaining our relationships with those who are dear to us. This personal "world" has little connection with the reality of the technical order that is no longer accessible to most people other than through the media.

Consider how the media keep us in touch with what is happening in our world. News shows, documentaries, and in-depth interviews gather what may be regarded as images of event fragments that must be "assembled" into a program that will work for an intended audience, by creating a suitable context for the advertising that will pay the bills or that will attract a sufficiently large audience to justify public subsidies.

All this becomes painfully evident when we take an inventory of all the images to which a person may be exposed for a significant period of time, which can never constitute the equivalent of the visual dimension of a symbolic universe. Any such inventory will reveal a collection of mostly unrelated and discontinuous image-stories that come out of nowhere and that disappear into nowhere after having been covered one or more times. Each image-story of an event is assembled from event fragments that have been taken out of the context in which they were filmed in order to be placed in a new context of other such fragments. A "talking head" may then add some words to help the audience make sense of the image-story. For example, images of a distraught person can mean any number of things, thus requiring a few words of clarification. None of the parties involved in the production of the news shows, including the film crew, the reporters, the news editors, the host or spokesperson, and the producer responsible for the overall direction, can come anywhere close to symbolizing the material because of a variety of constraints. The viewers of the program cannot symbolize it either and thus cannot fit these image-stories into their lives in the way that they fit non-technically mediated, daily-life events. They have learned to rely on the embedded clues provided by the talking heads as well as by the sound bites. When these are carefully examined, they turn out to be what has largely replaced the results of symbolization, namely a mythology based on the myths of a previous era. Such a mythology acts as a framework for the images, which provides the context in which everything will take on the sense so desperately needed by people to help them live in the reality of a technical order. The situation is somewhat analogous to what we experience in daily life. The reason we do not see the edges around our field of vision is that they have been interpreted as having no meaning, because there are no such edges in the world. Similarly, the mythology that frames each image-story constitutes the seamless extension of what we see on the screen.

We have already encountered most of the elements of this mythology. They include a kind of scientism that celebrates the unlimited power of science in the realm of knowing. They include a kind of technicism that marvels at every technical miracle and the bright future it will help to create. The mythology shows that democracy can overcome all tyranny, including that of a technical order, by giving every democratic society a mastery over it, thus making it liveable. We are kept informed of how modern medicine is delivering us from disease. We are reassured that the power of the large organizations that surround us on all sides can be matched by the way in which the internet is empowering everyone. Incidentally, it also tells us about the many growing pains that come with the accumulation of all this knowledge and power, but this will all be overcome by further "growth," although some of it may not happen during our lifetime. The next free trade agreement will further boost the powers of global markets and lift us out of our slow growth, unemployment, and under-employment. The growth of nanotechnology, biotechnology, and information technology will overcome the problems created by earlier technologies. The education of our best and brightest will keep us in the global race. In this manner, every image-story takes its meaning from, and constitutes a confirmation of, the mythology that depicts how the world works. This mythology is usually politically nuanced to satisfy the way in which a target audience desires its political illusions to be framed. The mythology thus ensures us that beyond each and every image on our screen lies an entire world that is just more of the same.

Since the media involve so little embodiment, participation, commitment, and freedom on the part of the audience, it is difficult to speak of "experiences" that people can actually live. To compensate, producers make use of human reflexes that respond to sensory "jolts." These take the form of frequent and sudden scene changes; multiple cameras that permit sudden and frequent changes in perspective; flashbacks; flash forwards; sound effects; music; and a great deal more. Such reflex experiences make daily-life experiences that are not enriched in this manner appear rather uneventful and boring.

Many news items and even entire programs have been carefully engineered by public relations firms on behalf of clients who wish to achieve a particular effect on a target audience in order to produce the kind of behaviour on which they depend. In assessing their effectiveness, it must be remembered that the people watching these shows have highly de-symbolized cultures that can no longer sustain individual and collective human life. They need and desire meaning, purpose, and direction for their lives. These are largely satisfied by the media in a technically engineered reality that is thus transformed into some kind of "world" in which people can live. In this gigantic public relations exercise – of making the technical order liveable by giving some direction and purpose to human lives that conform to it – language is not used as it was in earlier societies. Words become "tools" to obtain particular effects.[53] This language usage is no longer embedded in the double referencing system described previously. Words and phrases now take on powers that create desired behaviours, which involves an entirely new level of differentiation and integration (to be discussed shortly). Contemporary societies would not have survived the extensive de-symbolization of their cultures during the past few hundred years without the necessary social cohesion and desired behaviours having been engineered by techniques such as public relations, advertising, and group dynamics, which jointly constitute a social integration propaganda.[54] Its considerable success is due to our living no longer in symbolic universes but in a reality formed by the technique-based connectedness of a technical order. Human languages can no longer symbolically map this reality in the way they mapped the symbolic universes of earlier societies, because its architecture is not amenable to language.

These kinds of difficulties are sometimes experienced by scientific and technical experts who are interviewed on the media. They are being called on to make some sense of what is being shown, which means that the content of the images will not be symbolized by them but placed in the context of the domains of the disciplines they have mastered. Since these disciplines are autonomous from each other and thus cannot be integrated into a comprehensive scientific world-view, these specialists have no choice but to interpret their discipline-based knowledge by means of their highly de-symbolized culture. Doing so is inevitably affected by their own needs. These may include a justification of their employment, the necessity to advance their careers, and a desire to increase their chances of research grants.[55]

The old and the new media jointly helped to create the reality that has taken the place of the symbolic universes of the traditional cultures of the past. It marks a profound transformation of human life, which is now evolving into a "world" that is accessible only by image-stories and image-words. Its architecture is the diametrical opposite of that of symbolic universes, with the result that it can no longer be entered into and lived in by means of languages and cultures. Of course, we also experience this reality directly in all our daily-life activities. Shopping for groceries in a modern supermarket or a big-box store is typical. Nothing in these stores makes much sense to us, for the simple reason that almost every detail is a manifestation of the technique-based connectedness of reality as opposed to the traditional culture-based connectedness. Details, including the store lay-out, assignment of shelf space, pricing, packaging, and the physical features of the surroundings (including the music), are organized and reorganized by means of a variety of techniques backed by computer databases. The intention is to influence the behaviour of shoppers by making the local technique-based connectedness as efficient as possible in order to obtain the greatest desired outputs from all necessary inputs to the benefit of the corporation. For example, when shoppers complain to managers about having to walk around a large section of clothing in the middle of a supermarket, they will be politely told that these determinations are made by head office and they have no authority to adapt things to the wishes of local customers. In the same vein, phrases such as *new size* or *new and improved* are but a few instances of image-words, because what is new or improved is not the participation of the product in the culture-based connectedness but its participation in the technique-based connectedness that is frequently of no interest to the shopper. Endless sales can be created by redistributing profit margins on individual items, with little benefit to most customers but of some benefit to the store – that of increasing the throughput of products. As workplaces, these stores take no interest whatsoever in making local economies work for people. Businesses have lost interest entirely in helping to make local economies work by paying people living wages. Employees are just another "input," the cost of which is minimized by part-time employment with few benefits, leaving them with little option but to scramble for several such "McWall" jobs, and thus exposing them to the probability of irreconcilable demands from different employers. Moreover, they are the "human resources" that must arrive "just in time" when needed, which creates endless conflicts for people who have children. This contrasts sharply with the traditional grocery stores where many things did make sense according to the attitudes, practices, convictions, values, and choices of the storekeepers, all of which were culturally embedded and thus accessible to sense. Shoppers might complain about a storekeeper being dishonest, a little too greedy, or in other ways not respecting the values of the culture. A store's reputation also depended on how they treated their employees and whether or not this was in keeping with what was culturally acceptable. In sum, traditional stores were to a much greater extent an expression of the local culture-based connectedness. In contrast, the shoppers and the employees and managers of contemporary grocery stores are reified by a variety of techniques that rob them of the traditional social roles that made sense in terms of a way of life and culture. Moreover, these kinds of stores export as many costs as they can into the community, thereby imposing many economic burdens.

We experience almost all daily-life activities very differently from what we had intended, as a consequence of our having been transferred from a symbolic universe into the reality of a contemporary society and our being on the receiving end of a variety of techniques that structure these activities. For example, in shopping we consistently walk out with more than we intended to buy. Jointly, all such experiences leave us with a profound sense of our lives being under the control of forces that we do not understand and in relation to which we appear somewhat helpless. People respond to this very differently depending on the relationship that has been established between the demands made on them by the local technique-based connectedness and the resources they have developed to deal with them. For some people, it leads to a profound sense of helplessness and their lives being adrift and out of control; others are determined to stay on top of these demands, but this can significantly raise their adrenaline levels and in the long run will have some very detrimental effects on their health and lives. We have dissociated the current epidemic of anxiety and depression from our building of this reality with a technique-based connectedness, at the expense of an increasingly de-symbolized culture-based connectedness.

To examine this further, we will briefly highlight some of the difficulties encountered by children growing up in contemporary societies. As noted, toddlers develop a first referencing system by building up a great deal of metaconscious knowledge from everything that is immediately available to their senses, which then becomes a context in which other situations can take on a meaning. It is also in this context that vocal signs become differentiated from all other sounds during language acquisition. The double referencing system is developed when toddlers become exposed to situations that they cannot make sense of without language forming a foreground (with everything else relegated to the background) so that the language can transcend the situation at hand.

In this way, these language foregrounds can be differentiated directly from one another, thereby creating a second context through which language can transcend immediate experience to eventually map the symbolic universe of a community. A triple referencing system is required in response to the problems created by screen-based devices or any other direct manifestations of the technical order. Initially young children may not significantly differentiate these experiences from those dealing with family members, friends, and acquaintances in non-technically mediated, face-to-face situations. For example, the experiences of television watching may not be differentiated initially from those of face-to-face conversations because the image-stories contain a non-trivial language component. With much more exposure to both streams of experiences, children will metaconsciously learn that a language foreground is very different from the image-stories derived from a technical order. The language foreground has a dialectically enfolded order, while the image-stories are assembled from images of event fragments to which language is added in order to amplify and clarify them, thus constituting the order of reality. Image-stories may not have all the five characteristics mentioned previously, but their elements are separable and non-contradictory and form a simple complexity. It is worth emphasizing that these two streams of experiences cannot become differentiated as being fundamentally different until language acquisition has become sufficiently advanced that children can make some sense of the language that accompanies the image-stories.

Once children begin to differentiate their experiences with a language foreground from those with an image-story foreground, a distinction begins to be made between what may be referred to as language words and image-words. It is based on the fact that the former are directly differentiated from one another, while the latter are engineered by all kinds of techniques to efficiently create a desired effect. It is the conjunction of these techniques with images that creates these effects. Consequently, they complement the images rather than creating a language foreground. With image-words there are no speakers or listeners but only large organizations desiring to create certain behaviours. Image-words belong to reality, while language words tend towards the building of a symbolic universe unless this is blocked by de-symbolization. Image-words refer to an engineered reality, while language words refer to a lived world with a lived language rather than an engineered one.

While a double referencing system is developed by a semantic memory complementing an episodic memory, the triple referencing system splits the semantic memory into a differentiated cluster of experiences with a language foreground and a differentiated cluster of experiences with an image-story foreground. Within this latter, larger cluster the meanings of words and phrases are indirectly differentiated from one another according to their associations with images, thus creating the kinds of "plastic words" referred to earlier.

This complex and ambiguous development interferes with the way in which language would have developed in traditional societies. It is hardly surprising, therefore, that significant difficulties can occur. These correspond rather well to a great many learning disabilities and the way in which some children do not differentiate language from image-stories, because they appear to interpret written words as images.[56] The careful examination of these learning disabilities and the treatment of written language as images can potentially provide a great deal of insight into the way in which the development of a double referencing system may be adversely affected by the development of the triple referencing system.

The fundamental differentiation of experiences with an image-story foreground from experiences with a language foreground is greatly reinforced by children entering the "playground" of reality by means of computer screens. The software that generates these screens, especially in computer games, has the architecture of the five previously mentioned principles that constitute the order of what is real. Increasingly children have the choice of playing and doing things together with others or withdrawing into the reality of their screens. Their behaviour begins to imply a discernment of the differences between these two "worlds." They may be fascinated by the artificially enriched world of television or the even more reflex-driven world of computer games. They become torn between these two worlds. Shy and introverted children may prefer the much simpler complexity of reality to the more complex, ambiguous, and risky social world with others. In contrast, the more sociable and extroverted children may experience the opposite attraction: the social world offers them a much richer complexity and a great deal of ambiguity, but all of this is faced with the support of others. It also brings the risk of being vulnerable to others as relationships deepen.[57]

When children go to school, they are primarily being adapted to the technique-based connectedness of reality. One new technology after another is heralded by a majority of educators as the new saviour of education or the key to a better future. The current fascination with screen-based devices in the classroom is no exception. Many schools appear not to have any knowledge of or have summarily dismissed the studies showing how children's reliance on screen-based devices negatively interferes with their cognitive and personal development as members of a symbolic species. Children now encounter two streams of experiences. One stream enhances and develops their symbolic potential, while the other de-symbolizes and thus undermines it. In other words, schools are increasingly contributing to the strengthening of the technique-based connectedness of reality at the expense of the culture-based connectedness of individual and collective human life. They offer little or no alternative to the powerful de-symbolizing influences on the lives of children, let alone getting them started on a development based on the re-symbolization of the technique-based connectedness of reality in order to learn something about its meaning and significance for human life. Re-symbolization would create a distance between children and reality, to provide them with a margin of freedom to grow up as members of a symbolic species. Instead, they are educated in relation to the world of the computer, which is of little value because computers outperform human beings in this world. People are becoming peripheral devices to the technique-based connectedness of our civilization.

These developments in turn strengthen the preparedness of teenagers for learning and participating in the domains of scientific disciplines such as physics and chemistry in high school. Their experiences of entering into such domains have foregrounds with an architecture of reality, while the backgrounds correspond to a de-symbolized but dialectically enfolded daily-life world. Such de-symbolized experiences mark the beginning of a separation from symbolized experience and culture. The metaconscious knowledge built up with these de-symbolized experiences is also separated from symbolized experience and culture, thus contributing further to splitting young people's semantic memories: a part of their lives is embedded in symbolic experience and culture, and another part is separated from them. As a result the daily-life world of teenagers continues to transition from a highly de-symbolized and embryonic symbolic universe to a reality, as the triple referencing system develops. Increasingly the organizations of their brain-minds map their lives no longer as lived in a cultural order with a culture-based connectedness but as a highly reified existence in a universal technical order with a technique-based connectedness. Moreover, this existence becomes a weakly connected set of fragments corresponding to the various socio-technical roles that they learn to play in contemporary ways of life.

Each role is usually carried out with a different group of people, thus fragmenting their metaconscious social selves along with their lives. It is not only a divided existence but also one that is separated from symbolic experience and culture. In the past, people were able to live lives that were alienated in their entirety, thus making liberation a possibility. Growing up in contemporary societies reifies people's lives into fragments corresponding to various socio-technical roles that are organized and reorganized on the basis of a variety of techniques to fit into and serve the technique-based connectedness of reality. No simple liberation is possible any longer. We are engaged in a megaproject of re-engineering human lives, societies, and the biosphere as if all of life had the architecture of machines and technology. Of course, it may be objected that this view is much too pessimistic and one sided. I might be persuaded were it not for the responses of tens of thousands of students to whom I have taught this material for nearly forty years. The majority found this diagnosis to be a path towards a hopeful prescription, one that, if ever implemented, could ensure a more liveable and sustainable future. We need to understand the war that we have unleashed against ourselves, including its current battle for the human spirit. As noted, our social selves are becoming increasingly fragmented and reified because they are built up with a metaconscious knowledge separated from symbolic experience and culture and thus in the image of technique. It is calling into question everything that has made us human until now.

In sum, I have provided a few highlights of how discipline-based approaches to human knowing and doing began to de-symbolize our cultures, to the point that they had to be complemented by more "realistic" approaches in conformity with the reality of a technical order. In order for life to be made liveable within this new reality, many of the traditional cultural elements were replaced by secular equivalents. Today we have new secular myths that have transformed some of our creations into entities without limits, much like the way in which traditional cultures created their gods. These secular myths have produced new secular political religions, statistical moralities, and secular institutions, which are increasingly dependent on the technique-based connectedness of our society dominating what is left of a highly de-symbolized culture-based connectedness. Everything has been gradually turned into its opposite because of its dependence on a technical order with a completely different architecture.[58] It can be shown that discipline-based approaches to human knowing and doing have diametrically opposite characteristics to those of approaches based on symbolization, experience, and culture.[59] Economies have been transformed into "anti-economies" in the sense that they produce debt rather than wealth.[60] Contemporary societies have taken on diametrically opposite characteristics to those of traditional societies.[61] As a consequence of "technique changing people," what it is to be human has been re-engineered into something very different from what it is to be a member of a symbolic species.[62]

People of the Word

Ever since Max Weber examined the role played by Protestantism in the emergence of our civilization,[63] the influence of Christianity has been a subject of debate. Following the Second World War an analysis of the roles of Protestantism, Catholicism, and Judaism in the United States concluded that these three branches of the Judaeo-Christian tradition corresponded to three forms of the American way of life.[64] Similarly, the work *One Nation under God* carefully documented the influence of corporate America on Christian America.[65] In these and many other works, comparisons are drawn between the "spirit of an age" created by the vantage point and orientation of a time, place, and culture or a time, place, and technical order, on the one hand, and the mainstream interpretation of and beliefs drawn from the Christian Bible dominating the institutionalized Christianity of that period, on the other hand. When correlations are discovered, the analyses rarely take the next step by asking, Are these dominant representations historically and socially unique readings of the sources, or do they represent a distortion resulting from socio-cultural influences on these readings? In the latter case, the correlations found by the typical studies are hardly surprising and intellectually not significant. If Christianity is just another religion and morality that the cultures of our civilization have fabricated for themselves, the correlations are to be expected. If, on the contrary, Christianity is regarded as a revelation received from a source beyond all cultures, we need to probe a little further.

The present work seeks to reverse the usual perspective taken by these kinds of analyses. Assuming that the Jewish and Christian Bibles are ultimately dependent on a living god rather than on the gods created by all groups and societies through their cultures, an attempt can be made to re-read this revelation with the best possible critical awareness of the influences on that reading by the spirit of our age. Doing so will hardly result in a "pure" reading but hopefully in one that is less assimilated by this spirit. Simply put, if it turns out that there is a wide gap between the readings that have been freed from the influence of the spirit of an age to the greatest extent possible and the readings that are in the grip of this spirit, then the entire debate shifts to an examination of the extent to which Christianity has been assimilated by the spirit of the age, which in our case is dominated by technique, science, the nation-state (served through politics), and history. Based on my extensive prior study of our civilization in the grip of the tension between technique and culture, I will show that indeed Christianity has been assimilated by the secular sacred and myths of our civilization. It has been turned into a religion and a morality that are attempting to fill a supposed vacuum in our so-called secular mass societies. We depart from the assumption (or belief) that the Jewish and Christian Bibles have a source that lies outside of all cultures, in order to show that there exists an enormous gap between what passes for Christianity in North America and what its source declares it to be.

We have thus far argued that babies as members of a symbolic species totally depend on listening to human words for their development. The radical importance of this listening becomes evident when we compare the development based on listening to human words to a development without it, as in the case of being raised by animals, being kept in isolation, or having to access human words by other means, as in the case of deaf-blind children.

It is not until children begin to be suspended in the language and culture of their community that it becomes possible to communicate anything regarding God's Word. The Jewish and Christian Bibles tell us that, following the break between God and humanity, there no longer was any common denominator between God's Word and human words in the form of languages and cultures. The Word originated in a transcendent God communicating with members of humanity, following which it was transmitted to other members by speaking with them about it, using the language and culture required for their development as members of a community.

For those of us who believe that the Word is a communication from a transcendent God, this Word is not of our making and does not belong to our culture, or any other culture, for that matter. It involves our living the tension between the irreconcilable differences among the religions and moralities created by all cultures and what grows from listening to the Word as a non-religion and a non-morality. This is the task to which we now turn.

1 The Possibility and Impossibility of Living a Secular Life

How Secular Have We Become?

Why has every culture, without exception, created a morality and religion for itself? Perhaps this was a response to a universal necessity experienced by every human group or society. What could this necessity be? As will become apparent later, the most probable answer appears to be human finitude as a consequence of our being creatures instead of gods. For example, in our age we have difficulty accepting that our finitude puts limits on our scientific knowing and technical doing. In any case, the universality of morality and religion points to something structural about our relationships with our surroundings, as opposed to something intentional that can be either taken up or left.

The most common explanation, which has endured for centuries, is that morality and religion fill an existential void, a void that, we now believe, a universal and discipline-based science is better equipped to fill. However, the bloodbaths of the twentieth century created by the three great secular political religions (communism, National Socialism, and hard-line democracy) did not bear this out.[1] For example, Karl Marx was supposed to have scientifically discovered the laws of human history based on what was thinkable and doable in the nineteenth century.[2] In all of humanity it was thus only the Communist Party who knew what was truly happening and where everyone was headed. It alone had the truth about history, by which light they could guide all of humanity into a secular paradise. Everyone who stood in the way had to be re-educated or killed because they did not have the right to interfere with the destiny of humanity. It led to the slaughter of tens of millions of human beings on the altar of this truth, by the believers in this secular political religion. Similarly, National Socialism would guide the leading industrial power of its day out of the despair of crippling unemployment and inflation towards a glorious millennium that would eventually benefit all of humanity. Another bloodbath followed. In the same vein, hard-line democracy demanded that Americans unconditionally love the United States and serve the American way of life with all their heart, strength, and mind, with God on their side. If they had any doubts whatsoever, they risked being treated as secular heretics and labelled a "Commie," "tree-hugger," liberal, atheist, or whatever Americans were supposed to hate on that day. Had there not been a lingering remnant of the earlier influences of Judaism and Christianity on the mainstream of American life, the situation might have turned much uglier. Hard-line democracy continues to pose a threat in the United States and Western Canada. In sum, the events of the twentieth century are hardly a testimony to our having become rational and secular, especially since these three secular political religions were served by the three most modern and industrially advanced nations.

Had we listened to some of our foremost scientists, we might have been forewarned that our universal and discipline-based science was unlikely to fill the void created by the weakening traditional moralities and religions. Niels Bohr suggested that we are so suspended in language that we do not even know what is up or down.[3] Albert Einstein believed that we are able to observe only those facts of which our theories can make sense.[4] Thomas S. Kuhn found that, when this is occasionally not the case, a scientific revolution is usually triggered, resulting in a different theory.[5] Hence, we appear to be suspended in our scientific theories. Kuhn showed that, while we scientifically know a great deal more today than at any other time, we have no basis for claiming that we know our world any better. Bernard D'Espagnat believed that our search for reality may well be endless.[6] Similar conclusions have been reached by a variety of thinkers in the social sciences but especially by the three so-called masters of suspicion, Karl Marx, Sigmund Freud, and Friedrich Nietzsche.[7] It would appear, therefore, that the relationships we have with our world may be a great deal more complex than our popular scientism suggests, and our universe may well remain ultimately unknowable.

It is possible that we could have done much better by observing our children as they grow up. Provided that their creativity and curiosity is encouraged, they have a playful attitude towards their world – a world that yields an endless stream of surprises. These are not threatening because the children know that whenever they get stuck in their play, they can count on the loving care and support of a parent or caregiver who will help them and even console them if necessary. This playfulness gradually subsides when they go to school and become educated – an education that is too organized and planned to leave much room for playful initiative. When they grow into teenagers, they frequently exhibit signs of protest against the world of the adults, which makes little sense to them, and yet they learn to live in it. Initially the unknown is not a threat to toddlers and children, but by the time it can become so, they have learned to live as if the unknown were more of what they knew and lived, as a consequence of the development of metaconscious myths. These interpolate and extrapolate their symbolized experiences into a life and a cultural way of making sense of and living in their world. Their relationships with this acquired culture are somewhat analogous to those between fish and water.

From a historical perspective, it appears that humanity has been able to change its "cultural waters." Human life has evolved in relation to three life milieux. At first, there was the life milieu of what we call nature, in relation to which the food-gathering and hunting ways of life evolved. These eventually gave birth to the second life milieu, that of society, which interposed itself between the group and nature, thus creating a primary life milieu of society embedded in the now-secondary life milieu of nature. These societies evolved agricultural ways of life through which nature was transformed. Eventually, these ways of life gave birth to an entirely new life milieu, that of technique, as a growing number of relationships within society and between society and nature became technically (as opposed to culturally) mediated. As the density of technically mediated relationships continued to increase, they jointly formed a life milieu via which people experienced the secondary life milieu of what remained of a society and the tertiary life milieu of a substantially transformed biosphere.[8]

From these observations it follows that a life milieu is that entity in human experience in relation to which human life evolves as the provider of everything necessary for life and thus as the ultimate threat to that life if it withholds any of these necessities. It also entirely envelops that life, to the point that the people of a time and place cannot imagine who they would be, how they would live, and what their world would be without it. In order that this life milieu not become an all-determining force as a kind of destiny, human groups and traditional societies have always distanced themselves from their life milieux, creating a margin of human freedom in relation to this determination. They did this by means of symbolizing everything according to its meaning and value for human life, thereby building up cultures in the process. Doing so permitted their ways of life to evolve by opening up a variety of new possibilities and relationships. Our contemporary civilization is the only one that no longer engages in this symbolization of the current life milieu but regards it as one of our own making, thereby leaving the stage free for discipline-based approaches to all our endeavours. It has closed the door to all genuine solutions to our human, social, economic, and environmental crises since these all depend on symbolization or, more accurately, on re-symbolization.[9]

Humanity's three "cultural waters" may also be distinguished by the sacred (or central myth) and its accompanying myths, which jointly anchor and orient the associated human cultures in an ultimate unknowable universe. The food-gathering and hunting ways of life were anchored in a natural sacred surrounded by natural myths; the agricultural ways of life, in a social sacred flanked by natural myths; and industrial ways of life, in the sacred of capital supported by the myths of progress, work, and happiness, and later in the sacred of technique and the state-nation sustained by the myths of science and history.[10]

Since humanity is a symbolic species, each and every member is born into a dependence on a language and a culture, which includes becoming rooted in the myths of that culture. Even when these cultures are highly de-symbolized, we continue to be anchored in secular myths. Consequently, we cannot be born as a Jew or a Christian. What can happen is that when we grow up to become a member of a symbolic species, the acquisition of a culture may be extensively influenced by these traditions, but there is always a great deal that will escape them. It is obvious that, if we are born in a certain time, place, and culture, there is a high probability of our adopting a particular religion. The probability would be extremely low or non-existent if we were born in a different time, place, and culture. To put it in another way, there is no Jewish or Christian "human nature," although there are communities that will seek to permeate this nature by socializing their children into the tradition to the best of their ability.

With this background it may be a little easier to understand the radicality of the liberating message of the opening two chapters of the Jewish and Christian Bibles. Occasionally Jews and Christians understood this, but it appears hardly to be the case today. Nevertheless, there were times when the Jewish people in constant contact with surrounding cultures understood clearly that these had nothing whatsoever in common with the revelation. They knew very well that whatever neighbouring cultures held to be sacred – whether it be the sun, the mountains, the trees, the bulls, or anything else – these were nothing more or less than what they were created to be. The Jewish Bible constantly pokes fun at the make-believe gods of the Jews' neighbours by referring to them as "golden calves" or "lords of the flies."[11] Similarly, the early Christians in the Roman Empire, who were still close to their Hebrew roots, were regarded by others as atheists who were destructive of religion and thus enemies of the human race because they provoked the wrath of the gods.[12] Their Christianity could not simply be added to the collection of Roman religions, because it was against all of them. In the Jewish Bible it is never a question of a Jewish religion and morality against all others. Instead, in a creation brought into being from the outside, as it were – by a transcendent God who spoke – nothing physical or natural can be sacred. Instead, the Hebrew God was holy, meaning that he had set himself apart from his creation, with the result that there was nothing of him in anything natural or cultural. Although there are many polemical texts of this kind, those of Genesis 1 and 2 lead the charge. The sun is the sun and nothing else. So is the moon – nothing but a creation. The wind is simply the wind. There is nothing of God in anything.

Moreover, as creatures, human beings depend directly on their creator and indirectly on everything he has created. Human lives are thus relative in character, and no religion or morality can ever change this. The first two chapters of Genesis go to great lengths to explain the kinds of relationships between God and humanity, and between humanity and the remainder of creation, that made it possible to live without having to depend on anything sacred – including the religion and morality that bound a human group to such a sacred. It was the desire to be free from dependence on God and his creation that set humanity on the road of religion and morality. Before this happened, life was intended to be entirely secular without any sacred.

Although the early Christians lived in the conviction that there was nothing sacred when Christianity was declared to be the official religion of the Roman Empire, all this fell by the wayside. It now had to serve the religious needs of the societies of that time. Doing so required a sacred, and what could be more sacred than the vast organization that had become a necessity in order to manage Christianity and deal with the massive influx of converts?[13] It was assumed that the transmission of faith could be organized and managed by a religious institution.

By the end of the Middle Ages, corruption knew few limits. After the Reformation the Protestants continued the institutionalization of Christianity but on a national scale. With hindsight, the experiences of the non-institutionalized "house churches" of the first century were dismissed as impractical and idealistic. Catholic and Protestant congregations organized and ran sanctuaries in which consecrated priests and pastors exercised sacred authority and power. Undoubtedly, as people of a time, place, and culture, or people of a time, place, and universal order, all Jews and Christians share the same moral and religious needs as does everyone around them, with the enormous risk of confusing what is holy with what is sacred, confusing faith with religion, and confusing freedom with morality. As noted, there were times when this appeared to have been clearly understood and resisted, but today that does not seem to be the case. To understand this confusion we need to explore how the reading of our Bibles depends on our language and our culture, and thus on the sacred that anchors and orients them.

When we read our Bible, we enter into a reciprocal relationship with it. We inevitably influence that reading by what we bring to it, but we usually think only in terms of being influenced via our reading. We cannot read and make sense of our Bibles other than by using our language and culture, with the result that we risk imposing things on the texts that are simply not there. At the same time, we believe this text to be a communication from a transcendent God whose ways are entirely other than ours, implying that we may need some help in order to understand what we read. In human communication the parties must be similar enough that they can understand one another, and yet different enough that they can bring something into one another's lives. Such a dialectical tension does not exist with a God who is holy, that is, entirely other than ourselves. Hence, we need some help to understand what God says to us. This help is beyond what any institution can organize and manage, which is not to deny that some fellow believers (within or outside it) have a role to play in this understanding.

Why then do the Jewish and Christian Bibles from the very beginning insist on Elohim's speaking to us? The common theological answer is that God grants a connection with us, which is referred to as the breath of life, the spirit, and, in the case of the Christian Bible, the Holy Spirit. I must confess that these kinds of theological truisms never did much for me. For now, the point will simply have to be that, for there to be a true understanding, some co-operation from a transcendent God is required. In sum, because of this reciprocal relationship that we have with our Bibles, we run the enormous risk of reading something of our own time, place, and culture into it. We rarely accept a sufficient responsibility for this risk by doing everything possible to avoid it. We wave our theological wands and assure ourselves that God will break through all this with his Spirit so that the net influence moves from him to us and not the religious reverse.

From a historical and sociological perspective it is evident that the usual reading and understanding of Genesis 1 and 2 is unquestionably the result of having turned it into something that fits into our world. This is the case not only when we are persuaded that these chapters are a kind of flawed scientific account of how the world came into being. It is even more so when we believe that our reading is a faithful one because we oppose the world by suggesting that the Genesis account is an alternative answer to the theory of evolution. Such reading implies that these chapters must have a scientific validity, which is equivalent to bowing to a limitless science. It is equally the case when we suggest that the doctrine of fixism is untenable and must be replaced by something along the line of intelligent design. In all these cases what is really happening is that we impose on this text what we have brought to its reading in terms of the sacred and myths of our de-symbolized culture. Our imposition has completely obscured what the Jewish people and the early Christians understood from these texts, which was infinitely more important and far reaching than our silly debates about creation or evolution, which in one way or another are in submission to our secular sacred and myths.[14]

There is an additional matter that is worth noting. Georges Devereux has suggested that when social scientists encounter something that is deeply offensive or in any way troublesome from the vantage point of their time, place, and culture, what they usually take away from it has been modified by counter-transference reactions, which reduce the anxiety created by these situations.[15] If the Jewish and Christian Bibles are a communication from a transcendent God, they confront us with something that is entirely other than what we know and live. In other words, a simple litmus test as to whether we are comprehending what we are reading in our Bibles is a profound discomfort, because in one way or another these texts always call into question our cultural being and roots. Without counter-transference reactions these texts would push us towards relativism, nihilism, and anomie because of our strong connections to a particular time, place, and culture. We face the possibility of becoming a little less well-rooted by our secular, sacred, and myths, and this is deeply disturbing for all of us. Counter-transference reactions are utterly necessary. It is only to the extent and depth that we are convinced that we are loved and liberated by this transcendent God who reveals himself, that we are able to bear some uprooting from our time, place, and culture. As relative beings we need to be rooted, and it is only to the extent that we can live as belonging to God that we can give up a little of our dependence on the roots provided by our culture. On this point we must be totally clear. One cannot deal with the relative character of individual and collective human life by some kind of philosophical ontology, world-view, or moral principles. We must live it, and we can do this either through the secular, sacred, and myths of our culture or by struggling against them as we learn to trust our God and live our lives rooted in him.

These issues raise another difficulty. Theology has become one discipline among many in the modern university, with all the consequences this entails. One of the more obvious examples of our bowing down to our supposedly limitless discipline-based approaches to knowing and doing is the "historical Jesus" approach. It confronts the impossibility of dealing with the Bible entirely within the confines of disciplines such as religious studies and theology. The Bible must be stripped down to what a discipline can deal with, and the remainder must be left to the non-academics. The result is making a complete non-sense of the Christian Bible, in the same way that all other disciplines do to everything else when they exceed their limits. When theologians in the grip of discipline-based approaches pass these allegiances on to their students, especially those who become priests and pastors, it is not difficult to understand why churches have little to say to the world.

Similarly, the insistence on *sola scriptura* is a non-starter. It amounts to a kind of Christian magic that makes these issues disappear. Since our Bibles are translated into a particular language, and since this language is indissociably linked to a culture (de-symbolized or not), there is no such thing as a "pure" reading of the Bible decontaminated from the culture and world in which we live. Both the liberal and conservative branches of Judaism and Christianity have fallen into the same trap but for diametrically opposite reasons.

Superimposed on all of this are the considerable incommensurabilities between the Hebrew language in which the Jewish Bible was written and the contemporary languages in which most of us read it. These incommensurabilities are somewhat less in the New Testament of the Christian Bible, which, although it is written in a Greek strongly tied to its Hebrew roots, the Greek is closer to our own languages. However, the influence of Greek philosophy has created endless translation problems. Translating something from one language into another depends on how it can be lived, expressed, and thought in each one. In the introduction we noted that the meaning of a word or phrase depends on how it is differentiated from all other words and phrases, and how, jointly, all such differentiated elements symbolically map individual and collective human life in a symbolic universe associated with a time, place, and culture. For example, what can be expressed regarding the "world" of colour in one language may be incommensurate with the way in which colours are experienced by the members of a culture speaking another language. Dark shades of what we would regard as the primary colours have been differentiated in some cultures as being essentially similar, all belonging to the colour "dark," and light shades as belonging to the colour "light." Not all cultures have differentiated the colours of the rainbow into five primary colours. In these kinds of cases the translations of the names of colours can pose some difficulties.[16]

Similarly, different cultures have arranged individual and collective human life in time in very different ways, as is reflected in the tenses of the grammar of their languages. For example, if what happened earlier can no longer be experienced and lived as influencing people's lives, it may be differentiated as belonging to a past that is fundamentally different from the present. In contrast, the present may not be differentiated from the future as being fundamentally different, because it is lived as being constituted by what were once present events that helped to open the future by continuing to affect individual and collective human life for some time to come. In some cultures, the distant past and the distant future may be fundamentally differentiated from the present, while the present may be regarded as essentially continuing the immediate past that will also be carried into the immediate future. The deepest incommensurabilities between languages will occur when what can be lived, expressed, and thought is rooted in very different myths. As noted, this is the case for the myths of traditional pre-industrial societies and those of the industrial societies to which these traditional societies gave birth. The myths of the industrial societies in turn mutated into our contemporary societies whose highly de-symbolized cultures are overshadowed by the reality of a technical order. The first transition was accompanied by changes in the meaning of many words in the English language,[17] while the second appears to be accompanied by a growing vocabulary of what we have referred to as image-words.[18]

In addition, every culture will differentiate individual lives (as being essentially similar or fundamentally different) from the life of the group or society, will differentiate the group or society from all other life, and will differentiate all of this from the primary life milieu. For example, if the human group does not fundamentally differentiate its collective life from all other life in the natural world, it is possible to live as if everything around the group responds to language, that is, by having a spirit of some kind. However, a fundamental differentiation of humanity from a separate and distinct nature can evolve into living as if there were a separate and distinct environment "out there," from which we must derive everything we need as resources and to which we cannot help but return what we no longer need. In other words, these relationships are no longer symbolized as being highly enfolded, which makes it impossible to live as though they constitute the "environment" for other species as they do for us.[19] Language translation is thus inseparable from the cultures involved.

A great deal of difficulty has also arisen from the reading of the Jewish and Christian Bibles as a kind of intellectual resource for building a Christian philosophy or world-view. In such a case, these Bibles are placed on the level of, and in competition with, other philosophies and world-views, and this can lead to a distorted understanding of these texts. For example, early translations of the Christian Bible from the Greek were deeply influenced by Greek philosophy. It resulted in Genesis 1 and 2 being translated and read as dealing with the origins of the universe, since that is what Greek culture deemed all important. God became Platonic and later more Aristotelian, which completely distorted the kinds of relationships he could have with his creation. Eventually some Christians, including Pascal, began to realize that an image of God constructed by Greek philosophy had nothing whatsoever in common with the God of the Bible. More or less at the same time, Christians had given up on the immortal Greek soul, leaving a material world that could be expressed in terms of mathematics and envisaged as the most perfect machine of the time, thereby reducing God to the "great clockmaker." The universe mechanism ticked along according to its "laws" until Darwin's thought implied that there was little need for this clockmaker God. Greek philosophy was in the process of being replaced by the emerging discipline-based sciences as arbiters of what could be accepted from the Bible and what should be rejected by any rational and secular person. With a great deal of hindsight, it would appear that the philosophies of an age tend to push to the limits what is thinkable within the myths that sustain the people of a time, place, and culture. It is very rare that a philosophy is iconoclastic with respect to the myths of its time, for the obvious reason that powerful counter-transference reactions usually prevent this from happening. Certainly the "three masters of suspicion" were entirely rooted in the myths of their age or were just beginning to intuit something of the new myths that were taking their place.

Christian philosophies and theologies have been no exception; they are often permeated by the spirit of their age. Of course, this can become a certainty only with a great deal of hindsight. It cannot answer the question as to how Jews or Christians can introduce something radically other into their time, place, and culture by allowing their communities to evolve beyond their myths and thus opening up a new future. This would involve a discernment of what holds our communities captive, enclosed in myths that provide a distorted understanding of everything, including ourselves. Doing so requires a Judaism and Christianity without an ontology of any kind.[20] Genesis 1 and 2 could once again launch Judaism and Christianity in such a direction, one entirely other than as a morality or a religion.

This transformation cannot be accomplished by any philosophical or theological argument, which might proceed as follows. In the first three chapters of Genesis, God reveals to us that this universe and everything within it is his creation. Despite the break that occurred between him and humanity, he continues to love us and is busy saving us by delivering us from everything that enslaves us. Consequently, the unknown cannot pose a fundamental threat of any kind. On the contrary, what matters about the unknown is that God's kingdom is coming towards us as a complete reconciliation between him and his creation. There is thus no need for myths or for the religion and morality they anchor.

Moreover, when we respond to his love, there is no need for a morality, any more than two people in love with each other require their community to tell them what they must do for each other. With love all this comes spontaneously. If we no longer need a morality, we do not need the religion necessary to anchor it and to protect us from relativism, nihilism, and anomie. It is thus possible to come of age, and not only to live secular lives but to show the world how everyone can do the same. Surely the result would be a reduction in religious tensions and possibly the end of all religious wars, whether they involve traditional or secular political religions. The problem with these kinds of theological or philosophical elaborations is that they cannot contain truths. All they can be is more or less exact in relation to God's revelation, but our Bibles are all about living and not about a metaphysics that we derive from them. To Jews and Christians, truth is not something that can be achieved by means of discipline-based theology or philosophy. God is the only One who is true, and thus to be true requires a connection with him. For the Jews awaiting the Messiah, this relationship will be established by him. For Christians, it is Jesus Christ who is that Messiah: the way, the truth, and the life. Truth is not something theological or philosophical but a relationship that is lived. Hence, our reading of the Bible must not be confused with metaphysics, theology, philosophy, or science, because this will completely distort the message. Would any one of us read a love letter under these categories? If we did, it would certainly destroy our relationship with the one who sent it.

Language, Swearing, and the Sacred

A more positive way of attempting to clear away the many misunderstandings about Genesis 1 and 2, and everything this implies for the remainder of our Bibles, is to approach these texts as having been discerned by his people (and not by theologians) as the Word of God. Hence, we must read these texts as coming from the One who is entirely other than anything we know and live, including the myths in which we are suspended. It is not my intention to examine these texts in detail here, because this was done in an earlier book by Jacques Ellul.[21] My primary reliance on this study is due to the credentials of that author, who believed the biblical texts to be the Word of God and who was one of the leading sociologists of technology and our technique-dominated civilization in the second half of the twentieth century. Ellul did more than anyone else I know to make us critically aware of who we are in this time, place, and highly de-symbolized culture. As a result, his biblical exegesis is in constant dialogue with this interpretation, permitting him to avoid counter-transference reactions to a greater degree than anyone else I know. I will thus limit myself to some key aspects that are essential for the present study.

In this age what is so fascinating and important about the opening two chapters of Genesis is their description of human life lived in love and communion with God and everything that was brought forth by his Word. It is a perfectly secular human life; there is no religion, no morality, no magic, no sanctuaries, and no consecrated places or persons. There is a complete absence of the sacred. In our so-called secular mass societies all these human creations are a necessity, given our ongoing need for myths to close the door to relativism, nihilism, and anomie. Religion, morality, magic, sanctuaries, consecrations, and myths have taken on secular forms in comparison to the forms of their precursors, but this does not mean that we have liberated ourselves from cults of all kinds.[22]

The focus of the first two chapters of Genesis appears to be on the two ways in which God reveals himself (as Elohim and as YHWH) to establish relationships with us, all life, and our universe. They reveal what, in these two ways of his being, is essential for our understanding of the meaning of the situation in which we find ourselves, as described in the third chapter. Nothing in our lives and in the universe is any longer in the right place, with the result that the fabric of relationships within which we live our lives has robbed us of our freedom. As its slaves we have become incapable of forming relationships of love, for which such freedom is a prerequisite. As the first two chapters remind us, this is not what was intended and created.

Genesis 1 and 2 are not an account of the creation but of the establishment of and engagement in an architecture of relationships of love, freely participated in by God, humanity, and all creatures. In love the potentiality of this architecture enriches the lives of all parties. God launched all this by speaking it into being. In so doing, he risked everything because, in this creation of love and harmony, one of the parties could decide to break the relationship. This possibility was also taken care of in love in the days of the beginning. Without the Word these first three chapters could not have been written, because what occurred would not have been accessible to human language.

Possibly one of the most fundamental difficulties presented by this revelation is the insistence of the text on God's speaking. How are we to interpret this revelation, which was received at a time that the connection between God and humanity had been broken, with the result that his ways were entirely other than those of a humanity that had gone its own way? Does this situation not make it impossible to express anything God does by means of a human equivalent? What could God's speaking and our speaking possibly have in common? It is clearly not a matter of God's clearing his throat to begin to vibrate the air with his tongue in accordance with a language! The text surely intends to reveal something much more fundamental.

Before proceeding, it is essential to remind ourselves what we mean by *speaking* and *listening* as members of a civilization that has all but replaced traditional languages and cultures with universal discipline-based approaches to knowing, doing, and communicating. We can immediately dismiss everything that masquerades for speaking and listening because of a nearly complete absence of embodiment, participation, commitment, and freedom.[23] Much of the time we are on the receiving end of the mass media, where there are no genuine speakers but only spokespersons "communicating" an engineered message that has been created to achieve a desired effect of one kind or another with the greatest efficiency and power possible. On the new media, much of this filters down to all those who participate, as we "advertise" ourselves to gain "friends" on whom we wish to make the best possible "impressions," as they also do on us. Granted, the sophistication of the techniques involved is well short of that of the traditional mass media, but this probably makes the long-term consequences on our lives even greater because we spontaneously re-engineer ourselves in the image of technique, particularly that of the new media. In our texting we have been obliged to make the use of our language more efficient. With Twitter we have learned to speak and listen to sound bites. We are also becoming more and more accustomed to voice recognition, as if talking to our cars or any other device were much the same as speaking to another person. As noted in the introduction, all such developments are integral to a much broader and all-encompassing de-symbolization of our languages and cultures. In other words, these observations are neither a moral nor an ideological condemnation of others but a recognition that these are the necessities imposed on all of us living in our "anti-societies," in the sense that their characteristics are the diametrical opposite of their precursors.[24]

These kinds of experiences are foreign to our biblical texts, for the simple reason that they did not exist when the oral traditions were passed on and eventually written down, edited, and received as a Word from God. The people involved almost exclusively used their languages in face-to-face conversations with others, and all such conversations were embedded in a traditional culture and the symbolic universe interposed by it between their society and the universe. We must constantly remind ourselves that as a civilization we no longer see any essential differences between this kind of communication and what takes place between machines. This is evident from information theory, which excludes any possibility of a dialectical relationship because it cannot be mathematically represented. Similarly, cognitive psychology excludes any possibility of a dialectically enfolded human life in the world that is sustained by the organizations of our brain-minds. As noted, these kinds of "scientific" approaches appear self-evident only because we live in highly de-symbolized cultures, but from a historical vantage point this has been the case for little more than half a century. We must therefore be prepared for a counter-transference reaction regarding the role of language being intimately associated with creating and maintaining relationships. Nevertheless, this view of language is in part based on a great deal of research, of which the introduction has provided an overview.

The most prudent point of departure is revealed by our Bibles regarding the many negative aspects of our speaking human languages, because they tell us something of what our use of language should have been and what it will be again one day. The Epistle of James (as the most Jewish book in the Christian Bible) is particularly clear on this point.[25] This letter forbids Christians to swear an oath, which goes to the very heart of what is at stake in our use of language. When we as Christians swear an oath, we are thus regarded as people who have broken the unity of our persons and our lives. It is even worse when we swear on a Bible. Our words no longer correspond to our hearts or our actions, because the Christian Bible regards our words as coming from the depths of our hearts. Consequently, if our beings and our lives are no longer sufficient to guarantee that what we are saying is true, we are obliged to appeal to something else. In that case we do not take ourselves seriously and refuse to take full responsibility. We thus require another authority to which we appeal and behind which we hide in a refusal to commit ourselves. Since we live in a creation, no such authority can be found because nothing is more than what God created it to be. Consequently, the only other authority apart from ourselves would be God, but we have culturally rejected his authority and replaced it with something sacred. We will examine this in some detail in the chapters that follow.

Our swearing an oath thus takes on a religious character because swearing by anything in heaven or on earth involves attributing a religious character to it: we transform something that was created by God into something sacred, that is, something having religious authority. We turn into witnesses to our oaths things that are nothing more than creations of God, and religiously appropriate what does not belong to us. Worse, we in essence create a religious sphere within God's creation, which is forbidden as a transgression of life according to the first promise and commandment of the Decalogue. In sum, we attest to our hypocrisy when we swear an oath and show ourselves as divided beings whose words mean something else than our lives. We also engage in a religious act, which distorts the creation by introducing something sacred into it. The unity of our being, our words, and our life is broken, placing us in a condition that we will refer to as an inability to "be fully yes" to the other and to our God due to this broken unity.

This condition of hypocrisy must be distinguished from lying, which involves saying something that we know not to be true. Hypocrisy is a dissociation of who we appear to be according to our word and who we are in our being and our life. It was their hypocrisy that so deeply disappointed Jesus about the Pharisees.

All of this is in complete contradiction to what we experience in intimate face-to-face conversations with the person we love. The very first time we spoke with that one, we received two possibly different impressions in terms of how he or she looked and the glimpses of the life behind these visual impressions, which were revealed when we talked. It is by means of language alone that we gradually entered into that person's life and social "world." In a society like ours, where looks are almost everything, getting to know someone may well have been constantly prejudged by visual impressions. Nevertheless, it is by means of language that we are able to enrich each other's lives by bringing in something new. Doing so requires that we are sufficiently similar so that this enrichment can be fitted into our lives, but different enough that it is genuinely new and interesting. Initially, such enrichment may simply be interesting and thus reason enough to meet again. When this continues, a relationship may begin to grow, but this will happen only to the extent that we commit to it. The more we share of ourselves and our lives with the other person, the more we become vulnerable to the other by opening ourselves up to the possibility of being seen as flawed, inadequate, or in some other way not being what the other hoped for. In such cases the other person may feel free to share these concerns with acquaintances or friends, with many possible negative repercussions. In other words, the more the relationship deepens by our sharing more and more of ourselves with the other, the more we must be prepared to trust the other and commit ourselves to the relationship. When two people have shared everything in their lives, they become so fully embodied in the relationship that, in a delicate situation, the one can tell the other with a single look how they feel about it. Their lives work so fully in the background that even when they discuss the situation later, few words may be required.

At a certain point in an intimate relationship two persons may have come to know one another so well that there is little that the one can say to the other that they do not already know. At this point the dialectical tension between being similar and being different has weakened, and the relationship may be entering into a difficult time because there is less and less reason for one to remain involved in it. It now becomes essential to reinvent the relationship by opening up new areas for sharing. In our societies the risk of estrangement tends to be the greater one. Our lives are at best a bundle of weakly related social roles, of which the intimate relationship is but one. Consequently, there is a substantial risk of growing apart because the differences overwhelm the similarities, with the result that there is less and less reason for participating in the relationship.

Therefore, the sharing of a language is not a sufficient condition for the establishment of relationships. There must be a metalanguage held in common by the parties involved in speaking and listening. Moreover, the means of communication are always fragile and weak. Talking and listening in a face-to-face conversation is the weakest way of communicating. When speaking, we vibrate the air, and the sound waves reach the ears of the other, but they quickly die away to disappear forever. The other person needs to interpret what we are saying, which does protect their freedom; there is no obligation that a speaker can impose on the other to interpret and understand it in the way it was intended. Moreover, because the speaker's entire life is working in the background and is fully available by the greatest possible embodiment, participation, and commitment, much more may be said than the speaker is aware of. In the same way, the life of the listener is also working in the background, with the result that his or her understanding can enrich or impoverish what is being said by the speaker. In addition, if we are true to the other and to ourselves, we stand behind our words as expressions of who we are and of the life we live. To be true to the other, we literally give them our word each and every time we speak, fully backed by our being and our life. This implies an obligation and a commitment to the other person. Similarly, for the other to be true to his or her word and for there to be a true relationship, the other must treat what they hear as integral to the speaker. If (and only if) this is done out of love for the other, we will do the best we can for everything to work out as described. If we do not love the other, the worst possible things can happen. Our Bibles, and not only the letter of James, have a great deal to say about the false use of language.

If through language we can establish and sustain the most cherished relationships, we can also do the exact opposite, by not being true to the other and not standing behind our words with our being and our life. We are able to deceive the other by hiding behind our words or by creating an image of how we would like the other to see us. We can use language to spread rumours about the other person and, in the extreme, can destroy them, as is the case when bullying causes someone to commit suicide. We can also undermine and destroy relationships by lying.

This confirms how all of our lives began as members of a symbolic species. By being spoken to when we are babies and toddlers, we develop the double referencing system through which we can enter into the beginnings of the symbolic (though highly de-symbolized) universe of our community. Whether or not this use of language is embedded in a nurturing love can make a great deal of difference. The efforts of contemporary societies to use language to re-engineer all our relationships through public relations, commercial and political advertising, and social integration propaganda[26] are doing incalculable harm to all of us by diminishing these relationships; this is done by directly and indirectly destroying the capacity of human language to establish and sustain them.

Our use of language is indissociable from a culture, and a culture is indissociable from its moorings in a sacred (or central myth) and its supporting myths. This dependence continues in our contemporary so-called secular societies. However, there is no diminished dependence on swear words nor on cursing itself.

The discussion of the ways in which speaking and listening affect relationships generally also applies to relationships of love. However, what *love* brings to mind in our civilization has nothing in common with what this word means in our Bibles, for the simple reason that it is impossible for us to be fully "yes" to one another and to our God. Simply put, love has become the business of Hollywood and of technique. It has become a common topic of conversation and of popular music. It is a sign of our time when this talking and singing about love compensates for its absence in a civilization that has placed all human relationships on the rack of de-symbolization and technique, thereby stretching them until they break. If we could take relationships of love for granted, we would not have to endlessly talk and sing about them.

It is the same pattern that we observed earlier: when the air was clean, we simply breathed it, and there was no need to talk about it. When it became polluted as a consequence of industrialization and urbanization, artists began to pay a great deal of attention to how it affected the light. Eventually people began to talk about the things that went missing in their lives as symptoms of an environmental crisis.

Consequently it is quite difficult for us to avoid becoming a little frustrated or even cynical when reading biblical texts that insist on true and full relationships of love. It shows how difficult it is to avoid reading into our Bibles something of our own experiences, language, way of life, and culture. We simply cannot avoid counter-transference reactions.

It may be helpful to note that in our Bibles love never refers to sentiments or feelings. Instead it has everything to do with the quality of relationships and the commitments of the parties involved. For example, the usual translation to the effect that God loved Jacob but hated Esau suffers from a counter-transference reaction. It would be better to translate that God passed over Esau, in the way we pass over many people until we meet the person with whom we desire to share our life. This does not imply that we hated all the people we passed over but that we intended to establish a special relationship with one person to the exclusion of all others.

As will gradually become apparent, in our Bibles a relationship of love is total, all-encompassing, and exclusive of all other relationships. It demands that the parties involved in such a relationship hold nothing back from each other, to the point that it commits and defines each one's entire person, life, and being. Nothing must remain untouched by such a relationship of love. This relationship transforms everything, leaving nothing unchanged by it. Since this holds for both parties, each one totally identifies with the other in an all-defining commitment that includes a shared future. There are no limits to a bond of love since each party is fully "yes" to the other.

Based on what we have learned about our dependence on symbolization, language, and culture, even when these are highly de-symbolized, it is impossible for human beings to fully engage in these kinds of relationships following the break with God. As we will examine in a later chapter, people enslaved to the flesh and the principalities and powers lack the freedom to commit their entire being and life to being fully "yes" to their God and their neighbour. In earlier times slaves knew this only too well: two of them could commit their being and their lives to each other, but one of them could be sold an hour later by their owner, never to be seen again by the other. Neither Jews nor Christians escape being rooted in and defined by the enslaving, ultimate commitments imposed on them by the culture of their community as they grow up – in the form of a sacred and myths. Such commitments do not magically disappear when we commit our lives to God. It is thus impossible to be fully "yes" to our God and neighbour as well as to our cultural sacred and myths. What is possible is an engagement in a struggle against a divided loyalty, and the more we learn to live out of and through God's love, the more we are able to chip away at our cultural commitments without risking the engulfing of our lives by relativism, nihilism, and anomie. Such a struggle against a divided loyalty reaches all the way down to how we symbolize and thus make sense of all our relationships.

Our iconoclastic insights into our dependence on symbolization, language, and culture permit us to appreciate more fully what our Bibles tell us. When humanity loved God in the Garden of Eden, his Spirit dwelt in it. Human words were embedded within God's Word, thus eliminating any need for other kinds of support such as the ones that humanity created for itself following its break with God, namely our cultures. The original support has been partially restored according to Jesus's assurance to his disciples and followers that they would receive the Spirit that would permit them to dwell in him as he dwells in the Father. We will return to this in a later chapter.

What can we know about God's love of humanity? All we know is what God tells us, which is that nothing is impossible for him in his love. In other words, we can say with perfect confidence that the image of God's love made by liberal Christianity is absurd, as anyone would know who has lived through or been close to the break-up of a human love relationship. It is extremely painful and difficult to see one's lover develop a growing divided loyalty, involving someone else. Throughout the Jewish Bible, God tells us something very similar. The image of God's love made by conservative Christianity is also absurd. It resembles what happens in commerce and in the behaviour of the rich. The good and evil will be weighed on a scale, either before we are born or at the end of our life. Alternatively, faith is parcelled out on this kind of basis, even though our Bibles tell us the exact opposite. God's love cannot be limited by human decisions. We first learn that we are loved and pardoned. It is only then that we are able to understand anything else without developing counter-transference reactions. There are no preconditions of any kind, other than this: when we become aware of being loved as we are, we must accept and return that love. Possibly the greatest obstacle we encounter in understanding our Bibles results from our counter-transference reactions about God's love – as will hopefully become apparent as we advance in this study.

A Creation for Freedom without a Sacred

We can now appreciate the significance of the subject being inseparable from the verb, in biblical Hebrew. Hence, the phrase *Elohim created* corresponds to the sequence in Hebrew *he-created-Elohim,* which can be translated literally as "he-the gods-created" or as "he-the being of beings-created."[27] *Elohim* is a plurality acting as one because the verb is in the singular, as shown in the translation. In other words, the Hebrew grammar makes it unthinkable that there can be any distance between God and his speaking. Furthermore, what God speaks is backed by his unlimited power, with the result that his Word is at the same time an act of creation. Whenever God speaks to us, he makes something new and thus transforms the situation at hand.

When we examine Genesis 1 from this perspective, it becomes immediately evident that the first two verses set the stage for God's speaking. It was "within the beginning" or "in the days of the beginning" that Elohim created the heavens and the earth. For the Jews at the time this text was written, the Hebrew word translated by "earth" meant "the soil or land of Israel." Hence, the text begins with the God who created his own abode and established a covenant with his people.[28] This earth is thus different from the one referred to in verse 10. It has nothing to do with a cosmology or with a settling of the debate between creation and evolution. Having essentially been forewarned, we are then told that the earth was *tohu-wabohu,* which appears to be a Hebrew word that has no meaning and refers to no other word, either in the Hebrew language or those of the surrounding people. It may thus be assumed to be an arbitrary word to designate that before God spoke and established relationships by his Word, there was nothing expressible by words or language. As such it represents what is entirely indefinable for us.[29]

Next, we learn that God's breath or Spirit moves over the waters as it establishes relationships with what is not God. Doing so by means of the Spirit is encountered throughout the Jewish and Christian Bibles. Here it establishes a relationship with the abyss and the darkness over it. In other parts of the Bible the abyss refers to the depths of the sea where the great fish live, but it remains difficult to understand. What is meant by the waters is made clear throughout the Bible: the powers of annihilation and the nothingness that occur when things lose their created forms. This constitutes a kind of reconquest of the creation, which early Jewish readers attempted to understand by the way in which unbaked clay lost its form in water. Elohim forms the creation, but the waters can dissolve it. It is not an evil but a negative power capable of reducing the creation to nothing. This text is clearly polemical against the cultures of Israel's neighbouring peoples, whose mythologies generally regarded water as a positive force because it allowed things to grow in a dry climate.

These opening two verses of Genesis 1 do not tell us anything about what occurred before the creation, because it cannot be expressed in words, nor do we know how God began with nothing, as it were. From here on, everything becomes accessible to language because God begins to speak. It is astounding that the closest thing in human experience to what God did is our speaking. However, the God who is behind this speaking is the only living One and the Being of beings. Since he is fully behind what he speaks, we would have to be like him to fully grasp the meaning of what he says. Moreover, what he says cannot be contained in any human language and culture; we can only nibble around the edges of what he means with our language and culture. In the same vein, it is impossible for God to speak any human language because who he is and what he does have no equivalent in any culture associated with a human language. Nevertheless, God has chosen our speaking – our most fragile way of establishing a relationship – to give us some sense of what he is doing. We had better think very carefully about all the implications of that choice.

His creative Word establishes a distance between this all-powerful God, whose Word accomplishes what it says, and his creation. At the same time, this Word allows the creation the freedom to develop and respond to him. If God had used his unlimited power directly by his powerful arm and mighty hand, all this would not be possible. The creation is thus given the freedom to develop all manner of life in abundance, and God expresses his delight with the results, declaring them to be good. Since there can be no good independent from the only living One, the good is what God loves. In other words, despite the distance that God maintains between himself and his creation, everything is created by and maintained through his love, as confirmed throughout the Jewish and Christian Bibles.

Since the Hebrew language makes no distinction between God's speaking and acting, and since these are backed by an incomprehensible plurality acting in the singular, God is fully "yes" to his creatures and his creation. We can only back our words with our being and our life, but all this is very limited since we are creatures who depend on the only living One. We may not be able to accomplish what we say, or we may refuse to back what we say with our being and our life.

There is another significant difference between Elohim's Word and human words. The former is backed by a God who is unknowable other than by what he decides to reveal of himself. As noted, even this is constrained by the impossibility of God's speaking a human language and by our inability to grasp the full meaning of what he says by means of our language and culture. The most comprehensive meanings of our individual and collective human life are embodied in our myths. These are inaccessible to us as our deepest metaconscious knowledge. Yet they sum up all our experiences. We can at best intuit something of them, but they become expressible only with hindsight and then take on the form of a mythology. Of course, such myths represent a false anchor and orientation points that sum up the life and experiences of our society. Nevertheless, the only element in human experience in terms of which we can possibly understand something of God's Word is by our myths, except that God's Word expresses the fullness of being and of life and what he loves as the good. This can be understood only in terms of analogies by which we are able to construct some kind of paraphrase or metaphor of the meaning of his revelation.[30] When the living Word became a written text under the guidance of the Spirit, it gave us all that we have of Elohim's speaking. Whatever of God's Word is symbolically enfolded into this text is his being entirely "yes" to us, as is evident from the complete confidence Jesus placed in it. In other words, a connection is required between the Word and the words in the written texts. This connection takes the form of the Spirit.

If there were no distance between the Word and our text, we would become robots, directly conditioned by that Word because what God speaks is created at the same time. In other words, this distance creates a margin of freedom and choice for us as creatures. When we interpret the text and find a meaning in it, we are symbolically reaching back to the Word that Elohim spoke. As such, the reading and interpreting of the text involves us in reinventing what is required in order to listen to the Word. We need to live ourselves into the text and speak it, as it were. In other words, Elohim speaks, we need to interpret his Word, and we are called to speak it and, as witnesses, back it with our being and our life.[31] But one thing is certain: God's Word can never be fully grasped by any human language.

When God speaks the light into being, he has already differentiated it from everything else he is about to speak into being – otherwise what he speaks could have created anything or everything. Consequently, Elohim is unfolding something that is integral to his overall intentions for his creation. Moreover, speaking the light into being is backed by Elohim, the Being of beings, who is a plural acting in the singular. Without this backing, any spoken word could mean anything at all. In addition, everything created would not have been integral to and inseparable from the unity of his creation. There is thus an architecture of relationships that expresses the plurality of Elohim acting as one. The significance of any relationship, including its creation by speaking, cannot be understood in itself and must be grasped in relation to all the other creations and, jointly, to Elohim, on whom they all depend. In human experience, only languages have these kinds of architectures. This anticipates texts in the Jewish and Christian Bibles where the creation expresses itself as one, for example, when it groans in Romans 8:22–3. Our understanding of human languages also permits us to assert that nature is not a book written in the language of mathematics, because, if it were, its architecture would be very different. The creative Word is backed by Elohim, who creates a plurality that can express itself as one.

Since God speaks his creation into being, everything in it is "speakable" and thus open to human language. The first chapter of Genesis thus implies that human language is a gift from God. Humanity learns to speak and, by this most fragile of means, is to govern the creation, as we will see in the next chapter. When humanity dealt with the creation by means of symbolic languages and cultures, there remained a certain ability to respect its integrality, as is evident from the technologies invented by most cultures. Their technologies tended to be appropriate to their ways of life, and these ways of life were sustainable by local ecosystems as a consequence of symbolization. All this was lost when human knowing and doing were no longer embedded in languages and cultures after being reorganized on the basis of disciplines that de-symbolized these languages and cultures.

There is another important detail that is repeated each time God speaks into being all the plants and the living creatures.[32] In our translations they are created "according to their kind" or "after their kind." The Hebrew means the exact opposite, which can be translated better as "with a view to." It means a point of departure with a view towards its species. This implies an evolving in time. Furthermore, the translation that "Elohim saw that [what he had created] was good" is rather weak. A better translation would be that "Elohim sees: Oh, here is the good!" The Hebrew suggests a kind of astonishment on Elohim's part at what appears, and he explains that by saying, "Here is the good." This good appears towards the end of each day, except on the second and the sixth. The text never says that something is in accordance with the good; there can be no such good apart from God as a kind of objective standard. Elohim declares that what emerges is good: time, the land, the seas, the plants, the trees, the sky with all its lights, everything living in the water and the sky, and the animals on the land. In other words, everything around us in creation is what Elohim has declared to be good, and this surely implies limits to what we can do with them.[33] The good is in the material world and in the life of all creatures, not in a separate moral life. Everything in the human world is morally and spiritually good for God. All this suggests a dynamic unfolding of a differentiated and created good, with an architecture that reminds us of the development of language in babies and children.

Why does God appear to be so delighted about what he speaks into being and names? The answer to this question cannot be found in most of the translations we use, possibly because of the meaning of the word *day*.[34] The Hebrew word translated in this way can just as well mean "time." There would then be a period of time, or a passing of time expressed as a whole, that begins with the negative element (evening) and ends with the positive element (day). Associating this passage of time with twenty-four hours is to forget that for God a thousand years are like a day, as we are told in Psalm 90:4. It is the influence of Greek and Roman culture on Western civilization, and via it on much of the world, that makes us think in terms of the day beginning in the morning and ending in the evening. In the same way, we begin with life and end with death. For Jewish thinking, it is – and for Christian thinking, it ought to be – the exact opposite: we begin with death and end with life. This would also confirm why these texts were the last to be added to the so-called books of Moses. The point of departure for Jewish thinking was the situation in which the people found themselves: that of having been promised a reconciliation with God, and then working backward in history towards the way in which the need for this reconciliation had arisen. The seven days are thus seven periods of time during which Elohim made everything comprehensible.

This interpretation rests in part on the account of the creation of the light during the first period of time.[35] Elohim called the light into being. We can now know what it is, while before his Word there was nothing comprehensible about it. This light has nothing to do with the creation of the sun and the moon; that happened later. Jewish theologians associated the light with time (as we now tend to do as a consequence of the influence of relativity theory on our time and culture). The interpretation of light as time can be found in Jewish commentaries for some two thousand years. In other words, the entire creation is set in time as a preparation for human history, which will unfold during the seventh day. This leaves no doubt that a day cannot possibly refer to twenty-four hours.

There are two exceptions to God's declaring as good what he has spoken into being. The "ceiling" created between the waters is the first exception. The text does not say that the threat posed by these waters to the creation has been eliminated. It reminds us of the book of Job, in which there is a very important discussion of the powers of evil relative to those of matter and animate matter, represented respectively by the crocodile and the hippopotamus.[36] Furthermore, in the book of Revelation there are also hints of a greater battle that has raged, but we are not told about it until Jesus Christ gained the decisive victory, with the result that we need not worry about it.[37]

The second exception takes us to the creation of humanity.[38] It is preceded by a kind of deliberation or dialogue within Elohim to mark the gravity of what would come next, namely, the creation of Adam. The act of creation follows, but we are not told whether Adam's symbolic human qualities in general, and his consciousness in particular, were created all at once or whether these emerged over a period of time, as was indicated for all other life. It would appear that the Jewish and Christian Bibles have something much more important to tell us, and, in any case, they are not there to satisfy our intellectual or scientific curiosity.

All forms of animal life are created during the fifth period of time, and yet this revelation is repeated in the description of the "sixth day."[39] In other words, human beings are regarded as being different from all animals in the account of the fifth period, while they are included in the series of living beings "with a view to their kind" (or species) on the sixth day, except that humanity is not created with a view to its kind. It thus cannot be subdivided into races or any other diversity of differentiated groups. The text immediately explains why this is the case. Elohim declares: "We will make Adam within our image and within our likeness" (a literal translation). What this means is further clarified by the statement "Elohim created Adam within his image, within his image he created him, male and female he created them." As long as we do not separate any of these elements of the text in order to interpret them one at a time, the meaning appears to be that Adam is created within the image of Elohim, who is a plurality acting as one, and so it is for humanity.

All this has nothing to do with a free will, an intelligence, a microcosm of God, or a person endowed with a personality. What this text is clearly telling us is that God is man and woman in the sense that Elohim is a plurality acting as one. For this to be possible, this plurality must be one of love. In the same way, humanity is the only being created as one person separated into two forms joined in love.

This text later tells us that the two will become one flesh. We must take care not to separate a physical and a sexual love from a social and spiritual love in conformity to Greek conceptions, since this would be entirely foreign to the Jewish and Christian Bibles. Elohim as a plurality joined in love is able to act as one, and humanity was created in this image to do the same. The only other way a plurality can be a unity is by means of domination and power, but this would yield a forced unity, and it would be contrary to everything we learn about God in our Bibles.

What is so beautiful about this text is that as Elohim creates Adam, he reveals himself. Although the word *love* does not occur in this text, throughout the Jewish and Christian Bibles the love between a man and a woman that makes them two in one is taken as the key to understanding God, his relationship with his people, and the way his people should conduct themselves. This will be further clarified in the so-called second creation account, to be revisited shortly, as well as in the two "great commandments" that sum up everything about the relationship between God and his people. It should be noted that these two commandments are fully present in the Jewish Bible and were summarized by Jesus.

It should also be noted that, in Hebrew, Adam is a collective name, which does not refer to one man and one woman from whom everyone else is descended. Adam can just as well be translated as "humanity." Consequently, it is impossible to understand men and women by themselves; they are within the image of Elohim, from whom they cannot be separated. It also means that humanity is both free, as an image of Elohim, and not free, because humanity is an image. Similarly, humanity is both perfect, as a complete and finished being, and also imperfect, having been created on the sixth day (which signifies an imperfection tending towards perfection symbolized by the number seven). It explains why, following the creation of humanity, Elohim does not say, "Here is the good." What the text does say is that at the end of this period of time Elohim saw that everything he had made was very good, but this refers to the totality of creation. Within it, humanity represents an ambiguous and indeterminate factor.

Elohim does not pronounce a Word, charging humanity with bearing the good, for example. Humanity is oriented towards a history in accordance with the freedom that Elohim implies: he blesses humanity, telling them to be fruitful, to multiply, and to dominate the earth.

It is astonishing that being fruitful and multiplying has been reduced to a matter of having offspring, even though it clearly designates all the work of humanity, which includes this but is not limited to it. Similarly, to dominate the earth has been taken as a licence to do almost anything and everything. The text does not leave any room for this. Humanity created within the image of Elohim is the summit of his creation and is thus an intermediary between him and his creation by being capable of responding to his love and governing his creation in the way that Elohim does by his Word and love.

Humanity is to act in this manner in freedom. Doing so is possible because the creation is still empty of gods, evil powers, or any kind of higher forces. If we try to imagine how this text would have been read by the Jewish people at the time it was received as a Word of God, it must have been such a powerful polemic against the cultures of all their neighbours that little would be left intact.

We have already discussed the waters. The revelation that *time* was a creation of Elohim, no more and no less, constituted a fundamental challenge to an enormously influential Greek culture. An acceptance of this revelation would have required a secularization of Greek culture as a result of a cultural conversion, with far-reaching consequences for the way in which the Greeks made sense of and lived in the world. The revelation that the earth and the firmament of heaven did not come from the bodies of gods could have triggered a similar secularization of Babylonian cultures.[40] The creation of all the vegetation on the land before the creation of the sun was a polemic against all cultures that regarded the sun as a deity, because to agricultural people it was entirely self-evident that it was the sun that had made the people and their lands who and what they were. Taking this revelation seriously would have provoked a secularization of many other cultures, including the Egyptian one. It was one thing to recognize what all agricultural people knew from experience – that without sunlight nothing could grow – but this sun was something entirely different from a life-giving deity.

In the same vein, the creation of the sun, moon, and the stars to mark day, night, the seasons, and the years secularized any kind of astrology, divination, and calendar making. It would have undermined the religious authority of priests in almost every culture of those days. The same can be said about the revelation of the fifth period of time because no gods could be had from among any creatures on land, in water, or in the sky. It is no coincidence that, in the Hebrew text, the only animal singled out in the fifth period of time is the crocodile. The reduction of this Egyptian deity to a creature would again have triggered a cultural conversion towards secularization. The revelation also goes well beyond this, given the significance of the crocodile in the book of Job, as noted previously. Finally, the inclusion of humanity in the sixth period of time ought to have precluded the divinizing of human beings such as the Pharaohs in Egypt, the "divine kings" and emperors, and the saints created by religious institutions. Moreover, since humanity was to rule over all creation, no gods or any kinds of higher powers could be found there. The sixth period of time is a powerful polemic against all religions, including the transformation of Judaism and Christianity from architectures of lived relationships into little more than religions.

To sum up, each of the six periods of time may also be read as a polemic against every possible culture that, out of necessity, had to create gods for itself in order to make somewhat bearable a human life that was separated from the only living One. The price exacted was the very lives of the people who became enslaved to these gods through religious alienation.[41] What Elohim had in mind for his people and (through them) for all of humanity was something entirely different, which had no common denominator with any other culture. The Jews were to create a culture without false gods, idols, and everything associated with them. Nevertheless, they had been chosen as the smallest and weakest people in all of humanity, with whom they shared the break with God. They were called to pioneer a new, secular life and to share this with all humanity as the way in which God had chosen to reconcile himself with his creation.

Is any of this still relevant to a civilization like ours that considers itself rational, secular, and no longer in need of any traditional gods? I will attempt to show, based on a five-volume study,[42] that the revelation we are seeking to understand is possibly even more relevant today than at other times. Since discipline-based biotechnology cannot respect the integrality of our DNA pool, it will inevitably destroy it, with unimaginable consequences. What will happen to the power of matter when it becomes polluted with nanoparticles devised by discipline-based approaches? What will happen when the information-technology equivalents of almost everything human – our knowing, doing, expert intervening, remembering, using language, communicating, befriending others, and participating in communities – so dominate their symbolic equivalents that our future as a symbolic species is threatened? What happens to a civilization when most of its scientists cannot answer the question about what science is incapable of knowing either today or in the future? What happens to a civilization when there are few technical experts who know the limits of their expertise, thereby becoming like contractors who think that a hammer is the only useful tool? What happens to a civilization that regards everything as political, which implies that the state's scope and powers are unlimited? Is the threat of discipline-based approaches to the unity of creation not much greater than that of approaches based on symbolization and culture? The polemic represented by each of the "days" of creation against the cultures of the time is thus addressed to us as well – and possibly with a much greater urgency because the power of our means is so much greater.

We are now ready to briefly revisit the seventh day of creation.[43] This period of time is different from the preceding six days because it is open ended. There is no evening and morning. Consequently, we today are included in this period of time, and so will all of human history be. Moreover, it is the seventh period, which symbolizes its perfection. Elohim rests from all his work, and humanity enters into history.

Elohim is free to rest and no longer create new things, and this happens within human history. Elohim's rest provides humanity with its freedom, within a harmonious creation. This freedom enables humanity to respond to Elohim's love, as Elohim responds to humanity's love. This love is to weave the fabric of relationships of the creation. Elohim does not direct humanity but respects its freedom, as humanity respects Elohim's freedom in a communion of love. It is inconceivable that this God plans everything, directs everything, or predestines anything. He gave his creation to humanity, which was created free and was therefore able to do as it saw fit. It could either act within Elohim's image or not do so by breaking off the relationship of love.

By speaking, Elohim has made the seven periods of time comprehensible to us. He has revealed the tissue of relationships of love between himself, humanity, and the rest of creation in which humanity represents him in his image. It is the framework for human life. Elohim desires humanity to know more about this at the beginning of its history, namely, how he will be present in history as YHWH, who gives humanity his unpronounceable name. All of history is under the blessing of Elohim, who sets it apart. His rest makes possible the communion of love. We have strayed very far from this revelation by turning the Sabbath or the Sunday into something very different from a re-entry into God's rest.

For Christian readers, the first chapter of Genesis is complemented by the prologue to the gospel of John.[44] The latter informs us: "[1] Within the beginning [the Greek phrase here is exactly the same as the one used to open Genesis], there was the Word, and the Word was with God, and the Word was God. [2] The same was in the beginning with God. [3] All things were made by him and nothing was made without him." At a glance, the first and second verses of John appear to be more or less the same. However, the Greek word usually translated as "the same" is also used in verses 7 and 15, where the word clearly refers to Jesus. It is possible, therefore, to interpret the second verse as referring to the Jesus of history, which would mean that within the beginning Jesus was with God. Within the beginning, Jesus was the *logos* who was with God. The second verse is now very different from the first.

This interpretation, which goes back to the eleventh century, corresponds to texts informing us that in Jesus all things were created (Col 1:16), that he was before all things (Col. 1:17), and that we have known him from the beginning (1 John 2:13). The text in Philippians 2 gives this its full meaning. If we take these and other texts seriously, it means that the incarnation is an integral part of God's creative work, giving additional meaning to the two trees in the centre of the garden.

The same text also illuminates the curious repetition in Genesis 1:27, that God created humanity within his image, within his image he created him, male and female he created them. The repetition disappears, however, when the second phrase is interpreted as referring to the Jesus of history.

Both the Jewish and the Christian Bible reveal different ways in which God manifests himself. For example, the name *Elohim* refers to the plurality of God acting in the singular. Other expressions found in the Jewish and Christian Bibles include YHWH, the Spirit, Wisdom, God the Father, Jesus Christ, and the Holy Spirit. Christians have frequently grouped these expressions into a trinity. However, the concept of a God in three persons is an invention of medieval philosophy and is foreign to the Christian Bible.[45] In whatever way of being that God may reveal himself, he gives us his Word each time, and his entire Being of beings is behind that Word. It is in this context that we may interpret the seeming repetition regarding humanity within the image of God.

A Creation for Love without Eros

From the first chapter of Genesis it is becoming apparent that in Jewish thinking everything began with time. Consequently, the world was thought of as an event that had happened and continues to evolve. Other biblical books including Proverbs, Ecclesiastes, and the Song of Solomon develop this further: in his creation God was busy giving form to what had no form and was making comprehensible and expressible, through his Word, what previously had been *tohu-wabohu*. In these accounts it is a question not of how the creation came into being and what had been its origin, but of how this creation became comprehensible to humanity in order to make it liveable and to allow history to begin. Hence, the significance of Elohim's speaking.

Moreover, this revelation implies that the creation had already become unliveable other than in a condition of slavery. The Jewish theologians who received this oral tradition wrote it down and edited it under the guidance of the Spirit, which led to its being discerned by the people as a Word of God. They carefully examined the surrounding cultures as a way of clarifying how different this revelation was. In other words, it would appear that this chapter of Genesis both positively and negatively reveals the architecture of creation based on relationships of love, and how that love was diverted to other gods in the surrounding cultures.

A comprehension of this revelation created a variety of new insights, which made it possible to reach back once more to learn other things about this world as an event and about how it evolves. The second chapter of Genesis appears to do so in several significant ways to prepare us for understanding the third chapter, in which this whole architecture of creation based on relationships of love becomes adulterous.

Once more we must consider how the reading of these two chapters has been distorted by the imposition on it of something of our time, place, and culture. Doing so is unavoidable, but the problem can be greatly reduced by a critical examination of the prejudgments that we bring to the reading of our Bibles as a consequence of our being suspended in the languages and cultures of earlier societies or in the reality of our own civilization.[46] For over two centuries the first and second chapters of Genesis have been read as two relatively distinct creation accounts. Furthermore, as a consequence of the rise of discipline-based science and a scientism that is unaware of its own limitations, a "cult of the fact" has been created, which implies that these two chapters were read as accounts of the facts regarding the origin and creation of the universe.[47] It has become almost unthinkable that earlier cultures with low levels of de-symbolization would, without exception, have read these chapters as a single account transmitting two related meanings.

As a consequence of the influence of Greek culture and its invention of universal knowledge, we have lost track of the possibility that meaning can be neither philosophical nor theological. Meaning arises from living our lives. It comes from the way in which these lives are built up with differentiated experiences that are lived as moments of a life because that life works in the background.[48] As a result, meaning is embedded in individual and collective human life and thus cannot be transmitted directly; it must be passed on by an account of these lives or by an intellectual, philosophical, or theological reflection about such an account. No language or culture has ever been able to transmit meaning directly. As a result of the rise of discipline-based approaches and our being suspended in a reality created by such approaches, our civilization has become focused primarily on the facts and secondarily on their meaning. This means that we have completely lost track of these facts being established within a framework and a context in relation to which they take on the status of a fact, and from which they are thus inseparable.[49] From such a perspective, Genesis 1 transmits certain facts, and Genesis 2 provides others, and since many of them are contradictory, they must have been two distinct accounts that were integrated by a school of editors who simply did not have our scientific and intellectual development to understand that it is impossible to retain these kinds of contradictions.

However, if we accept that those who were involved in the receiving and transmitting of this revelation from God were people of a time, place, and culture who would regard these two chapters as an account necessary to clothe the meaning to be transmitted, it becomes highly significant that the details would change as the meaning to be transmitted is fleshed out. In this way, it becomes essential that the so-called first account describes the creation of the heavens and the earth, while the second describes the creation of the earth and the heavens with humanity at the centre. The first begins with water, and the second with a desert. In the first the animals are created before humanity, and in the second the reverse is the case. For the first it is essential that the universe be prepared to receive humanity, and in the second it is essential that humanity be created first, followed by the creation of a suitable habitat. In the first account it is Elohim who creates, while in the second it is YHWH who is busy forming and building and who gives his unpronounceable name to his people. In each case, the details are arranged to transmit complementary meanings.

In other words, we have uncritically imposed the scientific spirit of our age onto this text and have distorted it into two contradictory creation accounts of the facts. The "contradictions" are not the mark of intellectual and scientific inferiority or downright stupidity but of our so-called scientific approach being applied without any awareness of its limitations. These limitations have become virtually invisible as a consequence of our contemporary secular myths.[50] We bow down to these secular myths in exactly the same way that the cultures implied in the polemic of Genesis 1 bowed down to theirs. After all, if discipline-based science knows no limits in the domain of human knowing, it is our secular equivalent of a traditional god of human knowledge. Sacrificing these texts to this god is as useless as the sacrifices to the gods of earlier cultures. We will come away with nothing meaningful or useful. Worse, the revelation will have been submitted to our sacred.

The first two chapters of Genesis may thus be regarded as providing two meaningful and complementary ways of understanding the relationships between God, humanity, and the rest of creation in the context of the entire revelation as the story of salvation and reconciliation. It shows how the creation left no room for gods, evil powers, myths, or anything sacred, religious, and moral. Everything is a creation of God, and that is all it can ever be. If we make anything into something more, this will inevitably distort the fabric of relationships that is integral to a communion of love.

We need to discuss our understanding of how this text was "inspired," because it also involves relationships of love. God respects the freedom of his creatures, without which relationships of love are impossible. Hence, when he wishes to communicate with them, he does not mechanize them into dictating machines or word processors. By revealing that Elohim speaks, our text shows us that God has selected the most fragile of all means to communicate with us. As people of our time, place, and culture, we are not only limited in what we can know, understand, and pass on, but we are also enslaved to our myths, be they traditional or secular in character.

Similarly, the people who passed on the oral traditions, those who were involved in writing them down, those who edited them, and those who discerned the results as a Word of God all did so as people of their time, place, and culture. They could not take the place of God any more than we can, and speak his Word as if they could fully back it with their being and their lives. With a great deal of humour, the rabbis put this in perspective when they said that each and every text has seventy meanings, plus the true one that only God knows. In other words, all these people could do was to live this Word in so far as they were able to back it with their beings and their lives – but it remained the action of a creature backed by the Spirit of the Creator. All they could ever do was to become a witness of that Word to the extent that they were able to understand and live it. Nevertheless, we can have complete confidence in that Word despite all this human fragility. Jesus clearly showed this to us as the only one who fully lived it, thus becoming the incarnated Word.

The rather simplistic notions that have dominated Christianity about the inspiration of the Bible may well have been comforting to some, but they have been unacceptable to many others. It should be pointed out that the Jews never had these kinds of conceptions. God makes a connection with his people that is represented as the Spirit for the Jews, and as the Holy Spirit for the Christians. However, if we are to serve our God with all our heart, mind, and strength, there is a lot more to all of this than a simple affirmation of such a connection. It is here that the second chapter of Genesis reveals something that is equally essential as the first chapter, and, without it, what happens in the third chapter cannot be understood. Hopefully, we are now better prepared to briefly revisit some of the details previously set out in a more complete study.[51]

The above interpretation of the meaning of the first six days of creation could have been regarded as suffering from a speculative exaggeration of the role played in it by love if the meaning of the world as an event had not been transformed by the seventh day. Elohim ceased to create and withdrew into his rest, and human history began. Elohim had risked everything by creating a humanity that was free to respond to or reject his love. The only alternative would have been to create human robots or some other kind of mechanism. His rest was disturbed when humanity broke off its relationship with him, obliging him to create an entirely new kind of relationship in which people could call on him for salvation and reconciliation. For this purpose he gave them his unpronounceable name, YHWH. In other words, God freely decided to enter into human history because he had not broken with humanity the relationship of love – a love that he expressed by setting out to save and reconcile himself with humanity. For this reason these chapters were among the last to be added to the so-called books of Moses: to reveal what humanity was being saved from and how it came to be in need of salvation.

A brief revisiting of the world as an event during the first six days will show that there is no discontinuity, as it were, between Elohim and YHWH. Genesis 2:4 begins to make this clear. What is usually translated as "the origins of the heavens and the earth as they were created" really means the generations of the heavens and the earth in terms of the descendants born as the fruit of an act of love – the way a baby is born. In other words, this revelation is about the birth of the heavens and the earth as an act of love.

Similarly, Eden means sexual communion involving sensual pleasure and joy. Moreover, the Hebrew word usually translated as "east" always refers to the place from which the Messiah will come and from which he will return. When the word is vocalized differently, it means the glory of God. It literally means "what precedes" and "what was in the beginning." The east is also eternity from which comes grace, provided that we understand that in the Bible there is no relationship between eternity and time (as if the former were an infinity of the latter). Hence, the Messiah comes from where grace is, as a free gift of love.

The four branches of the river that flows from Eden appear to symbolize all the possible contradictions represented as positive and negative elements in the universe and arising from the presence of humanity. This revelation appears to be reinforced by the two trees in the centre of the Garden of Eden: the tree of life and the tree of the knowledge of good and evil. Humanity may eat of the tree of life but not the fruit of the other tree, which is better translated as "the penetration of good and evil." The good is what God says and does, and there cannot be anything good apart from him. In other words, the fruit does not symbolize the knowledge of an objective good but of deciding what is good and what is evil, and doing so apart from God, thereby putting oneself in his place. Since no tree can do anything more than what trees were created to do, this fruit symbolizes the outcome of humanity's declaring a sacred – a sacred capable of anchoring a religion and a morality as a penetration of good and evil. We must remember that it is God alone who can declare the good, but he cannot declare the evil, because his Word would bring it into existence. Only the gods that humanity creates can declare good and evil as the anchors of a morality.

In the Jewish and Christian Bibles the fundamental distinction is not between good and evil but between life and death. God is the only living One. Consequently, being in communion with him is to live and to be within what he loves, which is the same as being within what he has declared to be good. To break the relationship is to break with the only living One and thus to enter into death and evil. This is the fundamental choice that God puts before his people in Deuteronomy 30:15.

When God warns humanity not to eat the fruit of the tree of the penetration of good and evil, he is not saying that eating this fruit is morally bad and not eating it is morally good. He is referring to our being his creatures. We cannot live apart from the only living One, any more than fish can live out of water. It is no different from telling our children that if they touch a hot stove, their hands will hurt terribly and they may even not be able to play for a while. In other words, it is a comprehensible way of explaining to them that their skin cannot stand high temperatures because of the way it functions biologically. We must not transform this into a moral issue by telling them that if they touch the stove they are bad and will be punished by being sent to their room. Both Judaism and Christianity have constantly transformed God's warnings of this kind into moral commandments, a subject to which we will return in later chapters.

Following one of the early church fathers, Christians have read this text as referring to the cross, which joins the two trees into one. This would be the only way in which both could be in the centre of the Garden of Eden. In turn, this cross would refer to Jesus Christ because he is the only one who is both the fruit of life and the fruit of the discernment of good and evil. He discerns good and evil by separating the two, as seen in the book of Revelation.[52] In contrast, we are told over and over again not to judge because we cannot make that discernment; it would uproot both the wheat and the tares, as Jesus puts it in one of the parables of the kingdom of heaven.[53] Of course, this interpretation of the two trees is not possible other than within the context of the Christian Bible.

The relationship between the first two chapters of Genesis is now evident. The first reveals the meaning of the architecture of relationships between God the Creator and his creation. The second reveals the meaning of the architecture of relationships between God and humanity. The latter is ambiguous because humanity, born free out of love, can either respond to or reject this love, but it cannot avoid the consequence of being a creature. Consequently, the choice is between life and the good, and death and evil. Therefore, YHWH does not declare that this or that is good in the text; the text centres on humanity in order to reveal the ambiguities of this relationship. In the entire Jewish Bible, YHWH constantly advises his people about the consequences of being creatures. For this reason, the commandments trace the limits within which we encounter life and the good; if we transgress them, we encounter death and evil. It is a structural issue, as it were, but certainly not a moral one. We may be tempted to conclude that, in creating humanity, God gambled with the entire creation, but then we forget that he would never break his love for humanity. He would do everything possible (and, for him, everything is possible) to bring about salvation and reconciliation if that were necessary.

This text also further clarifies the relationships between what it is to be male and what it is to be female within the image of God. God declared that it was not good for Adam, formed from the soil and given his spirit, to be alone. He promised to make a helper to be "face to face" with him. God began by forming all the animals from the soil and then brought each one to Adam, and whatever word Adam spoke, that would be its name. Since these names would reveal their being, doing so would show whether the desired helper would be among them. It shows the importance of names, which for our contemporary cultures is next to impossible to understand.

In Jewish culture at the time that this text was written (and this was true in many of the surrounding cultures as well), a name corresponded exactly to the spiritual being that bore the name. Consequently, to tell someone your name was to provide them access to who you were spiritually.

To shed some light on this, let us return to our previous discussion of what was behind the interdiction against Christians swearing an oath. The words we speak must be fully backed by our being and our life. If there is a word that could designate this, it would be our name. Giving that name to someone else would be to tell them what kind of being and life is behind all our words.

In our highly de-symbolized contemporary cultures this sounds somewhat mysterious. In the introduction we suggested that the double referencing system acquired in the course of learning a language was the gateway to our becoming a cultural being, as an individual expression of the culture that binds the members of a community together. Before de-symbolization became a power of separation and division, the members of a culture were unique expressions of their oneness in that culture. It certainly was not the kind of oneness in love described in the Bible but it represented what made us a symbolic species until recently.

With the rise of the discipline-based approach to human knowing and doing and its development of a triple referencing system, an unprecedented challenge was launched against our being a symbolic species. It was the beginning of the end of the possibility of living in a creation, or at least in a world in which everything is related to and evolves in relation to everything else, without this interrelatedness being anchored in a sacred and myths. Although the names of everything may appear arbitrary to us, even today they continue to represent a version (albeit highly de-symbolized) of this interrelatedness, with each name meaning what all the other names in a language do not mean. There remains a very weak and highly de-symbolized dialectical enfolding of all these names, with the result that each individual name may appear to be arbitrary, but metaconsciously the names continue to be somewhat related. Of course, the growing vocabulary of names derived from the triple referencing system (in relation to what we have referred to as reality) is polluting the pool of names, with image-words being turned into image names. Especially when it comes to naming our children, we are much more concerned about the sensory quality of the name and the impression it makes on us.

In other words, even in our highly de-symbolized cultures with their many image-words and image names, there remains something of what was much stronger in earlier cultures. As a community was unfolding its symbolic potential by developing a language and a culture, a great deal of effort was sometimes made to find the kinds of names for everything that strongly designated what those things were in relation to everything else in the life of the community. The same appears to be true for people's own names. As these languages and cultures evolved in the course of the history of a community, the meaning designated by any name would necessarily evolve because it represented the meaning relative to all other meanings in dialectically enfolded relationships. Eventually, the distance between the name and the meaning of the thing it designated could grow quite large, as any etymological study shows. Consequently, it is still possible for us to imagine how, in the cultures of biblical times, giving someone your name was to give that person access to your spiritual being. It must also be emphasized that, in Jewish thought, the spiritual was not opposed to the physical and the social, because all of it constituted one being. Again, this can be understood from what we have learned about the development of language and culture: the organization of the brain becomes the organization of the brain-mind as a consequence of each lived experience being symbolized by neural and synaptic modifications to this organization, with the result that the organization of someone's brain-mind symbolizes the person's being and life.[54] All this was fundamentally changed by de-symbolization.[55] Prepared with this background in mind, let us now return to the text.

To summarize Genesis 2, following the generations of the heavens and the earth being born in love, YHWH creates Adam and then the vegetation and the animals. The focus is thus placed on the one who is formed from the soil, after which God blows the breath of life (his Spirit) into Adam's nostrils. God then plants a garden in Eden in the east and brings Adam to it. God plants all the trees, including the two in the centre of the garden. The river that flows from the garden divides into four branches that appear to signify the positive and negative possibilities open to human history. Adam is to cultivate and to protect the garden and is warned that he must not affirm good and evil. Next, God declares that it is not good for Adam to be alone and promises to make a helper who will be face to face with him. God begins by forming all the animals and the birds and brings them to Adam, and what Adam speaks to them, that will be their names. No suitable helper is discovered, and then God creates the woman. Adam is very pleased, and the two are entirely unaware that they are vulnerable as creatures.

As this biblical text was dealt with at length in an earlier study,[56] attention will be paid only to those details that are important for the present study. God has made everything speakable and meaningful. The attention is now on his forming and building, while Adam does most of the speaking by naming the animals as well as the woman. In Hebrew, *Adam* is both a noun preceded by an article (*the adam*) and a name unique to him. The text explains that Adam is made from the same red soil as the animals are, but Adam receives the breath of life and becomes a living person. Since, in Hebrew, *Adam* is both a generic name and a common noun in the plural, it designates humanity as one being in the singular and as all of humanity in the plural. It is a kind of anthropocentric interpretation of humanity's being within the image of God.

Adam lives by the Spirit or the breath of life. It is important to recognize that we cannot keep the Spirit, any more than we can hold our breath for a very long time. The breath of life and the Spirit are a connection with the only living One, and this guarantees humanity's freedom and life. The only thing that can threaten this freedom and life is to break the relationship with the only living One in order to affirm for oneself what is good and evil. This amounts to creating some kind of objective good apart from God and will lead to death and evil.

When closely translated, the Hebrew text is very clear on this point. It does not say that "on the day you eat the fruit of the affirmation of good and evil you will die." The Hebrew verb is in the imperfect tense, which literally means that "the very moment you desire to affirm good and evil you are already dead." This has nothing in common with a punishment that follows from a transgression of a commandment; it simply means that there is no life after breaking off with the only living One. At this point, freedom is lost as a result of an enslavement to evil and death (a condition referred to in the Jewish and Christian Bibles as sin).

In other words, God is not giving humanity a commandment and telling it that punishment will follow if anyone transgresses the commandment. God is warning that humanity's freedom depends on remaining in communion with the only living One. It may be objected that this amounts to an attempt on the part of God to compel humanity to love him. This kind of argument is equivalent to claiming that two people who are madly in love and deliriously happy together are forced into this situation, because if one of them has an adulterous relationship with someone else, this happiness will disappear. If these people nurture the love they share and spontaneously seek to please the other, there are no limits to their love. This love is indissociably linked to an unconditional physical, social, and spiritual commitment to each other, to the point that life without the other is simply unimaginable and unliveable. In the context of the love between God and humanity, humanity must eat from the tree of life and thus remain in the relationship with God by receiving the Spirit – a Spirit that comes and goes as an element of freedom but which is destroyed by any attempt to possess it.

In this context we can understand Adam's looking for a helper among all the animals by discerning what they truly were. It brings out a very important aspect, to which we will return later. As long as the creation was free from anything sacred and thus from moral and religious alienation, all relationships were in their proper place, permitting a true attitude to the creation without any false awareness of oneself, others, and the world. Moreover, in the communion of love, Adam, having received the breath of life, appears to have been capable of grasping the love of God that was manifested in these animals. He was able to understand the good that God had spoken into being. Therefore, he was able to name the animals, and what he named them was exactly what they were. It also showed him that there was no suitable helper among them.

It is possible and even likely that this text implies a great deal more. Naming each of the animals involved discerning how each one was different from all the others and how they were different from plants, from Adam, and from everything else. It would appear, therefore, that Adam was able to discern something much deeper and important about the creation than the nature of each and every animal. We have already been informed that God spoke all the animals into being, along with everything else in his creation. This speaking implies an embryonic design of sorts, with all kinds of potential that God had in mind. For example, when he spoke the light into being, there was absolutely no confusion between time, space, the land, and everything else that appeared. Each thing spoken into being was thus a unique and particular manifestation of the creation as a whole. After God had made everything comprehensible and meaningful, Adam, with the breath of life, was able to recognize this uniqueness and oneness. His knowledge and understanding as a creature was relative; he knew everything relative to everything else and the whole relative to God. He discerned the good that God had spoken into being on the level of each specific creation, as well as the overall good of the creation, of which each specific good was a unique expression. It was a harmonious whole that expressed God's love.

On the sixth day God gave humanity a kind of material domination over his creation. It now becomes clear that this material domination is inseparable from its spiritual domination and is realized by the human word in response to and with a love for God's domination by his Word. As noted, it is not a domination by power but by the most fragile of all means for establishing, maintaining, and evolving relationships. If Christians in the West, during the birth of our present civilization, had understood this text, their behaviour might have been less complicit in the emerging human, social, and environmental crises, by adopting approaches based on non-power. Instead, these texts were simply co-opted to legitimate a domination through the power of science and technology.

In this context we can understand Adam's task to work and keep the garden. The garden produced an abundance of fruit, with the result that there was no need to work it. Nor were there any threats to this garden from the outside that would make it necessary to defend it. It was clearly not an issue of necessity but of love. In other words, God made this request with no purpose in mind. It must therefore be understood as being within the communion of love between God and humanity. We may perhaps think of it as a couple that is madly in love going somewhere to enjoy one another's company. The woman may ask the man to wear something that really pleases her, and the man is delighted to oblige. There is no purpose other than pleasing the other. God asked Adam to do this, thereby declaring the good he loves, and Adam acted out of love. If Adam had responded by saying that it would serve no purpose and would thus be a waste of his time, he would be affirming good and evil, thereby separating himself from God. It was a matter of having full confidence that what God desired was the good for their communion of love.

Such an interpretation appears to be confirmed by the Hebrew word that is sometimes translated as "working" (i.e., in the garden). It means worship as a way of honouring and adoring the God who has spoken the good out of love for humanity. It is a response to God's creation that will be good for their relationship of love. Early Jewish commentaries recognized the importance of God's asking this of humanity, because it shows that he did not create humanity for nothing, but to give men and women a role to play in this communion of love. This role would bring the whole of the Garden of Eden before God in adoration and out of love. In this communion of love, each party would seek to please the other for no reason whatsoever other than love.

We must constantly remind ourselves that, even after our breaking with God, the greatest freedom we experience is in our love for a very special person in our life. This freedom completely disappears when the relationship of love begins to break down. At this point, what had once been done spontaneously for one another in love turns into obligation, necessity, and routine. Freedom disappears, and with it goes the joy that used to come with doing these things for one another. Too easily, the maintaining of the relationship out of mutual obligation may lead to resentment at a loss of freedom, and before long this may turn into hatred for the other. In other words, the best way even in our present situation is to exercise our freedom through love for the other.

The meaning of this text is further enriched by the unpronounceable name of God and the names of the man and the woman.[57] In Hebrew, the Tetragrammaton *YHWH* is not vocalized, which makes it unpronounceable. While Christians have become comfortable with vocalizing the Tetragrammaton (as "Yahweh" or "Jehovah"), the Jews never did, in order not to risk taking God's name in vain. The Tetragrammaton derives from the Hebrew verb that means "to be," "to arrive," and "to begin." This verb is in the first person, thus meaning "I am" or, more fully, "I am, I come, and I begin." Only God can say this because he is the only One who can back this name as the Being of beings and as the only living One. He is the God who establishes a personal relationship with his creatures, while *Elohim* refers to God's more objective presence, as it were – as the God behind this creation or the God of the nations. When God hands over his name to us, beginning with Abram, Moses, and all the prophets, he chooses to establish a contact with that person, with the result that this happens only when he reveals himself as YHWH. When he gives himself in such a relationship, we cannot fully take hold of him or influence him other than in a way that he freely decides in his love for us. We are incapable of doing anything other than taking his name in vain, for the simple reason that we are unable to back the use of his name with anything more than our being and our life. The best we can do is to be a witness to his Word by backing our limited understanding of it with our being and our life. YHWH is the hidden God until he decides to reveal himself to us, and when he does so, we become aware of his being a hidden God to whom we have no access other than when he reveals himself. When he does, all our preconceived ideas of him are shattered, as we discover that he is the One who is entirely other than anything we could have imagined or thought.

The name that Adam gives to the woman who was created by YHWH to be his helper is very significant: "She will be called woman, for from man was she taken." In Adam's naming of her as he did the animals, does this imply that he assumes a spiritual domination over her? Once again, our usual translations fail to convey what is really happening here. The Hebrew word translated as "man" is *isch*, which means "master." However, Adam now transfers this name to her as *ischah*, the one who will now be the master and dominate spiritually. The addition of the suffix to the end of *isch* means "in the direction of." Hence, the complete meaning of *ischah* is "in the direction of the man," with the result that it is now the woman who establishes the way towards becoming human. In other words, the man depends on the woman in order to become fully human in the direction of humanity. Furthermore, since the woman is recognized by man as "bone of my bone and flesh of my flesh," each one knows himself or herself thanks to the other. The Hebrew verb translated as "know" means "sexual knowledge, experiencing the value of the other, and participation." In other words, it is now possible to begin to understand why the first element that God declared not to be good in his creation was for man to be alone. Consequently, the evil in this case would be a break between man and woman, and this remains fundamental to our understanding of humanity throughout the entire Jewish and Christian Bibles. Too often, Christian churches have made this into a question of morality and a way of morally judging others, but it is entirely a question of what it is to be human: a relationship between *isch* and *ischah*. It constituted an affirmation of humanity in monogamy, which was highly unusual at the time this text was written.

Once again, Adam's ability to name the woman shows a deep communion with God, who had already identified his being alone as not good. Adam was able to set the first step on the road to becoming human in the direction of a humanity. Receiving the breath of life permitted a deepening of the communion of love between man and woman as a response to the love of YHWH. The woman had become a part of the spiritual direction of man, and this would be expressed later as the woman being the glory of man. The glory of man means revealing who man is. This is much more than two complementary beings. Within the totality of what it is to be human, there is a sharing of the feminine and the masculine, because both derive from the same root in the Hebrew language.

In his superb study Bible, which renders the Hebrew as close as possible to contemporary French, André Chouraqui notes that in the Hebrew the man is called Adam for as long as he is alone.[58] Once the woman has been created, the text calls him *isch*, which is the masculine form of the root; *ischah* is the feminine form. Each contains one of the first two letters of the Hebrew Tetragrammaton. A rabbinical explanation holds that in the union of the man and the woman these two letters are brought together, and thus the presence of YHWH is brought into the couple. When the couple breaks apart, the man and the woman separate these two letters and thus banish this presence. What then remains of *isch* and *ischah* is what, in Hebrew, designates a devouring fire. It should be noted that these details do not come through in the simplified transliteration of the Hebrew used in the above text by Chouraqui or in the one used in this work. It should also be noted that Adam does not name the woman as Eve until after their break with God. In Hebrew it means "the living one who transmits life," and it shares the last three letters with the Tetragrammaton. The omission of the first letter of the Tetragrammaton in the name Eve signifies that she now becomes the living one because she continues God's work on the level of nature, as it were, but the missing *i* indicates that she is not life itself, and life is not within her. In other words, she is alive, but she can never say "I am," because only God is the living One who can say this.[59]

The life of humanity in the Garden of Eden is summed up in the last verse of the second chapter of Genesis, where we are told that the man and the woman were naked and they were not ashamed. The Hebrew word here that is translated as "naked" is also used to describe the serpent at the beginning of the third chapter, where it is usually translated as "cunning."[60] In other words, it is also possible to describe the man and the woman as cunning and the snake as naked. Throughout the Bible, nakedness has nothing whatsoever to do with innocence; to be naked is to be weak and vulnerable as a result of a lack of strength and a lack of protection. The man and the woman did not know this because, in their communion with YHWH, he was the only protection they needed. Everything in their lives was a free gift from the God who loved them. There was no need to work and no need to fear anything whatsoever. Everything was grace and love.

Two aspects of this situation are important for our understanding of what was about to happen next. As there was no sacred, religion, or morality, all relationships served the communion of love without any distortion, veiling, or anything else that might interfere with a true awareness. In other words, no false awareness, no subconscious, and no unconscious were required to make these relationships liveable. As noted earlier, love is the only relationship that permits a complete awareness of the other and of everything else in creation, all to be dealt with through the human word. Any communication between men and women could be fully backed by their lives and beings, and in turn each life and being was fully backed by God's Spirit and Word, through which everything had become comprehensible and speakable to humanity.

The second implication of the man and the woman being fully protected by the love of God is the absence of any possible threat of the unknown. They lived in the Garden of Eden within the larger creation that, in communion with its Creator, posed no threat of any kind as long as they unfolded this communion of love in their history. Early on in this chapter, I suggested that toddlers and young children can safely play in a world of which they know very little. It is the kind of relationship that Jesus may well have had in mind when he said that his followers should imitate this playful trust in their heavenly Father. In such a case, the unknown simply becomes those interactions, with the creation as our home, that remain unexplored. Living this way requires that we are also fully conscious of being a creature who can never say "I am." Everything in our lives is integral to this creation's fabric of relationships, on which we depend from our conception to our death, when these relationships are severed as dust is returned to dust. For example, I am in relation to the DNA of my parents. My body developed in relation to my DNA in the womb as each cell became an expression of it. After my birth I developed in the social womb of the community to which my parents belonged and within which they raised me. I am in relation to all the experiences that helped to grow the organization of my brain at birth into the organization of the brain-mind that symbolizes my life lived in this community and in relation to its surroundings. I am in relation to my most significant others, especially my spouse and my children. I am in relation to the life that my spouse and I have passed on to our children through our DNA and the upbringing we gave them. However, I am also in relation to an advanced engineering education based on discipline-based approaches to knowing and doing. I am also in relation to my discovery, just prior to my doctorate, that my mindset was an integral part of the crisis of our civilization, and I am in relation to my decision that an intellectual conversion had to be worked out that would require lengthy postdoctoral studies. I am in relation to my having to come to grips with the secular religious attitudes that we have towards discipline-based science, technology, economic growing, and political organizing. All these things hide from our awareness the limitations of these approaches, thus opening the floodgates to their inappropriate use – with catastrophic consequences. I am in relation to tens of thousands of students who found some hope in my discovery that engineering and social science can and should be done differently if there is to be a more liveable and sustainable future. I am in relation to the recognition by my profession of my invention of preventive approaches, including my appointment as a fellow of the Canadian Academy of Engineering, and I am also in relation to my profession's prompt dismissal of all of this while engineering education continued "business as usual," despite all the growing crises. I am all of these relationships and more, and for this reason I will never be able to say "I am."

There is another reason for my inability to be able to say this. If my person and my life, being in relation to all the above and more, have determined me more than I have been able to influence all these things, then my "I" is diminished to the same extent. This remains the case even when we declare slavery to be an unacceptable form of human life. Thus enslaved, I am not free to love my creator and my fellow creatures, I am unable to have true relationships, and I am entirely incapable of being as true as I need to be in a communion of love. When my dust returns to dust, my person and my life will be entirely intertwined with this fabric of relationships. Hopefully, a little bit of wheat will be entangled among the tares, so that when the tares will finally be removed, whatever remains will be pure grace, that is, a gift from God. In other words, I am also in relation to what came from beyond my sociocultural world, which I learned to accept as having originated with the God of the Jewish and Christian Bibles. However, as with everyone else born into a particular Jewish or Christian religious tradition, growing up in it involves a discernment of good *and* evil, because our religious needs that are rooted in our being a member of a symbolic species are met by our living as if these traditions are the only true equivalent of the religion and morality created by any culture. In other words, the revelation that comes from beyond our culture is lived by us as mostly meeting our religious and moral needs, with the result that we think we can have it all: the Jewish or Christian religion and morality as well as everything else in our world.

In sum, what I am able to say, backed by my being and my life in this civilization, is that I am entangled in all these relationships, to the point that it may be difficult to see myself as a creature. All my experiences appear to point to my being little more than an evolving structure of all these relationships, with an occasional transcendence of it by means of symbolization, imagination, and creativity. Does this mean that most of the time I should simply abandon the use of the first-person pronoun in the singular? Should I simply acknowledge that it is all these structures of causal determinisms, determining influences, and correlations of factors that are speaking, acting, and thinking through me? Are the structuralists correct after all? Is all the talk in our contemporary civilization regarding freedom and love nothing more than a counter-transference reaction in an attempt to make the life that is reified by technique more or less liveable? We have new forms of these debates in relation to the assertion by computer science and cognitivist disciplines that, at bottom, we are nothing more than highly sophisticated "societies" of information processors, but this is mostly a question of our inability to understand and take seriously the limitations of discipline-based approaches to our knowing and doing. Since this way of thinking is extremely widespread, it is not difficult to understand the vast influence of political ideologies and philosophical world-views that simply begin with the assertion that we are born free and that in a democratic society we can continue to exercise that freedom for our entire lives. It is a necessary compensation for our lives being highly reified by discipline-based approaches of all kinds. The more we implement these approaches without any regard for their limitations, the more we re-engineer individual and collective human life in the world as if it had the architecture of a (dead) machine, whether of the classical or of the information type. We are thus a reorganization of life in the image of death. Consequently, to a considerable extent, the uncritical and widespread application of discipline-based approaches turns into a self-fulfilling prophecy that increasingly legitimizes them. An overview of the relevant research was provided in the introduction.

If human life in our contemporary civilization is diminishing our ability to use the first-person pronoun in the singular and to back this with our being and our life, we may be prepared to recognize that what the Jewish and Christian Bibles refer to as sin is always portrayed in terms of being a slave to higher powers and forces. This corresponds rather well to what is happening in our lives. It would appear that this situation is not merely an illusion that comes from an upwelling of guilt produced by the religions and moralities we have invented. We can now also understand why many of us listen to an endless stream of love songs and love stories on the media. We need to assert ourselves physically and biologically in the face of having lost much of our being as a symbolic species – a consequence of the de-symbolization resulting from discipline-based approaches for almost everything and anything. Our civilization has given an entirely new meaning to love, having made it into the "anti-sacred" (or sacred transgression) of the sacred of technique.[61] To put it simply, if almost all our relationships are re-engineered by technique, technique has enslaved our lives. In order to escape this slavery, we retreat into our physical and biological selves and assert ourselves in this manner. Doing so turns all physical appearances and biological behaviours into measures and performances of how free we are and thus how we are able to love. This is superimposed on what remains of our highly de-symbolized lives in our anti-societies.[62] In other words, instead of being close relationships of intimacy and love, these relationships have now been made into their diametrical opposites, involving strong aspects of performance, power, and conquest. To use biblical terminology, agape has been extensively transformed into Eros. The former is a love in which each party lives for the other and is even willing to lay down his or her life for the other, while in the latter relationship "love" is obtained by seduction and thus by conquest instead of being a free gift of one's life to the other.

As noted, especially in the Jewish Bible, God's love for humanity is often depicted in physical, sexual, social, and spiritual terms. We tend to brush over the many moving passages in which God is pleading with his people to listen to him. At one point God even has Hosea, one of his prophets, marry a prostitute to bring home to his people that he was a jealous lover. Of course, there is also the Song of Songs.

Why do we so easily read over these passages as a kind of poetic exaggeration? Have we forgotten the parable of the prodigal son? Can any human parent not identify with the dilemma of the father in this parable, who is completely unable to prevent his son from getting himself into a great deal of trouble? He could use force to restrain his child, in which case he would cease to be the loving parent and become the tyrant. When we as human parents conceive a child in love and then watch it grow in the womb, be born, and grow up, can we not be put in situations that are exactly identical to those of the father in the parable? What can we do when our teenager begins to mix with the wrong crowd and becomes possessed by alcohol or drugs? What do we do when our daughter falls into the hands of a human trafficker and becomes trapped because she does not believe she can ever come back to us, having been forced into prostitution? What do we do when our child joins a violent gang and ends up in jail for having committed violent crimes? Of course, these are extreme examples, and yet in the relationship between God and humanity they would be typical.

In the first two chapters of Genesis we learn that God spoke everything into being, made the creation comprehensible and liveable, launched everything towards a communion of love, prepared everything for the eventuality that humanity would love something or someone else, and warned people that as creatures they had limitations; despite all of that, he was unable to prevent humanity from breaking with him. As we will examine in the third chapter of Genesis, God then intervened to make the situation as liveable as possible. Later on he continually warned his people that if they chose this or that form of evil and death, they would harm themselves, but if they repented and changed their ways, he would take them back as his people. Throughout this and more, God was never tempted to cease submitting his unlimited power and justice to the direction of his love. This love was, and continues to be, his agape, which humanity always confuses with Eros.

Before we examine the third chapter of Genesis, it may be useful to point out that a creation made for freedom was the prerequisite for a creation made for love, which is another way of interpreting the relationship between the meaning of the first chapter and the meaning of the second chapter. It means that this creation is vulnerable when freedom and love are destroyed by the introduction of religion, morality, and magic, all anchored in a sacred and myths. As a symbolic species, humanity could symbolize anything God created as something else, thereby contesting the entire creation and God himself. This is exactly what is already anticipated by the polemical dimension of the first chapter of Genesis.

2 The Roots of a Non-secular Life: Religion and Morality as Symptoms of Evil

Uprooting and Re-rooting the Creation's Fabric of Relationships

For the Jewish people, the opening chapters of Genesis were an answer to the question, How did humanity in general, and the Jewish people in particular, find themselves in need of salvation or redemption? And exactly from what did they need to be saved or redeemed? As these chapters show, humanity's decision to break the relationship of love with its Creator completely shattered the communion of love that was the very order of creation. By breaking its relationship with the only Living One, humanity was as good as dead, and this would have been the end of human history were it not for God's undiminished love. Because of that love, he did not compel humanity to continue living in a relationship that it had rejected. We are told of a number of measures that God took to transform the creation's fabric of relationships, which could no longer be based on love and freedom. For God, this opened the door to his work of redemption, while humanity would go on living in a spirit of Eros that would enslave it to the object of that Eros. We have already noted that God had taken every possible measure to be able to respond in love if humanity rejected him.

The message of the third chapter of Genesis has become almost incomprehensible as a consequence of our highly individualistic understanding of humanity and an uncritical acceptance of our means of power, which negate our love. Typical results include a frequent use of the Bible as a kind of ammunition depot for "intellectual bullets" in the form of texts to "kill" all the evil in the world; a resorting to means of power by the use of the pressure of crowds on individuals and by the use of the media for spiritual advertising; a heavy reliance on concepts such as hell and damnation that have more in common with works such as Dante's *Inferno*[1] than those of the Bible; and with the continued use of the power of church organizations to manage the diffusion of faith and to raise money. In other words, in these practices there is very little, if anything, that is compatible with Jesus's parables of salt flavouring the food that is essential for living or of the use of yeast that, in the making of bread, makes the dough rise and disappears in the process.[2] From the perspective of these two parables, the media have enabled churches to throw so much "salt" at the food for the world that it has become inedible, to the point that everyone has become more or less allergic to it. The powers of churches have so transformed the "yeast" that it appears to be unable to make the dough rise, with the result that it has lost its purpose of sustaining life. Many people, including Christians, now cringe at the very mention of "being saved." We appear once again to be confronted with the situation in which the spirit of our age seems to have a much more decisive influence on our reading of the Jewish and Christian Bibles than their message has on us. Hence, before examining the third chapter of Genesis, we must be prepared for powerful counter-transference reactions.

Every translation of our Bibles must rely on the elements of languages that today are indissociably linked to our time, place, and universal technical order within highly de-symbolized cultures. At the same time, such elements are used to clothe the meaning of a revelation that does not come from that time, place, and universal technical order but from God, who is holy and whose ways are entirely different from ours. Thus, each verse and each word has one meaning when it is read in the context of a language and a highly de-symbolized culture, and an entirely different meaning when it is read in the way that language is used in the context of the revelation as a whole. The lives of Jews and Christians would be simplified a great deal if we could clearly separate these two meanings according to their origins, but this is no more possible than separating wheat from tares. To simply assert that we are going to receive help from the outside by means of the Spirit, or the Holy Spirit, is to resort to a kind of Jewish or Christian magic and a complete neglect of our responsibility to serve our God with all our heart, *with all our mind*, and with all our strength. Moreover, we would be sitting ducks for the most elementary counter-transference reactions. It would be all too reassuring to bring God's ways a little closer to ours by relying preferentially on the meanings of our time, place, and universal technical order. This would prevent the Word from calling our lives into question and would leave us at least something of which we can be proud.

In addition, a language is used to clothe a meaning in order to communicate it to others, which is all a language can do. In other words, a language depends on a metalanguage of lived relationships from which meaning emerges and which these relationships clothe. Hence the insistence on a language being indissociably linked to its context. Similarly, the meaning of a text and its words may be interpreted in the context of other texts and words and via them in the context of the entire Bible. However, this is a necessary but insufficient step. They will remain abstract ideas until they become clothed in the conduct of the Jewish or Christian communities to the extent that their members individually and collectively practise their faith. At the same time, it is in the members' individual and collective recognition of their failure to clothe the meaning of the revelation that they must entrust themselves to the Spirit to receive an understanding that far transcends what can be clothed in the conduct of their lives. In other words, their faiths will be strengthened. In the joy of having received a beautiful gift, they will seek to enrich their lives with it, in what ought to be a self-reinforcing cycle that marks the growth of faith. Since we do not see very much of this in our contemporary civilization, we have convinced ourselves that it is no longer realistic because we do not live in the days of Abram, Isaac, and Jacob or in the days of the early church.

For example, a few days ago my wife and I were walking in the downtown area of our community, where we were offered a pamphlet entitled "How to Be Saved." A few decades earlier such a pamphlet would have likely borne the title "Jesus Is the Answer." It is a powerful testimony to our possession by the spirit of our age. Christian pamphlets have finally joined the explosion of how-to books and videos, in perfect conformity to technique. In the time of scientism Jesus was made into an alternate answer, but the churches clearly had no idea whatsoever as to how this answer could correspond to the questions of the time.

In order to do our homework and protect ourselves as best as possible from counter-transference reactions that import the spirit of our age into the comprehension of our Bibles, we would do well to reflect on what they mean by terms such as *liberation*, *salvation*, and *redemption*. We have noted that the fundamental distinction in the Jewish Bible is between life and death (Deuteronomy 30:15). Since God is the only Living One, being in communion with him is to live and to be within the good that he loves; if you break this communion, you are separated from him and thus are within evil and death. There can be no good separate and independent from the good that God speaks into being. Since humanity decided to love something else, it entered into evil and death, from which it had to be saved. If we left it at this, we would again have the kind of biblical and theological truism that leads nowhere because it cannot survive as a "pure" meaning; it must be clothed. In the Jewish Bible this is made very clear in the book of Job (to which we will return later). In the Christian Bible the meaning is often clothed by reinterpreting the Roman legal concept of redemption, to which Job already refers.

The legal concept of redemption dealt with the situation in which a Roman citizen was captured by an enemy.[3] Under Roman law such a person was deemed lost to the community. The loss was radical and total to the point that the person became regarded as dead. Consequently, his marriage was dissolved, his wife could remarry, his children were distributed among his heirs, and his name was removed from the list of citizens, with the result that he no longer had any civil rights. Early in the development of this legal arrangement, it was the duty of the person's family to ransom him from the enemy. If he was set free, he would recover all his rights as a citizen upon his return to Rome, and he did not have to repay the ransom to his family. When this legal solution to a practical problem became increasingly difficult to implement as a consequence of family bonds having weakened, redemption became the responsibility of all Roman citizens, and the law was adjusted accordingly. Since the person had been treated as a slave by his captors, the Roman citizen who redeemed him bought a slave. His status as a slave could be changed in only one of two ways. The person who had ransomed the slave could go before a judge and legally set him free, or the slave had to repay the ransom himself, thereby setting himself free.

During the time in which the Christian Bible was written, the institution of slavery was almost universal, with the result that practically everyone could clearly understand this legal concept, which had been reinterpreted in the light of the revelation. When humanity broke the communion with God, it became the prisoner of the hostile powers that emerged in the gulf that had opened up between God and humanity. Until this gulf occurred, there had been no place for them within the creation, but when humanity broke with God, it became the prisoner of these hostile "principalities and powers." People became their slaves and completely lost their humanity. Jesus Christ redeemed humanity by paying the ransom, following which he remitted the debt by grace.

People regained their freedom and could become full citizens of the kingdom of heaven (distinguished from the kingdom of God, which appears at the end of time), having been fully reinstated in the position that they held prior to their break with God.[4] They were called to serve this kingdom in a world that temporarily remained under the control of the principalities and powers. Although these had been conquered and were on the way to their final destruction, their reign of violence and terror became all the greater, much as a tyrant who knows he has lost the war, but before the victors can reach him, brings as much revenge on his people as possible. The book of Revelation clearly describes this, provided that we do not read it through the spirit of our age.[5]

The concept of redemption can be further clarified in the light of the prologue to the gospel of John in order to understand to whom or what the ransom was paid and how this was done.[6] It rules out the possibility of God using his limitless powers to annihilate evil and death; he would have ceased to be the God of love who had always chosen the most fragile means, namely his Word. This Word was "within the beginning" and is still the means by which God accomplishes everything. There is no mention at all of this ransom having been paid to the prince of this world, who had enslaved humanity. It is simply unthinkable that God would make some kind of bargain with this prince. Jesus makes this quite clear when he is offered complete power over the world in return for prostrating himself before the prince, which would have put him in the same situation that humanity had placed itself. Jesus answers the prince by relying on the Word instead. God's being fully "yes" to humanity is summed up in the prologue to the gospel of John, which tells us that the Word *became* flesh (the translation of "was made flesh" is incorrect because the Greek verb is active). It sums up everything that God did for humanity after it broke with him, in accordance with the decision he had made in eternity. The prologue makes it very clear that the incarnation was integral to the creation "within the beginning."

The conclusion to the prologue (John 1:14–18) sums up Jesus's work of redemption, which begins with the Word making itself flesh. Once again, I will restrict myself to a few details derived from a previously published study.[7] The term *flesh* has several complementary meanings. In Paul's writings to the Romans it refers to what humanity is: corrupted and evil and thus separated from God. It concerns humanity's inner being, the heart, or soul (understood in the Hebrew sense), and it is this "heart" that involves the body in sin (Romans 1). In John's writings it refers to the human condition: weak and mortal. *The flesh* can also refer to what it is to be human following the break with God. In sum, the Word became fully human by entering into sin, which in the Bible always refers to a condition of slavery that results from breaking with the only Living One. Everything that humanity had become in seeking its independence was assumed in its totality by the eternal Son of God when he became flesh, including God's judgment of the flesh being evil. The Word becoming flesh thus includes this judgment by belonging to a humanity that has separated itself from God. It is the "nature" of humanity that resulted from the break.

Earlier on in the prologue to the gospel of John, we are told that the light came into the darkness, but the darkness did not receive it. The world of evil and separation from God had thus been penetrated. In other words, when light penetrates into darkness, the darkness vanishes. Similarly, when God in the flesh penetrates what is separated from him, it is no more. The purpose for doing so is made plain in 2 Corinthians 5:21, which tells us that he who did not know sin became sin for us. Jesus knew every human temptation and difficulty, but he faced them by living from the Word through the Spirit, thus penetrating evil and death. All that remained was their complete and total destruction at the end of time. In a sense, Jesus Christ entered into everything that was opposite to his father, thereby putting an end to everything that the powers and principalities represented. Doing so was impossible without paying the ransom for penetrating evil and death, which involved incomprehensible suffering and death itself in order to conquer death. After all, he was, is, and will be the Life.

God's way of non-power had scored the decisive victory, but humanity continued to cling to the principalities and powers in its ongoing separation from God. It is not until humanity fully recognizes that it has been redeemed, the ransom has been paid, and the debt has been forgiven, that this can change.

Even within churches this is poorly understood. For example, under the necessity of religion and morality, it was customary in many church services to read the Ten Commandments, followed by their summation in the two "great commandments," as a prelude to the members of the congregation being invited to confess their sins in order to receive the message of pardon and grace. Doing so entirely reverses and misinterprets the meaning of redemption. It is as foolish as the master of a number of slaves demanding that they tell him what they did wrong that week in order to be either punished or forgiven. It changes absolutely nothing to their being slaves. Once again, sin is a condition and not an endless accumulation of moral and religious transgressions. Jesus Christ entered into evil and death, thereby destroying them as entities separated from God. However, this work could not be entirely finished until the tares that had been sown by these principalities and powers could be separated from the wheat. Until that time, individual and collective human lives depended on both the tares and the wheat. This is not an observation limited to what in the Bible is referred to as "the world." It equally applies to churches and all their members, who are told that above all they must not attempt to judge in order to separate the wheat from the tares. This is why the language of the Bible is so profoundly dialectical as the members live the tension between their "old nature" and their "new nature." The latter derives from the new connection with God that is established by the Spirit and made possible by the Redeemer.

The caricatures of salvation and redemption that are commonplace today can be explained in part by our civilization having declared slavery as an unacceptable form of human life and having abolished this institution, thereby leaving the impression that we are all free and live in free societies. We are thus limited to understanding redemption in terms of the following kinds of examples. We can think of it as the liberation of a woman who has fallen in love with a man, but, after a brief romance, he begins to insist on her contributing her share towards their lavish lifestyle. Step by step, he finally turns her into a prostitute as he reveals himself to be a human trafficker. The whole process involves a high level of manipulation that eventually traps her into a situation from which many women see no escape because they are usually being blackmailed by their pimps who threaten to reveal everything to their former friends and families. An alternate example would be the liberation of a drug addict whose life has been completely enslaved by the necessities imposed by the habit. However, in both cases the liberation is purely personal and individual and thus a denial of our being creatures who can never say "I am." No institution is involved, and their humanity is not fundamentally affected. Nevertheless, the necessities imposed on the people who find themselves in either kind of situation tend to grow over time until they accumulate into the final necessity of death.

These difficulties of understanding the true meaning of salvation and redemption are multiplied by our civilization's obsession with freedom and love. This obsession is hardly surprising, given that our discipline-based approaches to scientific knowing and technical doing continue to uncover how deeply we are determined by the corresponding categories of phenomena in every possible way. Since we live with these approaches as if they were without limits, nothing can be known or done outside of them, which means that they imply an image of individual and collective human life in the world that is limited to what can be described or manipulated in terms of causal relationships, determining influences, statistical correlations, and the like. Anything that is done out of genuine freedom and love escapes these approaches and thus cannot be taken very seriously. As noted, this has resulted in unrestrained physical and sexual expressions of ourselves being lived as signs of freedom and love, only to be reabsorbed into the technical order as its permissible sacred transgressions.

In sum, concepts such as liberation, salvation, and redemption cannot be understood apart from the principalities and powers that rule our world, beginning with humanity – and that includes Jews and Christians. The ability to live in the world without belonging to it implies conducting a life that is entirely other than the ways of life of our societies, and this is no more possible than individual persons inventing their own cultures. As a consequence of being members of a symbolic species, we enter the symbolic universe of a community by means of a language and culture, and today we enter into the universal technical order by first being launched in the direction of what remains of our symbolic universe as a consequence of de-symbolization. To insist on salvation being exclusively personal and individual is equivalent to saying "I am," and thus no longer in relation to a symbolic species that continues to be dependent on highly de-symbolized languages and cultures – as if I take no part in and am not responsible for their adaptation and evolution. It also means that I do not participate in the principalities and powers, which is impossible. This participation is a component of what the man and the woman did in the Garden of Eden when they put themselves in the place of God by affirming good and evil.

We can readily dismiss the reading of the first three chapters of the book of Genesis as a kind of morality play related to nudity, innocence, sexual intercourse, shame, and guilt. This amounts to imposing on the text the spirit of a bygone age in which traditional religions and moralities reigned. It is also a complete negation of what the first two chapters reveal about the creation being entirely free from any sacred or any powers of domination, with the result that humanity was free. It was a creation that had no need of religion, morality, or Eros by seduction and conquest. Hence, the man and the woman being naked is neither a moral nor a sexual issue, and to associate this with sin imposes something on the text that is foreign to it.

Humanity lived in a creation that may be regarded as a fabric of relationships that were interdependent in their joint dependence on their Creator. This fabric was woven by and was to be unfolded in its potential by love. No fundamental choices had to be made because everything was within the good. There was simply an endless variety of possibilities within that good, which humanity was called on to unfold in its history, within its image of God, and in fellowship with him. Until that communion was shattered into pieces, no real choices had to be made between these pieces. Nor were there any possible contradictions within this good until it was fragmented. In love, God was fully "yes" to humanity, and humanity was fully "yes" to God. The kinds of dilemmas that haunt us today were completely unthinkable in such a creation. Every relationship was established and maintained through the most fragile of all means, that of human words anchored in and oriented by the Word.

Up to this point, human history was a playful and joyful unfolding of a communion of love, with the result that everything depended on the fellowship between God and humanity. When it was shattered, the entire order of creation was shattered with it because the whole fabric of relationships was affected: individual relationships were displaced, twisted, warped, strained, and broken to the point of being fundamentally altered. Nothing remained in its place within the good, as a consequence of alienation, domination, and seduction. It thus appears that the "structural" dimension of liberation, salvation, and redemption is rather poorly, if at all, understood in the context of the spirit of our age.

On the positive side, this spirit of our age, centred in our discipline-based approaches to knowing and doing, has indirectly shed a great deal of light on the roles played by languages and cultures in individual and collective human life as a consequence of its having extensively de-symbolized them. We are no longer able to take for granted that our lives work effortlessly in the background as we live each experience as a moment of our life and thus integrate our lives into our communities. It is the exact parallel of our civilization's no longer being able to take for granted the life-sustaining functions of the biosphere, which have been decisively weakened by ways of life that are organized and reorganized on the basis of disciplines rather than cultures. When cultures and the biosphere functioned well, they could largely be taken for granted because they required little or no attention from humanity.

When cultures became de-symbolized and we created the environmental crisis, they gradually began to attract our attention. Until the late-nineteenth century a concept of culture was virtually absent in the industrializing societies, and it was not until the twentieth century that we began to recognize ourselves as a symbolic species. This realization was quickly arrested by growing assertions that deep down we were *homo informaticus*.

Nevertheless, a critical understanding of our universal technical order has helped us to recognize our dependence on languages and cultures as a symbolic species. Since these languages and cultures are indissociably linked to traditional religions and moralities, there is a great deal in the Jewish and Christian Bibles whose significance can now be more deeply understood; this would be further augmented if the roles of their secular equivalents would also be more widely recognized. This in turn would make completely untenable the notion that we are spiritual people living in secular societies. Nevertheless, it may be possible to develop a new understanding of redemption that speaks more clearly to our situation.

The End of Secular Human Life

Hopefully, the foregoing discussion will help us to identify our inevitable counter-transference reactions as we briefly examine the third chapter of Genesis. Once again, we will limit ourselves to the most significant details drawn from a previously published study[8] in so far as they are important for the present work. Our text clearly tells us that the serpent was a creature that stood out because it was the most cunning. The Hebrew word translated as "cunning" can also be translated as "naked," meaning "vulnerable." This observation is another powerful polemic against the cultures of that time that regarded the serpent as a god. On the one hand, it was the most cunning, having seduced all the surrounding people, and, on the other hand, it was the most vulnerable (naked) because it owed its cunning to the people who were working out their religious intuitions inspired by the myths of their cultures, which were no more substantial than smoke or vapour. As these people lived in close contact with nature, the serpent may well have stood out as an animal that had to be particularly clever because it had no limbs. However, in our text the serpent cannot be anything more than what God had created it to be, given what has been revealed in the previous two chapters of Genesis. Adam had named all the animals, showing that he knew very well what a serpent was. For it to be anything more required the human intervention of recognizing it as something else, thereby going against the creation and its Creator. Only then could humanity imagine the serpent as communicating something that God had not said. Within a communion of love this would be unthinkable, unimaginable, and thus not expressible in words.

Nevertheless, those who passed on the oral tradition that gave rise to this text, those who wrote it down, and those who edited it received it as a Word from God, and their surrounding cultures made it as plain as day that the serpent was no ordinary animal, to the point of making the lives of the surrounding people unthinkable and unliveable without it. There is thus no point in speculating whether the serpent really spoke, whether it used a kind of serpent language, whether human beings could understand such a language, and so on. We know very well that our pets can communicate things to us without any language. To suggest that we concentrate on what the serpent said rather than on the serpent's doing the communicating is to separate two elements of the text that belong together. If we accept the polemical aspect of this text, which must have been abundantly clear at the time, we can cut short all these speculations. The serpent is both what God had created it to be and what humanity attributed to it, which for some cultures at that time was an image of the lord of life and fertility. As such, this image points to something symbolic that goes much deeper, namely, the need of a people to create a religion when they have separated themselves from the only Living One. Another source of life has to be created, and what used to be provided through grace must now be "produced" by doing everything possible to increase the fertility of the people and the land.

Our text establishes a clear bond between humanity and the serpent, as described by the Hebrew word that can be translated as "naked" or "cunning." This bond is further developed by the dialogue between them. It begins by the serpent putting words into God's mouth, words that he never spoke. The woman responds in a similar way. Instead of forbidding humanity to eat from the tree of the penetration of good and evil, God had described the limits of their communion of love, beyond which humanity would encounter evil and death. Each in their own way, the serpent and the woman, had already broken this communion by the question posed and the answer given. As previously noted, a choice between alternatives, or the forbidding of one of them, presupposes a communion that has already been fragmented in order to make this thinkable, liveable, and expressible. The exchange between the serpent and the woman thus led to a relationship, and even a kind of bond between them, that was entirely incompatible with all the other relationships and bonds in the creation that were revealed in the first two chapters of Genesis. It represents an embryonic beginning of casting doubt on what God had declared to be good, in order to imagine what it might be like to go beyond this good to explore the possibility of there being a good apart from God. If the woman had remained within the love of God and within the good, she would have exercised her dominion over creation, and things would have gone no further. Instead, she bestowed a certain legitimacy on the question posed to her by the serpent and took the next step in the same direction. At this point she had in effect transformed the serpent from being no more and no less than a creature into something entirely foreign to the creation, which in turn led to the necessity of now having to discern between good and evil. This discernment had been entirely unnecessary up to this point because everything in God's creation was within the good. It represented the embryonic beginning of religion, which needed to be worked out by means of a morality. It is exactly what Paul describes near the end of the first chapter in his letter to the Romans.

The new relationships and bonds that were thus introduced into the creation needed to be ordered and comprehended by a religion and morality because they were no longer the result of a playful unfolding of the good within a communion of love. The embryonic beginnings of an entirely new kind of world, and an enslaved life within it, were about to emerge. Everything that followed, as revealed in our Bibles, confirms this human "beginning."

We continue to experience some of this. Imagine something equivalent happening to a human couple deeply in love. If one of the partners begins to question what the other says and wonders if what the other has in mind is different, this partner essentially begins to place himself or herself outside of their communion of love, becoming a kind of detached observer to intellectually, morally, or legally examine what the other has said and the motives behind it. The trust is broken because it presupposes that the other's love is no longer full and complete and that things now must be done outside of that love, seemingly to protect it but effectively undermining and eventually destroying it. At the same time, the other partner faced with this situation will have little choice but to transform himself or herself from a lover into someone who also has to be judge and jury of whether the other is acting within their love or outside of it, thus having to determine a response not exclusively based on love. The relationship of love is now as good as dead and can continue only in the form of Eros.

As an alternate scenario, consider a couple equally in love but facing some difficulties, which a third party is willing and able to resolve provided that one partner acts as his or her lover for a single night. If the couple agrees, the communion of love is also broken as one of the partners goes beyond it by betraying himself or herself in the role as someone else's lover, and, having thus been transformed, makes it next to impossible to continue the love relationship as if nothing had happened.

Our civilization makes the understanding of situations of this kind particularly difficult because of our unlimited devotion to discipline-based approaches to human knowing and doing. It leaves no room for anything else but doing research *on* other human beings or creatures as opposed to doing research *with* them, thereby turning them into objects of investigation – which requires a suppression of their humanity or their being. Similarly, the technical approach to doing occurs within a triple abstraction that inevitably reifies all life. We experience this ourselves when we are stared at by someone of the opposite sex. It turns us into an object because the other person expects no genuine response from us. The other simply looks over what he or she sees and imagines what could be done with it. As a result, discipline-based knowing and technical doing have had an enormous negative impact on the social fabric of relationships.[9] In our songs, short stories, and novels we cannot get enough of the dream of love in which each party fully lives for the other, even to the point of any other kind of life becoming unbearable. Each one is fully "yes" to the other, and everything that each one does and says is fully backed by their being and their life. The two lives thus become one in a communion of love. It is only when this communion begins to break down that we get into spelling out what each one expects from the other in an attempt to once again learn to trust each other. Failing this, the last expectations will be stated in a separation agreement followed by a divorce settlement.

Returning to the text: The serpent continues the dialogue with the woman, telling her that God knows very well that she will not die immediately and that, when she eats the fruit, her eyes will be opened and she will become like the gods, knowing both good and evil. There is a unique construction in the Hebrew language that emphasizes the immediacy of an action, which is here translated by adding the word *immediately*. The serpent thus casts doubt on God's intentions, as if these did not fully back what he had said. Was God perhaps guarding his privileges by ensuring that others would not become gods? If that was the case, what were his real motives, and what was he not telling humanity? A distinction was thus introduced between the intellectual knowledge of someone who is more or less detached from the object of that knowledge, and the kind of knowledge that is backed by a full and unconditional commitment to the other, which orients the whole person and his or her life. The practical differences are immense. For example, if one party says something to the other that is not clear, a clarification will be sought, with the implicit conviction that it will be within the unconditional commitment; otherwise all kinds of possibilities and doubts can arise. As to the relationship between God and humanity, all religions substitute a relationship with their gods for a relationship with the only living God. All these gods are made either from what God created or from what humanity has fashioned (as in our secular age).

In addition, the serpent essentially promised a future in which humanity could live from the knowledge derived from the penetration of good and evil. Up to this point the will of God had been the good and there was no evil, since there was nothing other than this good. Humanity was now going to substitute itself for the Living One by deciding for itself what is good and what is bad. A community is obliged to evaluate everything by means of a culture and thus judge everything as good or bad. Hence, the expression *good and evil* can also be interpreted as having no moral content whatsoever and simply referring to everything in the life of this community.[10] The penetration of the knowledge of good and evil then signifies the ability to do everything and thus become like gods. It represents an encouragement for humanity not to respect any limits and to concentrate on developing the means necessary to overcome them. It would be something like opening Pandora's box. The current destruction of our planet is a good example of this.

Living by the power derived from the penetration of good and evil implies much more than the ability to do everything. It can also transcend the limits of human knowledge by means of magic in order to know the future and to unlock all the powers necessary for living it. For the people at that time, the serpent almost certainly represented both religion and magic. The Hebrew word translated as "serpent" derives from a verb that has two meanings: (1) to lead astray or to mislead with a view to the future; and (2) to practise magic and obtain knowledge by means of it.[11] Once again, there is an unmistakable polemic element in these texts against the serpent as the religious lord of all life and fertility. The text reveals that this serpent was the exact opposite: the instrument for bringing evil and death into the creation. Accepting this revelation thus implied a partial desacralization of the world of that time. It is also a powerful polemic against the moralities of the cultures that surrounded the Jewsthen. This becomes evident from several significant details in the text.

The text informs us that the woman saw that evidently the tree was good for food. In other words, instead of listening to the Word of God and remaining within the good established by it, she made the decision based on the evidence of what she saw. An opposition is thus introduced between listening to the Word and seeing the evidence derived from the world.[12] The text goes further. The fruit was not only good for eating but also beautiful to the eye and useful for intelligence. This triple temptation is the equivalent of what 1 John 2:16 refers to as the lust of the flesh, the lust of the eye, and the lust of the spirit. At this point her eyes were opened; she would live by this evidence in order to decide on her own and for herself what would constitute her food, her aesthetic, and her intelligence. Evil thus entered into the creation, as the good granted by God through his Word was replaced by something outside of it, thereby plunging humanity into evil and death.

As members of our scientific and technical civilization, we may well wonder if this condemnation of knowing and doing based on evidence was the outcome of a traditional culture suspended in a sacred and myths. We have become so absorbed by the cult of the fact that we have all but forgotten that every fact is exact only in relation to the theories that temporarily organize the domain of a discipline, and that, ultimately, scientific activities (like all other human activities) are today suspended in a secular sacred and myths.[13] All human knowledge is relative unless its status is transformed by a secular sacred, myths, and their related cults. A recognition of the relational character of our knowing and doing does not justify rejecting evidence. It merely relativizes it, thus opening the door to making more comprehensive decisions that will take into account any and all available evidence, but at the same time transcending it by subjecting it to further considerations. For example, our economic facts today are gathered within frameworks that have become entirely unscientific as a consequence of the emergence of discipline-based science and technique.[14] Basing economic policies on the extrapolation of facts in order to be "realistic" thus amounts to bowing down to the cult of growth, which excludes any genuine solutions for a global economy on a finite planet.[15] We have transformed the discipline of economics into our secular cult of scientific and technical "fertility," and this has resulted in a great deal of harm and suffering that could have been avoided if we had respected the limits of our economic knowledge.[16]

As a consequence of religion, morality, and magic the fabric of relationships that had been created and made comprehensible by God's Word was torn away from God by humanity, only to be recentred on the gods of the religions that humanity had invented, and to be reordered by the moralities and magical practices justified by these religions. Humanity thus dragged the entire creation into evil and death. It had been called to dominate the creation in the way that God had dominated it through his Word, but by breaking its relationship with God, humanity would now dominate the creation through evil and death. This possibility was an integral part of the risk God took in creating a humanity that was free to love him or to love something else.

By choosing death and evil instead of life and the good, humanity shattered the communion of love with its Creator and was now obliged to judge him as well as the good he had created. Doing so required moralities, and these in turn had to be absolutized and anchored in a sacred as the summation of the experiences of a community. The service of this absolute good necessitated a religion that submitted a community to the gods it had created.

In biblical language, God is the only Living One who can say "I am." As noted, no human being or any other creature can claim this equivalent because their being is relative, that is, dependent on a great many relationships that in turn depend on other relationships and eventually on the entire creation, and thus on the Creator. Breaking with God would have meant a complete relativism, nihilism, and anomie and thus a total impossibility of having any relationships, which for a creature means death. It is one of the two situations in the Bible designated as hell, the other being the garbage dump outside of Jerusalem (as the place for everything that was no longer of any value to life). Hell on earth is partially avoided by creating other gods, to whom communities relate as if these gods were the only living ones that could say "I am." It requires that something relative is treated as if it were absolute, as having life in itself independent from all relationships. It amounts to creating a kind of life support that, socially and historically, more or less holds together during an epoch in the history of a people. Following this epoch, with a great deal of hindsight, it becomes evident to everyone that this "life support" is nothing more than smoke or vapour blown away by the wind, never to be seen again. Nevertheless, as creatures we are individually and collectively dependent on our gods to prevent a complete impossibility of relationships. In the Bible this is humorously described by the prophet Isaiah, who tells stories of a person who cuts down a tree and uses the branches for firewood to cook his food, a part of the trunk to make the table and chairs in order to conveniently eat the food, and the rest of the trunk to carve an idol before which he prostrates himself in worship (Isaiah 44:9–20). Perhaps it is now possible, given what we have learned about our being a symbolic species suspended in the language and culture of our communities, for us to understand better the essential importance that the Jewish Bible attributes to our need to create other gods. In rejecting God's love, the communion with him, and his protection, humanity is now obliged to pursue its own autonomy, to protect itself by means of power, and to covet and conquer everything that was no longer freely given and received through grace.

Some commentators have argued that the situation that we have attempted to comprehend was inevitable. Sooner or later there had to be a break between God and humanity. For babies and children a complete and total dependence on their parents is quite normal. It does not interfere with their playful exploration of the relationships that they can make some sense of and engage in. As noted, this playfulness depends on their ability to turn to their parents or to others for help when they become stuck or too afraid to go on. As they develop, the relationships with their parents adjust along with this playfulness, especially when they are deeply loved. Their dependence on their parents gradually diminishes, and they increasingly live their own lives. When this is externally constrained, as by an economy that offers few opportunities to young people, the results are very difficult for both parties, and their love for one another may become strained. The problem with these kinds of analogies of humanity growing up, becoming rational and secular, and reaching adulthood simply confirms what we have tried to make sense of earlier. From the very beginning, God warned humanity that it was not going to grow up to become like him. Humanity was a creature, and that is all it could ever be, and God would always be the One who is entirely different from his creatures. The usual argument – that this situation began to change fundamentally in the nineteenth century thanks to the growing powers of science, technology, and economy as well as the emergence of secular mass societies organized by a state – is no more and no less than repeating the same situation first begun by the man and the woman. It is not merely a reassuring ideology;

it is an ideology that does a great deal of harm by blinding us to our limitations as creatures in our dependence on each other and on the planet and in our joint dependence on the only Living One. We will have much more to say on this in the next chapter, but for now we will continue our examination of the text.

God's Covenant and Humanity's Life Support

When humanity declared its independence from God, it was obliged to create its own life support in the form of other gods, who were now expected to deliver what humanity in its finitude was unable to achieve. This set humanity on a course of endlessly attempting to please these gods, which was impossible other than through an enslavement to them. As the book of Genesis shows, these developments occurred gradually. At the time of humanity's break with God, however, YHWH stepped in to rescue the situation and make life as liveable as possible for both parties in the relationship. Doing so was difficult because God knew that the man and the woman were now afraid of him. Finding themselves outside of the communion of love, they had begun to make their own protection in the form of clothing.

God questioned them in an attempt to have them respond and thus become responsible for what they had done. The man and the woman could not respond without accusing themselves. God himself would not accuse them, because he is not and never will be humanity's accuser, as the entire Jewish and Christian Bibles make plain. He remained fully "yes" in love and thus would not compel humanity to maintain a relationship with him under pressure or duress. YHWH revealed that the relationship between humanity and himself had changed and that this in turn had changed the relationship between humanity and the creation. He established a covenant with humanity that had to take the place of the former communion of love. This covenant had a kind of legal status, although on the part of YHWH it remained fully within and directed by his love. This limitless love could not be diminished by humanity's actions. What YHWH said not only was what he did but also revealed who he was. Consequently, what God revealed here must not be dissociated from anything else that is revealed about him in our Bibles.

Let us first examine the new relationship that YHWH established with humanity. The man and the woman now knew God outside of the communion of love in a manner that may be described as detached, objective, and without love. They had become sufficiently afraid that they hid themselves in the garden. They felt unprotected and they fashioned garments for themselves, which marked the beginning of making their own protection. Apparently, they were no longer sure whether God's unlimited power would continue to be directed by his love. This fear even makes the demons tremble, according to the letter of James.[17] The inability of the man and the woman to respond to God's questions may in part have been the result of their no longer having any idea of who they were and what they were doing; they had not yet worked out the reference points that permitted them to say that this was good and that was evil. Fully creating such reference points apparently did not occur until later, when humanity set out to build a city with the tower of Babel. Humanity's purpose was to name itself as a way of establishing its own spiritual mastery outside of the will of God.[18] Since this endeavour had failed, humanity was obliged to establish other reference points that would be neither absolute nor eternal. In any case, the text is very clear: the man and the woman were unable to respond to God's questions as to where they were and what they had done. Having broken with God, they were too terrified to accept responsibility and face the situation for what it was. As creatures they had seized their independence, but they were discovering how vulnerable and dependent they were, given that before this everything had been granted in abundance and in grace. They were spiritually lost and knew neither where they were nor where they were going. They did know that they had become irresponsible, that is, unable to respond to God's questions.

As God continued to love humanity, he could not impose his love on those who no longer loved him. The situation is well illustrated by the parable of the prodigal son. The father was powerless to do anything about his child's walking away and getting into all manner of trouble. Seeing no way out, the young man eventually decided to return home, only to discover that his father had continued to love him as before (Luke 15:11–32). God would not impose his presence on those who were now in fear of him, which could only drive them to utter despair and suicide. Out of love for his creatures God appeared to have made a terribly painful decision to withdraw his Spirit, because the man and the woman who were made from dust would now return to dust. Their human words would no longer be connected to God's Word by means of this Spirit, which eventually appears to have led to the languages and cultures with which we are familiar.

God's decision that our dust would now return to dust does not mean that he is going to ignore what his creatures do throughout human history. The Christian Bible makes it clear that in the new creation God will make everything new, but in doing so he will take into account and respect the wishes and aspirations of his creatures, whom he continues to love. He will do this in a manner that is fully "unto life," following the separation and destruction of everything that is "unto death." The new creation will take the form of the habitat that humanity desires to create for itself, namely, a city rather than another garden.[19] God was setting into motion not only the work of redemption but also the recovery from history of everything that would be useful to life.[20] It was all integral to a strategy whereby God sought to regain the love of humanity, for which he was going to risk everything, including himself. God could have chosen an entirely different path such as annihilating the creation and starting over with a new humanity created to be incapable of refusing his love. In such a case, he would have broken his Word and revealed himself to be a very different god.

Despite God's measures, human history quickly became a terrible struggle and a bloodbath. Every group and society was under pressure to create its own gods, to the exclusion of all others. Only its own gods were true. This has legitimated doing almost everything and anything to other groups and societies. In our conflicts God is never on one side or the other; only our gods are made to be so. There have been times of great religious tolerance, but these appear to have been the exceptions. Humanity has become incapable of understanding that it was created in and for love and without a view toward its species. We have attempted to base human rights, social justice, the dignity of all persons, and a great deal else on some kind of common denominator shared by all cultures and religions. This is necessarily doomed to failure. The only true common denominator that binds us together is that we are all creatures equally loved by God. For example, there are really no questions of social injustice. There is only a lack of love for God that manifests itself in a lack of love for fellow human beings, who are nevertheless equally loved by God. It is ultimately a question of the two great commandments that sum up all our relationships in terms of love.

It would appear that, from a biblical perspective, human history may be interpreted in two ways. First, there is the perspective of human experience and everything that this leaves behind, including records, artefacts, and human remains. From this we determine "facts" and arrange them as evidence, but ultimately these are suspended in myth as is everything else in human life. There is also the perspective of what is revealed to us. This includes, but is far from limited to, the horsemen of the Apocalypse, which represent how economic power, political power, and the powers of disease and death ravage human life – but these three are preceded by another rider who represents God's Word.[21] In other words, we can gather all the evidence about the three horses, but we can only discern the first by accepting this Word.[22] Hence, when the people living by the evidence of history complain to Jews or Christians about their terrible God who permits all this horror, we can only tell them that it is a little like looking at a complex woven fabric, which on one side exhibits a pattern and on the other side makes no sense at all. We may assure them of the pattern: they too are loved and redeemed, and a beautiful surprise awaits them. It is exactly as in the parable of the prodigal son. It is not the father who can be held responsible for the troubles of his son. No relationship of love between the father and the son could have existed without the possibility of one of the parties breaking it off. God created a humanity capable of responding to his love, and this involved the same kind of risk. By ignoring our limitations as creatures, we cut ourselves off from the only Living One, which has plunged us into a violent struggle between life and death.

Second, human history may be interpreted in the following way. Humanity has contracted a deadly disease not unlike cancer, which may be regarded as primarily the result of what we have done to the environment and thus to ourselves. We have become flesh, and it is killing us. God is offering to do life-saving surgery that is made possible by the work of Jesus Christ and which will remove everything that can kill us. Unfortunately the greater part of humanity does not trust him. It sees God as actively or passively behind what is causing all the suffering and death. In terms of the evidence, it is the only conclusion that people can reach. However, if we trust this God and have confidence in the surgery, the suffering and death has a very different meaning. If we understand history in this way, we become the only obstacle between God's love and a humanity in terrible suffering. Too often the Jewish and Christian communities have failed to share this love with everyone else. Worse, a constituent of the Christian community today is attempting to have humanity accept God's love, by blackmailing people with hell and damnation. In other words, they accept that they have been redeemed, that the ransom has been paid, and that their debt has been forgiven in grace. However, they cannot and will not forgive the debts of those whom they judge and condemn. Consequently, their behaviour has created an image of God who is no longer fully "yes" to humanity in his love. We will return to this point, but we must constantly be aware of the terrible baggage that we bring to the reading of these texts.

God also ensured that humanity could not re-enter into his presence. The return to Eden was blocked by those who, in the Hebrew language, are referred to as the "terrible ones." As humanity had rejected God's love, it could now only dread his power, and if it had access to the tree of life, it could be stuck in this situation for all eternity. Under these conditions no one can see God and live. God became the Invisible One, who reveals himself only by the Word.

Until the break between God and humanity the question of human responsibility could not arise. The man and the woman were in communion with God and thus alive and within the good. God implicitly responded on behalf of the man and the woman because he willed the good. Following the break, God's questions apply equally to us. Consequently, a conversion must lead to a transformation of our lives – a transformation that is ongoing, never complete, and in the direction of becoming more responsible, to the extent that we learn to live within his love and within the good.

A second response by God to the situation created by humanity's seizing of autonomy was to curse the serpent.[23] Moving on its belly, it would no longer be simply natural but a sign of shame. The serpent would now eat the dust from which humanity was made. When the text was received as a Word of God, this symbolism was much clearer than it is to us now. It was the custom of Semitic cultures to humiliate the people whom they conquered, by dragging them on their bellies over the ground. It was also plain as day that the religions in which serpents played a central role were absorbing the dust of these people by dominating and entrapping the material substance of their lives. To put it in contemporary language, the religions alienated the humanity of these people. It is clearly impossible to read these texts literally because the people of that time lived in close contact with nature, and they certainly knew that serpents did not live on dust and that they had not lost limbs somewhere along the way.

God also revealed that the serpent would be conquered by the woman's descendant (the Hebrew word is in the masculine and in the singular). Until then there would be enmity between them. The reference in the text to a single descendant of the woman, as opposed to all of humanity, gives this descendant an absolute character endued with majesty. Consequently, Christians have generally interpreted this text as referring to Jesus Christ as the Son of Man, who would kill the serpent by becoming flesh and penetrating evil and death. It is now clear that the serpent, which began as no more and no less than one of God's creatures, had become the instrument of the break between God and humanity: the power of accusation, the devourer of people's material humanity, and a combatant in the final struggle between the absolute Serpent and the absolute Man. In other words, the serpent had become the ancient serpent and the dragon that lived in the depths of the waters. As such, it was cursed and headed for destruction.

The text thus reveals that the serpent became a spiritual power, inserting itself into the "gulf" that had opened between God and humanity as a consequence of the break. Our Bibles show that this gulf would also become occupied by principalities and powers, for reasons that we will seek to understand later. It should be noted as well that the gulf will disappear when God re-establishes his relationship with humanity in the new creation following the destruction of all these powers.[24]

God also intervened in the internal relationships of humanity in general and between the man and the woman in particular. Humanity's decision to seize its independence and break with God completely shattered its being within the image of God. It had been created as one being and in two persons inseparably joined in love. This relationship was now broken as the spirit of accusation began to form within the couple. The man accused the woman and indirectly accused God as well because God had created her for him. The woman accused the serpent. The love between them was replaced by accusation as they opposed one another. God intervened. To the woman he said that he would multiply the pain that she would suffer in childbearing. To interpret this within the context of giving birth is certainly much too narrow, given the broad changes that took place. Moreover, it would appear that our civilization has made the birth process much more difficult than it was in earlier communities. In some cultures women even took care of it themselves. It is much more likely, therefore, that God referred to the break between the man and the woman as also negatively affecting their relationships with their children, and that this would be particularly painful for the woman. However, the text does not state this as a consequence of the break with God but as his decision, thus making it a sign.

Within the couple the relationships were changed as well. The woman's desire for the fruit had manifested a reorientation in her life that may be characterized as a spirit of desire. Again, to limit this to its sexual aspect appears much too narrow, given the broad context and scope of the text. Similarly, the man took back what he had passed on to the woman in terms of mastery and thus became oriented by a spirit of power and domination that he would also apply to the woman. God thus warned them that their love, which had made them as one, had been transformed from agape into Eros. It was now the man who would direct the couple by domination and not by love.

When God addressed the man, he reproached him for having listened to the woman and following her in eating the fruit from the tree. Hence, even though the woman had been given the initiative in directing the couple, the man had a responsibility for this direction, which he had failed to exercise. Hence, God held him responsible and pointed to the consequences. This intervention must not be confused with the man being cursed.

Finally, God made several decisions regarding other relationships within creation. Within the terms of the covenant that was to replace the communion of love, Adam had disobeyed what is now referred to in the text as something that God had ordered him to do. What had been God's warning before, made in love to prevent his creatures from transcending their limits by plunging themselves into evil and death, could now only be understood by humanity as a command, which God nevertheless continued to fully back by his love. For these reasons all God's commandments have this double aspect: a command accompanied by a promise that is fully backed by love. For example, "You will not kill" (in the future tense) is a spoken Word to his people, promising that, in communion with God, they are moving towards a time in which there will no longer be any need to kill. In the meantime, this commandment and the others trace the limits within which there is life and the good and beyond which is evil and death.[25] It also means that in accepting our redemption, we ought to attempt to live once again within the good, out of love for God and our neighbour, which implies an attempt to eliminate all need of killing. For this reason, in both the Jewish and Christian Bibles all the commandments can be summed up in terms of love.

Within the terms of the covenant the creation ceased to be sustained and directed by the communion of love between God and humanity. It was now dominated and directed by a humanity in the grip of a spirit of power, conquest, and desire. The creation that had been declared good by God was now dragged into the work of humanity and thus into evil and death. Hence, the break between God and humanity involved a corresponding break between humanity and creation. This does not mean that what we call nature is bad. The thorns and thistles mentioned in the text are not bad plants, but they would become bad when incorporated into the work of humanity (Genesis 3:18).[26] Human work became the instrument of the break between humanity and creation. The existence of this break is confirmed in the book of Isaiah 11:6–8 because it symbolically speaks of a reconciliation that is portrayed by the lion not harming the lamb, or by the serpent, the child.[27] In the meantime nature had become bad for humanity, with the result that human work was transformed by this new relationship with creation. Despite people's good intentions, things would always turn out differently because humanity had plunged itself into evil and death. Such a statement is usually taken as proof that Christians cannot be taken seriously because they are burdened by guilt and pessimism. I would argue that it is a realistic description of almost every attempt we have made at surmounting the many difficulties faced since the Second World War, which I have spent my entire life examining. There are also remarkable exceptions. The Bible is full of accounts in which God intervened in human affairs, warned of what lay ahead if people continued on their course, and promised forgiveness and reconciliation if they repented and changed their ways. If the Jewish and Christian people truly understood their task and incarnated the good in love, such exceptions would surely be more numerous. Our history is the consequence of the joint efforts of God and humanity, as symbolized by the four horses with riders, to which we referred earlier. It puts an enormous responsibility on Jewish and Christian people to become more useful instruments of God's intervention. Instead, these communities have frequently taken the legal approach inherent in the successive covenants that God made with humanity – as new duties, obligations, and judgments – forgetting that these covenants were ultimately based on God's love.

As a consequence of humanity's dragging nature into the break for which it is responsible, the character of human work was turned into its opposite. It had been a response to a request from God, as a token of humanity's love. There was no reason or need to do work. Work now became necessary for survival because the soil that used to yield an abundance of fruit as a free gift from God no longer yielded this abundance. Consequently, both the man and the woman had to play their roles in the maintenance of life, but they would now do so in suffering. The necessity of this work became a sign of the curse put by God on the creation. As the head of this creation, humanity had dragged it into its betrayal and become responsible for its suffering. Soon work became a reflection of humanity itself as it became organized by means of hierarchies of relationships maintained by domination, coercion, duties, and obligations, which became substitutes for relationships of love.

The man and the woman recognized that, under the covenant, life would now continue. Adam took the first step by naming the woman. The full significance of her name now becomes apparent. She had cut herself off from the only Living One and thus from the good and from life. She was now called on to transmit the life that she had received. With the removal of the first letter of the tetragrammaton, her name (HWH) fully expresses this. In naming the woman, Adam established his domination over her. Her apparent acceptance of the name confirmed that she also took hold of God's promises. They were now Adam and Eve and no longer Isch and Ischah, as two separate beings whose union in love had been lost.

Adam and Eve's acceptance of the covenant offered by God was further confirmed when they received the clothing made for them by God as a sign of his protection. In Hebrew, "the making of clothing" can also mean "the making of a sacrifice." This double meaning suggests that the clothing came from a sacrifice made by God as a sign of grace. Throughout the Jewish Bible the meaning and purpose of a sacrifice was to receive a pardon and redemption from God. In addition to being a sign of God's protection, clothing is also a sign that God no longer sees someone's sins when he clothes a person. For example, Isaiah 61:10 refers to a robe of righteousness, and Revelation 7:14 refers to people clothed in white who have been washed in the blood of the Lamb. The clothing given to Adam and Eve thus represented a prophetic announcement that humanity was headed for redemption and eternal life. Had the break between God and humanity not occurred, the "two trees" of the cross would have remained in Eden, but now they became the historical cross.

We have noted that God's decision that humanity was dust and would now return to dust seems to indicate that God had removed his Spirit. The implications are far reaching. Humanity had been created in time and not within eternity. Humanity was created finite and vulnerable, but it had access to the tree of life. In communion with God, a decision to partake no longer of the tree of life would have meant a completion of life without suffering or sadness. Life was entirely whole, to the point that a material life could not be distinguished from a spiritual life. There was a complete unity. When the communion with God was broken, the inner unity of human life was shattered, to the point that only a material life remained. Death became what the Bible has referred to as the "king of terrors." Nevertheless, all of this must be understood in terms of this covenant, the first that God made with humanity, to whom he extended his protection, pardon, and redemption. The Jewish people have interpreted these texts in this way for thousands of years.

Once again, it is important not to impose our need for religious answers on these texts. We would all like to know to the last detail how God is going to bring about our resurrection. There have always been different schools of thought among the Jewish people, as is apparent in the Christian Bible, which describes attempts to draw Jesus into the debate. The problem is that no matter what kind of theology of the resurrection we may invent, it would be a kind of "mechanism" according to which we expect God to act. As such, these theologies represent a negation of his freedom and sovereignty. Moreover, the Bible provides a bewildering range of possibilities: Enoch walked with God, and God took him. Job said that he knew he was going to his death, but his redeemer lives, and he would rise on the last day and see God. Moses died, and God buried him. Elijah was "taken up" by God. Faced with questions about the resurrection, Jesus pointed out that God referred to himself as the God of Abram, Isaac, and Jacob after they had long been dead. Jesus in his transfiguration was visited by Moses and Elijah. Following his own death, Lazarus was restored to his family. In sum, there is no simple and straightforward pattern here. All we know and can count on are God's promises, fully backed by his being God. He is the One who wills life and the good for us, and we may confidently leave the details to him.

It is also important to eliminate any idea of original sin because it would negate God's having created humanity as one being. Before God, we are integrated with everyone else who has come before or will follow after us, as well as with our contemporaries. Since none of us can say "I am" because our being and our life are relative to those of many others, and they to still others, and so on, our lives are inseparable from those of others. When someone dear to us dies, the portion of our life that we share with that person dies with it. It is helpful to recognize that we are currently living in what may be referred to as anti-societies because their characteristics are the diametrical opposite to those of all earlier societies.[28] The dialectically enfolded character of individual and collective human life has been enormously weakened as a consequence of de-symbolization.[29] In other words, we no longer see ourselves as individual, unique expressions of the spirit of our age that possesses our community. Moreover, collective human life is established by means of hierarchies maintained through domination, exploitation, obligations, duties, responsibilities, and everything else that has replaced the original communion of love. Within these hierarchies we encounter a variety of ways of making the situation perfectly normal, moral, and even justifiable. These are signs that our hearts are swollen with pride, conquest, and the like instead of being filled with love for God and our neighbour. Moreover, all of this and more is rooted in a language and culture, even when they have become significantly de-symbolized. As we will examine in greater detail in the next chapter, our lives are thus inseparable from a spiritual entity that can only maintain itself by its declaration of what is ultimately good and evil according to its own myths. Such myths correspond remarkably well to what is referred to in the Bible as vanities, smoke, or vapour. From the historical record we know that the moment these myths become incapable of providing a community with meaning, purpose, and direction, a society or civilization goes into a decline; if this is not reversed, it collapses and disappears.[30] Industrialization, modernization, and secularization have been accompanied by new generations of myths that are increasingly shared throughout humanity because they specify the ultimate relationships between our present universal technical order and what remains of local de-symbolized cultures.[31]

In sum, it is very important to be aware of our current vantage point from which we cannot help but read, interpret, and make sense of the text we have attempted to explain. Nevertheless, we are responsible for doing what we can to be critically aware of this, knowing full well that, according to our Bibles, we cannot uproot ourselves from these deepest spiritual powers that dominate human life on the planet. I believe this is essential for understanding the first three chapters of Genesis. The break between God and humanity entered into human history by one person, and it has been restored by another person. The waters continue to flow from Eden, but none of us can go back there because the road is blocked by the "terrible ones." Any attempt on our part to reach God by a religious, moral, or spiritual approach will fail unless God reaches out to us. This includes any Jewish or Christian form of doing so. We can only know YHWH because he is the One who revealed himself and gave us his unpronounceable name. Since the waters will continue to flow from Eden throughout human history, life will continue, but outside of Eden this life is only a material life that will return to dust. We cannot claim that we can take this material life, add to it some morality or religion (even when these are claimed to have been derived from the Jewish or Christian Bibles), and get back to a spiritual life that is capable of permeating it to make it one again. If there is to be a spiritual life at all, it is because God reaches out to humanity and grants an individual or a people his Spirit for a time to enable them to render a service through grace and out of love. This is the very best that dust can expect during its return to dust. For now, I can see no other interpretation of the implications that these first three chapters of Genesis reveal for human history. However, it is for all of us to discern whether or not this is so.

The Beginning of Human History

Before we continue our examination of what the book of Genesis reveals regarding the beginning of human history, we will briefly reflect on the significance of the first covenant that God established with humanity. Our current vantage point, when understood critically, leads me to the following brief meditation on these texts. During the last century we became increasingly aware of our being a symbolic species entirely dependent on a language and a culture, which suspend us and our community in a set of secular myths. The traditional gods have fallen from the sky, only to be replaced by secular gods that are also of our own making and for our own protection. Science has become the equivalent of a traditional god in the kingdom of knowledge because we refuse to recognize that the discipline-based approach to organizing science has obvious and far-reaching limitations. As I have shown elsewhere,[32] discipline-based approaches to knowing can only deal with situations in which the influence of one category of phenomena dominates that of all the other categories or where these are essentially static. The implications are that this approach is well suited to classical and information machines and everything built up with them, but it can only deal with living entities as if they were created in the image of these machines.

Similarly, technique (as in our discipline-based approaches to doing) cannot deal with complex living entities in which a multitude of categories of phenomena make non-trivial and thus non-negligible contributions, since everything is related to and evolves in relation to everything else. Similarly, when these approaches dominate all our institutions, our ways of life embody selective forces that drive human history towards reorganizing everything living as if it were dead. In other words, our civilization may well represent one of the most comprehensive attempts at cutting ourselves off from the only Living One by creating the most powerful systems for our own protection. Nevertheless, everything remains dust and returns to dust unless God re-establishes a connection with that dust. Having rejected him, we treat everything as dust. Despite all our talk about a universe, a biosphere, ecosystems, societies, communities, and everything else that lives and loves, the discipline-based approaches to knowing and doing (including their incorporation into our institutions) make it impossible for us to intellectually or practically deal with these living entities. Our civilization lives under the sign of separation and division. It is embodied in our discipline-based approaches and ways of life, which proceed as if these living entities did not exist as such. For discipline-based approaches there can be no creation, and there can only be life examined one category of phenomena at a time or a hybrid of categories at a time. These approaches have given our civilization unprecedented powers over our planet and all life on it, but at the same time it has revealed our almost limitless vulnerability and weakness. Our secular myths are blinding us to the limits of our means of protection. Our civilization recognizes that it faces some very serious issues including global warming, an environmental crisis, a persisting economic crisis, growing social inequality and issues associated with it, and extreme reactions to cultural and religious upheavals. However, we do not associate these (and everything else that we regard as necessary and beneficial) as being directly "produced" by our universal technical order. Once again, our secular myths neatly separate our successes from our failures, thereby making impossible any kind of human equivalent to negative feedback. We are locked into a course in which our accomplishments compensate for the problems created by earlier accomplishments, without addressing the real underlying issues. To sum up, our mesmerizing and spectacular achievements are increasingly separating and dividing the tissue of relationships that make up everything living. Even more than our weapons of mass destruction, we have turned ways of alienated life into ways of reified life that are inching towards death.

I am not suggesting that the opening three chapters of Genesis describe the setting of the stage for human history, which directly leads to our present situation. There have been a significant number of other civilizations with orientations that are very different from our own. What is new is that our civilization is building a global technical order because the discipline-based approaches to knowing and doing have all but eliminated the roles of language and culture in the public life of almost every society, as a consequence of de-symbolization.[33] Nevertheless, our reliance on language and culture has not been diminished in our raising of babies and children.[34] This contradiction poses a number of difficult questions. At what point will the process of de-symbolization become irreversible, thereby possibly contributing to the collapse of our being a symbolic species? Will our civilization disappear when this happens? Will the so-called singularity point, when our artificial intelligence outstrips human intelligence, come about as a consequence of our human intelligence becoming more and more like a machine-based intelligence (as opposed to the reverse)? These kinds of questions begin to expose why our civilization could possibly represent the summit of human fragility and vulnerability – if it disappears, there will be no other civilizations to take its place. Call this pessimism if you like, but doing so amounts to a secular-religious dismissal that refuses to use our intellectual abilities to question the secular gods that we have created and are serving in everything we do.

I offer this interlude as a brief reflection on the covenant established by God with humanity after it broke the communion of love with him and dragged the entire creation into evil and death. Unable to directly offer his love to his creatures, God did, as I understand it, what may have been the next best thing, namely, to offer humanity his protection. If humanity felt itself to be a little less weak and vulnerable (naked), this might limit the need to obtain by theft, murder, and lies what was no longer granted in abundance through grace. It could also limit the need for the means of power and protection such as weapons, armed groups, and fortified cities. It could even weaken the comprehensive character of the need for religion, morality, and magic in order to dominate the creation. The materiality of life that was severed from its spiritual connection to God (by means of his Spirit) exposed everything that was weak and vulnerable in humanity, but this could be limited only if humanity accepted God's protection. Otherwise these necessities of a weak and vulnerable creature might quickly take control over human life. God's strategy would have been incredibly relevant today. If our means of power based on division and separation amount to digging ourselves an ever deeper hole, will our situation convince us that we will need even more power rather than less? We will have more to say about this in the next chapter.

There are other ways in which the spirit of our age could block our understanding of the fourth chapter of the book of Genesis, which describes what could be regarded as a beginning of human history following the break. Such an interpretation would be incorrect, however, because this text was discerned as a Word of God, first by the Jews and later by the Christians. We need to remind ourselves that this Word cannot possibly be contained within any human language, because it is backed by God himself and not by a member of the Hebrew-speaking community. Consequently, this text cannot be written in the first-person singular, or in the plural with the verb in the singular. The transmission of this Word was mediated by people working within a Hebrew language and culture, and the results were discerned as a revelation. Consequently, the text tells us something about how God made sense of and related to what humanity was doing following the break. It is a perspective from eternity, related to the One who is entirely other than his creation in time. As such, the perspective offered in this fourth chapter of Genesis must be understood not in the context of what we know about human history but in the context of everything else God revealed throughout the Bible. When we attempt this, a perspective on human history will emerge that is quite different from the perspectives that are commonly found, particularly in the Christian community. As these latter conceptions could significantly hinder our reading of the text, I will attempt to clear away some common misunderstandings.

The Bible has a great deal to say about the role that the Christian community is invited to play in God's work of redemption and reconciliation. Moreover, this role is inseparable from the one to which the Jewish people were called. Although glossed over by most theologians today, the gospel of Matthew established a clear and consistent distinction between the kingdom of heaven, which operates within human history, and the kingdom of God, which will appear at the end of time.[35] The very first parable in the gospel compares the kingdom of heaven to a person who has sown good seed to yield a harvest of wheat, following which an enemy sows seeds to produce tares among the crop. There are thus two actions intervening in history and the world: one is carried out by the Lord of the kingdom of heaven, which exists within the world, and the other by the prince of that world. The servants of the Lord were not sufficiently vigilant to prevent the bad seed from being sown, and now it is impossible to separate the plants, whose roots are so entangled that uprooting the ones will destroy the others. In other words, good and evil has become completely intermingled in the world, and that includes the people. There are thus no good actions carried out by Christians, and bad actions carried out by everyone else. All this becomes very clear when the teaching of each parable is integrated with that of all the others. For example, the kingdom of heaven is also compared to yeast, which entirely disappears in producing the risen dough.[36] All these texts address a situation that began as described in the book of Genesis.

The book of Revelation symbolically represents the constituents of human history in terms of the seven seals that are broken by the slain Lamb in order to reveal the meaning of that history.[37] The breaking of the first four seals reveals the previously noted four horsemen. The breaking of the fifth seal reveals the role played by the prayers of those who act like witnesses in a trial, testifying to what is happening in the world, even at the cost of their lives. They have prayed for the triumph of the justice of God, the destruction of the powers represented by the last three horsemen, the judgment and separation of what is unto life and unto death, and the reconciliation of God with humanity in the new creation. These prayers are an integral constituent of the yeast that makes the dough rise. The breaking of the sixth seal reveals two sides of the same coin. One side displays all manner of terrible events, and the other a great calm, which nothing can disturb until all the people that God loves have been gathered as a consequence of the workings of the kingdom of heaven. This happens within history and thus does not refer to the final judgment at the end of time. The judgment is often confused with the work of the great divider that separates people, but this text anticipates the separation of the wheat from the tares. Finally, the breaking of the seventh seal ushers in the passage marked by the seven trumpets, which reveals the ultimate meaning of history by interpreting the life, death, and resurrection of Jesus Christ from the perspective of eternity. As we will see, Genesis 4 reveals a small part of this.

What these and other passages show us is that human history is constituted of positive and negative elements that we cannot and must not separate by once again penetrating good and evil on our terms, not even via theology or philosophy. To put this in another way, on the seventh day God entered into his rest to allow humanity its freedom. This freedom operates within the freedom of God in such a way that human decisions and actions cannot in any way change him. They cannot affect his love. They cannot affect the decision he made in eternity, represented by the two trees in the centre of the Garden of Eden. They cannot diminish his power to redeem humanity even to the last lost sheep. They cannot alter his willingness to forgive our debts and set us free. Most of all, they cannot affect his limitless patience that awaits our love in response. If any of this were possible, God would not be God.

Nevertheless, for some two thousand years the church has cast doubt on God's ability to accomplish this, by ignoring Romans 9–11 or by turning this text into a contrary message because of what it reveals regarding the relationships between the Jewish people and the Christian community.[38] Simply put, we cannot put ourselves back into the Garden of Eden by endowing ourselves with the capability of discerning life and the good as God sees it. God grants this ability only through his Spirit. The text in Romans is utterly clear. The return can happen only after we have undone all the harm that has been done by using these texts to undermine everything God promises because of seeing ourselves as predestined for salvation or damnation.

In chapters 9–11 of his letter to the Romans, Paul expresses his solidarity with his people, who for the greater part have not accepted the gospel.[39] However, the Jewish people are not in the Garden of Eden and thus not in a position to know what they are doing unless God grants them this ability by his Spirit. God's work of redemption cannot be limited by their decisions, because only the children of the promise and not their natural descendants have as yet been drawn into that work of redemption. In other words, God chooses those to whom he entrusts the bearing of his promise of redemption for the good of all. As the text tells us, before the twins were born to Isaac and Rebecca, God had decided that, against all the customs of that time, the younger one would bear the promise. Similarly, God chose Jacob over Esau, even though most of us would probably have found him a disagreeable person who cheated those who were dear to him. As noted, the translation of the text that God loved Jacob but hated Esau is incorrect. The Hebrew does not refer to the emotional aspect but to the action that God took. It would, therefore, be more accurate to translate this verse as saying that God chose Jacob to bear his promise but passed over Esau.

Everything we have discussed thus far has nothing whatsoever to do with salvation or damnation, as Paul explains in the context of the law. God sent his own son in the likeness of sinful humanity to be a sin offering, and thus sin was condemned in human flesh.[40] Hence, God held his wrath until it could be fully borne by his son. Consequently, God extends grace without any consideration of fault or merit, and does so by means of faith. This fundamental teaching of Paul has been almost universally misunderstood because of the belief that we can "have" faith, even though this is just as impossible as "having" our breath or Spirit, which comes and goes as it wills. The dust returning to dust cannot acquire the Spirit unless it has been granted from above. If we speak to non-Jews or non-Christians about hell and damnation, are we not like the servant in the parable of the kingdom of heaven who had been forgiven his debts but who could not forgive the debts of others?

It is clearly impossible to undo in a few lines the consequences of the neglect or the misreading of the crucial texts regarding the relationship between the Jewish people and the Christian church. I know very well how difficult this is, especially as a result of John Calvin's limited use of these and some related texts that his followers never bothered to correct. This problem has contributed to a terrible ambiguity in our understanding of the gospel. We accept that grace is extended to all because the Bible clearly says so, but we then think that it is our responsibility to come up with some faith. Many find this very difficult, especially in an age of science, because the church has never helped them to discern science's limitations. Any contradictions between science and the Bible have become impossible to resolve – as a result of the church's failure to discern the spirit of our age. Similarly, people become torn between their confidence in God's love and their moral doubts about their ability to overcome this or that sin in their lives. In the end, many people are divided between their knowing that salvation is by grace and their ongoing doubt that they have sufficient faith.

It is worth carefully rereading the account of the struggle that Job had with God.[41] His friends turned against him with arguments of the kind one is often faced with in churches when one has the courage to share one's concerns about terribly difficult questions. There are always many people with unsatisfactory answers. In the end, God not only convinced Job but gained his heart. His friends were condemned because they had made God appear unjust when they had claimed to explain his justice with their own concepts of it. They were back into penetrating good and evil on their own terms. Worse, Job's friends failed to relate God's justice to his love. Job never trapped God into his own theological, philosophical, or moral categories. When we do this, God becomes a kind of idea to us, rather than one with whom we have a relationship. In such a relationship we live in a way that must always be governed by love, as summed up by the two great commandments. This means that we are never right or wrong, but instead, to a greater or lesser degree, we fail in love. We must love God and our neighbour more than theological or philosophical truth because only Jesus Christ is the truth. Job had to intercede on behalf of his friends, and God forgave them in his name, even though these friends had been the devil to Job in their attempts to separate him from God. In the end there was a complete reconciliation between God and Job, between Job and his friends, and between God and his friends. It was a sign of the resurrection, since that is the reconciliation between God and everyone.

God's election of people is always for the purpose of their entering into the kingdom of heaven as his servants. There never is any reference to salvation or damnation, other than to warn us as servants that we should take our responsibilities very seriously. Nevertheless, I recognize that the Christian community is full of prejudgments that make a text such as Romans 9–11 difficult to read. I remember well that when I was asked to prepare a meditation on a portion of this text for a weekend during which no regular church service was scheduled, I had to confess to the small gathering (which included my French mentor, Jacques Ellul) that I had been unable to discern any good news in this text even though I was convinced it had to be there. It took me many years and a great deal of reflection to overcome these prejudgments, which so plague the Bible reading of many of us. It is important to remember that God is God, and thus his love and work of redemption cannot in any way be limited by our decisions and actions, no matter how often our churches cast doubt on this.

All this leads to a biblical perspective on human history in which both positive and negative elements play their role within God's being our God. Returning to Romans 9–11, the failure of the Jewish people to believe in Jesus Christ is temporary. They will be converted when the Christian church manifests so fully God's love, redemption, and forgiveness to everyone that they no longer want to be excluded. However, their temporary refusal to believe opened the door to non-Jews. We are very far from the Christian community's being able to bring about this conversion, but we must not assume that our actions can in any way limit God's love.

In other words, believers and unbelievers all play their role within God's work of redemption and reconciliation. This is possible only because he is God. Many biblical accounts are arranged in such pairs: Cain and Abel, Esau and Jacob, Pharaoh and Moses, Judas and Jesus,[42] to mention a few. God allows our actions and decisions to operate within his without them posing any threat or limit to his. Once again, if this were not the case, God would not be the God of the Bible.

The above perspectives on human history are further complemented by Ephesians 6:12, in which Paul shows that we are struggling not against flesh and blood (human beings) but against what has dominion (*archa*) over us: the authorities (*exousiai*), the princes of this world (*cosmocrates*), and the spiritual forces of evil (*pneumatika tes tonerias*).

We have already referred to the prince of this world and the devil, which are part of all these principalities and powers. Unlike other negative elements in human history, these powers will not be transformed, because they have already been conquered by Jesus Christ. They are now headed for their complete and total annihilation, according to the book of Revelation. The Bible is not talking about supernatural elements, fallen angels, demons torturing the damned, or similar fictions; it refers to a concrete reality, the significance of which is revealed from the perspective of eternity. God puts before us a choice between life and the good on the one hand and death and evil on the other hand. He first presented this choice to his people, whom he had liberated and assured of his presence and protection so that they could make that choice. No one in human history is ever put before this choice without the intervention of the Spirit. Under these conditions everyone would surely choose life and the good. Nevertheless, Paul complained that in his life and in ours our intentions to do the good often achieve the opposite result, and that our efforts to avoid evil frequently fail. In other words, our activities, lives, and world are full of entangled wheat and tares.

Think for a moment about the evil in the world and how we relate to it through our activities and our lives. The connections are usually difficult to make, and this has given rise to endless misunderstandings. For example, when wage earners purchased a loaf of bread or a litre of milk in the markets of the industrializing societies of the nineteenth century and the early part of the twentieth century, they did far more than enter into agreements with those who produced and sold the bread and milk. Each market transaction involved what economists refer to as market externalities, which are the consequences of such transactions that are borne by third parties, future generations, other life forms, and even the planet, even though none of these was party to any agreement. Millions and millions of market externalities added up to what have been referred to as market forces, which began to operate as selective and usually negative pressures on human history. Even the well-known market force of the "great invisible hand" excluded the needs of the poor because these people did not have the financial resources to translate their needs into market demands. They were excluded from this form of economic organization, which depended on a great many markets for goods and services of a kind rarely found today. Once the people of that time became aware of these market externalities, which their lives had helped to create, were they staring in the devil in the face? The answer is yes if we understand what the Bible means by the devil. The answer is no if we rely on the usual stereotypes that are so common in our world and even in the church.

Today our participation in the universal technical order creates similar unintended effects on third parties, future generations, other life forms, and the planet. Each technical decision made within the context of a discipline is based on a rational schema that distorts the ways in which everything is related to and evolves in relation to everything else. As a result, whatever is reorganized to become more efficient, productive, profitable, and cost-effective suffers distortions in its internal integrality and its external compatibility with everything else. Discipline-based approaches to knowing and doing divide and separate the fabric of relationships that make up our lives, communities, ecosystems, and the biosphere.[43] Billions of these kinds of technical decisions around the globe together constitute powerful forces that are pushing human history in a direction that has no relationship whatsoever to a public good and a common future.[44] This helps us to understand why it is very difficult to relate what in the Bible is called sin to our lives and our world. The gap in our understanding is commonly filled with references to the devil as a kind of contemporary metaphysics that has nothing to do with the revelation.

Hopefully, these examples can help us to understand what our Bibles are talking about when they refer to the principalities and powers. For example, Satan is the name given to the spirit of accusation, that is, the influence on individual and collective human life from each and every accusation that a person may bring against someone else.[45] It represents the totality of all actions of accusation that arise in our hearts. It is not an external power that tempts or drags us into these acts of accusation. Nevertheless, in so far as this spirit of accusation becomes integrated into our way of life, into institutions, universal technical order, and highly de-symbolized cultures, it becomes a part of what "orders" and "rules" our world. We implicitly recognize this when we say that power corrupts and absolute power corrupts absolutely. Any kind of power that people exercise over other people thus contributes to our becoming enslaved by the principalities and powers, which robs us of our freedom to love. Without freedom there can be no love; hence any spirit of power is demonic because it turns relationships of love into those of domination, exploitation, manipulation, and Eros.

In the same vein, the Jewish and Christian Bibles characterize as "the devil" all human actions of division and separation. These include driving wedges between God and people, between individual people, between people and groups, between groups and societies, and between societies and civilizations in the past, the present, or the future.[46] Similarly, political power that rules the nations of the world is named the "prince of this world." In the same vein, all human activities that are the opposite of grace because they are ruled by money are named "Mammon." The power of disease and death is called "the king of terrors." There are also powers that are not specifically named but whose destruction is described in the book of Revelation.[47] These include the state and the city.[48] In sum, from a biblical perspective there appears to be no difficulty in explaining the source of the devil, whether it be a fallen angel or some other created entity that rebelled against God. It is possible to speak of someone being possessed by a demonic spirit when a person's life is dominated by a will to divide and separate people, thereby inciting hatred, discrimination, humiliation, and everything else that undermines and destroys the relationships among people and between God and people.

In Ephesians 6:12, Paul reveals that the principalities and powers dwell in high places.[49] In order to understand this, we must briefly return to the break between God and humanity. The human heart, which was once full of love, became possessed by a spirit of coveting, beginning with the desire to be like God by penetrating good and evil, and then to have (by our own means and in our own time) everything that God freely granted in grace and in abundance. It is a spirit of power to want to possess and acquire from God, and from others and the world, whatever we desire. Warning against this spirit of coveting by the exercise of power not only concludes the Decalogue but also sums it up.[50] For example, you will not covet making a God who is at your disposal. You will not covet having God's name. You will not covet the well-being of others and steal from them. You will not covet someone else's wife and commit adultery. You will not covet another person's life and commit murder. Everything evil may thus be regarded as rooted in coveting.[51] With this spirit of coveting in our hearts we can be tempted by all kinds of different situations, as James 1:14 shows. It adds that God does not tempt anyone and that he cannot be tempted by evil.

We can now begin to understand what Paul is talking about regarding the principalities and powers. When we are tempted to act on our spirit of coveting in the case of an opportune situation, the results contribute to the evolving of the way of life, institutional framework, morality, religion, and aesthetic expressions of our community. Eventually they help to evolve its culture, including its reference points (commonly referred to as its myths).[52] In turn, this culture and its orientation guide all the matters of a community from "on high." From a historical and sociological perspective, I have shown this with regard to the first two generations of industrial societies: as people changed technology, technology simultaneously changed people, and later the same occurred for technique.[53] In these historical situations the members of the societies involved in the transformations responded to a vast range of evolving situations in a manner that frequently would elaborate and reinforce the very developments that had created them. This self-reinforcement resulted from their having experienced patterns that were integral to the way they lived their lives in the world, and these lived experiences modified the organizations of their brain-minds by means of the neural and synaptic changes that symbolized these experiences. For a symbolic species these organizations thus express these patterns, which in turn are reflected in the way that people respond to everything in their daily lives. It is only when societies and civilizations enter into a period of decline that this kind of self-reinforcement does not occur. In all cases, everything undertaken by the members of a society is suspended in a language and a culture oriented by myths. For the duration of a historical period these myths are as close as individual and collective human life can come to something absolute, that is, something that appears not to be influenced by everything else. It is not until an intuition of our dependence on everything else begins to break into human awareness that these myths gradually become like any other element of human experience by revealing how they too are dependent on and participate in the way everything is related to and evolves in relation to all other elements within our experience. This is how individual and collective human life is lived. In other words, what we are attempting to understand is what, in the Jewish and Christian Bibles, is named sin (a condition always likened to that of enslavement) and its relation to metaconscious myths – which puts it beyond the reach of discipline-based approaches to knowing. I am not suggesting that the above explanation exhausts the meaning of what the Bible attributes to our enslavement to Satan, the devil, the prince of this world, Mammon, the state, the city, and death. For now, my intent is only to show that, as a consequence of the massive de-symbolization of our cultures during the last half century, and because of the secular spirit of our age, we are able to weaken somewhat the strong prejudgments that we may have had against these kinds of texts. We need to develop a way of speaking about everything that exists beyond the limits of what a discipline-based science can know and beyond what a discipline-based technique can do.[54] Otherwise we will be encapsulated in the cults and secular myths of our time, place, and universal order. In that case, a revelation from God can have no meaning other than what is compatible with the ways of our culture.

We have noted that when humanity was in communion with God, there was no danger of relativism, nihilism, or anomie. Everything was within the good that God loves, and everything was oriented by humanity's response to that love. Following the break, humanity had to invent, on its own and by its own means, the reference points and orientation necessary for individual and collective human life. As a symbolic species, it did so by suspending itself in languages and cultures. The threats of relativism, nihilism, and anomie were driven from humanity's created symbolic universes by a few elements that appeared to be unaffected by everything else, as if they were autonomous and thus self-sufficient. In other words, these elements were as close to eternity as humanity could reach. Under these circumstances, symbolic cultures created a wide range of very difficult situations, and it was extremely tempting to deal with them by means of those elements that appeared to be autonomous, having limitless power to carry out their functions, because all the other elements seemed to be unable to affect and thus limit them.

As to our own civilization, its secular myths are posing the same kinds of temptations as did their traditional counterparts. Our indiscriminate use of discipline-based approaches to knowing and doing, as if they had no limits, has created an economic temptation to satisfy whatever human needs we experience or invent. Such needs are considered legitimate, thereby turning everything in the creation into natural, social, and human resources. Moreover, this makes it impossible for us to respect any limits of our planet. We must satisfy, with ever more powerful means and ever greater efficiency, whatever needs the advancement of technique can never satisfy. It has become an enslaving obsession to "live by bread alone" by harnessing everything to human needs. Of course, the needs that lie beyond those that can more or less be addressed by discipline-based approaches have become purely private, personal, and spiritual. It is not that such needs are not legitimate; it simply means that we insist on having everything – namely, penetrating the good *and* the evil. The means used to achieve this are the secular cults, including the cult of the fact, the cult of efficiency, and the cult of growth.[55]

In our civilization Jews and Christians may not serve these cults. The Word of God alone makes it possible for human life to be lived without relying on a secular sacred, secular myths, and secular cults. In order that they do not to bow their knees to them, God's people are called to live by the revelation that his Word is as essential for life as bread is for a person's physical and biological functioning. Hence the importance of the Spirit. And we are back to the opening chapters of Genesis. We may well be gaining a technical mastery over ourselves, our needs, and the world, but we are in danger of losing the human spirit, or what is left of it, under its enslavement to the principalities and powers.[56] If we truly desire a more liveable and sustainable way of life, we will need to be fed by God's Word to weaken our enslavement enough to enable us to reinvent ourselves.

Another terrible temptation that our civilization has been unable to resist thus far is that of political power and the state. Their growing influence is the direct consequence of the de-symbolization of our cultures. No longer can human life be lived in symbolic universes that are ordered by traditional values, moralities, and religions. Their symbolic ordering and ruling from above will now have to be accomplished in another way. Where this is headed has become increasingly clear during the last two hundred years. Before this development there was not a single moral, religious, or political tradition in the West that favoured the state, for the obvious reason that it excluded the possibility of free people. Either the people would make the decision, or the state would. To a large extent, the members of traditional societies were much more involved in evolving their cultures than we are today, thus making small local communities largely self-ordering and self-regulating, often to the point of not even requiring a policing function. This was clearly understood by every Western tradition.

As the self-ordering and self-regulating functions of local cultures became increasingly incompatible with industrialization, urbanization, and secularization, a growing range of difficulties could only be addressed by some form of central government. It was not long before everything became political, which implied that the business of the state had no limits. Whenever difficult situations arose, this limitless ordering and regulating capability of the state had to be called upon.

I am not in the least denying the growing role and influence of the corporation with its extensive technical planning, but corporations could not function without a constant and massive lobbying effort to ensure that the state would bestow the necessary legitimacy on their activities. No institution other than the state was capable of granting the corporation the legitimacy it required for its almost limitless exploitation of technique.[57]

As noted, the twentieth century produced three secular political religions, which provided the cults through which the state was to be loved and served. We must be willing to lay down our lives for it. We must also devote seven or eight months' earnings to it for every year of our lives as we pay our taxes. Our hopes for the future are entirely dependent on it as we look forward to electing the next government, which we know will be able to solve all our problems.

These are not merely a few sociological, political, and historical observations. The use of political power is nearly irresistible to each and every group, whatever its cause. To our shame, many Christians have found it irresistible to use political power to advance a Christian morality and religion in order to create "one nation under God."[58] It represents another way of coveting to do, by ourselves and with our own means of power, what God alone can grant in grace and in abundance: a truly secular society free of every cult, which therefore can no longer legitimate domination, exploitation, and destruction. The creation of a more liveable way of life and a more sustainable future cannot be contemplated without the destruction of our present secular cults.

The state cannot demand that we must love our sacred home with our hearts, minds, and souls, even unto death. We cannot assume that God is on our side or expect him to bless our nation when the state conducts the kinds of policies that inevitably divide everyone in political power struggles. We cannot leave it up to the state to morally dominate others by naming them as friends or enemies and, specifically, as communists, liberals, homosexuals, or anything else that threatens the secular political religion of the day. Nor can we allow the state to name other people as constituting evil empires. The nation-state, with its political power, divides nation against nation, people against people, and groups against groups. It represents the spirit of separation and division, which the Jewish and Christian Bibles name as demonic. It is the expression of our thirst for power and domination rooted in our covetousness. Here it takes the political form of advancing the kingdom of heaven by the prince of this world.

There is a religious temptation as well. As a symbolic species we were created with a connection to eternity by means of the Spirit. When that connection was broken, humanity was obliged to create its own eternity by sacralizing and treating as myth those elements in the world's interrelatedness that appeared to be unaffected; these elements manifest an unlimited power to execute their functions without being limited by anything else. By naming them as gods through religions, societies created eternity in their own image. It ensured not only that this eternity was accessible (unlike the Garden of Eden) but also that it could be religiously manipulated according to a society's own needs and aspirations. The sociology of religion has furnished us with endless examples of how this manipulation functions in a variety of cultures. Who or what could possibly stand against a society that was regaining an eternity of its own making and developing the means to bring this eternity under its control? This accomplishment provided a human community with the vitality, courage, and eternal rewards, even the domination of disease and death, for doing whatever it did.

Western nations attempted to regain access to eternity by means of the Christian religion. It began with Constantine, who made Christianity the official religion of the Roman Empire, with the most disastrous consequences imaginable. After the fall of the empire most Western societies followed suit by legitimating the political power of their kings or queens, emperors or empresses, by placing them at the head of a national church. As recently as the Second World War, many churches had altars draped with national flags, and some continue to display flags in their sanctuaries. Apparently, Western Christianity did not understand that Jesus Christ came to redeem humanity and not to legitimate its enslavement to political power. A number of influential theologians even believed that force was justified to compel conversions.

Jesus Christ was willing to be the least among us and counselled his followers to do the same. I have not yet experienced a church whose leaders do not hesitate for a moment to exercise a great deal of power over their "flocks." When they encounter objections from their members, they tell them that it is either unbiblical or impractical to do anything else. These kinds of leaders judge God's Word of love and non-power as being quite unsuited to this world. They and their congregations have utterly lost a sense of their complete dependence on God's Word illuminated by the Holy Spirit.

We may well have reached a time in which God turns his back, resulting in a great hunger and thirst for his Word.[59] It would explain why most churches are slowly but surely emptying while others can only stem this tide temporarily by threatening hell and damnation.

Within the Christian community there is a particular form of the religious temptation to use the Word of God outside of his will as a means to our own ends. Certain texts are separated out from that Word as being central and thus dominating all the rest, thereby creating a hierarchy within the Word. Here there exists the same demonic spirit to separate and divide the Word in order to legitimate and justify one denomination as being more faithful and biblical than the others. In other words, a demonic spirit is used to divide the Christian community, and this strikes at the very heart of the community's ability to bear the love of God among humanity. We confuse this with biblical virtue and Christian leadership, but it amounts to another form of penetrating the good and the evil. We are thus subjecting God's Word to our own judgments of relative importance as opposed to doing everything possible to listen to it in the confidence that, when we do, its creative power will renew our lives time and time again.

I am not suggesting that we are capable of understanding God's Word in its entirety or that, given the circumstances of our lives, some passages cannot speak more strongly to us than others. Intellectually and in our lives we are incapable of backing God's Word with our being. For this reason we need to complement one another and do so in love. Anything else is based on a spirit of separation and judgment that divides people against people. In the Christian community, truth is a relationship with Jesus Christ as the way to life. We are united by following this truth and this way and jointly submitting to only one authority, which is exercised in love and non-power. We must do everything possible to avoid the religious temptation that has divided the Christian community into a multitude of denominations that, without exception, name and judge one another based on the discernment of good and evil. I am making these remarks based on my long experience of encountering, in each and every congregation of which I have ever been a part, a remnant that attempts to be faithful by struggling with what it means to be Christian in our civilization. As far as I am able to understand the situation, these remnants have much more in common with one another than what divides them according to their denominational memberships. However, there is no institutional or organizational solution. It may be tempting to dream of what might be possible if some of these remnants could be brought into a fuller communion with each other, because their differences would complement one another in a spirit of love and non-power.

The historical and sociological functions of religions are well known. They have always added greatly to the principalities and powers, based on the coveting of a god to suit the ideas, beliefs, lifestyle, culture, and history of a people. Whenever Christianity sought to step into this role, it led to a great deal of violence and shedding of blood. We must also take care not to use the Word of God to satisfy our curiosity, because God has revealed only what we need to know for our redemption and for bearing the promise of salvation for all humanity.

It should be noted that the these three categories of temptation are symbolized by the three temptations to which Jesus was subjected during his life, as summed up at the beginning of three of the gospels (Matthew 4:1–10; Mark 1:12, 13; and Luke 4:1–13). This ought to come as no surprise. We are clearly told that like us, Jesus was tempted in all things, and these temptations show us how Jesus would suffer throughout his life.[60] I will limit myself to one detail in the remarkable study of Jacques Ellul,[61] namely, that these temptations always came through the intermediary of fellow human beings. In other words, it was humanity who tempted him to use his unlimited power, not in love and obedience to his Father, but to make sure that his ministry would not be ruined by a premature death due to starvation, to provide an effective means for reaching as many people as he could during his brief sojourn, and to use the Word to make this ministry more successful. We see this unfold throughout his life when he rebukes his disciples for being Satan whenever they engage in acts of accusation and separation. In many cases these temptations came from "on high" by means of the morality, religion, and institutions of his people. This situation resulted in profound suffering and isolation for Jesus. It should be noted that if Jesus had given in to these temptations, he would have done exactly what he had come to do, but he would have accomplished it by means of power and not in obedience to God's way of love and non-power.[62]

A New Beginning without God

The view of human history regarded from eternity that is becoming apparent thus involves an intermingling of the decisions and interventions of God and those of humanity. The result is a complex interaction of positive and negative elements. Cain and Abel embodied the elements of two different spiritual orientations that would increasingly be present in each and every human being.

Cain and Abel were the offspring of Adam and Eve, who had accepted God's protection and under it had decided to transmit life – a life that Eve acknowledged as having been received from God himself. The names that they gave to their children were significant. The name of the older son meant "the man who possesses."[63] The name of the second son meant "smoke, weakness, and inconsistency."[64] It is the same Hebrew word that is usually translated as "vanity" in the opening verse of the book of Ecclesiastes.[65] These names designate diametrically opposite orientations for human life, provided that we recognize that, throughout the Bible, people always exhibit elements of both.

Like their parents, Cain and Abel appeared to have accepted God's protection, at least to some degree, because they acknowledged it by making offerings to him. Abel brought the best of his flock, while Cain brought fruit from the land. Cain was rather put out when his brother's offering was accepted but his was not. God warned him, but the text of Genesis 4:7 is difficult to interpret.[66] It appears to mean that human beings have the ability to rise to a situation, but when they fail to do so, the fault lies in wait for them and is ready to pounce on them. When God did not accept Cain's sacrifice, rather than listening to God and repenting, Cain permitted his anger and jealousy of his brother to take hold of him. He spoke to his brother, but we are not told what was said. Following this conversation, Cain murdered Abel.

Abel vanished like smoke. As a result, all subsequent events are built on a murder. Cain appeared to be driven to repossess everything that he had lost as a consequence of the murder. He was almost certainly rejected by his family and lost his place in the community, and thus his place on the land. We must be very clear on the meaning of sin in this context. As noted, sin always refers to a condition as opposed to actions that can be judged as morally bad. Such judgments belonged to the penetration of good and evil. Sin is the condition that results from breaking with God and thus entering into the condition of evil and death. What we name as sins are the manifestations of this condition. Consequently, the rejection of Cain's offering meant that God was telling him that he was not within life and the good and that, unless he repented, his actions would manifest evil and death.

Following the murder, God cursed Cain but also offered him special protection – a prophetic sign that the curse would not last forever. Cain's punishment was thus little more than his own banishment from his tribe and land. As a homeless person, he was terrified of being killed by whoever would find him. Nevertheless, Cain was not satisfied with God's special protection. He went out from God's presence to live in the land of Nod to the east of Eden.[67] The land of Nod is the land of wandering, a condition under which life is lived; it is not a geographical place. Spiritually, this condition of life is found "east of Eden." In the Jewish and Christian Bibles the east is the point of departure for human journeys, with different orientations characterized by an opposition or a faithfulness to God. Cain decided to settle in the east, thus putting himself into a situation of perpetual departure.[68] He was stuck there and could never finish his journey as a wanderer. Moreover, this happened "east of Eden," which signifies that he had his eye on the lost communion of love with the only Living One, whom he had rejected.[69]

A vicious cycle was thus initiated. The more Cain rejected God and his protection in order to begin his own life, and shielded that life by turning to means of power to ensure his own protection, the more he longed for what he had lost in terms of his connection with eternity. He had set out on a journey that, as a creature, he could never complete without his Creator, whom he had rejected. He therefore condemned himself to making his own substitutes, but these would never satisfy his longing for eternity. The search for a home in Eden was in the end a longing for God's presence.

Cain thus made his own beginning by transmitting his life to his offspring and making his home in the form of a city that was entirely of his own making. It became the locus of his spiritual wandering and the material proof that he had taken responsibility for himself and the life of his family. This position made it impossible for him to answer God's questions, any more than could his parents. At the same time, in taking charge of his life, his family, and his surroundings, he reinforced his break with God because it compelled him to deny his status as a creature.

It was God who had named humanity and thus set its spiritual orientation. Cain had now taken the first step towards humanity's naming itself and setting its own spiritual orientation. This step is evident from the name he gave to his son and to the city he built: Enoch, a name that meant "to initiate, to dedicate, and to inaugurate." It marked his own beginning and spiritual orientation in a rejection of God and his creation. It was a rejection of everything that came before.

The spiritual significance of the city in general constitutes a theme that receives a great deal of attention throughout the Bible.[70] This city, into which humanity poured its aspirations and expectations of its seized independence, is something that God nevertheless respects and takes seriously. Cain's beginning without God and without the creation, in so far as it could be excluded from the city, is carefully taken into account by God's work of redemption. God's new creation will be a city, with the difference that in it God will be all in all. It is another sign of his love and respect for humanity.

In Cain, humanity rejected God's love and protection in order to make its own beginning by developing what it deemed necessary for its independence in terms of its own protection and maintenance of life. An orientation by necessity thus replaced one by love and freedom. The possibility of walking with God was carried on by a small remnant, of whom Enoch and Noah are mentioned in the first genealogy of ten generations. These generations jointly spread the evil that ended in death by the flood.[71] The number ten is almost certainly symbolic since there were also ten generations between God's making of a second covenant with Noah and his descendants and the making of a covenant with Abram. It was Abram who became the father of a people that God set apart to represent him and to share his love and redemption with all of humanity. I will conclude this chapter by briefly commenting on several aspects that are important as preparation for the next chapter, which will examine the account of the tower of Babel and its consequences for all of human history.

The first genealogy contains a strong polemical element against some of the cultures of the people surrounding Israel at the time these texts were written. The fathers of those who lived in tents and raised cattle, those who played the lyre and stringed instruments, and those who forged iron and bronze were human beings who invented and named these activities. In parallel genealogical accounts of the surrounding cultures, these human capabilities were always handed down by the gods. Consequently, attributing these capabilities to people was highly desacralizing with respect to these cultures.

In his speech to his two wives, Lamech boasts that he has killed a man and a boy and that he will be avenged seventy-seven times – instead of the seven times that Cain would be avenged. It is the first indication of the spread of violence and killing following the murder of Abel.

The Genesis text informs us that people began to call on God, but it does not tell us whether this was a religious attempt to regain Eden or a true worship of God. It is also worth noting that the Hebrew verb usually translated as "to know" (as in a man knowing his wife) literally means "to penetrate," thus probably signifying that the kind of love that had made a man and a woman "two persons in one" had disappeared.[72] Moreover, the Hebrew language did not distinguish between the roles played by men and women in the passing on of life. Hence, a literal translation would require the invention of a new verb such as "to children" similar to the French verb *enfanter*.[73]

The view from eternity of human life on earth during these ten generations is that the rejection of life and the good opened the flood-gates to evil and death. According to Chouraqui, the meaning of some of the Hebrew text is uncertain.[74] One possible interpretation of Genesis 6:3 is that God's Spirit cannot remain with humanity forever because even though its flesh is weak, it resists him. Another possible interpretation is that God's Spirit may become flesh (and faulty) if it remains with humanity for a long time. In any case, this verse implies that God occasionally makes a connection with "dust returning to dust," which requires his Spirit (for the reasons discussed earlier), and that such connections have grave consequences. Genesis 6:5 and 6:6 add that "God saw that humanity was spreading evil over the earth and that everything that sprung from its heart was evil." He regretted having created humanity, and it grieved his heart. He therefore decided to wipe humanity from the earth, along with the animals and the birds. He would no longer hold back the waters but would limit them, excluding them from the ark that would carry a faithful remnant of humanity as well as animals and birds. The Hebrew word usually translated by "ark" occurs only twice in the Jewish Bible.[75] In the other usage, the word refers to what protected Moses as a baby from the waters of the Nile; and through his life God delivered Israel and established his covenant with it on Mount Sinai. In any case, it represented a containment of the waters that threatened a remnant of life in the creation.

According to Chouraqui, some rabbis held Noah responsible for not pleading with God to save humanity as Abram would some time later.[76] God's decision as well as his regret are also difficult to understand for many of us today. We must resist any theological truisms that so frequently descend from our pulpits. God is God, and we can at best understand something of what he reveals to us. In the final analysis it is a question of whether or not we learn to love and trust him in all matters including those that provoke strong counter-transference reactions in us. It would be much easier to invent some way of rationalizing the death of most of humanity or to judge God by our cultural values, but this is exactly what always plunges us into evil and death because we are his creatures, now made up of both wheat and tares.

It is essential to recognize that these opening chapters of Genesis frame the entire revelation set out in our Bibles. God had intended his creation to be a communion of love. When humanity refused his love, God took the two trees from the centre of the Garden of Eden and put them in the centre of human history, as the structure of the book of Revelation shows symbolically.[77] As God began to implement his work of redemption, he steadfastly showed his love for his creatures by making the broken-down situation as liveable as possible for all parties – by means of a succession of covenants. These used what may be called a legal approach: delineating a variety of obligations coupled with promises in order to permit life without love to proceed. It was his steadfast and sometimes jealous love that constantly framed his interventions. Nevertheless, the portion of humanity that believed itself to be faithful to God generally mistook its "legal" obligations under these covenants for rules, although throughout our Bibles they are always summed up in terms of love for God and our neighbour. For example, the Torah became an endless burden of obligations that completely lost track of its original purpose: to reveal the limits within which life and the good were possible and beyond which reigned evil and death. Again, within these limits, everything could be summed up in terms of love. This was usually understood by a small remnant within the community, which thought of itself as being faithful to God. In the way they lived their lives, this remnant bore the promise of life and the good for everyone else belonging to God's people and his church and, via them, for all of humanity. If we cannot frame everything that we do (and that we do not do) in terms of love for God and our neighbour, we are trapping ourselves into a Jewish or Christian morality and religion. There are a number of moving texts that confirm this, in which God pleads with us, such as Isaiah 65:1, 2 (which is also cited by Paul in Romans 10:20, 21). God complains that he continuously spreads out his hands to us in our rebellion. There is a kind of frustration and impotence there to which we, as human beings, can relate. It is like a situation in which a man is told by his lover that she needs to go and "find herself," or in which a woman is told by her lover that in mid-life he has finally encountered true love with someone half his age. Nevertheless, God renews his promise that for the sake of the remnant he will not abandon us and that, following the resurrection, this rebellion will be remembered no more. It is this faithful remnant that in the Christian second testament is compared to yeast in dough, salt in food, and the bearers of light in a world of darkness. However, the Jewish people were the first of the "two witnesses" called to this task.[78]

3 Language, Myth, and History

Making a Name

The account of the tower of Babel is of the greatest significance for all of human history because God put limits on the efforts of humanity to secure its independence from him. He is the only Living One, which implies that such projects inevitably lead to spiritual self-destruction and death. In his love for humanity God set limits to this enterprise, and humanity responded by making it liveable through an even greater enslavement to the powers. Humanity built a city with a tower that God named Babel. In order to understand what happened, it is essential to examine the revealed significance that the book of Genesis attributed to the city, which is confirmed and developed further throughout the Jewish and Christian Bibles. This revelation regarding the city culminates with a description of its destruction as one of the powers that holds humanity captive. I will draw on the insightful but widely misunderstood study of the biblical message regarding this city that was undertaken by Jacques Ellul.[1]

To avoid further misunderstanding of his work, I will make a distinction between a revealed myth and a cultural myth. The former corresponds to the concept of myth used in Jacques Ellul's analysis,[2] and the latter corresponds to the myths created by symbolic cultures. Within a revealed myth the meaning of a fact or an account is the meaning that such a fact or account takes on by virtue of its having been incorporated into the biblical revelation. In other words, its revealed meaning, though expressed through a human language and symbolic culture, derives not from them but from what God reveals about their meaning from the perspective of eternity, as it were. Such a fact or account thus bears his revelation, although in its linguistic and cultural context it does no such thing.

Jacques Ellul's definition of a revealed myth presupposes that we do not read our Bibles in the way that we read historical and literary documents. The meanings of such documents refer to their linguistic and cultural contexts as well as the etymological and historical developments that formed these contexts. Whatever the cultural or discipline-based approaches to knowing are able to discover about the linguistic and historical context remains very important, but the revealed meaning can never be reduced to what is learned through such approaches. Nevertheless, it can help us to appreciate the polemical character of a text, how the people of the time in which these texts were written would likely have interpreted them, what their acceptance of these texts as a revelation added to them, and whether it transformed them.

The practical implications are that when the believing Jews and Christians discuss these writings with others, they must be prepared for their own counter-transference reactions as well as those of the others. Consequently, any communication with others is vulnerable to the possibility that these counter-transference reactions will drive the meanings of what is being discussed towards the meanings of their linguistic and cultural contexts, and thus towards a moral and religious distortion of the revelation.

Following the account of the flood and the establishment of the second covenant with Noah and his family, the tenth chapter of Genesis names all the people who constituted humanity. They are arranged in three groups according their descendants from one of the three sons of Noah. Particular attention is paid to Nimrod, the son of Ham. Ham had been cursed to become the "slave of his brothers' slaves" for what he had done to his father, Noah. Nimrod did everything in his power not to become such a slave, by founding a kingdom and building the cities of Babel, Erech, and Accad in the land of Shinar. Nimrod was a mighty hunter before God. Being "before God" is a biblical designation of a person's life being separated from God but not escaping his presence. For Nimrod, God was not the One whose love he reciprocated, and yet the all-powerful One saw and knew everything he did. The relationship was the opposite of communion as a consequence of the break that had occurred. Nimrod was a hunter of animals and men. He plundered and conquered the latter by military might in order to establish his reign in opposition to the good that God willed.

From Shinar he extended his military and political control to Assyria, where he built Nineveh, Rehoboth, Calah, and Resen. From a historical perspective, it is almost certain that Nimrod did not build all these cities, but they symbolize the revealed meaning of the work he began.[3] Nimrod established an urban civilization based on military power and domination. From the perspective of human history, it would also become the centre of commerce and trade, banking, political power, religious power, and, most recently, the centre of industrialization, technology, and technique. The accusation launched against this civilization in the book of Revelation is that it trades in the bodies and souls of people, thus constituting a historical power of enslavement whose spiritual quality is symbolized by Babylon the great.[4] Given the enormous growth of the urban phenomenon and our recognition of being a symbolic species, it is easy to appreciate that our Bibles are not exaggerating in the least. As we build cities, cities simultaneously "build" us by their vast influence on the experiences that in turn build our lives through the organizations of our brain-minds.[5]

This interpretation is amply confirmed by the meanings of the names of the cities and their lands.[6] The land of Shinar designates the spiritual condition of human life: it is being thrown down, shaken, and subjected to fury, and thus it is everything that is opposite to peace. In other words, the name refers to something much more fundamental than a geographical location, and this is confirmed by the subsequent references to it in the Bible. For example, Abraham defeated the king of Shinar, who had captured his nephew Lot, and Melchizedek, the king of Salem (righteousness and peace), blessed him for it. Throughout the history of the Jewish people Shinar represented a spiritual power and a temptation to evil. It was the land to which Nebuchadnezzar took the vessels of God's temple. Daniel specifically refers to it as Shinar, and not as Babylonia, to signify that its meaning is far more important than its geography. The clearest example is the vision in Zechariah 5, in which Shinar designates the land of sin. Similarly, the names of the cities symbolize the city of eternity, the city of vastness, and the city of force, showing the conquest of and the attempts to dominate time, space, and energy.[7] For example, Resen means "a bridle bit," representing the domestication of the horse as a natural force put into human service; the cavalry was one of the most fearsome weapons of those days. Every subsequent civilization has marked its birth by the building of cities as the symbols of its power over humans beings and over nature. In other words, the city is the exact opposite of everything that God had intended as a communion of love sustained by grace. Nothing is free; everything has to be paid for. There are no relationships of love in its public life, only those of hierarchy, domination, and enslavement. Nature also is drawn into the city's orbit, becoming the hinterland that must be dominated to extract what is necessary for the city. All the city's interests must be protected by force, indissociably linking it to military power and war. Without this, its economic and political power could not be expanded and defended. In sum, the city is an assembly of people that is the diametrical opposite of the assembly of God's people joined together by their redemption, which makes freedom and love possible.

The message of our Bibles regarding the city thus has little to do with an urban habitat or with its advantages or disadvantages over the countryside. It is the symbol of what happened when humanity refused God's love, declared its independence, and thus needed to procure for itself what had been freely given in love and grace. Humanity was compelled to turn to all means of power in order to acquire what, in its weakness and vulnerability, it deemed necessary and desirable.

Babel was the centre of Nimrod's kingdom. Its name means "the gate of the gods." Everything was now ready for humanity to make a final push, to build a "city of cities" that possessed a tower with its top in the heavens, and thus make a name for itself. In other words, despite the usual interpretation of this account, the city and the tower were the means for humanity to earn its own name. We have already discussed that God named the first man and that Adam in turn named the animals and the woman, and why Adam later renamed her Eve. Except for the latter name, these names reflected who and what they were within the good that God willed. Hence, what remained for humanity to gain its full independence from God and to seize control over its spiritual being and direction was to reject the name that God had given it and to name itself. All it had to do was to take the next step: construct the city of cities with a tower penetrating the heavens. Humanity would thus seize eternity, name its own spiritual truth, and be like the gods, exactly as the serpent had predicted. It would be the final step in uniting humanity because all its members would live by the same truth of its own making. Such a truth would be all in all, in its exclusion of God. No longer would God be able to call humanity by its name because humanity would no longer recognize it and would have no reason to respond. God would no longer be its lord. Since this would take place in the land of Shinar, its borders would vanish. Humanity would appropriate the entire creation as a hinterland for its "city of cities." This would be the ultimate choice of evil and death, to the exclusion of life and the good. In sum, this city of cities with its tower in the heavens would become the spiritual locus of the triumph of evil and death over God. He had created humanity to rule over his creation by the human word nested within God's Word and the good. Humanity now desired to embed its word within its own truth separated from God, thereby turning it into the most terrible weapon: a system of communication and coordination of human efforts that, because it was within evil and death, would lead to humanity's own destruction unless God intervened.

It was thus hardly surprising that, before this could be accomplished, God came down to look at the city and the tower that humanity was building, and he made the astonishing observation that whatever humanity thought of, it would henceforth be able to carry out. God thus confirmed the ultimate significance of this city and tower, which far transcended its physical manifestations. God intervened in an equally decisive fashion. The rejection of the Word (which named the good by which humanity was to rule) and its replacement by a system of communication and action was halted by a confusion of their language (i.e., a mixing together of elements), thereby making it impossible for the people to understand one another. It should be noted that the Hebrew text does not say that a single language was divided into many languages. Only small groups could understand one another, to the exclusion of understanding all other groups.[8] The confusion was accomplished by a mixing together, presumably of the language's elements, which no longer could be clearly differentiated from each other, resulting in a complete loss of meaning. There was no choice left but to abandon the building of the city and the tower and to get away from the others who had become a threat due to non-communication.

When we put God's intervention in the context of the entire revelation, it becomes clear that once again it was an act of love. If humanity had succeeded in transforming everything into the land of Shinar, first of all, it would have separated itself from the only Living One, thereby assuring that evil would completely spiral out of control and end in the death of humanity. In his love, God could not stand by and watch humanity destroy itself. Second, God's work of redemption and liberation to bring about the freedom of humanity, and thus the possibility for it to respond to his love, would become a great deal more difficult and painful for humanity. The two covenants that God had made with humanity as a whole had been rejected. God was about to change strategy by setting apart the weakest of all the people on the earth as his own by means of a covenant with Abraham. They would learn of their redemption and liberation as well as the limits of life and the good within which, as a liberated people, they could love God and their neighbour. Within this people of God there would be a remnant who would understand that there was much more to the law than a mere legal approach to their relationships – those between God and his people as well as those among his people. The law was an attempt to recreate a limited possibility of loving God and one's neighbour. This remnant would bring forth the Messiah, who would be fully flesh but living by the Spirit, thus penetrating evil and death and thereby destroying them, because they would no longer be separated from God. However, this penetration could only be achieved with unimaginable suffering and death. Having been overcome, evil and death could no longer hold the Messiah, resulting in his resurrection. Following his return to his Father, a new bond would be created between the resurrected Christ and his followers by means of the Holy Spirit. As Jesus promised them, they would be in him as he is in the Father. This would be beautifully symbolized on Pentecost by the tongues of flame and everyone hearing the Word in their own dialect. It meant the beginning of the reversal of the confusion of human language and the total reconciliation of everyone with everyone else and with God. In sum, his intervention in the building of the city with its tower assured this ultimate triumph of redemption, grace, and the resurrection.

God's intervention thus precluded the development of a new unity and solidarity of humanity with evil and death as a complete separation from the Living One. When this unity and solidarity could not be achieved, it could not be named, thus leaving open the door to his people hearing and bearing the news of redemption and liberation to all other people; within this people, it could be borne faithfully by a small remnant. The covenant with Abram and later with Moses would in turn lead to a new covenant with all those who would follow the Messiah as the way, the truth, and the life, back to the Father. Throughout this entire development it was essential that the wheat not be separated from the tares, for this would remove the yeast that would make the dough rise into the kingdom of God, to lead to a complete reconciliation with him and with all people. In the meantime, first the Jews and then the Christians would still be held captive by the powers of enslavement that ruled the city. However, there would be many cities, none of which would have the complete spiritual character of Babylon the great but would have only tendencies in that direction. The Jewish and Christian communities were to await God's interventions, which time and time again would prevent any threat that the coming of his kingdom would be thwarted. As they waited for these interventions, they knew that the city was not a battleground between people but between people and the powers that robbed them of their freedom and love by enslaving them "from on high." Owing to one Man, the walls of these cities would not protect them from God's interventions, nor would their powers any longer be a means to seize what belonged to God.

There is a rather important detail in the Hebrew text that is missing in all our translations. Genesis 11:1 literally says that the whole earth spoke with the same lips, with uniform words.[9] The Hebrew language could just as well have said that all spoke the same tongue, which is an expression that also occurs in the Hebrew Bible. By choosing the external lips as opposed to the internal tongue, it would appear that, up to that point, language was still somewhat tied to God who, as the Creator, had made everything speakable. However, humanity had been subverting this gift of language by the evil in its heart. As a result, humanity was gradually bringing language under the control of the heart that expressed itself through the tongue. Had humanity succeeded in naming itself, it would have completely broken what little connection it had to God, who had made his creation speakable – with the result that human language would then have been in reference to humanity's own name and the spiritual truth designated by it. Humanity would then have closed itself to hearing the Word, with all the consequences mentioned earlier. As we will see later, human languages will indeed be in the service of the heart by means of the flesh, but this remains open to the Word. It would appear that all these changes are implied in human language being transferred from the lips to the tongue. When language was related to the lips, its external reference was to God, which made it the same for all. When it became related to the human heart, language became embedded in and referred to the life and history of a group or society and was thus unique to a time, place, and culture. Until then, human words had been nested within the Word of the one God.

By means of a play on words in the Hebrew language, God named the city of cities Babel, designating the condition of confusion. Subsequently, humanity spread over the earth, and once again there was no sign of repentance and conversion. It continued the work necessitated by its separation from God but with one important difference. Now individual groups and societies sought to make a name for themselves by "building" their own ways of life. Given their very different situations, they would need their own languages and cultures. The resulting names and the spiritual truths they designated would forever remain partial and thus open to being contested. However, this partiality would not be recognized by the group or society that lived it; the group or society would go about its way of life and make its history as if there could be none other. Doing so would plunge all groups and societies into spiritual conflicts with each other because they would all have mutually exclusive names and truths. They would condemn themselves to endless conflicts and wars, from which they would seek to protect themselves by developing all means of power. In order to understand this more fully, it is essential to pay careful attention to the details of the account.

Of all the details that could have been included in the account, why was the offering of bricks and mortar for the project mentioned? Given the scope of humanity's undertaking, would it not have been more appropriate to speak of the architectural design principles or the way in which this enormous effort was organized and executed? Having arrived at an overall interpretation of the account, it is important to verify it by carefully examining how all the details fit and then to understand why the bricks and mortar (instead of a great many other things) were selected to bear this revelation, whose meaning is as deep as a myth. At the time these texts were written and accepted into the canon, there was no cult of the fact. What we would regard as facts were the necessary details for clothing the meaning. If we reread Genesis 11:3, 4, we are exposed to a counter-transference reaction that reassures us that at least some of the historical details appear to be in line with archaeological findings. Nevertheless, the meaning clothed by these details is related to a widespread discussion that involved everyone and without which no plans could have been devised, no collaboration assured, no control over the work exercised, and so on. In other words, human communication by a language was the key to this entire enterprise. To put it in modern terms, what we are observing is a symbolic species naming everything in its surroundings in accordance with the meaning and value that those things had for individual and collective human life. Before anything can become bricks and mortar, and before people can even begin to work out some technology and a way to organize the work, they must symbolize some natural elements as such. Whatever they symbolize must be communicated, whatever is communicated must be understood, and whatever is understood must be translated into action; therefore they need language to become a complex system of communication that orders everything being done. This association of language with what people saw greatly contributed to its breaking up. In a penetrating study of human language and its de-symbolization by technique, Jacques Ellul discusses this aspect of the account of the Tower of Babel,[10] and I will elaborate it further with my own work on our being a symbolic species that was once suspended in language and culture.[11]

In order to avoid any misunderstandings, it is important to acknowledge a few possible counter-transference reactions that may stand in the way of our comprehending the Biblical texts. For any Israelite reading them, the mentioning of bricks and mortar must have been a powerful reminder of how as a people they had been enslaved in Egypt to supply the bricks and mortar for the cities that Pharaoh was building for economic reasons. It also would have reinforced the strong link between cities and enslavement that was first established by Nimrod.

Most of us would have the exact opposite reaction. A number of commentators happily draw a connection between the implied methods of construction and what archaeologists have discovered in one of the "cradles of civilization." After all, we tend to admire civilizations for the cities and monuments they leave behind. We do not immediately connect this to the multitudes of slaves or near slaves who must have been involved in these gigantic construction projects. If a civilization was highly egalitarian, with the result that it could not and would not enslave large numbers of people, it would be unable to construct the kind of grandeur we admire. Nevertheless, we would almost certainly prefer to live in the latter kind of civilization than in the former, especially if our social position were such that we would likely have been drafted into the making of bricks and mortar. In sum, as modern people reading these texts, we are likely to side with the genius and creativity involved in the planning and execution of these massive projects and public works, even though our values would probably not condone the human and social price that had to be paid by the majority of the people involved. It must not be concluded that, if humanity had not broken with God and remained within life and the good, we would still be food-gatherers and hunters today without any permanent settlements. This is ruled out by the very revelation that God will make all things new at the end of time and that the new creation will take the form of a city. God is going to make the city, and that city will be within life and the good. Had humanity remained within its original relationship with God, it is entirely possible that cities might have been built by unfolding this life and the good. In such a case, the cities would not have become the loci of rebellion, evil, and death.

The Word, Human Words, and Cultures

The interpretation of various portions of Genesis 3–11 can be deepened and enhanced by elaborating some of its key components in the context of the entire revelation. I will begin with Jacques Ellul's interpretation of Qohelet (Ecclesiastes), in which God is referred to as our Maker or Creator.[12] The historical implications are far reaching. Because we did not make ourselves, we and our history go back to an origin that gave us a certain kind of being within a unique world that was not of our own making. Each and every human generation simply borrows a certain indebtedness to this origin, which it has received from the previous generation and which it in turn adapts and evolves and passes on to the next generation, and so on all the way back to the beginning. The same is true for our planet. We inherit it from our parents and pass it on to our children. All of this happens in the presence of our Maker. In this interdependence we can never say "I am." We cannot be the masters of our situation but can only be its stewards, and that imposes limits on our desires, our projects, and our expectations. When a group, society, or civilization forgets this, these limits inevitably impose themselves. The results are almost always disastrous. For example, our present civilization is under the illusion that by proliferating and advancing means of power in every area of human life it can transcend all limits.[13]

The future of humanity is also affected by God being our Maker. Because our origin makes us a certain kind of being in a world that was made comprehensible and speakable by being created through the Word, certain kinds of futures are opened to us, and others are closed. We may ignore this, but there will be inevitable consequences. For example, the current de-symbolization of human languages, primarily by our organizing and evolving everything through discipline-based approaches, is equivalent to putting the fabric of life on a rack that is busy distorting, twisting, stretching, and breaking each and every relationship. Consequently, everything is no longer related to everything else or evolving in relation to everything else in the way it had before industrialization, urbanization, and secularization.[14] As we continue to bump into limits, we are reminded of our origins. Also individually, we must know what is possible and what is not possible as God's creatures.

Being individually and collectively mindful of our Creator is not a call or some kind of abstract pietism, metaphysics, philosophy, or theology. It is something fundamental and essential in the way we live each and every daily-life situation. It is again the question of our inability to say "I am." We are relative to everyone and everything else and thus suspended in an infinitely complex web of relationships. Hence, we have no "built-in" orientation and reference points for our individual and collective lives. When we respond to the love of our Maker, all this presents no problems whatsoever. He is the One who is fully life, love, freedom, justice, knowledge, and understanding. When granted his Spirit, we can (figuratively) reach for and hold his hand long before life can become too perplexing, bewildering, intimidating, or foreign to a community of love. He is a heavenly parent who has offered to be our counsellor and reference point, with the result that our weakness, fragility, vulnerability, and anything else related to being a creature never needs to stand in our way. After all, our Maker spoke ourselves and our world into being. When we have done everything possible but have reached our limits (of what is comprehensible and speakable to us), we are not stuck in an ultimate sense, because there is nothing about this being and this world that God cannot grant us as wisdom if we ask for it. Hence, our being suspended in language and culture and not even knowing what is up or what is down may be a scientific, technical, philosophical, or theological problem, but it is nothing that can stand in the way of our living full lives. God will permit us to discern what is up and what is down, as it were. It is for this reason that Qohelet is so utterly important for our civilization – a subject to which we will return.[15] Qohelet reminds us that we can do all kinds of things, but we cannot create something new under the sun. Only God can do this by his Word. Nevertheless, we (humans) always act as if we are the creators capable of speaking and bringing into being our life and our world (beginning with the building of the city with its tower to the heavens so humanity could name itself, followed by every human group, society, and civilization naming itself by a sacred and myths). The results can only be disastrous, both on the individual and the collective levels of life.

Keeping all this in mind, we can better understand why the Spirit or the breath of life needed to be added to the dust from which humanity was created. This dependence becomes clearly evident throughout the Jewish and Christian Bibles whenever God grants the Spirit to his people or to those who were called to intervene on his behalf. Later, it was his granting of the Holy Spirit to those who were called to be the witnesses to redemption, pardon, and love in their participation in the kingdom of heaven.[16]

The Spirit or breath of life performs three primary functions to make possible our lives as creatures.[17] First, it enables us to establish and participate in true relationships by nesting human words within the Word. In this way, we are able to be fully "yes" to our Maker and to our fellow creatures. Everything we know about ourselves derives from our relationships. As a consequence of the ability to establish true relationships, we are able to live lives that are complete – that is, a life in which our bodies, our cultural-historical "souls" (understood in the Hebrew and not in the Greek sense), and the Spirit each play their roles without dominating any of the others. Whenever God grants his Spirit to people, it becomes possible for them to participate in human history and in God's work of redemption that is moving this history towards a complete reconciliation. At the same time, such people themselves become a personal history. It is true that what the Spirit has to work with are beings made up of "wheat and tares." Nevertheless, this provides us with a glimpse into what a communion of love might have been and, more importantly, what it will be again one day.

The breaking up of the communion of love was not inevitable. Humanity knew life and the good by listening to the Word, and in turn human beings established relationships, lived lives, and made history by means of human words nested within this Word. This permitted Adam to undertake the incredibly complex task of establishing relationships with all the animals and naming them. He was able to grasp their place and role within the good. He also understood that he had no helper among them, thereby recognizing his unique task to represent God in his creation by ruling over it with human words, as God did with his Word. Adam was free to do so because there was nothing "above" him that could enslave him; there was nothing sacred, and there were no principalities and powers.

In essence, the serpent proposed to the woman that this "architecture" of creation could be lived in very differently than the way in which she had lived in it. Up to that point, she had listened to the Word in order to participate in and unfold the enormous potential of the communion of love between God and humanity. The serpent in effect suggested that she ought to take another look at the limits of this way of life. It was fine to listen to God's Word, but she should also pay attention to what her senses presented in terms of hard evidence: the fruit was good for eating, beautiful to the eye, and useful for intelligence. It corresponded to a coveting of the flesh, the eye, and the spirit (or cultural-historical "soul"). She thus set out on a very different way of life where she would do it all; she would listen to the Word of God and would also be guided by the evidence presented to her by the world. It quickly became apparent that this approach to life was unliveable. Our Bibles pay a great of attention to the reason for this.[18] As noted, the woman's decision to penetrate good and evil separated her from God. Consequently, the evidence she could now draw from the creation was limited to what that creation meant apart from its Maker. It implied that the meaning and value of everything in the creation could be found within it. Hence, the creation now had life within itself and required no reference to its Maker. Similarly, everything within it was no more and no less than what was available to her senses. She could now deal with everything without having to take into account that God loved what he had created and had declared it as very good. For example, she could now do with animals as she saw fit.

This situation is the exact opposite of that of Adam naming the animals in communion with God. Whatever evidence the animals presented to his senses was not sufficient in and of itself, because these were creatures that God had created and presented to him. In naming them, Adam took this into account to gain an adequate insight into what God had intended, and how this gave a deeper meaning and value to what he was observing.

When humanity broke with God, a rupture occurred between what was real in human life and what was true for human life. In our Bibles the former is identified with seeing, and the latter with hearing. The former is associated with what presents itself to our senses, as if the meaning and value of everything were fully contained within itself; the latter is associated with transcending all of this to take into account what cannot be accessed by our senses and can only be learned by listening. Even in our separation from God we continue to live our lives by implicitly recognizing this distinction. We do not leave our babies to discover the world according to what they observe and experience. We know very well that if we do not talk to them as a sign of our love for them, they will not grow up as members of a symbolic species. Children who have been brought up by animals, or who have been deprived of human contact and language during a critical period, grow up to be barely recognizable as members of a symbolic species. The effects of such a partial or complete deprivation are largely or entirely irreversible.[19] The reasons are well understood. No group or society has ever lived in the world of its immediate experience. Without exception, groups and societies have lived in a symbolic universe that they have interposed between themselves and the world. These symbolic universes can be entered only by listening to the members of a group or society. They cannot be discovered by carefully observing the world.

Similarly, Adam entered into God's creation in communion with him. It made all the difference in the world. We can assert this without any doubt whatsoever because, following the break with God, each group and society had to develop a substitute for the lost relationship with its Maker. We will examine this in detail in the next section.

This is made clear in our Bibles. When humanity is fully reconciled with its Creator at the end of time, what we see will be restored to its rightful place, that is, as a complement to what we learn by listening. What is real and what is true for human life will be reunited. This is shown in the last section of the book of Revelation that is marked by the sevenfold occurrence of the phrase "and then I saw."[20]

We are once again discovering something about relationships of love. When we deny other life forms their status as creatures, we cannot have a full relationship with them. For example, even if we do everything possible not to be cruel to be animals, we will still not love them as God does. In communion with God, our current agrobusiness practices related to animals would be unthinkable; it simply would not occur to our minds to treat fellow creatures in this way. Similarly, it is inconceivable that groups and societies would have created unsustainable ways of life. What is true for other life forms is even truer for fellow human beings. In communion with God, the knowledge that they are loved as much by him as we are, makes any relationships of power, domination, and exploitation unthinkable. We can perhaps begin to understand a little of why our Bibles consider all evidence, and what we see in particular, as untrustworthy and fundamentally misleading. Any evidence always takes on its full significance relative to the myths of a society. We are back to our inability to be fully "yes" in our relationships. This inability to love applies to all of us, enslaved as we are by the principalities and powers, and divided as we believers are into wheat and tares.

Just as human babies must transcend their immediate experiences by listening to the people who love them, so humanity will one day listen to the Word again in order to be fully "yes" in all its relationships.

Listening to the Word is as essential for human life as are the food we eat, the water we drink, and the air we breathe. Human history would have been unrecognizably different had humanity remained within the communion of love based on relationships of being fully "yes" to God, fellow human beings, and the creation. One of our many failures has been in making the revelation about the Spirit into little more than a theological truism that we may intellectually accept but that we do not live. We thus deny ourselves any possibility of living with the Spirit to make our relationships less false.

Whenever God grants his Spirit, it will participate in the lives of the people who receive it. As a result, it will envelop something of their lives, and this aspect of their lives will return to God whenever the Spirit returns to him. Hence, something of these lives would be inscribed in this breath of life, with our "dust" being only a temporary support, as it were. It is in this manner that God receives what is unto life from these people, and nothing of this will be lost because he has promised to incorporate it into the new creation.[21] Qohelet said that all of life was vanity, smoke, and vapour, and therefore it did not count for much. What little it may be will be received by God.[22] We have noted that, in spite of some difficult translation problems, Genesis 6:3 appears to suggest that God posed the question as to how long his Spirit could be with the flesh without weakening or injuring it. We must not make much of this informed guess at the meaning. What we do have is Jesus's teaching regarding the Spirit. Jesus told Nicodemus that all those who are born from the Spirit are spirit, and all those who are born of the flesh are flesh. He also said that the Spirit behaves like the wind, coming and going as it wills in freedom. To his disciples Jesus said that his words were breath (or Spirit) and life. Before he died, he placed his breath in God's hands. Furthermore, in the gospel of John, Jesus gave us the only comprehensive teaching on the Spirit, just before his betrayal, crucifixion, death, and resurrection.[23] We will revisit this in a later chapter.

We must keep all of this in mind as we carefully read the account of the so-called tower of Babel; it holds the key to understanding how human language became confused. Within the communion of love, human words had the Spirit as their reference point. Following the break with God, it appears that humanity entered a transition period in which human words still referred to God's Word to some degree, but in disobedience. In other words, humanity was busy penetrating the good *and* the evil. It desired to have it all, but when this increasingly turned out to be impossible, it decided to make a clean break and to name itself. As a consequence, an attempt was made to "unhook" human words from the Word and to harness them to the making of a new beginning according to the spiritual meaning and direction that humanity intended to name, independently of God. It must be remembered that God had made the creation speakable and thus comprehensible to human words. It may be assumed, therefore, that these human words had some of the same capabilities that we refer to as symbolization: a way to understand how everything was related to and depended on God and how this interrelatedness evolved in communion with him. There was no possibility of a threat of relativism, nihilism, or anomie because it all included God, who is fully life, love, justice, peace, truth, and everything else that a creature may need as references for life. When humanity decided to name itself, it lost all these reference points, with the result that there was a complete collapse of all meanings and values. Everything became confused in the face of relativism, nihilism, and anomie. Nothing was speakable any more, and confusion reigned over human language "from the lips" and, via it, all human actions. There was thus no choice but to abandon the building of the city with the tower reaching to the heavens.

These observations seem somewhat speculative, but what emerged following the confusion is not. People had to find ways of making themselves understood by a few others, and if they were successful, they would almost certainly have formed groups. Since the small groups formed on the basis of the shared experience of their members would have little in common with other groups, they dispersed all over the earth. In other words, for these groups to make sense of and live in the world, they now had to invent languages and cultures unique to their shared experiences and circumstances. The result is well known and has been extensively studied as the history of groups and societies.

Little can be known about the transition period that followed the confusion of human language. At this point, we may benefit from a rare, positive counter-transference reaction. Our current situation may be somewhat similar to that of the Jewish people who were reading the Genesis text shortly after it had been written down and discerned as a Word of God. For them, the many polemical elements in this text would have been readily understood, given their contact with and knowledge of the surrounding cultures. However, if they had done little more than read this understanding into the text, they would have masked its deeper and more fundamental revelation. In the same vein, our understanding of our being a symbolic species that mediates all relationships with others and the world by means of a symbolic language and culture can illuminate the social and historical significance of humanity's making a name for itself. However, if we confused this understanding with the revelation itself, we would be terribly mistaken. In other words, our current understanding of language and culture can illuminate some biblical texts in terms of their social and historical events and developments, but that is all. What it can never do is to provide their revealed meaning in the sense of how such events and developments were selected as details to clothe or to bear a revelation that was received and discerned as coming from beyond any culture or society.

As noted, the role that symbolic cultures played in individual and collective human life was discovered at a point in human history when their ability to sustain that life had become severely weakened as a consequence of de-symbolization. Until then, symbolic cultures, somewhat like the biosphere, had worked almost unnoticed in the background. With hindsight, it is astonishing that, beginning with the opening verses, our Bibles emphasize the uniqueness of God's speaking: how through his Word and the Spirit he establishes a relationship with a symbolic humanity. Recent developments have given us a much greater appreciation of the importance of this, given our present understanding of how we are suspended in a language and culture.

Every human group and society has distanced itself from its surroundings by interposing a symbolic universe, which transcends the immediate experience of these surroundings by symbolizing everything in terms of its actual and potential meaning and value. For example, the observation of a dead tree trunk floating down a river with some birds sitting on it would have to be symbolized in terms of its meaning and value for the life of a group: a way of travelling on water, of fishing, or of hunting water-borne animals. Once such an idea came to someone's mind, it would have to be discussed with others. If they agreed that it was a good idea, working it out would depend on symbolizing a tree branch as a potential paddle, a sharp stone as a carving tool. Fundamentally, certain rituals would have to be devised for gaining the permission and cooperation of the powers that ruled in nature. In other words, the symbolization of a constituent of nature as a potential canoe could not proceed without symbolizing a great many other things, and these would require the symbolization of still other things, and so on. It ultimately would rest on a comprehensive effort of symbolizing the individual and collective life of a group in the life milieu of nature. In order to create a measure of freedom for itself, a group (and later a society) had to distance itself from its surroundings by imposing a symbolic universe, and this could not be done in a piecemeal fashion. Moreover, the organizations of the brain-minds of the members of our symbolic species had to be capable of sustaining such a comprehensive effort to create a language and a culture. No animal group has ever expanded its system of signs into a symbolic language. We do have some very creative accounts of how human groups may have achieved this with a strategy that was necessarily piecemeal at the outset; these are fascinating but far from definitive.[24] The conviction that the world is comprehensible and speakable may not have been obvious or compelling to people separated from God. Moreover, the strategy to achieve this would be a daunting task.

Whatever the case may be, all human groups and societies have symbolized everything in the individual lives of their members and in the collective life of the community by means of languages and cultures, thus making worlds for themselves. However, in developing a language and a culture, a group committed itself to a strategy of inadaptation by distancing itself from its surroundings, from which had come everything necessary for the maintenance of its life, and from which had also come the threats to that life. The opposite strategy – making life easier by adapting to the surroundings – appears to have been sacrificed for one that created a margin of freedom, with survival in the balance. Without these developments, groups and societies could not have sustained themselves with very different ways of life in more or less similar surroundings. However, once a margin of freedom was achieved by symbolically distancing the group from its surroundings, this freedom needed to be mastered and organized. A margin of freedom could thus be lived within a host of constraints that included the necessity of doing so in an orderly fashion. Consequently, any freedom could be lived only in a dialectical tension with every necessity capable of enslaving human life. Since all such efforts of symbolization leave few traces, the transition period from the confusion of human language to the establishment of very different human languages and cultures will likely remain shrouded in mystery. Possibly one of the most challenging aspects of making sense of it is related to explaining the co-development of the organizations of people's brain-minds and of their brains as the genetically formed organs that sustain them. Brain-minds are able to adapt and change at a much greater rate than brains as organs. It constitutes a fascinating puzzle with many missing pieces, and that is likely to remain so. With the emergence of societies and civilizations, the ways of our being a symbolic species became a great deal more accessible to us because of the much more extensive traces they left behind. Hence, the part of human history immediately following the break between God and humanity will probably remain out of reach of a definitive understanding. I will thus restrict my attention to traditional societies and the civilizations they helped to constitute. In turn, this understanding will form the basis for making sense of the birth of our own civilization built on a universal technical order.

Socially and Historically Naming Ourselves

As noted in the introduction, our being people of a time, place, and universal technical order has led to an awareness of ourselves, others, and the world that is so permeated by everything being expressed and understood in the image of technique in general, and of information machines in particular, that it is almost impossible to explain what we mean when we speak of living a life. Implicitly and explicitly we think of our senses as information-processing transducers, not unlike digital cameras, microphones, loudspeakers, and a robotic skin, via which the body-machine feeds information to the computer-soul that processes it, which reacts by sending appropriate information back to the body-machine. Researchers who have undertaken studies of how people *live* this have found that we appear to be having an identity crisis not unlike the crises that occurred when Western civilization adopted the Greek soul, then the Cartesian mind-soul, and now the information-computer-soul.[25] Nevertheless, when we go back to people living their lives prior to extensive de-symbolization, and examine how a variety of social and historical developments affected the roles of symbolization, language, and culture, very different interpretations present themselves. The introduction to this work has outlined one way in which we can remain socially and historically grounded – by not losing track of what has made us human until now.

Although what it is to be human has varied, and continues to do so, we do not have any difficulty recognizing it unless we are prevented by prejudgments or ideologies. Every society establishes and evolves a unique collective identity that includes cultural commitments defining every aspect of individual and collective human life, unless this process is limited as a consequence of de-symbolization. Each established relationship is thus unique as well as culturally typical. It is made speakable by a unique language that grammatically organizes such a relationship along the lines of subject, verb, object, indirect object, and additional qualifications. There is a great deal that a language cannot express directly about a relationship simply because not all of it is available to human experience because of its dependence on metaconscious knowledge. For example, the living of a life refers to the establishment of relationships, the resulting modification of situations, and the symbolization of all of this by neural and synaptic changes to the organization of a person's brain-mind. This modification not only symbolizes an experience but also evolves one's awareness of oneself and the world. In other words, in living their lives, people modify a situation, and the situation simultaneously modifies them as a consequence of the influence it has on them. Whenever a situation involves more than one person, others also affect that situation, and they themselves will be affected by it.

These reciprocal interactions help to constitute a group or society, which in turn provides each of its members with a collective identity and a binding commitment to its time, place, and culture. This creates a unique relationship between each and every individual and the collectivity. Each member helps to constitute the group or society for all other members, as they in turn do for that member. Hence, each member is both an individual person and an individual manifestation of that group or society. This is possible only because the life of each member is dialectically enfolded into the collectivity, and the collectivity is simultaneously enfolded into the life of each member. In other words, each member expresses the collectivity by living its way of life, institutional framework, and reference points and adapts this collectivity according to the experience of living it. There is thus a dialectical tension between individual diversity and the cultural unity of the collectivity. Each one limits the other. For example, if individual diversity gradually begins to overwhelm the cultural unity of the collectivity, a group or society begins to disintegrate. Alternatively, if the cultural unity imposes itself too strongly on the individual diversity, the ability of the collectivity to invent and absorb successful responses to new situations into its working culture may become inadequate and critically damage its ability to adapt and evolve. It is impossible to reconstitute these kinds of dialectical relationships in the image of technique, which is slowly but surely leading to anti-societies under the universal technical order.[26] Moreover, these kinds of dialectically enfolded sociocultural "worlds" cannot be understood by means of discipline-based approaches.

Owing to a person's collective identity and cultural commitments, substantial constraints are placed on the way in which relationships may be established in love, hatred, or indifference. If an attempt is made at establishing a relationship in love, care must be taken to serve and enrich the other person, other life forms and the world. As noted, to be fully "yes" to the other, one commits oneself and one's life. Doing so may thus conflict with one's collective identity and cultural commitments, and the same holds true for everything else participating in the relationship. Consequently, establishing a relationship in love is extremely difficult, if not impossible, because a culture's way of life, institutional framework, and reference points have emerged from ecologies of relationships based on power, hierarchy, and exploitation. When we "fall in love," we seek to transcend these constraints and circumstances to live entirely for and through the other, but this is next to impossible to sustain. These difficulties are particularly great in our anti-societies that have highly de-symbolized cultures.

We now turn to the heart of the matter: how can we cope with our being vulnerable and weak as finite beings living in an ultimately unknowable universe? In the introduction we emphasized that babies and children do not learn anything absolutely but only relatively. Everything they experience can take on a meaning and a value only relative to everything else they have lived. In turn, everything they live is relative to the others who endeavour to love them and who, through their relationships, begin to weave the lives of babies and children into their lives and, via their lives, into the collective life of a group or society. In other words, those who nurture babies and children form a kind of social womb in relation to which these children develop; this environment gradually includes the way in which the collectivity deals with the relativity of human life in the world, and the way in which this relativity is defended against relativism, nihilism, and anomie.

A few details may be helpful. In a previous study an attempt was made to synthesize what is relevant to our understanding of the way we live our lives by interpreting the findings of a great many disciplines in this context.[27] It led to putting centre stage what later became known as *brain plasticity*: the living of each experience as a moment of a life made possible by the modification of a person's organization of the brain-mind by means of neural and synaptic changes. Much of this could be summed up in terms of two fundamental processes that are essential for sustaining the living of a human life: namely, a process of differentiation and a process of integration. The former ensures that no two situations will be confused when their differences matter for a person's life. Each new experience is dialectically divided from all the others and enfolded into a person's life when it symbolically takes its place among all the other experiences of that life. This happens metaconsciously (transcending the individual experiences that we can remember) and thus in the context of both a person's collective identity and his or her personal life. These developments are inseparable from those in the process of integration. Simply put, the process of integration builds on the way in which all the experiences in a person's life have been dialectically divided and separated from each other according to the differences that matter for that life, its collective identity, and its cultural commitments. Thus arranged, the experiences of a person's life symbolically imply its "structure" or "organization," which may be thought of as the interpolation and extrapolation of all these experiences into a life. A great deal of metaconscious knowledge corresponds very well to what is implied in a person's behaviour, even though no one has, for the greater part, learned it explicitly. In the assumption that each experience is directly differentiated from those that most resemble it, clusters of symbolized experiences will be "mapped" by the organization of the brain-mind. The differences between the members of a cluster matter a great deal less for the life of a person than do the differences between any one of them and the members of neighbouring clusters, and even more for *their* neighbours, and so on.

The body of experience or the life of a person may be conceptualized as a symbolic and metaconscious network with clusters of symbolized experiences at its nodes, where each cluster generally corresponds to a particular kind of daily-life activity. The acquisition of metaconscious knowledge in each cluster, and jointly in the network, may be thought of as follows. The cluster of the eating experiences of a toddler will include those in which everything went more or less according to what the adults expected, with the result that these experiences were relatively emotionally neutral. There will be others in which the toddler did not like the food and messed around with it, triggering negative emotional reactions from others. In this way, the cluster of eating experiences may imply at first that the members of the immediate family "do not like it when I mess around with food." More such experiences will show that, generally, people do not appreciate messing with or spilling food, and eventually this will imply a kind of objective metaconscious knowledge that food is not to be spilled or messed with. A metaconscious value thus becomes implied in the cluster. The same kinds of developments occur in all other clusters and also in the network of clusters. In this way, children acquire the metaconscious values of their group or society, to the point that in a traditional society they will spontaneously learn to obey the laws that correspond to these metaconscious values.[28] Many of these values may be reinforced explicitly by what constitutes the morality of the group or society.[29] In other words, each and every cluster will eventually develop metaconscious values as to what is normal and acceptable behaviour and what is not, what is a good way for dealing with deviations and what is a bad way, and so on. The network of clusters will symbolically map a hierarchy among these metaconscious values and will point to the greatest metaconscious value as well as the way in which all this fits into a personal life as the expression of a collective identity with its own defining cultural commitments.

Other features can be understood by comparing different symbolic cultures as ways of making sense of and living in the world. Each of them has made the world comprehensible and speakable according to a language and a culture. It also becomes evident that every culture avoids cluttering the lives of its members with distinctions that contribute little to obtaining and maintaining a good existential grip on what is happening in their lives. At the same time, a culture also avoids the opposite: glossing over distinctions that do matter for the lives of its members. In other words, each culture avoids under-generalization and over-generalization in a manner that makes it possible for most people to live relatively meaningful and purposeful lives in accordance with its collective identity and defining cultural commitments. A vital and dynamic culture maintains a balance between over-differentiating and under-differentiating to keep its members in touch with their lives and the world.

In contrast, highly de-symbolized cultures fail to maintain that balance. For example, our contemporary societies are bogged down in over-generalizations related to understanding their economies. We do not sufficiently distinguish the markets of the nineteenth century and the first half of the twentieth century from those that emerged following the Second World War, when economies came into the grip of discipline-based approaches. Nor do we distinguish either of these two kinds of markets from those that make money from money without any intervening economic activities. Nor is there any clear-cut understanding of how these economies function within these societies because we are confused about the kinds of societies we live in (whether these are post-industrial, post-capitalist, consumer, information, mass, service, spectator, or any other kind of society).[30] This has far-reaching implications for our being able to live responsible lives, and for our contemporary societies, whose economists suffer from the limitations of discipline-based approaches.[31] We have also failed to come to grips with the so-called computer and information revolution, because we do not see it as the extension of preparatory developments that have been in the making for nearly two hundred years – all related to the gradual shift from our societies relying on symbolic cultures to their relying primarily on discipline-based approaches that de-symbolize these cultures.[32] As a result, we appear to have little appreciation of what we have had to give up in order to gain what fascinates and even mesmerizes us.

There appear to be three successive ways of dealing with our finitude as human beings as we grow up. Initially, babies and toddlers are protected from being swamped by the "noise" of stimuli that does not yet have a meaning in their lives. They are slowly relating everything to everything else in their lives, and to this they can add only what has some meaning and value in this context. Everything else remains "noise" – random stimuli that are still void of any significance. It appears that the daunting task of making some sense of their lives and the world requires the assurance of an enveloping love, which transforms this task into one of reaching out towards and responding to this love. It is love that provides the deeper meaning and value in their lives. If this is indeed the case, then our current practice of involving day care in children's lives as soon as possible may well have far-reaching consequences, especially because so many more activities will have a de-symbolizing influence that could potentially contribute to the development of learning disabilities.[33] Contemporary societies that have effective policies encouraging parental care and social equality may well have enormous advantages.[34]

Later on during this first phase the organizations of the brain-minds of toddlers will have constituted an adequate metalanguage to begin language development through a double-referencing system. Much interference can come from too much exposure to visual screens of any kind, with their image-words and their de-symbolizing influences.[35] Possibly now more than ever, toddlers need an enveloping love in their playful discovery of others and the world. It ensures that they can confidently play in the full knowledge and security that, when they are stuck, they can turn to someone to help them, console them if necessary, and be a reliable and loving support.

A second phase in which children learn to deal with their finitude occurs when the body of the experiences that make up their lives in the world converge with those of the people who love and take care of them, in the sense that the organizations of the brain-minds of children have become embryonic beginnings of those of the people in relation to whom they live their lives. This development generally commences following a more turbulent transition from a life without a metaconscious awareness of one's physical self to a life with such an awareness; this metaconscious awareness of a physical self develops into that of a social self, and eventually into that of a cultural self. Although the unknown continues to present children with new discoveries and situations, children can now mostly deal with them by cumulative expansions of the organizations of their brain-minds. They are still sufficiently shielded from the threat of the unknown by their reliance on adults, and thus on the collective identity and the defining cultural commitments of these people. However, the children have not yet developed to the point that all this has become their own. It is during this phase that adults who betray the trust of these children can do incredible harm, given their dependence on others.

Finally, long before children might be threatened by the unknown bringing experiences that could trigger significant doubt about their being in touch with their lives and the world, the organizations of their brain-minds begin to acquire the deepest metaconscious knowledge. It corresponds to what are generally referred to as myths in such disciplines as cultural anthropology. As noted, the unknown becomes symbolized as simply what teenagers know and live by interpolating and extrapolating all the experiences of their lives in the world. At this point, their lives are able to work in the background with a great deal of independence from adults. In traditional groups or societies this occurred by the organizations of their brain-minds acting as a symbolic "mental map" that permitted them to locate and find their way in the world. Alternatively, in contemporary societies with highly de-symbolized cultures, these organizations of people's brain-minds function as a symbolic radar, scanning what everyone else is doing in order to determine what is "normal," and turning this into what is "normative" in order to help them find their way in the world. Examples include the development of a public opinion that has largely replaced private opinion, and a growing statistical morality in which what is right is defined by what most people do. At this point, a complete, symbolic universe has been interposed between them and their surroundings. Any future discoveries, events, or developments are symbolized as missing details and will thus pose no threats whatsoever to a person's life or to the collectivity. People now know where they are going and are symbolically in touch with whatever is still to come. The door to relativism, nihilism, and anomie is now closed for most of the time. Metaconsciously, people have acquired a firm ground on which to stand in an ultimately unknowable universe. There is no need for any kind of ontology. The acquired myths have provided people with a defining commitment that binds them to the time, place, and culture of the collectivity.

In sum, in traditional groups and societies, these developments amount to an impressive spiritual accomplishment. The organizations of the brain-minds of the members of traditional groups and societies did not merely sum up the experiences of each member; they also summed them up in relation to those of everyone else. Moreover, the acquisition of myths completed this summing up by including everything that could possibly be thought and lived, and by excluding everything that was radically different. In this way, the body of experience of a community became the ultimate reference point, the measure of all things, the anchor in a universe that was only partly understood, and the only possible spiritual orientation for human life that could make sense. A traditional group or society metaconsciously named itself, its orientation, its past, and its future. Its collective experience became its ultimate spiritual triumph, against which the unknown could not prevail. A certain spiritual autonomy was thus established by the group or society in a world that was of its own making. As we shall see later, it also included its own gods and thus excluded the need for a transcendent God.

Today, the symbolic universes of most societies have been de-symbolized to the point that those societies can no longer sustain them by the spiritual accomplishments described in the previous paragraph. The symbolic universes have been replaced by what we have referred to as "reality." We build, maintain, and evolve this reality by means of discipline-based approaches instead of symbolic cultures. The visual dominates the aural, and this requires a de-symbolization of language to produce more and more image-words and image messages.

Nevertheless, children continue to learn to make sense of and live in the world by listening to their parents and others speaking to them. However, the development of a double-referencing system that is required for language acquisition is under pressure from a stream of de-symbolizing experiences whose foregrounds have the architecture of reality and whose backgrounds have the dialectically enfolded character of a world. For now, the de-symbolization of myths appears to affect the exclusion of anything radically different to a lesser extent than it affects their role related to metaconscious values. This role has become much less important because of the complementary role of integration propaganda that is diffused and sustained by the mass media as well as the new media.[36] It appears that the spiritual accomplishments of contemporary societies continue to be effective as a consequence of a combination of a highly de-symbolized culture and the pressures of integration propaganda.

The way in which traditional groups and societies named themselves through their myths has never endured beyond an epoch in their histories. It can never become absolute, because the unknown is always found to be different from what it was symbolized to be during a historical epoch, and this is associated with the desacralization of its myths. This desacralization can occur for one of two reasons.[37] For some time a traditional group or society may encounter a growing range of events and discoveries that cannot readily be "fitted" into the life and world it has made for itself. Although such events and discoveries may initially have been symbolized in the usual manner, the members of the community may individually and collectively intuit that there is something amiss; there is too much that no longer makes good sense. This may attract a great deal of creative attention, which may lead to attempts to approach these kinds of situations somewhat differently in the hope that they will make more sense. When such initiatives begin to interact and feed on one another through the lives and the world of the community, embryonic patterns for making sense of the overall situation may emerge, If such efforts persist and become increasingly successful, they may give rise to new metaconscious knowledge that begins to weaken and undermine the previously established metaconscious knowledge. In time, a cultural minority may champion the new patterns throughout their lives. In the course of a century or more a new sacred and myth may begin to assert themselves. To the extent that they do, they will desacralize those that had ruled the life and world of the historical epoch that may be coming to an end with the success of these developments. A new historical epoch ruled by the new sacred and myths will then be ushered in.

In the second case, the attempts at reinventing a culture, in order that more and more events and discoveries will make sense again, either do not get off the ground or they remain unsuccessful and are eventually abandoned. The disorder within the life and world of a community grows without being checked and will further weaken the ability of the community to sustain the lives of its members. When this disorder continues, a general decline sets in. Unless the decline awakens the community to realize that it must make an all-out effort to survive, it will continue and eventually cause the community to collapse.

The histories of societies and civilizations can thus be described as the establishment, growth, decline, rejuvenation, and renewed growth of their cultures in terms of the abilities of the societies and civilizations to spiritually name themselves and sustain human life. Each historical epoch is characterized by a life and a world summed up by a sacred and myths that cannot be named explicitly because of their metaconscious depth. A decline that is not arrested and reversed will result in the collapse of the community. When this happens, the former members of the community will go on living, but it usually marks a period of social chaos, violence, and the unchecked exploitation of the weak by the strong. The only way out is through the establishment of a new culture capable of giving meaning, direction, and purpose to life, and thus attracting more and more followers.

Each of the three life milieux in which humanity has lived is associated with unique forms of a sacred and myths. In the life milieu of nature, the sacred summed up its life-sustaining and life-destroying powers over the community. Once societies had become established, the sacred and myths were related to the primary life milieu, that of society, as well as to the secondary life milieu, that of nature. The sacred tended to sum up the powers that ruled over society, while some of the myths added the natural powers that still made their presence known. With the rise of the universal technical order and the dominance of discipline-based approaches to knowing and doing, the primary life milieu became that of technique, with society becoming the secondary life milieu, and nature the tertiary one. The secular sacred was technique and the nation-state, with the supporting myths of science and history.[38]

Metaconsciously identifying the all-powerful and limitless forces that rule over individual and collective human life and its world represents the greatest necessity. Such forces have to be brought under human control or at least have to be made to cooperate significantly. Consequently, all traditional groups and societies have invented religious and moral institutions to accomplish just that. If these efforts fail, everything else can be called into question by these limitless powers. There have been no exceptions in human history. There has only been the appearance of exceptions because, following the establishment of a universal technical order and the de-symbolization of cultures, the sacred and myths became secular in form but not different in kind.

The approaches to domesticating and influencing the limitless powers that have been symbolically detected as ruling over life and the world have always been more or less the same. Individually and collectively, people metaconsciously discovered and intuited the entities in their experience that were so significant and important that life and the world would be unthinkable without them. Who would the people be, how would they live, and what would the world be like without them? It was simply unthinkable and unimaginable. The limitless powers thus identified had created life in the world as it was, and they were able to sustain or threaten it. This metaconscious knowledge was intuited within what was true for a community, but in order for the community to grasp them, these powers had to be represented within what was real. In other words, these powers must be represented in some physical form and housed in facilities in which cults to these powers could be organized. In this way, a priesthood could conduct rituals that often had both a religious and a juridical thrust, to oblige the powers to be kindly disposed to the people and to cooperate with them in response to everything they did. The powers with which a community became acquainted by symbolizing everything to establish what was true for its life and world, and the idols that were the visual representations of these powers in what was real for the community, must not be confused. Every member of the community knew very well that these statues, sacred poles, altars, and everything else were a means to reach the powers that ruled over their lives and world, as revealed by symbolization. It should be noted that the same confusion has often affected the interpretation of biblical texts regarding false gods and idols. The idols made the existence of the powers self-evident; in themselves the idols were nothing.

It should be noted that when a community's sacred and myths are desacralized towards the end of an epoch in its history, it will become easier to name them explicitly in a mythology. At this point, they do not have the influence over human life and the world that they once had, but it can still be significant. For example, the sacred of capital, which was created by the first generation of industrial societies, lives on. It is perpetuated by the political illusion that money has the power to make any problem go away, and thus all one needs to do is to allocate money to it in a budget. Similarly, the myth of progress influenced advertisements for decades following the Second World War: bring in this brand of beer, you will be immediately surrounded by beautiful friends and you will never be lonely again; brush with this toothpaste, your dazzling smile will attract the partner of your life and end your loneliness. In other words, material progress had the power to bring social progress, and social progress could be turned into spiritual happiness. Even the best thinkers of the nineteenth century, whose lives were ruled by this sacred and these myths, were unable to conceive of a life and world outside of capital, progress, work, and happiness, by which they spiritually named everything.

In sum, the complex symbolic developments commonly referred to as the living of our lives can also be thought of as *the spirit of an age*. This latter term designates the collective identity and defining cultural commitments that enslave a people during a certain time by possessing the minds and lives of its members. With hindsight, the spirit of an age can be judged in terms of a variety of criteria and values. For example, the Christian Bible states that the nations will be judged according to how they treat their poorest and most vulnerable members. This is affirmed in the letter of James by the statement that the only religion acceptable to God is the care of widows and orphans (the most vulnerable people in the societies of that time).[39]

There are three categories of experiences that prevent the members of a group or society from summing up these experiences into lives, and then these lives into a community with a collective identity and defining cultural commitments. By spiritually naming itself, a traditional group or society necessarily denied this possibility to all other people. Those people had to be named "the barbarians" or something equivalent that would dismiss them. It was impossible to symbolize the experiences of the ways of life, institutions, and cultures of other people like the experiences of one's own. The gods of other people could not be permitted to challenge those that ruled over one's own life and world. A measure of coexistence was often possible, however, given that these gods had territorial or other specific jurisdictions.

Generally speaking, contacts between cultures engaged in trade and commerce usually relativized them. For example, these interactions began to relativize Greek culture because, although the Greeks did not educate their women, in other cultures with which they traded the women negotiated all commercial transactions. The success of these women thus questioned Greek practices. Socrates, with the aid of Plato and Aristotle, attempted to salvage Greek culture by discovering the rules that were supposed to underlie best practices, but the process only led to further relativization, and Socrates was put to death for corrupting the youth. Plato and Aristotle had considerable influence on the development of Western philosophy, and this philosophy was generally destructive of any culture, including their own. The project of attempting to discover the "foundations" of human activities and communities lasted almost two millennia and had an enormous influence on Western civilization. As noted, this search was continued by knowledge engineering and the early phase of the development of artificial intelligence. With a great deal of hindsight, it is now possible to understand more clearly the reason that all such attempts relativized traditional cultures, and the enormous damage that this did to the liveability of such cultures in terms of their abilities to give meaning, direction, and purpose to the lives of millions.

As Western civilization began to move towards ways of life that eventually were named by the sacred of capital and the myths of progress, work, and happiness, contact with traditional cultures became particularly disastrous. It became next to impossible for Western people to regard the ways in which traditional societies named themselves (by their defining cultural commitments) as just different forms of doing what Western people necessarily had to do themselves. Everywhere in the world today, native peoples who continue to cling to naming themselves in the ways that all traditional groups and societies have done, have had their cultures relativized to the point that those cultures have become unliveable, thereby producing a catastrophe to which there are no obvious solutions. It is impossible nowadays to overlook the dreadful mistakes made by Christian churches in their contact with indigenous groups and native people. Oblivious to the way in which they had named themselves through the secular cultural commitments of their own societies, these churches thought of themselves as more civilized, rational, scientific, and advanced than native people. Failure to distinguish between (visible) idols and the (metaconscious) false gods by which these groups and societies had named themselves made any empathy next to impossible and justified a kind of cultural sabotage. Worse, being unaware of their own defining cultural commitments in secular form, Christians suffered from a metaconscious "blackout" that made them oblivious to the extent to which they had allowed Christianity to become closely identified with the way in which their own societies had named themselves; that is, they were essentially oblivious to the religious and moral functions performed by Christianity within their own cultures and societies. Owing to their own defining cultural commitments, Christians were generally unable to take seriously what their Bibles had to say about the effects of commerce and trade on humanity.

All these examples illustrate the consequences of humanity's breaking apart, when each group and society had to name itself, and that these divisions are at the root of much of the violence, domination, exploitation, bloodshed, and wars – not to mention their diminishing of the liveability of people's lives by relativizing what made these lives possible in a broken situation.[40]

The second category of experiences that could not be included in a traditional group's or society's naming itself was related to the deaths of its members. Since death is unlike anything that people live, death cannot be symbolized in terms of life, hence its meaning and value must be established in other ways. It had to be inserted into the symbolic universe of any group or society as a religious construct expressing death in terms of lived experiences. For example, it could become a passage to another life in another world, a rebirth or reincarnation into the same world, the soul ascending to the eternal, and so on. Death also affected the survivors. Parts of their lives, the ones that enfolded the experiences that had been shared with someone who had died, had ceased to evolve and in effect were dead as well. What we have noted about the experiences related to death often also applies to the experiences of birth. If a birth was interpreted as the gift of life by a god, a religious interpretation had been made, because symbolization was impossible. The same is true if a birth was regarded as a rebirth or reincarnation. Rarely were births regarded as the result of the transmission of life from generation to generation by sexual reproduction of the kind found in other life forms.

A third category of experiences that could not be incorporated into a traditional group's or society's naming itself was the experiences of what people believed to be a revelation from a transcendent God. Such a God thus introduced something into the culture of a group or a society that was not of its own making. In other words, the conventional distinction between faith and religion cannot have any meaning apart from the necessity of a group or a society naming itself. Religion is an integral part of this naming by establishing a relationship with the powers that rule over the life and world of a group or society. It is entirely a cultural creation like any other constituent of a way of life, institutional framework, and collective identity with defining cultural commitments.

In contrast, faith is a discernment that a communication that has entered into a symbolic universe is radically different from anything that a group or society has brought into being by symbolization and its culture. The difficulties in distinguishing faith from religion arise because the members of a group or society have no way of dealing with a revelation other than by using their cultural resources. Only by faith can they discern that what they are dealing with via these resources is something holy, that is, set apart from their culture by a transcendent God. Holiness always refers to something that God sets apart for his service. It has nothing whatsoever in common with the sacred, which is a cultural creation. Consequently, the Jewish and Christian Bibles can be read in two ways. They can be read as literary manuscripts produced by earlier cultures that were retained because of their extraordinary ability to inspire large numbers of people. They can also be read as having been discerned by earlier people and cultures as a revelation, but this can only be done in faith. The practical implications are significant. For example, there are a great many texts in our Bibles that are extremely difficult to understand because even after a thorough reading they appear to have very little that speaks to us as people of a time, place, and universal technical order. When believing Jews and Christians come to such a conclusion, the matter ought not to end there. In faith they know that their God is not one to waste his and people's time, because he loves them and is busy redeeming them. When faced with such a situation, we need to go back to these texts and wrestle with them until we become aware of what God is attempting to reveal through them. It is entirely understandable that many intellectuals who apply their disciplines to the analysis of difficult texts come away with nothing. It is not only that a discipline-based reading of the text will distort it (including doing so by means of a theology), but that it takes more persistence than can reasonably be expected from someone who does not believe. Those who do read it in faith have been called by God to perform a service for him that, for Christians, is summed up in the teachings regarding the kingdom of heaven.[41] They know in faith that there is something in the text that is essential for life and the good, and they also know that when they have done everything possible to understand it, they can call on their heavenly parent for the Spirit if they are stuck. Only in this way do they learn how to live differently and to loosen their enslavement to their defining cultural commitments. Once again, this is not at all a matter of salvation or damnation. They are to be the salt that flavours the food that sustains life, the yeast that makes the dough rise to produce the bread necessary for life, and a light for others to show them that this life can be lived, not as a slave to the defining cultural commitments but as a redeemed person. In other words, they are to bear and hold out faith, hope, and love to their community and beyond.

Once again, the practical implications are far reaching. Western civilization still has not recovered from the tremendous blow dealt to its Christian community when Christianity became the official religion of the Roman Empire. The immense practical problem of dealing with all the converts and educating them in the faith was impossible without an organization and an institution. They were a necessity, but one in which faith lost out. Eventually, the reformers saw no solution but to start again, but each and every one of them failed to deal with the fundamental underlying issue that faith can never serve any cultural function; that would involve it in the group or society naming itself in rebellion against God. To permit Christianity to serve as the morality or religion of a society would necessitate its institutionalization, and its institutionalization would make it next to impossible for the Spirit to play its part.

As a simple example, imagine an annual meeting of a congregation during which it plans its objectives and strategies for the coming year, including the necessary financial resources set out in a budget. Following an opening prayer, which asks for guidance by the Spirit, the meeting moves through the agenda and generally approves what the leadership has proposed. We know very well that institutions need to operate in this way to function and be effective. Just because this is a necessity, however, does not make it conform to what a group of Christians is called to do as redeemed people in freedom. If we were truly serious about the Spirit playing a role, we would have to proceed with a bottom-up strategy. It would be essential to examine the gifts that had been bestowed on the community. Following an inventory of these gifts, a discussion would have to take place as to how they could be used as a salt, yeast, and light for the entire community. Next, a consensus would have to be arrived at as to what would be possible with the gifts received, and then a budget would have to be drawn up to verify that the financial gifts would enable those actions. And yet, some people might object that it would be better to do what they felt called to do and to trust that whatever was necessary would be granted. At this point, my reader may correctly object: with this kind of approach, how is the leadership of a congregation supposed to pay the mortgage on a building, the operating costs, and the salaries and to feed the hierarchy of the denomination what it needs? The dilemma is obvious, but I am convinced that it is the result of our being backed into a corner as an organization and an institution. In any case, the way in which Christian communities are conducting themselves at present seems to be entirely in the hands of organizational and institutional necessities. However, the solution certainly does not lie with a naive kind of Pentecostalism either. We have somehow convinced ourselves that the early churches constituted some kind of Christian utopia, although our Bibles tell us plainly that this was far from the case. One of the fundamental differences is that these small groups of Christians did not build organizations and institutions and thus had the flexibility that made them open to their efforts being sustained by the Spirit. Despite their complete organizational and institutional ineffectiveness, they brought faith, hope, and love to the world of their time, even after Jesus's resurrection when many of his followers were initially more than a little confused as to his teachings.

In sum, human history as we know it is a cultural creation. It also has largely escaped the need to come to grips with our being a symbolic species suspended in a language and culture, one group and society at a time. Every epoch in the history of a group or society represents an attempt by that group or society to name itself by giving itself a collective identity with defining cultural commitments, without which it could not sustain the lives of its members. Doing so comes with a heavy price tag – an enslavement to the very commitments that make the collective life of the group or society possible. Although each and every group and society needs to name itself, the results have divided and separated each one from the others, thereby producing a history of unimaginable suffering, violence, and death. Socially and historically, these outcomes are rooted in our being a symbolic species.

Culture and Revelation

We have suggested that believing Jews and Christians are necessarily involved in their societies' naming themselves. Doing so became a necessity that humanity imposed upon itself following the confusion of its language, in order to avoid again taking control over its own spiritual being and orientation. In other words, had humanity succeeded in this control, it would have enclosed itself in evil and death. Being unable to establish a universal and eternal name for itself, it would now have to live with the fragmented and temporary names that each group and society would make for themselves, which would leave a tiny measure of spiritual openness for a revelation.

Whenever God came down to see what any group or society was doing and decided to intervene by his work of redemption, his revelation had to penetrate the cultural shield of a group or society – a result of its symbolization and culture having left no place or opening for him. Whenever God penetrated this shield to establish a relationship with someone, or with an entire people, he set that one apart for a service. Those who were called in this way then faced the daunting task of interpreting and living out a revelation by means of their cultural resources, without transforming that revelation into something that conformed to these resources. The gap between what they could achieve and what was required to maintain the integrity of the revelation would be bridged by the Spirit. It is impossible to avoid making a cultural image of a transcendent God, but they knew that such an image would necessarily be false. Similarly, counter-transference reactions would have to be overcome to avoid people's bringing the ways of this transcendent God as close as possible to the ways of their culture. Since God has always respected the freedom of the people whom he called, despite their enslavement, the transmission of a revelation always included the voluntary commitment of the people involved. Never does God use the Spirit to simply take over, which would have amounted to substituting enslavement to a culture with enslavement to the Word, which would have made "redeemed robots" out of them. At the same time, these people who were called by God had to respect his freedom, which meant that the Spirit was also free to come and go as it willed. In other words, it was impossible to restrict the role of the Spirit in a tradition, in a theology, and certainly not in a lineage going back to an ancestor who had been called directly. The interactions between God and the people he called were fluid in their complexity, and the results were unpredictable, given the freedom of the participants. Whenever a group or society thought it could organize this on its own, things turned out very badly.

For example, the Jewish religious establishment was constantly criticized by the prophets who intervened on God's behalf. The book of Amos is a particularly vocal example.[42] I hasten to add that Christians have learned very little from this; they did exactly the same thing following the organization and institutionalization of Christianity as the official religion of the Roman Empire. Within and outside these Jewish and Christian religious establishments, however, there has always been a faithful remnant who understood and thus found itself at odds with them. These few had to bear the revelation for the entire Jewish people or the entire Christian church, as they were supposed to have done for all of humanity. Any claims to being the descendants of Abram or the followers of Calvin, Luther, or Knox (or anyone else, for that matter) or to being the champions of this or that theology amount to the same dreadful mistake. For Christians, Jesus made it plain that they could neither possess the Spirit (or breath of life) nor organize it. We cannot take care of things by means of confessions of faith, catechisms, doctrinal statements, or anything else – as if we could take God's place in denial of our complete dependence on his Spirit. Similarly, the Christian denominational divisions require the equivalent of naming themselves as a denomination, which implies a judgment on all others as practising a less faithful form of Christianity. It compels a denomination to identify itself as "the Church," with disastrous consequences for its members and doubly disastrous consequences for couples who originate from different denominations.

Since Christians are always members of societies that have spiritually named themselves, Jesus's advice to us to become like children takes on another meaning in this context. As noted, until the teenage years, young people have not yet acquired the cultural shield that makes anything other than the life and world of their culture unliveable and impossible to take seriously. From an early age, children can joyfully play in a world of which they can make only a very limited sense, because they know that when they are baffled, stuck, or lost, they can turn to a loving parent to help them. For adults to live like children, they need to know that they can turn to their heavenly parent when they have done everything possible and nevertheless have become stuck. As persons having acquired a collective identity and the defining cultural commitments of the societies in which we are born, we can now appreciate how difficult this is. After the Garden of Eden, none of us can live in a genuinely secular world without anything sacred and thus void of any gods. Attempting to do so in obedience to the first commandment of the Decalogue will constantly remind us of our finitude and weakness as God's creatures.

We have suggested that any communication between God and his creatures encounters two limitations: God cannot be a creature, and a creature cannot be God. In other words, when God decides to communicate with his creatures, he cannot simply adopt their language. Such a language is indissociably linked to a culture and thus to a society's attempts at naming itself by a sacred and myths. If God adopted such a language, it would be impossible for him to be fully "yes" to these people because of two issues. First, his Word could not be contained within a human language, and even if it were forced into it, it would be falsified in the process. The only way God can communicate with human beings in a language is by becoming flesh, as he did in Jesus Christ. Second, the human beings with whom God seeks to communicate cannot receive his Word as a revelation without culturally appropriating it. Consequently, any communication between God and his creatures requires a mediation by the Spirit, but this does not relieve these people of their unique responsibilities. They must endeavour to weaken their cultural shields as much as possible in order to be open fully to the Spirit, who comes and goes at will.

As a consequence of our being a people of a time, place, and universal technical order, and having named ourselves by means of a secular sacred and myths, it is very difficult for believing Jews and Christians to understand the meaning of the first commandment of the Decalogue. Under the ideology of being secular and rational, the traditional gods have vanished from the skies; hence, we do not look for them in other places or in other forms. Nevertheless, this Word of not serving any gods but the only Living One is possibly even more decisive today than it was in earlier times. In different ways, both the so-called conservative part and the so-called liberal part of the Christian community appear to be stuck on this point. The former believes that it is the most faithful because its members read their Bibles relatively literally, making it possible for them to believe that no cultural input is involved. The latter is more culturally aware but uncritical of the implications, which, as we have seen, results in its members' culturally appropriating the gospel. Neither component appears to understand that it is stuck on the same issue and that what divides the two is simply their different approaches.

As a consequence of God being God, and ourselves being creatures, the Spirit must mediate. God's Word must be put in the form of a metaphor, as it were, in order to reach out towards what the members of a cultural community can understand.[43] At the same time, believers must take the text that is the remnant of God's past communications as a context for understanding a revelation that transcends the cultural resources at their disposal. They must live it as witnesses, and this necessitates another kind of metaphor that reaches towards the living Word.[44] The creation of these metaphors and the mediation between them requires the intervention of the Spirit. Owing to this mediation, God's Word will not turn us into redeemed robots. After all, this Word is the same by which he brought the creation into being. Of course, this is only a tiny glimpse into the work of the Spirit, but it flows from what Jesus revealed to his disciples just prior to his arrest and death.[45] We will return to this in a later chapter.

It is also in this context that we should probably understand Jesus when he declares that he is knocking at our door, waiting to be allowed to enter. It surely is not a matter of our willingness to accept or reject him. With such an interpretation, we would endow ourselves with the capacity to limit his love and work of redemption. If we were able to limit his love, God would not be God. Surely what Jesus is saying has both a personal and a collective dimension. Individually and collectively, we are responsible for symbolically creating a door in our cultural shields to make a place for God to enter as well as for making a place for him in our lives. Since this involves how our societies have spiritually named themselves, the decision to make and open a door can never be a purely individual one, any more than we can make our own personal cultures. It is this precise function, I believe, that organized and institutionalized Christianity is incapable of undertaking, and the day may come when the faithful remnant within it will have to leave.

It should also be noted that our civilization, based on highly desymbolized cultures, is imposing additional difficulties on the understanding of the revelation for believing Jews and Christians and on their attempts to explain it to others. We have noted that with the penetration of good and evil came a split between what was real and what was true for human life.[46] Following the confusion of the language of humanity, a bond was created between the two by any culture. What were discerned to be the powers that ruled over a group or society, by the symbolization of everything in terms of the meaning and value it had for human life, metaconsciously established what was ultimately true through a sacred and myths. This lived truth was then introduced into what was real by the visual representation of these powers as idols, and by the religious cults through which the powers were served. In other words, by transferring the ultimate lived truth into the lived reality, people could grasp it, just like anything else they could see and thus act upon. If it had been left as the ultimate lived truth, little could have been done to appease these powers or convince them to co-operate with the way in which a group or society named itself.

Our civilization is moving towards the elimination of what is true from public life. Discipline-based approaches, with their autonomous domains, can neither respect nor understand how everything is related to everything else. Hence, it is impossible to determine by means of discipline-based approaches what something means or what its value is for individual and collective human life. Somehow, by means of our secular sacred and myths, we live as if making everything as understandable and as efficient on its own terms will somehow translate into happier lives, viable societies, and a sustaining biosphere. As a result, individual and collective life adapts itself and evolves relative to what is "real."

Reality has the radically opposite architecture of what is true. As noted, the former's architecture can be described in terms of the principles of non-contradiction, separability, closed definitions, openness to measurement (and thus quantification and mathematical representation), and a simple complexity. In contrast, the architecture of what is true continues to be a dialectically enfolded one. These differences have far-reaching implications. Due to the architecture of what is real in our civilization, its simple complexity permits us to know and deal with everything one constituent at a time. Consequently, it commoditizes and reifies everything. This simple complexity means that when one of the constituents disappears, nothing "essential" can be lost. For this reason we do not become very upset when hundreds of species are disappearing. We cannot sufficiently appreciate how integral they are to the functioning of all life. Similarly, there was no problem whatsoever when the traditional gods were first limited to religious holidays and then vanished altogether. We are fascinated by all the new additions to reality, but its simple complexity makes it impossible for us to associate their appearance with what we have to sacrifice for them. Moreover, the way we recreate life in the image of the Googles, Facebooks, Twitters, and internets of this world is widely believed not to do any harm, and Google states this explicitly. Nevertheless, these jointly represent the most powerful de-symbolizing forces that humanity has ever unleashed on itself. If Judaism and Christianity are the faiths resulting from a God who speaks, permitting what is true in human life to be dwarfed and distorted by what is real will inevitably limit our ability to understand and to transmit the gospel. No one can see God and live. We must therefore rely on language and our cultural resources, for better or for worse.

In sum, the Jewish and Christian faiths must first and foremost be lived in relation to the cultural entities into which we are born and which spiritually name us through a collective identity and defining cultural myths. It is these entities that trap us into the service of false gods and the rebellion against God by establishing a name for ourselves.

We need to understand as clearly and concretely as possible how we are enslaved by the cultural homes we have symbolically made for ourselves. In relation to this enslavement, we can then begin to appreciate being liberated in so far as we learn to trust God and orient our lives by him and his Word, as opposed to our defining cultural commitments. In this regard Christian theology has done a great deal of damage, especially after becoming yet another discipline in our institutions of higher learning, including the theological schools and seminaries that are now entirely in the grip of discipline-based approaches. Having become aware of humanity's being a symbolic species suspended in a language and culture, believing Jews and Christians must face their responsibilities with a greater awareness of the significance of serving a God who speaks and of the cultural factors involved in understanding, living, and communicating his Word.

The Subversion of Symbolization

It is now becoming apparent that the break between God and humanity involved a complete transformation in the roles played by symbolization in individual and collective human life. The strong attack on language in the letter of James ought to come as no surprise in the context of what we have discussed.[47] The roots of this criticism lie in the opening chapters of the book of Genesis. Language was the most precious gift that God bestowed on humanity. It was by human words nested within God's Word that humanity would represent God and rule in his name over the creation after he had brought it into existence by his Word. Humanity's attempt to name itself, and God's response of confusing this language, led to the development of the languages and cultures we have been discussing.

James 3:1–12 deals with the power of language, a kind of theology of language, and some ethical implications.[48] The text does not mince words over the power of our languages. Their abilities to control are compared to a bit in the mouth of a horse and to a rudder on a ship. They are also compared to a spark that can burn an entire forest. Moreover, what such a spark can do to a forest is compared to what languages can do to human lives. James gives a number of practical daily-life examples of how, by means of language, we can explain to others what is happening, get their passions aroused, poison situations, and a great deal else. In our contemporary anti-societies, where highly de-symbolized cultures are complemented by integration propaganda, we know very well how language can do even more, thanks to techniques such as public relations, commercial advertising, political advertising, group dynamics, psychotherapy, and semiotics. These are intensified by the mass media, now enhanced by the new media.[49] Our language profoundly affects our relationships by revealing what is in our hearts, by offering a cover when we hide behind our words, or by helping us to project a certain image of ourselves to others. Language can bring out the best and the worst in us as we use it to bless, curse, or bully others.

The reason that a language has these powers is revealed in the opening chapters of Genesis. Since God brought forth the creation by his Word, he made it comprehensible and speakable for humanity. Language was thus of fundamental importance to humanity and constituted a tremendous gift. It was essential for maintaining a communion of love between it and God. It was also the most fragile means for doing so, thereby allowing both parties their freedom and permitting Adam to name the animals and the woman.

Following the break with God, language continued to play a fundamental and decisive role as humanity desperately searched for a way to establish itself outside of the communion of love with God, no longer wanting to depend on his grace. Following the confusion of the language of humanity, every group and society had to create its own language, which James refers to as an absolute evil and a world of iniquity. This judgment is no poetic exaggeration. Language had become inseparably linked to the groups's or society's naming itself in an attempt to fully break with God and thus plunge itself into evil and death. Moreover, all such languages divided humanity into competing groups and societies, thus manifesting a spirit of division, separation, and conquest. This spirit is the diametrical opposite of that of love, and of God's creative acts of division and separation to bring forth again a communion of love. As noted, in the Jewish and Christian Bibles, all *human* actions of division and separation of people, groups, and societies, and their division and separation from God, are called the demonic. We must not personify this any more than we have personified the spirit of an age. The demonic is the opposite of love because it destroys relationships, drives people apart, and causes all manner of hatred and violence in addition to separating humanity from the only Living One. We may therefore regard the making of languages and cultures as indissociable from the demonic in human history. It is indeed an absolute evil, a world of iniquity, and a power that can defile the entire being, to repeat once more the pronouncement of James. It is clearly a deep structural issue and not a moral one.

By means of languages and processes of differentiation and integration, humanity names everything. From birth onwards, these processes order every person's life and, through it, all the lives of the members of a cultural community – not in a spirit of love but in a spirit of coveting and power. Language thus remains a decisive force in individual and collective human life, but it now moves in the opposite direction, away from God. The letter of James gives a glimpse of what our Bibles refer to as the principalities and powers that reign from on high, to which we will turn our attention more fully in the next chapter.

It is important to contrast this teaching regarding language with that of the opening two chapters of Genesis. There can be little doubt that humanity was created as a symbolic species. Moreover, its language must have had the capabilities that come from symbolization, as a way of understanding God's creation. Everything within it was a creature and thus depended on other creatures, and jointly all creatures depended on the Creator. Nothing could be understood on its own terms, independently of everything else and of God. The fact that Adam was able to name the animals that God brought to him, and to do so with some understanding of God's intent as their maker, implied that their symbolization had to transcend the mere differentiation of one from one another in terms of what mattered for human life. This would have implied a denial of doing so as a fellow creature. Consequently, symbolization would have to be done in a way that did not rely ultimately on anything equivalent to a sacred or myths as a way of naming oneself and, via this, naming everything else. A very different point of reference was required, and, for a creature, this could only be God himself. Adam understood that, according to the being of the animals, none of them could be a suitable companion for him. It also meant that he understood something of his own being and what God meant when he said that it was not good for him to be alone.

How is it possible for symbolization to have God as the ultimate reference point in his being fully life, love, justice, and peace? I believe the text gives a clear answer. God had provided Adam with the breath of life. Consequently, God had established a connection with humanity through the Spirit. It was therefore possible for Adam to know the One who was the fullness of everything. For example, if something was true, it meant that it was understood and dealt with in relation to the One who is Truth, and in relation to everything else in creation. It reminds us of what Jesus said when he told his disciples that he was the way, the truth, and the life – the way back to the Father. By means of the Spirit, he promised his disciples that they would be in him as he would be in the Father.

There is a very important counter-transference reaction that stands in our way of understanding the foregoing. Beginning with the Greeks, truth became associated with universally valid knowledge. It was thus associated with science, mathematics, and a certain kind of philosophy. Universal knowledge was an invention of Greek culture and referred to knowledge that was independent of the context and vantage point from which it had been gathered, although for some it could be contaminated by human experience. When Greek culture went into decline, Socrates and his students sought to save it by assuming that it was founded in part on universal knowledge. By the discovery of this foundation, the culture could be stabilized and defended against its relativization.

When the Jewish and Christian communities rapidly grew apart during the first century, the latter lost touch with its Hebrew roots, making it relatively defenceless against Greek philosophy. To many Christian thinkers, a convergence between God's revelation and the universal knowledge or truth appeared almost self-evident. Since God is eternal, so is his Word. Hence, the Jewish and Christian Bibles could be "mined" by philosophy and theology for eternal universal knowledge. Attempts could then be made to create a foundation for Christianity based on these truths, which could be set out in statements of faith, catechisms, and other such documents.

This view is completely foreign to our Bibles. There can be no truth outside of God by means of which his actions can be evaluated. God is fully truth. Consequently, humanity is within the truth when it is in communion with him. In other words, truth is a relationship with God, and the same is true of life, love, justice, and peace.

In sum, when humanity was in communion with God in the Garden of Eden, it was within life and the good. Moreover, having been endowed with the Spirit, it knew the One who was fully God. Consequently, the language of humanity was developed by the Word from the One who was fully life, love, truth, justice, and peace. It is in this sense that we can think of God's Word as a revealed myth – the fullness of meaning that can never be entirely put into a human language but which can provide that language with everything it requires to understand and communicate the true meaning and value of anything. As a result, human language was anchored in this revealed myth and had no need whatsoever of the equivalent of cultural myths. As such, it was the language of human lips and not of the human heart.

In communion with God there was no threat of the unknown and no need to symbolize it. Humanity had full access to the One who had created everything and could turn to him if it was stuck with something it could not understand or deal with. Consequently, any symbolization occurred within the context of the revealed myth that was maintained by the Spirit. In this way, God was all in all to his creatures, as he will be again one day. There was no room for anything sacred or for the principalities and powers that would begin to occupy the gulf that had opened up between God and humanity when the latter broke with him. These principalities and powers enslaved humanity, and God is busy redeeming it from this enslavement. In the meantime, our dependence on God's speaking is so fundamental that what the Jewish people feared most was his silence.[50]

I will attempt to summarize my findings thus far by suggesting that, if we could glimpse into and beyond our secular myths, we might observe the following differences between a truly secular humanity in the Garden of Eden and a humanity that claims itself to be secular by the spirit of our age. The difference between the two is undoubtedly as great as that between children whom we see around us and children who have not been brought up to participate fully as members of a symbolic species. For lack of listening to a language, the latter children have almost nothing in common with normal children other than certain superficial physical similarities. For readers who have not read any accounts of these children, it may be highly instructive to read the stories in detail. One of the best documented ones is the story of a boy who was referred to by his custodian doctor as the "man-plant" because, as he observed, even his dog had a greater emotional capacity to relate to people.[51] It is a very moving but also extremely depressing story because, despite the ingenious attempts of the doctor to bring this child into the human world of language and culture, he did not succeed. Given everything that our Bibles reveal, I believe that this comparison can help us to imagine the differences between a humanity in the Garden of Eden that is unfolding its symbolic potential within the Word of God – and thus is entirely free of any sacred, principalities, and powers that could interfere with that freedom – and a humanity whose symbolic potential is undermined in our time, place, and universal technical order, where this order represents the rule of discipline-based approaches, and where a powerful state has brought everything under its control by making it political. This gives us some idea of the extent of our reification and alienation.

The revelation goes further by putting much of what we do in the context of the creation as actions of de-creation.[52] In the Jewish Bible,

God told his people that they must hold certain things to be impure and that acts of purification may be needed. He declared them to be impure, which is an entirely different matter than their being impure in themselves.[53] In his act of creation God divided, separated, and formed things in order to establish an order in his creation, which was designed to make possible and sustain relationships of love. By implication, a disordering of the creation can result when incompatible elements are brought into contact with each other, thus undermining it. As noted, the demonic represents all human actions of division, separation, and forming that create relationships that are the opposite of love and thus undermine the creation.

The elements that are compatible as a consequence of God's act of creation constitute a purity that was disturbed by the break between God and humanity. God thus declared some elements to be incompatible with one another, to be impurities and defilements of the creation. At one point, it became theologically fashionable to associate the concepts of impurity and defilement with magic. Simply put, having named itself, each group or society orders its world by linguistically and culturally orienting the lives of its members and its universe through acts of division, separation, and forming; it thereby brings about an order of a "pure" sacred as well as an "impure" sacred of transgression and defilement. To touch certain objects or to get involved in activities associated with the impure sacred was regarded as being capable of bringing a curse upon a person by means of magic. This concept of impurity and defilement has nothing in common with the revelation; beginning with the opening chapters of Genesis, religion, morality, and magic came under attack.

From the very beginning, therefore, the Jewish people dissociated defilement and impurity from magic. Since God had told his people to regard certain things as impure, those who touched them became defiled – as a consequence of their disobedience of this commandment. Defilement was thus a matter of incurring a debt towards God.[54] In the same way, God commanded that certain elements of his creation were not to be mixed and declared the results to be impure. This mixing was to be regarded as an action in opposition to God's creation because it involved a return to the confusion of incompatible elements in the direction of *tohu-wabohu*.

In the letter of James, impurity and defilement are related to the world in which we live.[55] It is the world that a group or society has formed within creation as a result of naming itself by means of a sacred and myths in an attempt to shut out God. Consequently, it is impossible to love both this world and God at the same time.[56] Once again, this has nothing to do with the world being impure or defiled in itself; instead, it is a matter of the incompatibility between the Spirit of God and the spirit of such a world. The opening chapters of Genesis show that God is not his creation, nor is the creation God himself. When people receive the Spirit, their bodies become its temples. But if such people live in conformity with the world, they confuse its spirit with the Spirit of God, and this amounts to a mixing and a confusion that belong to evil and death.[57] The letter of James explains that the love of our world amounts to enmity against God. We cannot love both God and the principalities and powers that rule the world. In sum, what is pure corresponds to God's acts of creation, and what is impure undoes the creation by producing a confusion – a kind of return to the *tohu-wabohu*. Our world is the result of the demonic, which establishes elements that are incompatible with one another, in order to produce hatred, exploitation, power, and everything that is the opposite of love.[58] Our civilization has put its own unique stamp on the demonic by confusing the actions of living beings with those of dead machines through the use of concepts including language, memory, cognition, knowledge, expertise, and intelligence in relation to both. We thus confuse life with death and good with evil. Similarly, institutionalized Christianity tends to seek either an absolute spirituality that seeks to escape the world, or a worldliness in which God's Spirit is eliminated.[59] God is the Holy One, which means that he is set apart from his creation. Consequently, when he sends his Spirit, those who bear it must also separate themselves from a world that has named itself in order to shut God out. In sum, it is a question of whether we love this world or its Creator. We must maintain a distance between the two to avoid defilement. It is a matter of creation and de-creation. God's creation is for love, while our unfolding of its potential in the world is for hatred, hostility, and everything that undermines and destroys love as a work of de-creation. Whenever Christians seek to separate themselves from the world, they engage in their work of division and separation. The letter to James suggests that separating ourselves from the world begins with submitting ourselves to God's love and his ways of reconciliation. Doing so causes the demonic to be pushed back, bringing about a distancing from the world.

4 Born Neither Free nor Equal, but Loved

An Enslaved Humanity

Following the break, God established two covenants with humanity. The first was granted through Adam, and the second through Noah. He thus attempted to make the situation as liveable as possible. (We may regard them as two successive separation agreements.) Humanity responded by attempting to sever all ties, by naming itself and thereby rejecting the name God had given it. Humanity would have plunged itself fully into evil and death were it not for God's intervention to prevent this by confusing its language.

Each group or society now had to create its own language. First, it had to name itself to establish the necessary point of reference for a life apart from God. Each name was necessarily exclusive of all the other names, with the result that humanity became divided into opposing groups, societies, and civilizations. Each entity loved what it had named, to the exclusion of what all the others had named.

God responded by electing one people from among all the others for the purpose of setting it apart as the one that would bear his Word of love, grace, pardon, and redemption. To the extent that his people lived this Word, all other people could learn the good news that was intended for all of humanity. Once again, God's election was for the performance of a service and not for salvation. In other words, God's intervention in Babel led not to the repentance of humanity but to each group's or society's continuing to name itself apart from all the others. The resulting division and separation of humanity was now going to be used by God in a different approach to his work of liberation and reconciliation.

What God now began did not bear any resemblance to a separation agreement. He first entered into a covenant with Abram, whose descendants would become God's people. Following the liberation from Egypt of these descendants, God established a second covenant with them through Moses. Thus began a *lived* relationship between God and his people that must never be separated from what became the Torah and the law. The aim of that lived relationship was to restore its character of love between God and his people and among his people, as a witness to humanity. Everything needed to be understood by, and referred to, this lived relationship of love.

I believe that an insistence on such a broad interpretation of the revelation is confirmed not only by everything that followed but also by the law itself. As part of the Torah and the law, the Decalogue of ten "words" that God spoke to the people whom he had just liberated enabled them to tackle the cultural shield that the Israelites (like any other society) had made for themselves out of a need to make life liveable apart from God. After God had introduced himself as their liberator, his first "word" was both a promise that one day they would have no other gods in his presence, and an invitation to them to begin living out from that promise here and now. Reducing this to no more than a commandment contradicts everything that was happening. Why would God liberate his people only to enslave them in a religion and a morality? Moreover, such an enslavement had been revealed to be the consequence of the break between God and humanity, which God was busy healing with his people.

The first "word" of the Decalogue is an extraordinary liberation. From then on, God's people did not need to worry about anything sacred or religious in their lives and the world. He promised that the freedom and love that characterized the relationship between himself and humanity in the Garden of Eden would be restored. In the meantime, the Israelites would struggle against powerful forces in their lives, but that is all those forces would be. A drought would be a drought, a rainfall just a rainfall, and an invasion of locusts a threat to their crops, unless God revealed that there was more to it. In other words, the Israelites were invited to live by the covenant that God had established with them, and to the extent that they were able to live out of love for God and their neighbour, they would not need a sacred or myths as reference points by which to name themselves. After all, such a sacred and myths would simply represent the deepest meaning that they could establish apart from God, by metaconsciously absolutizing their body of experience as their all-defining commitment and orientation. They were now offered a commitment to and a relationship with the only Living One, who promised to set them free from their enslaving collective identity and defining cultural commitments.

The second "word" spoken by the Liberator to the Israelites was a promise that one day they would no longer need to visually represent the powerful forces that they had metaconsciously identified in their lives as idols and to which they were obliged to prostrate themselves; that was the only way they had known to appease and coexist with them. They were therefore invited to stop doing so. From that moment, because the vast influences on their lives and their world were not gods, there was no need for the Israelites to bring them into what was real (as idols) and thus to enter into enslaving cults. These influences were nothing more unless God told his people that they were a sign of something else.

The third "word" spoken by the Liberator to Israel was a promise that one day his people would no longer use his name in a "harmful manner" (a literal translation) and that they were invited to stop doing so immediately. It is absurd to reduce this statement to the idea of cursing. The most harmful way in which a people can use God's name is a religious one. Most likely, this was clearly understood by the Israelites as a result of their contacts with other cultures.

Skipping to the tenth "word" spoken by the Liberator to his people, we note that it too has a collective and thus a cultural dimension. It sums up all the other words. It is understood to mean that Israel was not to covet the gods of other cultures, the idols of other cultures, the religious powers of the sacred names used by other cultures, and so on. It was also a promise that one day there would be no need to covet any cultural alienation because the reconciliation between God and humanity would be complete. In the meantime, the promise included the permission to struggle against all cultural enslavements in order to reveal that this could bring a measure of freedom and love.

If the Torah and the law were so full of promises of liberation and love, why did things turn out for the worse, as described in our Bibles? The simple answer, which we will seek to explain further in the remainder of this chapter, is that first the Jewish people and later the Christian church were enslaved by the flesh and by a world ruled by the principalities and powers. God promised his people a different world so that they would know their spiritual orientation and future. For that journey, their collective identity and defining cultural commitments would be of no use in guiding them. Instead, God called Israel to live by faith and to be guided by his promises. In other words, to the extent that Israel trusted God, it could let go of its cultural moorings and discover its condition of enslavement (sin). However, the pressures of the flesh and the world would constantly bring the opposite results: the making of religious and thus cultural images of God, the transforming of his service into religious cults, and the changing of obedience to the law into obedience to a morality.

It may be argued that I have yielded to a powerful counter-transference reaction: to have the revelation correspond to what we have discovered about our dependence on language and culture. We must constantly question ourselves about such possibilities, and respectful disagreements within a community of believers are essential to ensure that we keep counter-transference reactions to a minimum. As I have shown, it appears that a reversal has taken place in our understanding of the dependence of the revelation on human cultures. In the past it was commonly believed that many biblical accounts (such as the creation story) were inspired by parallel accounts from neighbouring cultures. Gradually, we have become aware that the Jewish people used such accounts in an iconoclastic fashion to show that the revelation was entirely different from anything that the surrounding cultures believed and lived. We attempted to explain this with regard to the first chapter of Genesis, and the early Christians appeared to have understood it extremely well. At the same time, there is an opposite development that makes people of our time, place, and universal technical order much less aware of the role that culture played in traditional societies and still plays in our own lives. When we began to move towards the building of this universal technical order by means of industrialization, urbanization, and secularization, much of traditional cultures and religions was dismissed as superstitions for which we no longer had any need. From a biblical perspective, I wish this were the case, but the evidence is overwhelmingly against it. We have a collective identity and defining cultural commitments that are of a secular kind, and although these are no longer found in the sky above or in nature below, we must not assume that what the Bible speaks of has disappeared.

There exists another possible counter-transference reaction that comes from our living in highly individualistic so-called mass societies. Christians have picked up on this individualism and read it into their Bibles. Groups of people are seen as collections of individuals who are essentially making their own decisions, especially concerning salvation. This dreadful mistake has made many biblical texts virtually incomprehensible. All I can do is to continue to insist on our being a symbolic species, on how this awareness undermines our present secular collective identity and defining cultural commitments, and on how this opens the way to the Word being able to penetrate more deeply and radically into our lives. Having spent my life attempting to understand our secular collective identity and defining cultural commitments, I have experienced a gospel that is infinitely richer, deeper, and more liberating than anything I have ever learned in churches. Hence, all I can say is that I hope my reader will have the same experience.

In sum, a relationship with the only Living One has nothing whatsoever in common with a cultural religion; nor does his law have anything in common with a cultural morality. God's Word comes from beyond all cultures. In everything we have attempted to understand, we discover that God remains fully "yes" to humanity, even in its rebellion. When, time and time again, his people Israel gives its love and freedom to other gods, he laments, pleads, and even begs them, like someone who has been abandoned by a lover. He refers to himself as a jealous God and compares his feelings to those of any human being who is betrayed by a lover and is compelled to watch from the sidelines – sometimes in frustration, at other times in anger, and always in a kind of impotence. We humans then turn around and accuse him of being the nasty God of the Jewish Bible. We are back to what our Bibles mean by love. As people who have all been born into a collective identity and defining cultural commitments, be they of a traditional or a secular form, we become divided beings and live divided lives as we begin to take God's promises seriously. We become torn in two different directions. For Christians, this represents the cultural dimension of being wheat and tares, flesh and spirit.

Even though Jesus Christ, in becoming flesh, won the decisive victory over the flesh and the principalities and powers, humanity remained completely entangled in them. Consequently, their annihilation will have to wait for God's decision to intervene and to separate what is unto life from what is unto death in all of us. Any actions taken by Christians to hasten this process by judging others is thus detrimental to all of humanity. At the same time, if God had decided to use his unlimited power to destroy the flesh and the powers, humanity would have been destroyed along with them. In that case, God would have ceased to be the One who revealed himself as love, humility, and non-power.

The structure of the book of Revelation reveals this in considerable detail.[1] Its second part, marked by the breaking of seven seals on a scroll, reveals that the meaning of human history is entirely centred in Jesus Christ, in whom all things were created and in whom all will be reconciled. A third part, marked by the sounding of seven trumpets, reveals from the perspective of the heavens (and thus eternity) what the gospels describe from the perspective of creation and the earth. A fourth part, marked by the pouring out of the contents of seven bowls, describes the final separation of humanity from the flesh, the world, and the powers in preparation for the new creation. This new creation is revealed in the fifth part, which is marked by a sevenfold repetition of the phrase "and then I saw," signifying the reconciliation between hearing the Word and seeing reality. The first part, marked by the seven letters to the seven churches, reveals how they will play their part in this as yeast in the dough. Doing so requires putting relationships of love in centre stage, as Jesus made abundantly clear when he spoke of how his followers ought to relate either to mammon or to family.[2] This was further clarified when the Spirit came to illuminate all Jesus's teachings.[3]

From the first two chapters of Genesis it is clear that God regards humanity as a creature and thus in its relationship to him and to his creation. There can be no "human nature" because of this relatedness. How is it possible that an all-powerful God, whose Word is one and the same as his actions, can relate to his creature, made in his image, without overwhelming, dominating, or mechanizing it and thus destroying this image? It is possible only if this relatedness is one of love within his love, one of freedom within his freedom, and one whose words are within his Word. As noted, relationships of love must be total, all-encompassing, and exclusive of loving anything else but God and one's neighbour. Such relationships of love commit and define human beings in their entirety. These relationships can be shattered when anything is withheld from them. They bind two parties in an all-defining comprehensive commitment that includes a shared future. Where the one will be, the other will be as well. In this kind of relatedness there can be no division of human beings into bodies and souls, of worldly life and spiritual life, of life during the work week and life during the Sabbath or Sunday – or any other kind of dualism.

The Flesh and the World

It is difficult to imagine a biblical teaching that has been more subverted by counter-transference reactions than what our Bibles mean by "the flesh." The opening chapters of Genesis reveal humanity's being a single creature in two persons. As a creature humanity was finite in time, as the entire creation was within time. It was finite in space as a consequence of bodies having been made from dust. It was finite in all its relationships as an image of God, referring to him through the Spirit. Hence, in the Garden of Eden, its finitude in time, space, and in all its relationships distinguished humanity from God as its Creator. Again, this finitude of humanity is referred to as the flesh, which, being in the image of God, prevented it from being the equal of God.

Within the communion of love, being flesh was entirely positive because human life was within a relationship of love with the only Living One. Human freedom was within God's freedom, human justice within God's justice, human peace within God's peace, and so on. Humanity had one language within the Word. Consequently, being flesh had no negative implications of any kind.

With the break between humanity and God, what it was to be flesh changed in every aspect.[4] The flesh became the mark of being separated from God and of a boundary that humanity could no longer bridge in love. From that point on, humanity's refusal of God's protection transformed its finitude into a vulnerability, weakness, and openness to all manner of influences that threatened humanity with becoming a nothingness. Everything that humanity now did could be undone by the influences of time, space, and social relationships. From a historical and social perspective, we know this with a great deal of certainty because of the universality of the institutions that each group or society had to create for itself in order to respond to and dominate such influences. The universality of legal institutions is a clear example that I have explained elsewhere.[5]

From a biblical perspective, which is a great deal more radical, humanity no longer wished to be within God's love and turned its love towards other gods. The result was a dreadful enslavement by all manner of religions that exacted a heavy price from each and every community in return for false meanings, values, and comforts in life and death. Humanity no longer wished to accept God's grace and protection, thus bringing down upon itself the rule of economic forces. Humanity no longer wished to live with God's protection and peace, thus bringing down upon itself the rule of war, and this necessity for war was indissociably linked to a necessity for political power and the rule of the state. Humanity no longer wished to live within the life and the good that God willed, and thus brought down upon itself the servitude of cultural moralities. In sum, humanity was no longer able to live playfully and joyfully in the creation as children of a heavenly Father, who would have had no burdensome cares in the world because they could have turned to him whenever they were stuck. Humanity now lived in fear of becoming nothingness; it was like grass or a flower in the field that withers and disappears (Isaiah 40:6–8).

From a historical and social perspective, every group or society lives under the threat of relativism, nihilism, and anomie, which can make it disappear in chaos. All that stands between it and chaos is its cultural shield of a collective identity and defining cultural commitments. These are ultimately based on nothing but living as if the collective experience were limitless, and yet this is based on the nothingness of myths.

This situation can be summed up by the serpent's promise to the woman in the Garden of Eden. She would become like the elohims if she penetrated into good and evil. From the historical and social perspective of our being a symbolic species, each group or society found it necessary to live as if it were a god with its own body of experience giving the ultimate spiritual direction and reference points, but this view rested on nothing but myths. In other words, each group or society transformed the weakness and vulnerability associated with its finitude into the opposite by referring only to itself as the ultimate measure of everything and the only possible point of reference. It covered over its nothingness with myths. Nevertheless, since this approach was founded on myths, it was constantly undone towards the end of each historical epoch, necessitating either a complete reconstitution of a group or society or its total disappearance.

We would fall into a very serious counter-transference reaction if we stopped at this apparent convergence of certain aspects of what our Bibles reveal about the flesh, and what we currently believe to be our situation from a historical and social perspective. The biblical revelation always goes much further than what we can know from historical and social evidence. Our fear of nothingness, as a consequence of refusing God's love and protection, leads to covetousness – also referred to as the lusts of the flesh. Covetousness is the desire to take what belongs to God or to others in order to cover our weakness and vulnerability in a denial of our finitude. The reasons are clear. God is the Creator of everything, and thus everything belongs to him. Within the communion of love this did not affect human life in any way, because God freely gave in grace and abundance whatever humanity needed. However, when the communion of love was broken, humanity began to appropriate everything as it saw fit, by means of power, conquest, and domination.

Hence, the flesh became the seat of covetousness. It was this spirit of covetousness that now dominated and possessed the flesh.

Reciprocally, in its weakness and vulnerability, the flesh is a provocation to covetousness. The flesh will use a variety of situations as opportunities to reduce its weakness and vulnerability by seizing what it deems to lack. According to the letter of James, the flesh has taken possession of humanity, and in this way we have become possessed by sin. Consequently, the flesh now constitutes a power within us that governs us and rules over our actions (James 1:12–18).[6] In sum, the break with God has turned the flesh into its opposite: from our being a finite creature to being something that is against God and seeking to possess God in order to overcome our creaturely finitude. Before the break, the flesh was within the life and the good; following it, the flesh was within evil and death.

The flesh appearing as a power within humanity is closely associated with pride and egotism.[7] When humanity rejected God's love and protection, it put itself at the centre of everything. Everything began with humanity, which also meant that everything could end with it. It opened up human life to anxiety, especially regarding the future. We are the civilization that should have quieted this anxiety to the greatest extent possible, given the proliferation of our scientific and technical means of ever greater efficiency and power. The opposite appears to be the case: anxiety and depression are widespread.[8] This anxiety further incites the flesh and the power it has over us and our lives.

The Jewish and Christian Bibles thus reveal the first power that has taken possession of humanity, even though it originated with humanity. Individual and collective human life is ruled by the flesh. From a biblical perspective, humanity is neither nature nor nurture but flesh expressed through both nature and nurture. Consequently, all religious attempts to save humanity by its escaping the body in order to become more spiritual – by having the soul depart from the body after death, by splitting human life into a good and a bad part and using the former to deal with the latter, or any other such religious schemes – are utterly useless. Humanity is ultimately qualified by its relationship with God and by the relationships between its members.

Jacques Ellul summarized Paul's teachings on the flesh as follows.[9] The flesh is a power in human life that resides in our bodies (understood in the Hebrew sense, which includes all of our being), and it is via the flesh that we are enslaved to sin. Flesh designates our entire being, which, separated from the only Living One, becomes a non-being in the grip of sin and death. Our being lives in the world by means of what may be referred to as an existential project that binds our being to others in a joint attempt to succeed in the world. By adapting and evolving this project of existence, a group or society makes its history. What the flesh fails to do is to provide individual and collective human life with true meaning, purpose, and direction; this weakness and vulnerability turns the power of the flesh into one that covets everything in the world. As a result, the flesh covets to do for itself and by itself what God intended to accomplish by the law. Every group and society has coveted access to the gods by creating a religion, access to justice by creating a morality and legal system, access to the future by magic, and so on. Each group or society regards its works of this kind as superior to all others and also to God's law, and thus in opposition to that law. It is for this reason that the opening chapters of the book of Genesis attack religion, morality, and magic as the antitheses of the revelation. Paul shows that all those who live by the flesh ensure that everything they think and do, and thus their entire lives, is in its service. Consequently, this commitment to the flesh amounts to a love of the flesh. It is a love of non-being and therefore a hatred of God since he is the only Living One. This is already implied in the opening chapters of Genesis, which set the stage for understanding the decisive importance of God liberating his people from Egypt and then providing them with his law through Moses. In every respect the flesh is the opposite of the law, which teaches the true meaning of life in a conduct of humility, love, and non-power. This leads us back to what God loves and what he declares to be good. The law reveals the difference between the way of the flesh and the way of God, thereby showing our enslavement to sin. It compels us to acknowledge that we cannot escape our enslavement, set ourselves free, and then follow the law. The result is an impasse. The law is unable to overcome the power of the flesh within us, otherwise we would be able to obey it. God cannot eliminate this impasse by destroying the flesh, because he would then use the way of power, which is the way of the flesh. God is going to fulfil the promise of the law and follow his way of non-power. Jesus Christ became flesh, and, by penetrating flesh and death, he destroyed them once and for all. We will return to this in the next chapter.

A non-religious and non-moral understanding of the law is incompatible with the conventional Christian terminology of an *Old* and a *New* Testament. This terminology is partly the result of countertransference reactions – an attempt to bring the revelation closer to the collective identity and defining cultural commitments of various historical epochs. For example, this terminology implies that the God of the Old Testament, who commands his people to do all kinds of things of which we disapprove, is very different from the God of the New Testament, who loves everybody in accordance with our values. All such attempts have involved the church in a dreadful mistake. As Jewish theologians have pointed out, there is almost nothing new in the New Testament. They are largely correct. Jesus did not come to invent new things; he came to fulfil the law by living it through the Spirit without abolishing any of it, and, by doing so, he gained the victory over the flesh and death. Of course, once this victory had been achieved, a fuller understanding of the law was possible through the life of Jesus Christ. Consequently, there is a total and complete inseparability between the Old and New Testaments. We will henceforth refer to them as the first and second testaments. There can be no third testament, as the warning against adding anything, which is found in the book of Revelation, makes clear.

As noted, the flesh enslaves human beings to the point that their lives in the world are in complete conformity to it. There is thus a close interdependence between the flesh and the world. This world is the result of each group and society appropriating the creation according to the flesh, which brought about a fundamental transformation. The creation that was entirely free of anything sacred and religious became what our Bibles refer to as *the world*, ruled by enslaving powers that, like the flesh, originated with humanity and that, once generated, ruled it "from above." Consequently, every historical epoch will generate countertransference reactions that undermine people's ability to understand the biblical meaning of *the world* by reinterpreting it in such a way as to bring it closer to the collective identity and the defining cultural commitments of the group or society to which they belong. However, the original use of this term was the complete opposite of the most influential mythology of the cultures of that time. We will begin by explaining this before we turn to the way in which theologians reinterpreted it as a consequence of the mythologies of the twentieth century. The concept of a world represents another beautiful example of the way in which our Bibles reveal a message from God. It begins with an iconoclastic use of cultural concepts, beliefs, and world-views to show that this revelation is entirely other and, at the same time, transcends the limits of what is knowable and believable in any culture.

Biblical authors, including John, Paul, and James, use the word *cosmos* in a very concise manner. Their usage implies a distinction between the creation before humanity broke with God and the world in which we now live, which is rejected and condemned in its entirety. For example, in the letter of James, the term *cosmos* occurs four times. Each time it refers to the world in which we live and in which we encounter the destructive powers that rule over it.[10] In the fourth chapter, the cosmos is where we encounter commerce and the accumulation of wealth. The fifth chapter associates the term with employers and their use of wealth. Next, the text discusses material happiness, following which it turns to trials and judgments. Moreover, there are recurring references to pride and the spirit of power. The meaning is clear: when Christians are told that they must separate themselves from the world, they must distance themselves from activities of this kind. It is all about the societies in which we live and the world they help to constitute. According to Paul's letter to the Romans, the world remains God's creation, but it suffers and groans in the pains of childbirth and waits to be delivered (Romans 8:22). Once again, we must not divide this world into what, according to our mythology, is good and apply these teachings only to the part that, according to this mythology, is bad.

In James and John the cosmos is radically condemned, which has been interpreted as meaning its separation from God. This is true, but there is a much more immediate explanation, with vast and concrete implications for the lives of the readers of that time.[11] There was a growing competition and an increasingly influential ideology of a kind of popular stoicism. According to this ideology, the cosmos was the highest spiritual value known to humanity because it revealed the perfect order through the stars, and this perfect harmony was taken to be God himself. The ideology had a dreadfully destructive influence on human life and society because it implied that as long as people lived within the harmony of this cosmos, they lived within the order of its God and therefore could conduct their lives as they saw fit. It is not difficult to imagine how economically and politically destructive this was for the societies of that time. In sum, this ideology implied that all meaning could be found within the cosmos, while the revelation taught that the cosmos was God's creation; therefore, the meaning of that creation must refer to him.

The consequences are far reaching. Since the cosmos belongs to its Creator, people cannot live their lives within and in relation to it as they see fit. With regard to bringing up children, the stoic ideology implied that all parents and others had to do was to clear away any obstacles that stood in the way of their growing up, following which these children would have meaningful lives because they could discover all the meaning within the cosmos. For Christians, children are the transmission of life that God has given, with the result that the meaning of their lives in the cosmos refers to him, as does everything else in the creation. Consequently, the biblical use of the word *cosmos* was polemical and iconoclastic with regard to the stoic ideology and its influence on cultures, reminding Christians that nothing good could come of it. This is beautifully summed up in the letter of James when he reminded his readers that their quarrelling came from their attachment to the world (*cosmos*), and that their love of this world meant enmity towards God. People, including Christians, who attach themselves to the world are attaching themselves to the rule of the destructive powers over it. In other words, an attachment to the world produces an attachment to the powers that enslave and destroy human life as well as the creation. Once again, we are back to the biblical teaching regarding love: we will be attached to whatever we love, and that will have inevitable consequences. If we are passionately attached to our world, we are attached to everything that enslaves it. There is thus a correspondence between our covetousness – which expresses itself as the will to power, domination, accumulation, and the exclusion of others – and the kind of world that this covetousness produces. There can never be an end to this relationship, because what we have will never be enough, in part because it is never secure. As our Bibles put it, we desire what we do not have, and we do not have because we do not ask God (James 4:2).

For example, the consumer societies of the second half of the twentieth century could not make us happy. They were entirely based on our coveting whatever could be achieved and produced by technique, thereby expanding our desires in its direction and enslaving us to it. In contrast, the revelation teaches us that what can truly satisfy us belongs to God, and that he will not let us seize it. Instead, he freely grants it for the asking. We are thus confronted with the conflict between the way of the flesh and the way of the Spirit: that of asking in prayer and awaiting a response. In the final analysis, what we ultimately need is God, but he will not permit us to take hold of him by any religious means, even when they have a Jewish or Christian orientation.

Hopefully, we can now better understand the conflict in which many theologians found themselves during the second half of the twentieth century. They were torn between the teachings of the Bible and the mythology of the first generation of industrial societies that was spreading throughout the world. How was it possible that the advancement of science and technology, and the growing economic output that they made possible, would not benefit humanity, especially the substantial portion that lived in dire poverty? Surely this would do a lot more good than harm. It resulted in a theological dilemma that could only be resolved by dividing the world of that time into the societies in which people were making good headway towards reducing and hopefully eliminating poverty, and the cosmos of the principalities and powers, a solution that the theologians could not accept because these principalities and powers were rejected and condemned in the Bible. Theologies of all kinds were thus produced to eliminate the tension by dividing the "world" into what people were attached to by their myths and what the Bible condemned.

Every age puts us in this kind of dilemma because of counter-transference reactions. The tragedy is that the so-called liberal sector and the so-called conservative part of the Christian community deal with these counter-transference reactions in diametrically opposite ways, neither of which is a faithful response to the situation. Both ways make it a little easier to be a Christian and to live in the world, by means of our collective identity and defining cultural commitments while at the same time convincing ourselves of the opposite. I will give one more example related to our current situation.

The biblical teachings on the flesh and the world will remain theological truisms unless we apply them to our lives and the world in which we live. How can we detect our enslavement to the flesh and to the powers that rule our world? We can begin by putting to the test the ideology of our being rational and secular people: by searching for entities that we deal with as if they had no limits. Such entities would be the secular equivalent of the traditional gods of the past. As noted, in the creation everything is related to everything else and jointly dependent on the Creator. Anything that appears to escape a dependence on everything else will in effect be dealt with as being omnipotent, self-sufficient, and thus good in itself. It is one way of detecting the secular sacred and myths of our contemporary societies.

How did we ever manage to get into our current relationship with discipline-based science and technique? How is it possible that something that is entirely of our own making has become the object of our secular religious attitudes? These kinds of questions are not new. In the nineteenth century it was suggested that the economic organization referred to as capitalism had enslaved everyone, rich and poor alike.[12] In the 1960s some economists suggested that consumer societies had ended up serving the very economies that they had created to serve them.[13] Around the same time Jacques Ellul argued that technique had become an autonomous force in human life and society.[14] Although widely misinterpreted, what he meant was that from a historical and social perspective the influence that technique had on people was now much more decisive than the influence they could exercise on technique. It would be incorrect to suggest that these kinds of enslavements to our own creations only occur from time to time. Our Bibles suggest that this is a permanent state of affairs. We will attempt to understand it in the case of our own civilization.

A World Ruled by Principalities and Powers

In the previous chapter I attempted to show that following God's intervention in humanity's seeking to name itself through the building of a city with its tower in the heavens, each society made its own world by symbolically appropriating the creation through its language and culture and everything associated with them. In the present chapter we are examining the consequences, namely that these worlds are ruled by what the second testament refers to as the principalities and powers. We must avoid any confusion arising from apparent contradictions. God, being God, cannot be affected in any way by what humanity does, with the result that what we do is in his presence and within his will, even when we go against it. Our attempts at excluding him from his creation cannot change his will to reconcile himself with humanity, otherwise God would not be God.

This biblical teaching has provoked countless misunderstandings in the lives of Christians. As a result, their message to the world has been frequently confusing and ineffective. The consequences flowing from the rule of the principalities and powers that we help to bring into being and sustain by our daily-life activities are a plunging into evil and death, and thus a going against God's will, which desires life and the good. We know that life and the good will triumph, but in our daily lives we often see the exact opposite. If we understand how we are ruled by the principalities and powers, our lives may be less contradictory. For example, when his people desired a government headed by a king, God gave them a dire warning of what would happen. When the people insisted, the resulting government could hardly be considered an expression of God's will. Similarly, Christians have been endlessly confused as to whether to obey God or to obey the state, for example when the latter used infant baptism for civic and legal purposes, or when it conscripted Christian men. Countless

Christians have thanked God when events in their lives turned in their favour and questioned him when they did not, as if God were micro-managing everything done by his creatures in violation of his desire to set them free and thus restore their ability to love. We will return to these matters. For now, it is important to understand that everything we do operates within God's will, which it cannot alter in any way. Nor can we in any way call into question God's work of reconciling himself with humanity.

This also explains why, from the opening chapters of Genesis onward, the first and second testaments distrust the evidence of what we see around us. It is the world we create by symbolically appropriating God's creation, which is ruled over by the principalities and powers. Hidden within and behind it, as it were, is God's work of reconciliation. Consequently, Christians must decide whether they will live by what appears self-evident according to the world around them or they will live by faith that discerns God's hidden rule, which expresses his will for reconciliation. In other words, we must live either by serving the false gods through religions and moralities or by serving the living God through love and freedom.

Regardless of what happens in God's creation that is within time, and regardless of what happens to the fabrics of relationships woven by each and every group and society, it will not change God's being God. It also means that there can be nothing beyond God or above him to which he is subject. Hence, when God declares that this or that is justice, that is what it is. The same is true for freedom, love, peace, redemption, and reconciliation. It is important not to misinterpret the implications. It is not a matter of nothing being powerful or influential enough that it can affect God. We are not talking about a power struggle. On the contrary, God always reveals himself as the One who liberates us because he loves us, and who never uses his unlimited power to force his way. He always warns us of the consequences of what we do, given that we are creatures living in his creation. Consequently, our freedom is within his freedom, our love is within his love, our justice is within his justice, and our peace is within his peace. This was harmoniously the case in the Garden of Eden as a communion of love, and it is still the case following our break with him, but each group and society has sought to name itself and thus give its own significance to freedom, love, justice, peace, and so on. For example, within the Garden of Eden, humanity's responsibility was within God's. When the communion of love was broken, God attempted to make humanity take responsibility for itself – which it refused to do.

Consequently, humanity's break with God meant that the total fabric of relationships comprising the fabrics of each and everyone's lives was no longer enveloped in God's being the only Living One. It thus became open ended and vulnerable to relativism, nihilism, and anomie, leading to chaos and nothingness. It plunged humanity into evil and death as a consequence of humanity's being separated from the only Living One. However, the separation was never complete. Within humanity there was always a faithful remnant that, through the Spirit, maintained a kind of "umbilical cord" with Life.

If Christians are to responsibly act on their calling to render a service to God, we must be *in* the world but not *of* the world. To be in this world requires that we understand how all of humanity, including ourselves, is enslaved to the principalities and powers, which, according to the first and second testaments, include the demonic powers, the satanic powers, the prince of lies, the prince of this world, Mammon, the three riders of the Apocalypse (which accompany God's Word), and the city. Without understanding the depth of our enslavement to them, we will not know from what we are being liberated, and we will be unable to tell others that, out of love, they are being saved from this enslavement. If we do not use this revelation as a lamp to guide our feet in this dark world, it will remain a set of revealed abstractions that will have little concrete meaning in our lives. Worse, it can make us complicit in turning the gospel into a religion and morality.[15] The remainder of this chapter is devoted to a study of the principalities and powers as they rule over our contemporary societies.

The Demonic Powers

We have discussed how God began his creation by dividing and separating light from darkness, the sky from the waters, the land from the waters, and all of this from an abundance of differentiated life forms everywhere in the water, land, and sky.[16] His work of creation ended with humanity, which would represent him in his creation, and humanity would rule over it by the human word that was developed by listening to God's Word. In sum, God's division and separation in his work of creation led to the communion of love in the Garden of Eden.

Following humanity's break with God and the confusion of its language, each group and society continued to name itself. It did so by making its own sense of, its own way of, and its own benchmarks for living in its own world, and thereby developed a language and culture.

This human work depended fundamentally on symbolization, which began by dividing, separating, and reintegrating everything through processes of differentiation and integration.[17] However, this dividing and separating gave rise to the opposite of a communion of love. The human world had to be integrated by a sacred and myths that alienated a group or society in its commitment to false gods, to which it responded not in freedom but out of necessity through religions and moralities. As noted, the letter of James refers to this world as one of absolute evil and iniquity, created by people listening to language. This is hardly an exaggeration. In its separation from God, humanity's flesh became evil, and the works of the flesh created a world of enslavement by many powers. It became the complete opposite of everything God had intended and loved.

Moreover, within this human world appropriated from God's creation, all manner of additional divisions and separations occurred as a result of each group and society naming itself. Since these names were mutually exclusive as lived truths, humanity was divided into competing groups and societies. Within them were socio-economic divisions based on relationships of power, exploitation, domination, and exclusion. Every social relationship became subject to a play of forces.

In our Bibles the devil represents all human actions and decisions that undo God's work of creation by establishing and evolving human life and a world that are the diametrical opposite of the communion of love in the Garden of Eden. These actions include all works that divide God from humanity, and human beings from one another, thus setting individuals, groups, and nations against one another and exploiting the world by means of power and domination. As noted, it is important not to personify the devil. Human life enslaved by the flesh and driven by coveting is in the grip of a demonic spirit, much like the ways in which a group or society during one of its historical epochs manifests its enslavement to the spirit of that age.

Once again, from a social and historical perspective, an iconoclastic examination of what is happening to individual and collective human life that is possessed by a sacred and myths (represented as the gods ruling over this life) converges with a great deal that is revealed by our Bibles. Everything that groups and societies accomplish by means of symbolization, experience, and culture is contrary to humility, love, and non-power. Again, by looking at any human culture, we can learn a great deal about the opposite of the revelation. However, this is as far as we can go with a social and historical perspective. The revelation goes much further by showing that this destruction of life is the direct consequence of humanity's breaking with the only Living One and thus no longer living within his freedom, love, justice, and peace. Consequently, cultural values always produce the exact opposite whenever a group or society chooses evil and death over life and the good.

To avoid theological truisms, it is important to examine how our societies unleash demonic forces on the world by naming themselves. Despite the participation of contemporary societies in the building of a universal technical order, they continue to depend on a symbolic language and culture to allow babies and children to grow up as members of a symbolic species. Babies and toddlers begin by dividing, separating, and then integrating everything in their experience in order to get a grip on their lives in the world. Despite high levels of de-symbolization in their cultures, this comprehension continues to be possible. Moreover, adults can still make some sense of expressions such as *living a life* or *living in a world*, and that all of this contributes to the collective life of our society and its making of a history. As adults we can still appreciate that babies and toddlers live lives, and we talk to them accordingly, which is utterly important.

As noted in the introduction, when toddlers begin to make sense of vocal signs by listening to language, they develop a double referencing system. It marks the beginning of the division between what is real and what is true in their lives. They also encounter a stream of image-based experiences that have a considerable de-symbolizing influence on their development as members of a symbolic species.[18] This encounter prepares the way for the development of a triple referencing system, which divides what is true in their lives. On the one hand, there is an ongoing development of everything related to language and culture, and, on the other hand, there is a parallel development of everything that has been separated from experience and culture.[19] This latter development includes exposure to image-words, image language, the domains of television and computer screens, and eventually the domains of cell phones and disciplines. All associated experiences are characterized by deep divisions. The customary division between foreground and background according to the way in which children direct their attention becomes discontinuous when screens are involved. The foreground will have the architecture of what is real, while the background will continue to have the architecture of what is true in their lives even when it is highly de-symbolized. Superimposed on this division may be another division, where what appears on a screen is arranged in a foreground and a background as well. The metaconscious knowledge that is built up with these kinds of experiences is no longer related to the metaconscious knowledge that is associated with the living of one's life in the world as a member of a symbolic species. The new metaconscious knowledge is associated with a disembodied life that is related to what is real and what is separated from experience and culture. Consequently, the metaconscious knowledge built up in the brain-minds of children that corresponds to the developments under consideration is discontinuous with the metaconscious knowledge built up from their symbolized experiences of living in the world. As a result, the accepted distinction between their episodic and semantic memories becomes more complex.

These deep discontinuities that develop in the lives of children continue into adulthood. Nevertheless, we can continue to live them to some extent because of our secular sacred and myths. The sacred of technique and the nation-state, and the myths of science and history, together transform these discontinuities into something that is normal and desirable.[20] After all, if there are no limits to discipline-based scientific knowing, technical doing, and political organizing, then the parallel ways embedded in experience and cultures, even when highly de-symbolized, must be lived as being purely personal and subjective and thus of little or no value to a way of life entirely based on discipline-based approaches. Moreover, living these parallel ways makes it possible to "live" the experiences of domains as if they alone implied a reliable vantage point and perspective on our lives and the world, even though they can have neither because we cannot live embodied lives in these domains; we can only enter into them via our scientific, technical, or mathematical imaginations. Consequently, our present secular sacred and myths make our disembodied lives more real and valuable than the embodied life lived by symbolization, language, and culture. Moreover, the "normality" of this disembodied life completely transforms our participation, commitment, and exercise of freedom.[21]

If we wish to belong, if we desire to make a useful contribution to our way of life, and if we wish to live by its meanings, values, and orientations, we will have no choice but to suppress to the best of our ability what remains of ourselves as members of a symbolic species. Doing so would be impossible unless anything that was radically other was made unliveable and unimaginable by our secular sacred and myths. For example, when politicians, economists, and social scientists speak of our becoming knowledge workers in a new knowledge economy, they are implying that we would be making a greater use of some of the gains that we have made thanks to discipline-based approaches. However, they fail to understand that this requires our relinquishing more and more of what has made us human as members of a symbolic species. Our gradually becoming disembodied *homo informaticus* appears to be accompanied by significant learning disabilities, mental disorders, and new forms of mental illness.[22] It is too early to know whether this is transitory as humanity adapts more fully to the new life milieu of technique, but for now the growing incidence of mental disorders in our university students is deeply troubling. This is equally true for other disorders that appear to affect negatively our ability to maintain social relationships. Some children are even acknowledging that face-to-face relationships make them uncomfortable. In sum, the evolving relationship between technique and culture in a life milieu of our own making continues to rely on symbolization, language, and culture, but in the context of domains these are subjected to unprecedented levels of de-symbolization. This has given rise to very different forms of metaconscious knowledge and thus to intuitions of an emerging new humanity, but many of the existing accounts are highly contradictory and selective in what they consider. Very few include a discussion of the possibility of our enslavement to new secular myths.

Despite unprecedented levels of de-symbolization, humanity continues to make sense of and live in the world by dividing, separating, and reintegrating, as it did in the two previous life milieux. Much of this now occurs by means of discipline-based approaches that dominate symbolization, experience, and culture everywhere in contemporary ways of life. For example, discipline-based approaches have permitted these ways of life to penetrate more deeply into matter, life, our knowing, and our doing, as manifested by nanotechnology, biotechnology, and information technology. Like all other branches of technique, these approaches are spectacularly successful in increasing our powers over everything, but they exact a heavy price of incompatibility with everything else. Nanotechnology will create an entirely new frontier of pollution because the biosphere has no functions, processes, and cycles for dealing with nanoparticles. Biotechnology has opened up a new frontier of polluting the DNA pool, with as yet unimaginable consequences. Information technology is "polluting" our being as a symbolic species with a variety of developments that are separated from experience and culture, thus producing all manner of new tensions in our lives.

As interpreted from the perspective of division and separation, discipline-based approaches to knowing and doing represent the ultimate of what can be accomplished by means of de-symbolization. These approaches amount to the re-engineering of everything. What I mean by this is that everything is dealt with as if it had the architecture of classical or information machines and of the systems built up with them. From a scientific perspective, discipline-based approaches imply that whatever they study or improve has an architecture that can be expressed in terms of the principles of non-contradiction, separability, closed definitions, measurability (including quantification and possible mathematical representation), and a simple complexity. It is the diametrical opposite of the architecture of everything living, in which the whole of an organism is enfolded into each cell by means of the DNA. This gives rise to a variety of relationships that simply cannot occur in classical or information machines. In a symbolic species this biological enfolding is complemented by a dialectical enfolding by which the brain becomes the brain-mind that enfolds a person's life, collective identity, and defining cultural myths into each moment of that life. In re-engineering everything, we are gambling that whatever discipline-based approaches cannot know or do will matter very little for the future of humanity and this planet. Proceeding as if this were the case is becoming increasingly irresponsible, since the evidence shows that most of our deep structural crises of an economic, social, political, legal, and environmental character are the direct consequence of "collisions" between whatever has been made more efficient and powerful and everything else – with which it is no longer compatible. These collisions can be directly attributed to making everything as efficient and powerful as possible by internally transforming received inputs into the greatest desired outputs by means of the latest discipline-based approaches, as if the architecture of biological and cultural life were that of reality. Moreover, discipline-based approaches will never be able to offer humanity the enormous benefits of a secular way of life; they have merely exchanged a traditional collective identity and defining cultural commitments for their secular equivalents, which superimpose reification on alienation.

Consider mathematical modelling and computer-based simulation as a key example of what is happening. We tend to forget that the rapid growth of mathematical modelling during the Second World War took place in a unique context of killing or being killed, where efficiency and power were all important and the broader implications were ignored out of necessity. During peacetime the techniques of operations research began to diffuse into a great many areas, and today we find them everywhere. They tend to work very well within a technical system that has the architecture of reality, but they produce all manner of difficulties when applied to anything in which human beings and social structures play a significant role.[23] The growing necessity of operations research is rooted in our creating technical systems of such complexity that participants can no longer grasp them intellectually by means of symbolization, experience, and culture. In other words, we have entered into a positive-feedback system. Discipline-based approaches diffused rapidly in areas where the limitations of symbolization, experience, and culture became evident, as in the chemical and electrical industries. Their immense success in areas where they could be used with scientific validity led to their use in other areas where this validity did not hold. All kinds of difficulties occurred, to which new techniques were applied, and so on. We have now created entities on such a scale that we have little choice but to turn to these kinds of approaches, because the alternate cultural ones cannot grasp intellectually what is happening. Moreover, the mesmerizing performance and power is instant, while the effects take some time to manifest themselves. In addition, the psychopathic character of the system of technique has largely gone unnoticed. No government or senior executive can resist the promise of an even greater efficiency and power if only the next step is taken.[24] Our secular gods must be served and the necessary sacrifices made. Again, there is nothing new under the sun.

The more the life milieu of technique advances, the more human beings will be turned into human resources for the system of technique, acting as the disembodied peripheral devices that connect complex technical systems to their non-technical surroundings. The possibility of a liveable future that can be sustained by the biosphere is not threatened by our technical systems taking over, phasing us out, and starting their own "history." The danger is most likely going to come by our permanently tipping the balance between "people changing technique" and "technique changing people" in favour of the latter, thereby remaking ourselves in the image of our technical works. For a growing number of practitioners in certain technical disciplines, this appears desirable, a future that ought to happen, but I hope that some believing Jews and Christians will discern the danger and wake up from their slumbers.

As explained in the introduction, the practitioners of technical disciplines are suspended in a triple abstraction, which makes it completely impossible to deal with human life in the world *as life*. They can only deal with life one category of phenomena at a time, whether or not this is scientifically and technically justifiable. It is here that their secular religious commitments become as plain as day to those who understand the limits of discipline-based approaches. Without such commitments, it would be self-evident to use the discipline-based approaches where they are scientifically and technically valid and to develop others where they are not.[25] Until these limits become obvious to a great many people, that is, until we desacralize our secular religious commitments, a liveable and sustainable future is completely out of the question. By dividing and separating everything and lacking any acceptable equivalent to symbolization, experience, and culture, we have committed ourselves to a path of destruction that is unprecedented in human history.

Where in all this are we to find the secular equivalent of the idols of the past? The simple answer is that idols are no longer required, because technique operates entirely within what is real in human life by excluding, to the greatest extent possible, what is true. Moreover, it is by techniques of all kinds and in the image of technique that we engineer what is portrayed as reality on the media. Our cultures have become so highly de-symbolized that they can no longer adequately sustain human life by giving it meaning, direction, and purpose. Cultures must be complemented by integration propaganda that, by means of images (and thus within what is real), shows us how we must live, how we must think and develop the most plausible opinions on everything, how to recognize the technical specialists we need for our lives, and so on.[26] Owing to the de-symbolization of our cultures, we are utterly dependent on and need this integration propaganda, and this need deeply bonds us to the building of the universal technical order. It gives us our collective identity and defining secular commitments.

Instead of building a civilization that utilizes approaches based on symbolization, experience, and culture for everything living, and approaches based on disciplines for everything technical, we have become possessed by our secular sacred and myths to the point that this obvious solution to many of our current difficulties remains something that is radically other and thus impossible to take seriously. If we persist in the cult of the fact, the cult of efficiency, the cult of economic growth, the cult of the democratic state, and the cult of disembodied life (individual and collective), we will subject ourselves to the same kinds of results that humanity has always experienced in serving its gods.[27] Whether these gods have taken on traditional or secular forms makes no difference whatsoever. To avoid any misunderstandings, it must be emphasized that the traditional approaches based on symbolization, experience, and culture had their own limits, collective identities, and defining cultural commitments, as do our discipline-based approaches. In other words, it is ultimately a question of desacralization that needs to take place to make apparent the limits of both approaches. In human history this kind of desacralization tends to come about towards the end of a historical epoch, or with attempts to live the first three "words" of the Decalogue. Since there is no foreseeable end to the current historical epoch of our civilization, believing Jews and Christians who understand these first three words (which is impossible without the Spirit and a Jewish or Christian defining commitment) have their work cut out for themselves. A great deal could depend on it. It would involve living the potential complementarity between the two kinds of approaches because the strengths and weaknesses of each one are the diametrical opposites of those of the other. If this fails, the members of our civilization will continue to be possessed by the demons of their own making.[28]

From the perspective of the revelation, what we are discussing is the limits of our being creatures within the limits of a creation, all depending on our Maker. Consequently, nothing can be intellectually grasped or responsibly dealt with as if it were autonomous, self-sufficient, and good in itself. Doing so necessitates treating it as a god by means of religious attitudes that block out its limitations. Even the most comprehensive effort of symbolization cannot encompass the entire interrelatedness of the creation – and certainly not its dependence on its Maker. Whatever has been symbolically interrelated will necessarily remain open ended and thus vulnerable to relativism, nihilism, and anomie on the way to nothingness. Therefore, any symbolization no longer enveloped by the Spirit of our Maker has always done and continues to do the only thing possible: summing up the individual and collective experience of a group or society by means of a sacred and myths and thus absolutizing it as the only possible point of reference, essentially symbolizing the unknown as an extension of the known and lived. In this way, the sacred and myths are the all in all as a collective identity and its defining commitments, outside of which nothing can be lived or be taken seriously by our imagination and intellect. There is no possibility that a new discovery or lived situation could call everything in the life of a community into question. What this implies is that a group or society is provided with meaning, direction, and purpose by its own collective experience. Given our finitude, this is impossible in the long term. It is for this reason that we have spoken of a cultural shield. Anything that is radically other can penetrate through that shield only if it can receive some kind of meaning, direction, and purpose that conforms to the collective identity and its defining commitments. Nevertheless, doing so will involve "stretching" them to a point where some members of the community may intuit metaconsciously that things do not quite fit. When this situation snowballs, the end of an epoch in the history of a group or society may be in sight.

As we have attempted to show, the same is true when a revelation from a transcendent God penetrates this cultural shield. Without the intervention of the Spirit, the revelation would quickly be turned into a religion and morality of the kind that all cultures have created for themselves in their separation from God. In this way, God's ways are appropriated once again by the elimination of what is radically other through counter-transference reactions – unless we ask for and await his wisdom.

There is an important additional dimension to this. In ordering each of its experiences in relation to all the others to create a culture as its body of experience, a group or society discovers the meaning and value of everything for its life. The resulting interdependence of all values may be imagined as a kind of hierarchy whose summit symbolizes the most valuable element in the life of the group or society, beyond which nothing more valuable can be imagined or lived on the basis of the group's body of collective experience. When something more valuable appears to gradually emerge, everything needs to be reordered in accordance with it, which amounts to a process of desacralization and resacralization.[29] Consequently, the meaning and value of everything in the life of the group or society remains true only as long as new experiences confirm its collective experience. Once a new sacred and myths are established at the beginning of a new epoch in its history, it becomes apparent that all previous meanings and values were false relative to their successors. Similarly, all current meanings and values will one day turn out to be false relative to their successors. Jointly, all these meanings and values will have given a false purpose and orientation to human life relative to what comes after. Hence, all groups and societies move from one body of collective experience to another without ever achieving any lasting meaning, purpose, and direction.

As a consequence, the limitations of symbolization, language, and culture, as well as those of discipline-based approaches and de-symbolized cultures, complemented by integration propaganda, will be permanent features of any group or society whose body of collective experience is necessarily finite and thus dependent on a sacred and myths to cover over its finitude and nothingness. Only if a group or society were itself a god would it have no need of a sacred and myths. It would then have an unlimited life within itself, an unlimited independence, and its own claim on everything that is good. Failing such god-like qualities, the life of any group or society will necessarily be an alienated and possibly also a reified one.

The accomplishment of our civilization is the creation of an illusion that our finitude and nothingness have disappeared without any reliance on gods and idols. Since this is based on proceeding as if there were no architecture of enfolding or of dialectical enfolding, the local technique-based connectedness has a simple complexity. This complexity includes flows of matter, energy, their composites, labour (embedded in or separated from experience and culture), capital, and discipline-based knowledge (scientific or technical). Hence, each node in this technique-based connectedness with the architecture of reality may be represented as an autonomous domain within which we only need to occupy ourselves with the transformation of the received inputs into the desired outputs that we seek to augment. Moreover, this transformation can be organized according to the same architecture, which makes it possible for it to be based on repetition rather than on the adaptation and evolution required for life. The only connectedness we need to be concerned about is how this domain received its inputs from others, and how the desired outputs will be transferred to another domain. Anything else is of no concern whatsoever. Discipline-based approaches thus neglect everything outside of the domain under consideration other than the inputs received and the desired outputs produced. That there are human lives, groups, societies, ecosystems, and a biosphere beyond this domain has absolutely no effect whatsoever on the workings of discipline-based approaches.[30]

In sum, discipline-based science and technique intellectually and practically divide and separate everything they touch into autonomous domains beyond which nothing has any influence. It is the ultimate human work of undoing what has always been at the very centre of the adaptation and evolution of all life, including human life, according to the way it was related to and dependent on everything else. This relatedness is the expression of the finitude and creature-like architecture of everything. Nothing could be autonomous in this relatedness unless it were sacralized and treated as a god.

Symbolization may thus be regarded as a strategy of making the most possible use of context, while discipline-based approaches may be regarded as based on a minimal consideration of context. For these reasons human history and the evolution of the biosphere have fundamentally changed in character and direction in the course of the twentieth century, when humanity began to build a universal technical order. As I have attempted to show, the relationship between technique and culture has changed almost everything. For example, we are losing ground in having adequate vocabularies in our languages to grasp intellectually what is happening to us and our world. We are increasingly living as if a disembodied life in relation to the discipline-based domains and the screen-based domains that connect us through the internet could truly satisfy us. Some even hope for an eternal digital life! We have created a whole new range of secular cults by which we bow down to our limitless accomplishments. Possibly the most tragic aspect of it all is that we are becoming the very resources and peripheral devices for the socio-technical systems we are building, thus superimposing reification on alienation. Any study of the relationship between technique and culture shows that we are gambling with our future as a symbolic species. We are gambling with the possibility of creating liveable and sustainable ways of life. In sum, our works of division and separation are capable of slicing through every fabric of relationships essential to all life. Never before has any civilization imagined a future by imitating (dead) technical machines, processes, and systems. We have made life into the all-pervasive externality of our discipline-based approaches to knowing and doing – that is, non-life.

Before my reader has enough and closes this book as something that is too unbearably pessimistic, deterministic, Calvinistic, or generally too hard to take, may I point out that it is the very opposite of my intention. From my diagnosis comes a prescription. Modest beginnings in engineering, management, and the regulation of technology have been proposed towards creating a synergy between re-symbolization and discipline-based approaches.[31] Similarly, university reforms have been proposed that would do the same kind of thing beyond my own original intellectual and professional "backyard."[32] Suggestions of how to overcome the cult of the fact, the cult of efficiency, the cult of economic growth, and the cult of individual and collective disembodied life have been based on a diagnosis of what is happening in the corresponding areas of human endeavour.[33] At one point, these proposals were being given serious consideration by the Province of Ontario and the federal government of Canada. There is thus no need whatsoever to throw up our collective hands in defeat. We could begin an intellectual and technical conversion tomorrow. However, unlike Marx, I do not promise a secular paradise but simply suggest concrete strategies based on what works and what does not, which could greatly reduce the harm we are doing to ourselves, to others, and to other life forms and the planet. These strategies could replace the current ones, which are pushing largely preventable harm to its extreme limit as a consequence of our intellectual tunnel vision that limits everything to one domain at a time.

If we place this in the context of God's Word, there is an obvious convergence between the human work of division and separation, which we have examined from a social and historical perspective, and what is referred to as the demonic in the revelation. From a social and historical perspective, it is clear that when groups and societies recognize that their members are creatures who neither individually nor collectively have life within them and thus depend on their Maker, there is no need for a sacred and myths in a culture. This need came about as a consequence of humanity's break with God. As a symbolic species, we cannot live without symbolization, experience, and culture, but believing Jews and Christians appear to be generally unaware of how deeply we are implicated in the human work of division and separation that is so destructive of life. Hopefully, this reflection will help us to take a more seriously the texts that speak of the devil and the demonic in human life.

Of course, it suits us much better to interpret the demonic in terms of the images and fantasies of our cultures, which have nothing whatsoever in common with the revelation. They get us off the hook because all the demons poking their forks into the damned are not of our own making. A genuine conversion experience includes a struggle to transform the demonic in our lives as we learn to comprehend the first three words of the Decalogue. We are once again back to relationships of love that do not permit any dualism. We must be fully "yes" to our God as he is to us, and we must treat our neighbour accordingly.

There is an additional component to the demonic that is uniquely Christian. It is rooted in a number of theologies and interpretations that rain down from many pulpits. They divide humanity into the saved and the damned. It may be well for Christians to reread Romans 9–12, which (astonishingly) has been at the root of the nonsense of predestination and double predestination.[34] How could people like John Calvin and his followers not understand what Paul says so plainly? In the

Spirit he is deeply troubled that his fellow Jews do not believe (Romans 9:1–5). Paul speaks in the way that Jesus Christ spoke, with infinite compassion for those who do not believe. He is even willing to be cut off from Christ for the sake of his people. What has always disturbed me, from my teenage years on, is how easily many priests and pastors can speak of those who do not believe and essentially damn them without the slightest trace of compassion. I cannot understand how Calvin, who was generally very careful, could take the text that follows Paul's declaration out of this context to show that God is not really God, his love is not for everyone, Jesus Christ was not the absolute sacrifice demanded by the law, and so on. Worse, this interpretation implicitly endows humanity with the capacity to decide to accept or reject God's grace and God's pardon as if, following the break with him, humanity continued to be able to discern life and the good without entirely depending on the Spirit. Moreover, humanity is then capable of limiting God's love, grace, pardon, and redemption. If humanity has this power, God is not God. Despite the warnings against judging others, the majority of the Christian community has taken upon itself to judge the overwhelming majority of humanity. These people, however, are their neighbours, whom God loves as much as he loves them. However, liberalism forgets that God reveals himself as God, which means that his revelation cannot be limited. In one way or another, the limitless love of God keeps seeking us, and even the hardest of hearts will one day come to recognize that this love is the best thing that ever happened to them. However, by remaking Christianity into a religion and morality, all this is unthinkable; religion turns it into a justification that those who believe are set apart as being the only ones loved by God, as opposed to having been set apart for a task they appear no longer to understand.

Of course, I do not expect to change anyone's mind on this subject in a few lines. But there is no doubt in my mind that if Calvin had carefully read Romans 9–11 and the book of Revelation, he would have changed his mind on his nonsense of predestination. His followers should have noted that these texts were not adequately integrated into his overall understanding, and they should have held themselves accountable for not doing so. I cannot even begin to imagine how much suffering could have been prevented for Christians whose whole lives were deeply affected by this misguided interpretation of the gospel. All of us are wheat and tares, yeast and dough, and light and dark. What is predestined for destruction is the flesh and the demonic within us. Some will be saved even though, like gold being passed through the fire for purification, nothing else will remain. We have completely turned things around: we can never *have* (i.e., *own*) faith. It is a gift from God that is free for the asking, with the result that faith has us. It can never be the other way around, as with anything in God's creation.[35]

We have been discussing a particular instance of a much more widespread occurrence of the demonic within the Christian community, related to the division and separation of the Word. There is the constant threat of a temptation to emphasize certain texts and to play down others in order to justify and legitimate divisions within the Christian community. Every theological system or statement of doctrine is necessarily false because it seeks to permanently reconstruct the Word by works of division and separation. I am not speaking of our experiences in which specific passages speak to us much more strongly than do others, particularly during certain times. If we remain open to the Spirit, we can in obedience open ourselves up to struggling with passages that have been obscure or seemed not to speak to us. We must also remain open to fellow believers' sharing their perspectives with us. In other words, the communion of saints remains a vital and dynamic interplay of the limitations we all have, and we can help one another to come to a fuller and more mature understanding of the Word. However, once closed theological or philosophical systems are constructed, our dependence on the Spirit and fellow believers becomes obscured, and membership in a denomination becomes a kind of intellectual participation in these theological constructions. It shuts us into religious cages, with disastrous consequences for the body of believers and the kingdom of heaven. I recognize that every religious institution has a need to reconstruct God's Word in its image in order to name itself, but this does not legitimate this demonic work. Obeying a necessity will always be contrary to living in the freedom made possible by the love of God.

The book of Revelation appears to hint that there may well be much more to the demonic than what I have suggested. If that is the case, it is important to remember that this hint appears only at the very end of the Bible in the context of the assurance that the total and complete victory has been won and that only a few details remain to be settled. As noted, the very structure and organization of the book of Revelation symbolizes the complete and total reconciliation of God and humanity, with the implication that if there is more to the demonic, it is of no consequence whatsoever to our lives and our responsibilities because our God is fully "yes" to us in his love. There can be no hidden agenda or details of any kind that could make a decisive difference. We are thus learning something more about relationships of love. We may be a little truer because there is no need to veil anything by a false awareness of ourselves and the world. Love requires that everything is included. Hence, the more we trust God's love, the more we can liberate ourselves from our dependence on and commitment to our collective identity and defining secular myths. It engages a struggle to gradually weaken our metaconscious "blackout" in order to become more aware of ourselves and the world; such awareness is desperately needed in order to face the demonic in the spirit of our age.

The Satanic Powers

Just as the demonic designates all human acts of division, separation, and disordering that are destructive to the relationships within humanity and between it and God, so the satanic designates all acts of accusation. This satanic power includes all acts of self-justification and legitimation, because these necessarily involve a denial of responsibility by transferring it to others and to God.

The Jewish and Christian Bibles make it very clear that God never accuses anyone. Following humanity's break with him, human responsibility was no longer within God's responsibility. God attempted to make humanity responsible by asking where it was and what it had done. God's action made humanity recognize that it could not answer these questions without accusing itself, and that it refused to do. As a way out, the man and the woman accused one another and implicated God as well, but God never accused anyone. Humanity continued to make its own decisions without backing down, with the result that to this day God's questions remain unanswered. A spirit of accusation was unleashed that would occupy the gap that had opened up between God and humanity and that would rule "from above" throughout human history.

Following the break with God, people could no longer be fully "yes" to one another and to their God. There would always be the suspicion that God or others did not fully mean what they said or that something crucial was being held back. It was impossible to live with this brokenness. People needed to justify themselves, and there was no way of doing so than by accusing the other and God. Individually and collectively, the members of each group or society did so as part of naming themselves. Their absolutized body of collective experience, which had created its collective activity and defining cultural or secular commitments, placed the group within its own life and the good and thus all other groups and societies within evil and death. The only responsibility that remained to a group or society was to deal with those members who violated its good and its way of life; this was done by means of its morality as well as its legal and religious institutions. The same happened to Israel when it refused to be directly ruled by God and demanded a king, but this unleashed the political and religious powers on itself. God made this consequence very clear in his warnings to his people (1 Samuel 8). The necessary self-justification of each group's and society's actions affected and permeated the way in which that group or society symbolized everything as it named itself through false meanings, values, and reference points that were anchored in its sacred and myths. In this way human life became possessed by a spirit of accusation, which ruled over it through the cultures by which groups and societies named themselves.

Before returning to our Bible, it is important to point out how its revelation regarding the demonic and satanic powers has been undermined by counter-transference reactions. By personifying these powers, we essentially create an independent party to which we can now attribute full responsibility, thus turning ourselves into unwilling victims of the powers. This distorts the revelation by bringing it a great deal closer to our own ways as shaped through our cultures. It makes the situation a little more bearable and liveable. However, the revelation is actually much more radical and decisive: all of us as members of humanity have unleashed and sustain the demonic and satanic powers that rule us. We do this by our acts of division, separation, disordering, accusation, and self-justification rooted in our collective identity and defining cultural or secular myths.

In the prologue to the book of Job, Satan approaches God with the suggestion that Job's love is due to the many blessings he has received from God. From what we have learned about our dependence as a symbolic species on language and culture, we may interpret this text as Job's person and life calling into question all the names that the groups and societies of the time had given themselves by evolving and adapting their collective bodies of experiences. The demonic and satanic spirits are thus fighting for their survival. If Job truly loves God, then these spirits are threatened with nothingness. God knows this very well, and he does not need to do anything; the spirits attempt to deal with Job as one who is radically other and thus a threat to them. There is absolutely nothing metaphysical occurring. We only need to read the endless discussions between Job and his friends to recognize that these spirits are nothing more nor less than the actions of the members of groups or societies anchored in a sacred and myths.

The letter of James rules out any other explanation. He admonishes his readers never to say that God is tempting them, because God cannot be tempted by evil, and he does not tempt anyone else. The reason follows immediately: everyone is tempted when they are enticed and dragged away by their own evil desires. Then, after desire has conceived, it gives birth to sin, and sin, when full grown, gives birth to death (James 1:13–15). These verses are an integral part of a discussion of the temptations experienced by Christians in relation to their love for Jesus Christ. We are back again at the exclusive character of relationships of love. If we love Jesus Christ more than something we covet, we will be able to resist pursuing it. For example, in the case of mammon, we need to decide whether or not we love our riches more than our Lord. Jesus warned us that we are bound to what we love, and hence we will be either where he is or where our wealth is. In passing, it must be noted that the words in the Lord's Prayer usually translated as "do not lead us into temptation" are a distortion. A more literal translation would be "do not make it possible for us to penetrate into our temptations." The dilemma of our translators is clear, but surely that is not sufficient reason to turn the meaning of a text into its opposite in order to make good English out of it.

In other words, whenever we are tempted by something or someone, we are really discovering who or what we love most in our life. Intellectually we may know this very well, but living it involves our entire person and our life. We constantly fail to respond to God's love. In the short term it is often much easier to maintain our self-respect and justify our actions than to admit that once more we have disappointed the love of our Father. For those who do not yet know that they are loved by God and have been fully pardoned, the course of self-justification and blaming others is usually a necessity from which they can rarely escape.

There is a strong parallel between the prologue in the book of Job and the summation of the temptations experienced by Jesus during his life that we find near the beginning of three of the gospels. Once again, the spirit of accusation implied in the culture of every group or society, including Israel, was threatened by Jesus's love for his Father and his fellow creatures. His love threatened everything that humanity had done, and would continue to do, by all the societies naming themselves. I am inventing nothing. In the central part of the book of Revelation that is marked by the seven trumpets, chapter 12 reveals the woman who was pregnant and ready to give birth. She was confronted by the dragon who was prepared to devour the child from the moment it was born. From the perspective of heaven, a battle ensued between the child and the dragon, as had been announced in the book of Genesis.

Let us briefly consider the summation of all the temptations that humanity would hurl at Jesus during his life, as found in Matthew 4:1–11. This account refers to the temptations of demonic power until, following the third temptation, Jesus dismisses this power by telling Satan to be gone, after which the text tells us that the devil left him. In the same vein, in Matthew 16:21–3, Jesus addressed Peter as Satan in response to his rebuking of Jesus for having informed his disciples that he needed to go to Jerusalem to suffer, to be killed, and to be raised up on the third day. Peter responded: "God forbid, Lord, this shall never happen to you." Jesus replied: "Get behind me, Satan; you are a hindrance to me for you are not on the side of God but of people." In both these situations, the demonic spirit sought to divide and separate Jesus from God and his disciples. Doing so was integral to the implicit accusation that Jesus was not using any means of power available to him in order to advance his ministry as effectively and rapidly as possible. What if he had died of starvation as a consequence of refusing to make bread for himself? Why would he not use political power to establish his reign over the whole world, since this is what he had come to do? Why would he not speed up things and shorten the suffering of humanity by providing God with the earliest possible opportunity to show that he was indeed the Messiah? Why would he not postpone being killed in Jerusalem, because his ministry had just barely begun? All this and much more were tests of who or what Jesus really loved. In this manner Jesus experienced both the demonic spirit of division and separation and the satanic spirit of accusation at the same time. The two frequently overlap and interpenetrate. As relationships of love are turned into relationships of power, domination, conquest, and exclusion, we must either accept full responsibility or justify ourselves by transferring the responsibility to others in acts of accusation.

From a social and historical perspective, the building of the universal technical order during our age integrates the demonic and satanic powers in new ways. (The evidence for this conclusion comes from my five-volume analysis of the relationship between technique and culture, which I will not repeat here.) Developments in North America are a humbling reminder of our enslavement to the powers acting in our lives and our world. Particularly in the history of the United States, wave after wave of immigrants escaping difficult economic, political, and religious conditions came to a land of new beginnings that was full of promise because of its potential to fulfil their hopes and aspirations. For the Christian groups among them, comparisons to a new kind of exodus to build Christian communities and a God-fearing nation proved irresistible. At the time, the immigrants' economic, political, and religious ambitions were quickly and deeply plunged into all manner of contradictions. Their freedom meant the enslavement of the native peoples. Their working together frequently involved leaving behind cultural differences by participating in a new and growing technology that was built not on craft embedded in experience and culture but on interchangeable parts, assembly lines, and a great deal else. This was exemplified by the Fordist-Taylorist system of production, which quickly made the United States the leading technical power in the world. There was also a complex reciprocal interaction between agricultural development and industrialization. For a host of reasons, in agriculture and industry the dependence of technology on experience and culture was minimized to the greatest extent possible. These developments received an enormous boost from the efforts in support of the Second World War, following which they spread into American society. The discipline-based approaches that had been developed in Germany diffused rapidly. Such changes put enormous de-symbolizing pressures on the cultures of the immigrants, which in turn facilitated the building of a unique American way of life.

The de-symbolization of experience, language, and culture necessitated an ever-growing dependence on what we have referred to as integration propaganda – the bath of images into which the mass media plunged the American people and which collectively portrayed how life was to be lived.[36] At the same time, the growing effects of "technique changing people" resulted in an entirely new kind of dominant personality type, referred to as "other-directed."[37] This personality type essentially uses the organization of the brain-mind as a kind of symbolic radar to scan what everyone else is doing in order to "go with the flow." Consequently, other-directed people complement their dependence on culture with a dependence on image-based integration propaganda. Thanks to this dependence, the influence of the state and the large corporations increased enormously, even though it was contrary to traditional values. These institutions began to use the techniques of public relations to explain and justify their actions as an integral part of integration propaganda. This is but a snapshot of the many forces that have plunged American life into a host of contradictions that have to be made liveable for society.[38]

One of these contradictions was between the beliefs and values of the Christian and Jewish traditions and the powerful forces that were shaping American life. Of course, corporate America had an enormous influence on Christian America.[39] In many respects this influence was but a symptom of much deeper, underlying currents, which may be summed up as America's growing reliance on technique in parallel with a declining reliance on culture. In other words, corporate America would not have been nearly as successful were it not for the growing need of the American people for a moral and religious component within integration propaganda to replace what was being lost as a consequence of the de-symbolization of experience, language, and culture. The Jewish and Christian communities felt the pressure of a growing other-directedness of its young people, which led to the communities' adopting a statistical morality as well as public opinions on many subjects. Moreover, what was real in their lives was becoming much more important than what was true, with devastating consequences for the way in which these traditions had relied on the Word expressed and understood via the human word. Creative pastors and rabbis reached out to these young people, but any success in their attempts had to bow to the need to "translate" what had once been exclusively related to what was true in human life into what was real. In other words, on the grassroots level there was considerable experimentation in reaching young people by re-engineering the Christian and Jewish message into what was real for them. Supported by powerful counter-transference reactions, God and his Word were brought closer to what was real, with the very best of intentions.

An influential study of that time showed the results of all this "re-engineering": based on a great deal of evidence, Protestant and Catholic forms of Christianity as well as Judaism had become three forms of "the American way of life."[40] This study amply confirmed that Christianity and Judaism were being transformed by the emerging secular sacred and myths that, as Jacques Ellul showed, were beginning to possess the most industrially advanced nations.[41] The new sacred and myths led to the birth of a new secular political religion based on democracy.[42] It was becoming impossible for this secular political religion to coexist with the Christian and Jewish religious traditions, further adding to the need to "re-engineer" them. The evidence shows that, within the emerging collective identity and its defining secular myths, the secular political religion of democracy was dominating the American way of life in a Protestant, Catholic, or Jewish form.[43] This development is very difficult for non-Americans to understand. We must not forget that what really matters is how the American people lived it. We are not dealing with a world-view, a religious ideology, or an ontology. It was, as always, an absolutized body of collective experience that guided the nation and provided the American people with an overwhelming sense of unity despite their differences. This collective American identity and its defining secular commitments were able to sustain a strong sense of superiority over other people and serve as a benchmark of freedom and enterprise. It formed a framework for daily life, as cultures had once done. It had its beliefs, ideals, values, aspirations, and standards for conduct in which people had an unshakeable faith. In the eyes of the American people, no other nation had been able to establish or match the U.S. standards of freedom, goodness, and enterprise. When God was added to this mix, a religious spirit was unleashed that had no equal in the world because the other secular political religions had either disappeared or been decisively weakened. The statistics showing the opinions that American people have of themselves confirm this in great detail.[44]

In many respects the American way of life as expressed politically in the constitution, economically in free enterprise, and socially in a unique egalitarianism is a remarkable accomplishment of a highly culturally diverse people gathered from all over the earth who had no common culture and history. To the mix of contradictions in this American way of life, we need to add the sacred transgressions (the "anti-sacred") of technique by sexual intercourse and of the nation-state by social deviance.[45] Owing to its contradictions,[46] the American way of life can be lived very differently in the centre and the south from the way it is lived along the coasts. Almost every election shows this division. Nevertheless, the nation remains united in the belief that in its new world a new beginning has been made, and this conviction nurtures what is probably the most idealistic nation in the world.

The United States is an equally unparalleled self-righteous nation that, in its foreign policies, believes that its innocence and virtue must be defended against the corruption and godlessness of the remainder of the world. The American way of life, as a highly successful synthesis that is made possible by the re-engineering of its principal moral and religious traditions, has always emphasized lived deeds at the expense of intellectual creeds. In this manner the Jewish, Protestant, and Catholic traditions became Americanized as legitimate expressions of the American way of life, and Christianity and Judaism became the religions of democracy. Gradually, this way of life became more inclusive as other religious traditions were integrated.

The American way of life is possible because the various groups of American people, outside of their participation in churches, synagogues, and other places of worship, are largely undistinguishable in their daily-life behaviour. Everyone serves freedom in all spheres of human life through the secular political religion of democracy. Every religion that serves freedom can find its place within it. We must remember that this belief is based on the dominance of the other-directed personality living in mass societies that has accompanied industrialization, urbanization, and secularization everywhere. These developments make it almost impossible to practise Judaism or Christianity faithfully.

The American way of life has thus become a civic religion served by a variety of rituals such as the pledge of allegiance to the flag. It borrows Jewish and Christian values as well as Christian prayers and anthems. For many Americans, God stands right behind the president, in the way that he stood behind kings in the past. For them, the purpose of the nation and the ways of God are closely intertwined. The purpose of the nation must become the purpose of humanity. The gospel of democracy, with its political freedom and free enterprise, must be brought to all the nations in the world. This proselytization represents what Jacques Ellul has referred to as a false presence in the world.[47] We appear to have learned nothing from the experience of the Second World War, when priests, pastors, and rabbis accompanying the armies on all sides prayed to the same God for victory.

As with any religion (traditional or secular), democracy has its "heretics." They threaten the American way of life. Over time, they have included "godless" communists, socialists, tree-huggers, feminists, people with a "different" sexual orientation, liberals, ethnic or cultural minorities, and other nations with different cultures and values. However, this is but a symptom of a deeply embedded spirit of accusation of anything and everything that does not measure up to the American way of life. My own experience may be illustrative. I spent a year as a distinguished visiting professor at a Midwest engineering school. Before my arrival on campus the student newspapers were already ringing the alarm bell over the Canadian socialist who was coming to teach. When my public lectures quickly became popular, things went more smoothly. However, I found it practically impossible to teach a fourth-year seminar for engineering students about the social and environmental issues related to modern technology and its engineering. To the students, every issue was always black or white without any middle ground to allow respectful and informed discussions of very complex issues, which always indissociably linked the positive and negative effects on human lives, societies, and the biosphere. I was deeply troubled by this kind of polarization. It reminded me of what I had read regarding the effects of totalitarian propaganda on the populations of the nations engaged in the Second World War and in the totalitarian communist societies that followed. As a neighbour from the north, I had the feeling that I was looking into our own future. These attitudes are already emerging in western Canada and in some Jewish and Christian conservative groups in eastern Canada.

The spirit of accusation is also strongly present in the decisions of our courts. Our legal institutions find their legitimation and their reference points for pronouncing justice in the collective identity and defining secular myths of our society. They define what the courts take to be a "reasonable" person. In a society dominated by technique a reasonable person is very different from such a person in a society having a traditional collective identity and its defining cultural myths. For example, organic farmers are not reasonable if they refuse to take advantage of the latest agricultural techniques in a supposedly hungry world. An injured worker who refuses to undergo a highly risky operation is deemed to be unreasonable for refusing the benefits of the latest medical techniques. Any person who has serious concerns about the agreements that we are obligated to sign when we need a new operating system for our computer, a music system for our phone, and a software package for an application, for example, is simply excluded on the grounds of being unreasonable. I am inventing nothing; preliminary research has clearly unveiled these biases on the part of the courts.[48] Until now, funding for the completion of this important research has been refused. This is hardly surprising, because the only kind of expertise recognized by the courts is founded on discipline-based approaches. Such expertise is so lacking in context that it can be used by both the prosecution and the defence, for contrary purposes. It would be quite a challenge to have a court recognize the hidden biases of this expertise. Worse, being seen as an unreasonable person is but a small step from being seen as a kind of secular heretic.

The spirit of accusation has taken on unprecedented forms in our contemporary police forces. I could fill pages with personal examples even though I am a white person, highly educated, and live in the right part of town. During the last G20 summit meeting in Toronto my fellow citizens were treated like dissenters in totalitarian societies, with unprecedented brutality and a complete disrespect for democracy and human rights. Based on my own experiences, I no longer have any respect for the police. I know very well that there are some very good people working in these forces, but I also know that when these forces commit errors, they immediately resort to false accusations. When one of my children, during a period of unemployment, was contemplating joining the Royal Canadian Mounted Police, I asked her if she was willing to club, humiliate, and arrest me in the way the police did to others in recent events.

In conclusion, the demonic and satanic powers have merged in a new synthesis of technique. In the past, the symbolic cultures of groups and societies helped their members to resist deviance and crime. With the de-symbolization of all cultures by technique, however, we are increasingly creating societies in the grip of the spirit of accusation and litigation. We now require far more lawyers than practically any other professionals. All this is rooted in our building of a universal technical order of non-sense; that is, it is constructed with little or no reference to sense (cultural meanings and values).[49] Corporations have been granted the status of legal persons, with far-reaching consequences. If you or I behaved like they do, we would quite justly be classified as psychopaths or sociopaths.[50] The problem does not stop there. These corporations are in the grip of the spirit of technique, which, owing to its discipline-based organization, is in itself psychopathic in character.[51] The spirit of technique represents the historically unique combination of a demonic power and a satanic power, which externalizes and imposes so many difficulties on others that a growing number of institutions have learned that the best proactive approach is one of accusation. For example, SLAPP lawsuits (strategic legal action against public participation) are a typical example of suits that threaten even editors of scientific journals, who have done their due diligence in refereeing articles on controversial subjects. A lawsuit was brought against an editor-in-chief of a journal who had the courage to publish the first two volumes of a series documenting the health effects of wind farms on people – facts that the industry and governments had been denying for years. In a world that no longer makes much sense to people, actions of litigation are very tempting, and, judging by the advertising, it must be big business. Furthermore, many governments are aligning research funding more closely to their agendas, with the result that it is becoming almost impossible to find funding for a comprehensive examination of the many issues related to the use and application of discipline-based approaches and everything built up with them.

The entire "system" is closing up on all fronts. For believing Jews and Christians, these developments ought to have sounded many alarm bells. It means that our civilization acts as if the system were good in itself and self-sufficient in its regulation. This view is absurd, as any competent engineer knows. Anything in this creation regulates itself in relation to everything else, and the systems we bring into existence are no exception. To understand this point, think of a ship crossing an ocean. Without a compass, references to the stars, or satellites, the captain cannot make the necessary course corrections. If our collective identity and defining secular myths make unthinkable and unliveable anything that is radically other, we have essentially surrendered ourselves to the powers and forces that now rule our lives and our world. This surrendering has been going on for decades. We keep talking about an environmental crisis and a need for a more sustainable way of life, but nothing essential has changed in the engineering, management, and regulation of technology. No course corrections have been or will be made in the near future.

Some people think that the next generation of "green" technologies will solve the problems of today's generation, but this is the irresponsible naïveté of a "reasonable person" in the grip of a collective identity and its defining cultural myths. However, a faithful remnant within the Jewish and Christian communities who understand the fundamental importance of the first three words of the Decalogue may discern (at least in principle) that what we have brought into existence has been sacralized – thus we have been compelled to serve it with all our hearts and minds – and that this sacralization is the source of our enslavement and the eventual destruction of the planet. Their discernment represents another dimension of being yeast in the dough and salt in the food: to put ourselves between humanity and its course of destruction and death.

In churches we tend to hear that it is God who will bring the world to an end, but now, with the unprecedented powers we have unleashed, we can do it ourselves. We used to concern ourselves about the possibility of a total nuclear war, but with our current system we have the power to accomplish almost the same destruction, be it at a much slower rate. My reader may feel that I have far too much confidence in a faithful remnant who, by having a living relationship with a transcendent God, will be able to provide the necessary outside reference point to permit the desacralization of what holds us captive, to bring us to our senses, and to begin a project of re-symbolization.[52] We may form any concerned opinion we like on these matters, but it will hopefully make us more aware of the seriousness of what our Bibles reveal regarding the demonic and the satanic.

All of this is made a great deal more complex because most of us are distracted by our conventional perspective on what is happening in our lives and societies. We are paying far too little attention to what is happening in the developing anti-societies of the disembodied "relationships" mediated by the Facebooks, Googles, Twitters, and Apples of this world. Jointly, these initiatives represent the most powerful project of de-symbolization ever undertaken by humanity. They divide, separate, justify, and accuse people in ways that are entirely new. We do not appear to appreciate the risk we are taking as, without our knowledge, these systems enclose us in our own worlds by custom-tailoring them to our preferences. It goes far beyond determining what is real in our lives and further suppressing what is true. We are in danger of becoming spoiled children who will only tolerate what they like and want – and without delay – as determined by the growing capacity of these systems to track everything we do. We are thus shut into our own private worlds, which inevitably will make it more difficult for us to comprehend and tolerate the worlds of others that are unlike ours. There are increasingly powerful algorithms to identify what we "love" and "hate." It is not simply a matter of the kinds of products we are interested in, the subjects on the news that we favour, or the "friends" we collect on our "walls"; we are increasingly enclosed in what we love and comprehensively divided from what we hate. As we lose the daily-life experiences of dealing with what our Bibles refer to as "our neighbours," we will lose the very skills that have always been essential for the maintenance of any human community. Our works of division, separation, self-justification, and accusation are being taken to entirely new levels, with unimaginable consequences for our being a symbolic species and thus for our ability to relate to our God.

Three Horsemen of the Apocalypse

As noted in chapter 2, the second part of the book of Revelation, which is characterized by the breaking of seven seals on a scroll, shows us the major constituents of human history. They collectively symbolize its meaning in relation to Jesus Christ, who breaks these seals. For the broader context I refer the reader to the remarkable study of Jacques Ellul because I find it to be the least bogged down in counter-transference reactions.[53]

When the slain Lamb breaks the first seal, a white horse appears with a rider carrying a bow and wearing a crown. It represents the Word of God, as Ellul persuasively argues. The breaking of the second seal reveals a red horse with another rider. The colour signifies human blood because this rider is given the power to take away peace and make war. Once again, there is no metaphysics of any kind. We know that the different "causes" that provoke wars have economic, social, political, religious, and territorial dimensions. The revelation goes further: we can conceptualize the red horse as a spirit of war capable of taking hold of people and nations. It is what our Bibles refer to as one of the principalities and powers (an *exousia*). Although these powers act on a material plane, they exist within the gap that opened up between God and humanity following the break. They are thus rooted in the collective identities and defining cultural or secular myths of every group and society. As such, they express themselves via the spirit of an age. When that spirit becomes warlike, war may indeed break out, but we will never be able to fully explain its cause to our satisfaction.

Then we are told that the rider has been given a sword. This detail would be redundant if it simply referred to a necessary weapon. The sword is the traditional symbol of the power over life and death that is wielded by any authority, even in its exercise of justice. The rider receives this power, but we are not told from whom it comes. As I have attempted to show, I believe that this power originated in humanity's breaking with God. In any case, since this rider is distinct from the first, the sword is not used in accordance with the Word of God but by the rider's own authority and power.

Following the break, God intervenes from time to time in human history; and he occasionally uses war to punish a people. This power, like everything else in the creation, is ultimately under God's authority, but it originated from humanity's decision to break with him. We may therefore conclude that the second rider represents all authority capable of making war, and thus the state with its political power and justice.

We need to confront a common counter-transference reaction – the idea that all authority is from God – which is ultimately true but historically false. This idea is based on a few texts' having been taken out of the broader context of what our Bibles reveal regarding the authority of the prince of this world, who offered Jesus all the kingdoms of the earth in return for service to him. Jesus refused his offer but did not challenge it. When God's people desired a king who was like them, they refused God as their king, as well as his rule through the judges. It unleashed the political power of an authority that from then on would make its own decisions. In his mercy God made sure that the king would meet face to face with a prophet who would speak on God's behalf. Nevertheless, the dreadful consequences of unleashing the political power of this new authority were described in great detail in God's warning to his people (1 Samuel 8): the king would take their sons for his armies and conscript them for his personal service; he would take their daughters for a variety of services; he would take some of their best property for his purposes, including the enrichment of his favourites; and a 10 per cent tax would be levied to support this authority. In sum, the people would become the slaves of the new authority, and their property would be at its disposal. They would cry out soon enough, but God would not listen to them when they complained. I cannot imagine a more concise and moving description of the evil of all authority and political power.

This revelation regarding political power and authority is confirmed over and over again by examples such as the Jewish people's slavery in Egypt, their captivity in Babylon, and their submission to Rome. We are clearly told in the book of Revelation that this power will be destroyed at the end of time. When the full reconciliation between God and humanity has been achieved, there will no longer be room for any of these principalities and powers. It is inconceivable that, in a great many nations, a Christian denomination became the official church of a political authority; it had already begun in the Roman Empire. I cannot understand how national symbols can be present in any place of worship. I cannot comprehend how a pastor at a wedding can pronounce that the Christian Bible recognizes three institutions of God: marriage, the church, and the state. I was shocked when someone told me that he had been kicked out of his church because he had asked the pastor to have his children registered as conscientious objectors; he was accused of being a coward. Have we not read what happened to God's people once kings were set over them, and how it led from one disaster to another? As noted, Paul clearly includes authority in the same category as the principalities and powers. Like the demonic and satanic powers, political power exercised over people by the state is a necessary evil following the break with God.

The breaking of the third seal by the slain Lamb leads to the appearance of a black horse whose rider holds a scale in his hands. It is said that this rider has the power over a measure of wheat for a denarius. He thus represents the power over the minimum necessary to keep someone alive. This measure of wheat was the minimum intake of food required for a family and cost a day's wage, a denarius. The power of controlling whether the poorest people would live or starve was derived from the power of weighing that was necessary for commerce and trade; since money was in the form of precious metals, its weight had to be determined as well. In sum, this rider represents the economic powers that rule the world following the break with God, when grace no longer reigns.

The economic powers are limited, as shown by the command to not damage the oil and the wine. Many possible explanations have been given of this limit, but none of them appears to be decisive. Hence, its importance may well be the limit itself. In any case, the principal instrument of this economic power is money, which, elsewhere in the Bible, is referred to as Mammon and is thus a power in its own right. When we put all of this together, the rider appears to symbolize the power of our economies and the power of money, and therefore the power to distribute wealth and poverty and to determine full bellies and starvation, as well as every kind of scarcity.

The economic systems that were required to sustain industrialization, urbanization, and "development" during the last two centuries have taught us a great deal about the powers of this third component of human history. It has surely put to rest any doubts that the very strong language used in the Bible in relation to trade, commerce, money, and the city was and continues to be prophetic of what is happening around us. No metaphysics is required. This text represents an iconoclastic realism of what we are doing to one another and the world.

We all make a great many decisions about how to earn, spend, or invest our money. In so far as these decisions lead to purchases of goods and services, they may contribute to so-called market forces in cases that do not involve transnational corporations. In so far as they are not deeply influenced by advertising (a major component of integration propaganda), they contribute to "people changing the economy." Another contribution to this influence is made by the producers of the goods and services, who monitor the demands for them and modify the allocation of capital in order to increase profits. Each market for one of these goods and services mediates between producers and consumers by establishing a market price at which the supply equals the demand. Although these markets have been the best means devised for regulating the distribution of goods and services, they have far-reaching influences on people, societies, and the biosphere.

Many economists agree that the market price of a good or a service is a relatively poor measure of its value for human life and society. This is hardly surprising since a culture establishes this value by relating everything to everything else in human life, while a market establishes the value of one good or service at a time and thus is largely independent of all other markets and their evaluations. Despite this important limitation, industrializing societies had no choice but to entrust the role once played by their cultures in establishing the values of everything to the market economies. Moreover, for a good or service to be traded in a market, it must be commoditized and reified; that is, it must be treated as if it were not an integral part of the interrelatedness of everything in human lives, societies, and the biosphere. For example, a "chunk" of biosphere had to become a piece of terrain that could be described on a deed, and human work had to become labour, as if it could be detached from the lives of the people who sold it for a wage.

In sum, one effect of a market economy on human life and society was a de-symbolization of the culture by which these lives were lived and by which the society had evolved. The consequences became serious very quickly as these de-symbolized cultures were less able to oppose and delimit greed, which was so richly rewarded by the markets. This represents another example of market externalities: the effects that market decisions necessarily have on third parties who have had no say in agreements between buyers and sellers. These third parties include the other members of a society, future generations, other life forms, ecosystems, and the biosphere. For example, when a person trades in an old car for a new one, and the old car is sold to someone else, there will be an additional vehicle on the road that will contribute to raising the pollution level. The result will be a negative impact on third parties such as poor people who cannot afford a car, and people who cannot obtain a driver's licence because they are too old or have a disability. In the market economies of the nineteenth century and the early part of the twentieth century there were innumerable such market transactions every day. Together, they had an enormous effect on the way in which everything related to everything else, and on the way in which everything evolved in relation to everything else within the organization of a way of life, an institutional framework, and a culture. We have already seen that these collective influences act as market forces on this interrelatedness, of which all but one (the so-called invisible hand) are negative in character. The environmental crisis is an obvious example.

Another important market force produces structural unemployment. Since the scarcity of natural resources and energy is not priced, it has progressively made them cheaper in comparison to human labour. For centuries, entrepreneurs attempting to remain competitive by lowering their production costs have been encouraged to economize labour by mechanization, automation, computerization, and enterprise integration, while paying a great deal less attention to the productivity of natural resources and energy. This has created economies that "over-consume" nature and "under-consume" people.[54]

When human knowing and doing separated themselves from experience and culture and became organized by means of disciplines, corporations had to reorganize themselves in order to take advantage of these developments. It was not long before all business processes had to be re-engineered, and eventually the entire corporation had to be reorganized in the image of the computer.[55] The technological cycle (invention, innovation, and development; application and production; diffusion and displacement) then had to be planned in its entirety, with the result that corporations could no longer rely on markets for many of their inputs and outputs. It created what has been referred to as the planning system, which became largely autonomous from what remained of the market economy.[56] Market forces became overwhelmed by the overall influences of the externalities related to the application of discipline-based approaches, which permitted the new corporations to maximize systematically the costs that they could externalize and impose on their communities, societies, and the biosphere. The problems became so serious that, as some studies have shown, the costs of the corporations significantly exceeded their profits, with the result that they became wealth extractors.[57] Moreover, economies also became wealth extractors: the costs incurred in the production of wealth overtook wealth creation as a consequence of the widespread use of discipline-based approaches, which took no context into account other than the domains of the disciplines being used.[58] These developments created anti-economies that extracted wealth to everyone's detriment in the long run. In the short term, however, they are making 1 per cent of humanity wealthier beyond anything that could have been imagined in the past.

In sum, our daily-life decision making contributes to, maintains, and develops massive forces and pressures on the evolution of our civilization and human life within it – forces that are almost entirely negative. It is a first component of the ways in which economic power and money rule our world. Our daily use of money has similar far-reaching consequences. Money and currency systems are much more than mutual means of exchange. Even some prominent economists admit that ultimately money remains a somewhat mysterious force in our lives.

Even if money were a neutral means of exchange, the necessity of everything taking on a monetary value imposed by more and more people's becoming wage earners as a consequence of industrialization led to the previously noted consequence of money becoming the common denominator of all values. This inevitably undermined and eventually destroyed the value systems of groups and societies that had been created and evolved by symbolization, language, and culture. Everything became for sale as it took on a price, which was very destructive of human relationships and cultures. Many of the present currency systems were created just prior to industrialization in order to sustain growing trade, commerce, and centralized production.[59] Social exchanges were increasingly mediated by money, and this mediation was so lacking in neutrality that its ability to alienate human lives and communities was once widely recognized.

The new currency systems necessitated the creation of central banks capable of injecting funds into the reserve accounts of the commercial banks they served. With these reserves and the deposits received, the commercial banks can issue loans, except for a small portion that must be kept in reserve. For example, if the rate to be kept in reserve is 10 per cent, one billion dollars of deposits can be turned into 900 million dollars' worth of loans. Borrowers use these loans to pay for goods and services, and their payments become deposits in banks. All but 10 per cent of such deposits can again be turned into loans that result in more deposits from which more loans can be made, and so on. If all the borrowers defaulted on their loans, the banks would still owe their depositors. Consequently, the original commercial bank creates 900 million dollars of fiat money, on the second round the commercial banks create 810 million dollars of this fiat money, and so on. The fiat money disappears when all the loans have been repaid. These fractional reserve systems have created numerous bank crises and failures when, for whatever reasons, too many depositors wished to withdraw their funds at the same time, and the bank simply did not have enough in reserve. This creation of fiat money has done incalculable harm to many individuals, families, communities, and nations.

The consequences do not stop there. Since interest is charged on all loans, borrowers must compete with each other to procure this interest because the financial system deliberately does not create the matching funds ex nihilo. It is compelled to make money scarce in order to make it valuable. Assuming that the central bank does not add to the money supply, the economy must grow the stock of goods and services to pay for this compound interest, or some borrowers will have to go bankrupt. In other words, our use of compound interest compels us into the limitless growth of our economies, which in the long term is impossible on a finite planet. Moreover, these kinds of currency systems in effect put a price on the future as a consequence of discounting it due to compound interest. It has been argued that our financial systems have transformed societies from fabrics of reciprocal obligations into a competition of everyone against everyone because our credit ratings are essentially determined by our ability to compete for scarce currency in order to avoid bankruptcy.

The entire situation has been made much worse by the growing development of financial techniques that have gradually transformed economies since the 1970s.[60] This has created an entirely different category of economic activities that make money from money without any of the intervening economic activities that would normally have been required. It has been estimated that these new economic activities now account for some 97 per cent of the global economy.[61] The financial techniques have transformed economies into anti-economies that extract rather than produce wealth.[62] In other words, the economies that our governments, politicians, and media speak of most of the time account for less than 3 per cent of what is economically happening to us.

This brief overview needs to be further nuanced to incorporate the effects of tax systems and free-trade agreements. The latter make the world safe for technique and unsafe for people, by permitting an almost unlimited exploitation of technique in those areas where social, health, and environmental costs can be externalized to the greatest extent possible, thereby draining from many cultures a staggering number of desperately needed jobs, especially for their young people. This kind of trade is not free, because there are very few reciprocal benefits for society at large. It is the consequence of the international mobility of capital, which was non-existent when economists first began talking about the advantages of free-trade agreements. Free trade with genuine reciprocal benefits is good for everyone, but we have replaced it with forced trade, necessitated by making the world safe for building the universal technical order. This trade is based on the dubious assumption that in the long term it can save our global civilization and the planet.

Another aspect that we need to add to our understanding of the economic forces and the power of money that we have unleashed on ourselves and the planet is the instability of our financial systems. According to the International Monetary Fund, between 1970 and 2010 there were 145 banking crises, 208 monetary crashes, and 72 sovereign debt crises, which total an average of more than ten crises per year.[63] It represents a level of human misery rivalling that of many wars. Moreover, the reliance of these systems on compound interest and currency speculation has led to the most unprecedented concentration of wealth ever seen in human history, and this concentration is increasing every year. Perfectly reasonable solutions have been proposed, such as the Tobin tax or the reduction of our dependence on fiat money by increasing the percentage that banks need to keep in reserve, but the vested interests are so powerful that the defenders of a public good and a civic society have been rendered impotent. Has anyone recently heard a politician speak in support of the public good or a common future?

After this limited overview and with this very partial evidence, I hope we are ready to entertain the hypothesis that our economic decisions and our daily-life activities create forces and powers that touch almost everything on our planet in a manner that is destructive for the overwhelming majority of humanity in the short term and for everyone in the long term.

Returning to the perspective of our Bibles, we are hopefully prepared to be less surprised at the strong language used in the Epistle of James with respect to these topics.[64] Moreover, the severity of what Jesus said about Mammon is hopefully more comprehensible, given how implicated we all are, without exception, in these economic and monetary powers and forces.[65] Finally, to portray these forces and powers as some of the primary constituents of our human-history making, as symbolized by the black horse of the Apocalypse, is no exaggeration of any kind and involves no metaphysics whatsoever. Our Bibles provide us with an iconoclastic realism of what is happening to our lives, our societies, and our planet. We are all implicated in the way that we engage in our economic activities and financial decisions.

I am ready to forgive my readers if they think that I am just another one of those Canadian socialists. It is much easier to invoke countertransference reactions in order to deny the gospel its real force in our lives than to accept it. This denial has permitted the American way of life to triumph over Christianity and Judaism. In Canada, it is increasingly permitting what used to be the Reform Party, and now the Conservative Party with its provincial counterparts, to dismiss the gospel's message and remain politically involved as Christians. I can understand this very well; it reduces the pains of anxiety, depression, and disillusion. However, the worst result of my attempt to lay things on the line as to whom or what we should love would be to involve our congregations in politics. This would be nothing short of bowing down to the secular political religion of our time. The entire political spectrum, from left to right, has absolutely nothing to contribute to the deep structural issues regarding technique and the efforts of the nation-state to organize, control, and advance technique. When it comes to politics, everything that has been tried by Christians, without exception, has failed miserably. The inevitable result is our bowing to false gods.[66]

When the fourth seal of the scroll is broken by the Lamb, a pale sickly horse appears whose rider is pestilence or death, reflecting the thinking of that time. This rider is given the power to kill by the sword, famine, plague, and wild beasts. Behind him follows the habitation of the dead, which gathers together all those who have been killed. The limit set on this rider's power applies equally to the red and the black horses, since they also cause a great deal of death. In contrast, no limit is placed on the white horse. We have been assured that the Lord holds the keys to death and to the abode of the dead. There are no limits whatsoever on God's work of redemption and liberation because Jesus Christ in the flesh has conquered death and has penetrated the abode of the dead.

Regarding human history, the breaking of the first four seals on the scroll thus reveals the interwoven character of the actions of God's Word and those of the political, economic, and all other destructive powers, including death. With the exception of God's Word, all these powers have their origin in the break between humanity and God and operate in the gap that resulted from it. They indiscriminately affect everyone who shares in this break. It is not a question of "good" people being spared, and "evil" people being punished; it is a structural issue that has nothing whatsoever to do with morality. The sun shines and the rain falls on everyone alike. The four horses gallop all over the earth in ways we can neither fully explain nor control. The play of these powers remains the same, with the result that we must rule out any ideas of a steady march towards one goal or another or some historical laws that we can discern. There is simply the interaction between political, economic, and demographic forces delimited in their destructive powers by God. Of course, there is more to history than this, as the breaking of the fifth and sixth seals reveals.

The City as the Seat of the Powers

Now I will return to Babel, the city of cities, through which humanity intended to name its own spiritual direction, take hold of its future, and shut out God permanently and definitively. Unchecked, it would have become the land of evil and death where this name would have been "all in all." As such, it would have become the complete and total opposite of the kingdom of God. However, God intervened and put a limit on this undertaking by confusing the language of humanity. Nevertheless, the revelation consistently tells us that the city remained one of the principalities and powers that would jointly rule humanity from above until its liberation at the end of time.[67] Among the powers, Babel takes a central place: from the beginning, it was the seat of political, military, religious, economic, social, and cultural powers. A strong case can be made that, in so far as the deepest penetration of the demonic and satanic powers into human life is through groups and societies naming themselves, cities also became the seat of these powers, following the disappearance of the food-gathering and hunting ways of life and the appearance of societies. The unleashing of the powers of the flesh and of the other powers (*exousia*) that were integral to humanity's break with God coalesce in Babylon, whose destruction is described in great detail in the book of Revelation.[68]

In Revelations 17 and 18 we are told about the destruction of Babylon the great, which begins with the great prostitute who sits by many waters, with whom the kings of the earth commit adultery and whose wine makes humanity drunk with its adulteries (Rev. 17:1–2). In other words, the destruction of the city is set in the context of humanity's loving other things than God. In the desert, Babylon the great is then portrayed as a woman decked out in jewellery, bearing the name of Babylon written on her forehead, and sitting on a scarlet beast. It is once again a matter of whom and what humanity loves. We are also told that she is the mother of prostitutes and that she is drunk with the blood of God's people. Babylon the great is thus revealed as the prison and execution chamber of those who love God and Jesus Christ. The waters beside which the prostitute is seated represent the people, nations, and languages of the earth, all of which are in evil and death. As the great city, she rules over the kings. The symbolism of the hills and the kings represents an extension of the political and historical situation of the time in which the text was written, to something that can only be revealed.[69] It is fascinating and complex but not essential for the present argument: that the great city is the locus both of all human works in rebellion to God and of the *exousia* generated and sustained by these works. In every respect, these works are the opposite of those of God, which are characterized by love, freedom, non-power, justice, and peace.

As the judgment of the great city gets underway, chapter 18 tells us that humanity has listened to the call to leave the city. Even the kings watch from a safe distance as the city burns. They mourn her loss, as do the merchants who see their trade in all manner of riches disappearing with the city. They all continue to love the city and its great wealth, which have now come to nothing. Those who were responsible for shipping all these riches across the seas are also stunned by what they see. All the activities of the cultures and civilizations that took place within her will be no more. The power of the great city has been destroyed, but the destruction of the flesh is yet to come.

The impressive list of the riches that were traded and accumulated in the great city ends with the trade in the bodies and souls of human beings (Rev. 18:12–13). The last phrase appears redundant. Jewish thought knows no distinction between bodies and souls because the entire being is indivisible and thus implicit in either body or soul. Moreover, this unity is also implied in the reference to *human beings*. Hence, there is a kind of triple repetition. At that time it was generally accepted that slaves had bodies but no souls because they were objects that could be bought and sold and thus were not complete beings. Presuming that our Bibles do not waste our time with repetition, *souls* would therefore refer to free people who did have souls but who were nevertheless traded. It means that free people were also possessed, not in the way of slaves but in their inner beings as alienated people (to use the sociological and historical concept).[70] In other words, there were no free people in Babylon the great. All those who participated in its life loved other things and thus were possessed by what they loved. The text, in its description of the reactions of kings, merchants, captains, and sailors, as well as its comprehensive list of riches (the separation from which they all lament), shows once again that their hearts are with what they love.[71] This is exactly what Jesus said with regard to the relationship between people and Mammon. It is for this reason that the book of Revelation turns next to the separation of humanity from the power of the flesh.[72] Humanity would have to be divided and separated from the powers that had their seat in Babylon the great, because this action would clear the way for the next step in God's work of redemption and liberation and the ushering in of his kingdom. This amply confirms the good news about the flesh and the powers that rule our lives and the world. They have been conquered, but they remain so entangled in our lives that their immediate and final destruction would destroy us along with them. Hence, God patiently and carefully divides and separates humanity from what it loves and from what has enslaved it, in preparation for its redemption and freedom, at which point people will be able to experience the love that has sought them throughout human history. Until then, the people possessed by their wealth in the city have killed the prophets in their vain attempts to shut out God. We are back to Babel, which means the door to the gods and to power and wealth, and the negation of God's Word. Once the great city with its powers has been destroyed and the flesh taken away, humanity will encounter what is true in its life and history. Everything it has loved and to which it was attached has gone, and humanity will now meet the One who truly loves it.

We have attempted to show how humanity, in its enslavement to the flesh, creates a world ruled by the principalities and powers, collectively designated as the ruling prince of this world. Once again, the prince is not some metaphysical entity but the concrete incarnation of the principalities and powers in the actions of people in particular situations. Such actions exhibit the attitudes of what, in our Bibles, is designated by "the world." For example, when Jesus warned his disciples that the prince of this world was coming, he was referring to the group of people, including soldiers, who were about to arrest him. If we cannot understand how, in our enslavement to the flesh, we create the world ruled by the principalities and powers, our Bible reading will remain stuck in abstractions rather than penetrating into our daily-life behaviour and our lives. The flesh, the world, and the principalities and powers are what remain present in our lives to signify our separation from God and thus from his love, freedom, redemption, justice, and peace. If we cannot understand our lives in terms of this revelation, we will remain stuck in our theological truisms and will be incapable of bearing the light so that it penetrates the darkness of this world.

5 The Law, the Spirit, and the Kingdom of Heaven

The Law and the Jewish People

It is astonishing how little Christians have learned from the experiences of the Jewish people, who (according to the second testament) remain the ones chosen by God and with whom the Christian church ought to have had and continue to have a very different relationship than is currently the case. If, for some two thousand years, the Christian church had not ignored texts such as Romans 9–11 and Revelation 7, we might have understood why Jesus always spoke with great compassion to the crowds but often with extreme warnings to his followers who were to continue his work on this earth. It represents the diametrically opposite attitude of those churches today who preach hell and damnation to the world, while more or less sustaining collective identity as an institution.

The first testament provides us with a warning in telling of what happened as soon when the two tablets of the law, written by God and given to Moses, encountered the consequences of the Jewish people in Egypt naming themselves (just as the other people had done in the wake of the confusion of language). In Moses's absence, the people felt a strong need to reaffirm their name by relating to the powers and forces that, according to their experience in their separation from God, appeared to rule over their lives and their world. From a social and historical perspective, this was hardly surprising, but from the perspective of faith, it represented the dilemma of all God's people, Jews and Christian alike.

For some time God had been immediately present in the lives of the Jewish people through Moses as his intermediary. However, when Moses stayed on the mountain, and the people were not sure as to his whereabouts, it was not long before they had to deal with the threats of relativism, nihilism, and anomie. They had nothing to fall back on but their own body of experience. The gods whom they had discerned needed to be dealt with, and this required transferring them from what was true in their lives to what was real in order to take hold of them, establish a relationship with them, and coexist with them as best they could through a religious, moral, and juridical arrangement. Hence, the golden calf was the traditional equivalent of entities such as a flag, a constitution, or a national anthem in a contemporary secular society. These connect us to the political forces and powers that we have discerned in our bodies of experience as ruling our lives and our world, just as much as the golden calf did in those days. Any other interpretation would go against everything that is revealed in the first and second testaments about our human finitude, the flesh, and the world ruled by the principalities and powers.

How else is it possible to understand what Moses did when he came down the mountain, discerned the significance of what the people had done, and responded by destroying the tablets of the law that he had received from God's hand? He made it radically impossible for the people to simply exchange the golden calf for the two tablets of the law. These would have become the ultimate religious images and the radical negation of the first three "words" (commonly referred to as laws) of the Decalogue within the Torah. God would have become the only true religious god, his law the most advanced religious and moral precepts for life, and everything bound up with it the cultural appropriation of the Jewish people. God's ways would have become their ways, and his transcendence and holiness would have become the ultimate cultural satisfaction of human finitude as the only true penetration of good and evil. All God's work of redemption would thus have been turned into its opposite. Moses discerned this risk and acted in faith, and the struggle of God's people serving two masters began. Any possible synthesis of the people naming themselves culturally through their gods and naming themselves by faith had been avoided, at least for now.

Moses's discernment and response to the situation confirm once again what we observed earlier in relation to the Genesis texts' being polemical with regard to the surrounding cultures of that time. For those who walked by faith and not by the orientation of their culture's naming itself, there could be no serving of two masters. The love for their God and their neighbour was all defining; nothing sacred, religious, or moral could be tolerated, because it would represent the service of another master. It is very important to be clear on this point.

Whatever insights we may have gained of our human finitude and our dependence on symbolization, language, and culture are nothing other than our own attempts in a so-called secular age to understand better the kinds of discernments that can only be made in faith. From a social and historical perspective, the Jewish people were a traditional society with a traditional culture and everything that this implied in terms of a collective identity and defining cultural myths. Anything that appeared to be self-evident could only be transcended by means of faith freely given to a small remnant who constantly bore the revelation within Israel for its benefit and that of all humanity. Throughout the first testament the Jewish people were warned that their religious and political establishments, as well as their culture as a whole, represented a constant straying from the Law of the Torah. If this were not the case, the regular interventions of the prophets would not have been required. They resulted in an occasional repentance on the part of the people, but these were short lived. This fickleness can be explained by the necessities imposed by Jewish culture.

As Christians we have learned very little from this history, which represents the interplay between the Word and the powers of the flesh and the principalities that ruled the world at that time. Our institutionalized churches and denominations have generally behaved as if they represented the body of believers on earth, much as the Jewish religious establishment did then. Due to institutional means of self-justification, even the most excessive abuses rarely led to institution-wide repentance and iconoclastic changes. The Reformation, of which some denominations are so proud, was assumed to be faithful to the gospel in every respect, thus requiring little or no repentance in future. Indeed we have not learned much from our Jewish brothers and sisters who worked to keep the faith, as if the powers of the flesh, the world, and the principalities had no influence on us other than on some theological abstractions.

Moses simply broke the tablets of the Law, but he burned the golden calf, ground it to powder, mixed it with water, and had the people drink it. This manifests the difference between something that is holy and something that is held to be sacred by a culture. For something to be holy, God has to set it apart from everything else for a special purpose, and its meaning resides in that purpose alone. It has no religious value of any kind. In contrast, the golden calf was an image representing what the Jewish people had discerned as the gods that ruled their lives and their world. It had been made sacred in their culture, possessing all the well-known attributes, which have been so extensively studied. To demonstrate that it could not possibly have any such qualities, Moses reduced the golden calf to something that the people could drink like any other liquid. He thus destroyed the sacred and religious character of this object. However, it did not alter in any way the metaconscious and cultural developments that had been brought, by means of this idol into what was real for the people.[1]

Today we face many of the same kinds of issues. Is there not a considerable overlap between God's law, the Christian morality we have derived from it, and the laws that many Western societies have made for themselves? This was to be expected, since the Jewish and Christian traditions formed one of the pillars of Western civilization.[2] However, we must go further. As noted, in a society babies and children grow up by listening to human words spoken by parents and significant others. Doing so leads to the formation of a double referencing system that is required to learn a symbolic language and culture. Children thus enter into a symbolic universe made up of what is true for their individual life and for the life of their community, which includes but far transcends what is real as presented to their senses. One form of metaconscious knowledge that develops within the organizations of their brain-minds is that of metaconscious values. These values become a constraint on the kinds of laws that will be spontaneously obeyed by the community because they make sense to most of its members.[3] In traditional societies, the art of law-giving was to "stretch" these metaconscious constraints in a desirable direction according to a common good embodied in a collective identity and its defining cultural myths. If the metaconscious values were stretched too far, lawgivers risked the possibility of the new laws not making sufficient sense to a non-trivial portion of the community, thus leading to growing levels of disobedience. Whether these laws were an elaboration of a common-law system administered through judges or enacted by elected representatives made little difference. Owing to high levels of de-symbolization, it is a great deal more complex today. Contemporary law has taken on a more organizational and technical character, making it much more arbitrary in the eyes of many people.[4] Obeying the law in an anti-society has taken on an element of assessing the chances of getting away with violating it, as opposed to seeing the law as having a dominating element of right and wrong.

In contrast, the law given to Israel by God through the intermediary of Moses had no cultural origin. It initially came by listening to the Word and also indirectly through the human words of others who passed on the Torah from generation to generation. In addition to God's law thus having a completely different origin than that of laws made by a society through its culture, the context in which this law is to be understood is also radically different. In other words, although there may be a great deal of overlap between God's law and human laws in their forbidden actions such as lying, stealing, or murdering, the apparently common denominator disappears when we carefully consider the context. Human laws are generally obeyed because they correspond to the metaconscious (cultural) values that are acquired by listening to human words; following such laws is inseparable from being a person of a time, place, and culture based on a collective identity and defining cultural myths.

None of this applies to God's law, which includes but is far from limited to the Decalogue. It promises that, because of God's work of redemption and reconciliation, the day will come when his people will no longer have any need of other gods, idols, the religious use of God's name, lying, stealing, killing, coveting, or any other behaviour associated with evil and death. The law thus invites people to live out of this promise and to conduct their lives by faith rather than through the evidence provided by symbolization, experience, language, and culture. People have been granted the permission *not* to do what is necessary based on this evidence but to act as free people who have been liberated from their enslavement. They are reintroduced to their Creator and his creation, and both they and this creation belong to the One who gives them the promise of another life, a life lived by faith. As liberated people, they are once again able to struggle to love him and therefore to love others, as people who are equally loved by him. However, because of a divided loyalty – to their Liberator on the one hand and to the flesh, the world, and its powers on the other hand – they are not yet able to be fully "yes" to their God and their neighbour. Everything in the Torah can be summed up in terms of love for God and for one's neighbour. The law steps in as a law only when this love is broken. God calls his people to live for him and their neighbour instead of for the maintenance of a collective identity, tradition, and defining cultural commitments. In sum, a person does not steal from another because it is morally wrong, but because stealing is not something one does to someone whom, God promises, you will be able to love as he loves that person. Therefore, there is no need of cultural values such as social justice in the Bible. What we refer to as social injustice in our culture is (from a biblical perspective) a lack of love for God, which manifests itself as a lack of love for others.

For Jews or Christians, living their lives through love means not living according to one's experience and culture. The former orientation is that of a life lived for God and others, while the latter orientation is to live according to the meaning and value that the gods and other people have for your own life. In the case of the former, we essentially offer our life to the other, while in the case of the latter we seek to enhance the ways in which everything is related to everything else in our own life. Consequently, to live from love for the other is the diametrical opposite of living one's life according to the values, morality, and religion of one's culture. The latter involves surrendering to the necessities imposed by the flesh and the principalities and powers that rule the world.

The first fulfilment of the promise of the Law came through Jesus Christ. In him the flesh was fully dominated by the Spirit. This domination changed everything because it destroyed what the flesh had become as a consequence of humanity's break with God. The break was bridged because of the Spirit. In Jesus this was accomplished without destroying humanity, which continued to be flesh. Similarly, when Jesus made himself flesh for us, this flesh was condemned, crucified, and killed. This flesh dominated by the Spirit penetrated into death, thus destroying its very separation from the only Living One. God had made himself flesh dominated by the Spirit, thus providing the ultimate sacrifice. It satisfied the Law and destroyed all the evil and death of humanity (past, present and future) by penetrating and thus obliterating them; it redeemed humanity by paying the ransom. The Law had been fully accomplished in Jesus Christ. What remained to be done was to bring the gospel of redemption to all of humanity in a way that would eventually show God's love to be unlimited, otherwise he would not be God. Passages including Romans 9–11 and much of the book of Revelation show how God promised to proceed.

As the second chapter of the letter to the Philippians and similar texts make clear, the historical Jesus took on our flesh, but kept it in submission to the Spirit even unto death. In other words, Jesus was a person of a time, place, and culture but with one decisive difference. Led by the Spirit he was fully "yes" to God and his fellow creatures, which meant that he did not enslave his life to the collective identity and defining cultural myths of the Jewish people of that time. I am suggesting not that Jesus was not fully human, but that everything, including his deepest metaconscious knowledge, was fully enveloped by the Spirit. As a result, there was no place whatsoever for anything sacred, religious, or moral in the life of Jesus. In terms of his daily life, this meant that anything he encountered in his society or in creation was no more and no less than what it was. For example, a terrible storm that threatened the lives of his disciples and himself was just what it was: an element of creation that could be calmed through the authority of the Spirit. As a fellow Jew, Jesus understood and experienced the power of the flesh, the world, and the principalities and powers embodied in the lives of others. Everything his fellow human beings said and did represented a temptation for him to intervene by the Spirit according to his own will instead of the will of his Father. It is probably for this reason that three of the gospels speak of the three temptations, which may be regarded as the totality of all possible and specific economic, political, and religious temptations.[5] If he had followed the example of almost every successful evangelist today, he would have given in to the temptation to use all possible means of power to advance the ministry that he had been sent to accomplish.

As a result of obeying the will of his Father, which represented everything that he loved and was good for humanity, Jesus was in constant conflict with anything that was sacred, religious, and moral in his society. From the first testament it is abundantly clear that, with few exceptions, the way of God was entirely opposite to the way of the Jewish people. The book of Amos is particularly vocal on this point.[6] What constituted the way of the Jewish people? It originated with Abram as their ancestor, to whom God had revealed himself. As descendants from this ancestor (confirmed by the circumcision of all male children), they had substituted their descendance in the flesh for descendance through the Spirit. Moreover, they had expended a great deal of energy on putting the Torah into practice, which led to a moral and religious tradition of what they regarded as the most faithful practices. They thus had substituted the approaches of any traditional culture to creating and evolving a way of life, for living the Law out of love for God and one's neighbour.

In sum, they had culturally appropriated the revelation, thereby turning it into its exact opposite. The clash between the Jewish ways of practising the Law and God's intervention through the prophets is fully evident in the life of Jesus as well. We only need to recall the debate over the Sabbath, which Jesus insisted was made for people but which had been turned into something that religiously enslaved them. There was nothing sacred, religious, or moral to Jesus. We need to keep in mind the attack on religion, morality, and magic in the opening chapters of the book of Genesis.

What Christians ought to have learned from the revelation of the first testament was to do everything possible not to repeat the mistakes of the Jewish people. But they did. When Christianity became the official religion of the Roman Empire, it was being turned into its opposite. When the Roman Catholic Church became the sacred institution of medieval societies, the mistakes of the Jewish people were repeated. The apostle Peter was substituted for Abraham, and a Roman Catholic religious tradition was created and evolved that also culturally appropriated the revelation. Nothing essential changed with the Reformation. Despite the texts from Paul insisting that there were to be no divisions according to whom people followed (1 Corinthians 3 and 12), the Reformation gave rise to the followers of Luther, Calvin, and Knox. New religious traditions were elaborated, and the same old problems were repeated.

In sum, what Jewish and Christian brothers and sisters have in common is that they forget the aftermath of the confusion of language at Babel. Their societies needed to name themselves by creating a collective identity and defining cultural or secular myths. Although both Jews and Christians had received a revelation from God, not only did they borrow all the cultural means for putting it into practice and elaborating the most faithful ones into a tradition, but they also did not recognize that they were serving two masters, with the flesh and the world ruled by principalities and powers generally keeping the upper hand. In other words, the conflict that Jesus had with the religious and moral traditions of his day equally applies to us as Christians.

When Jesus destroyed the flesh, evil, and death, the enslavement of humanity was broken, and its freedom was assured. He paid the ransom, and, because of grace, humanity did not have to repay its debt for this redemption. All the sins of humanity, jointly constituting the break with God, were forgiven. However, Jesus had come incognito, with the result that almost everyone (including most of his disciples) did not really understand what had just happened before their very eyes. It was the Spirit, through whom Jesus would dwell in his followers, and they in him following his resurrection, that would fully explain the decisive victory.

How could this victory be lived? Salvation was freely offered to everyone through the means of faith. Once again, institutionalized Christianity turned this into a terrible dilemma: salvation is granted to everyone, but we ourselves are responsible for coming up with faith, which we then "possess." This is nonsense. Human lives continue to be enslaved by the flesh and by the principalities and powers that rule the world, as long as human beings continue to live by their collective identities and defining cultural or secular myths. When people discover that they are loved and have been redeemed, they can only enact this love and redemption by means of faith, which is the opposite of living by their collective identity and defining cultural or secular commitments. The conviction that somehow we can come up with faith on our own and have it for ourselves amounts to a repetition of Adam's actions. When Jesus promised to send the Spirit to his followers, he assured them of the possibility of their living by this Spirit and thus of dwelling in him as he dwelt in the Father. In other words, the Spirit makes it possible to live by faith as the means to engage the struggle between dwelling in our collective identity and defining cultural or secular commitments and dwelling in Jesus Christ through the Spirit. Faith makes it possible for us to live not by experience and culture but by the love for God and one's neighbour. As noted, the two ways of living are diametrically opposed to one another in relation to the quality and commitment involved in relationships of love. We dwell either in our culture or in our Lord through the Spirit, even though we are as yet incapable of being fully "yes" to our Redeemer.

This brings us to God's strategy following the destruction of the flesh and death through Jesus Christ. We will first discuss this strategy in relation to the Jewish people as revealed in Romans 9–11. We will then turn to the role played by the Christian community through its participation in the kingdom of heaven, which the gospel of Matthew systematically distinguishes from the kingdom of God. Finally, we will review the overall architecture of the reconciliation between God and humanity as set out in the book of Revelation.

Recall that, within the beginning, God created the life and the good by dividing and separating opposite elements in his creation. Romans 9–11 suggests that God continues this strategy by temporarily dividing yeast from dough, salt from food, light from dark, and those called to a task from those passed over. Without such a division and separation the dough cannot rise, the food necessary to sustain life cannot be flavoured, and the kingdom of heaven cannot lead to the kingdom of God at the end of time. I believe this is the thrust of Romans 9–11.[7]

There is thus a continuation of the way in which God had set apart the Jewish people from all other people, whom he had passed over. Within the Jewish people, many did not believe, but there was always a faithful remnant that bore his Word for everyone else. Within this remnant, God chose some to carry out a particular task, while passing over others. By the time Jesus was born, this faithful remnant appears to have been exceedingly small. In any case, the Jewish people refused to believe in the Messiah, but our text makes it clear that this disobedience is not permanent. Paul goes to great lengths in the opening verses of chapter 9 to show that he is not mistaken about this point. He is even willing to be cut off from Christ for the sake of his people. He emphasizes importance of the people and insists that God's work has not failed. This becomes obvious when we recognize that the Jewish people did not descend from the natural child of Abram, the one he had with his slave, but from the child he conceived in faith. A distinction is thus drawn between the natural descendants of Abram and the spiritual descendants who lived by the promise in faith. Paul also reveals that God loved Jacob but passed over Esau, and thus that God always set aside a faithful remnant for himself within his people. He continued this strategy when the followers of Jesus Christ in the Spirit were set aside as the new faithful remnant that would bear the good news for all Christians and for all humanity. If this remnant was capable of showing that God's love and redemption truly led to life and the good, the Jewish people would eventually no longer accept their exclusion. Following their conversion, they would be the first to pass into the new creation, as Revelation 7 clearly shows.[8]

Paul makes it abundantly clear that he is not discussing the salvation or damnation of the Jewish people. In the opening verse of chapter 10, he declares that it is his desire and prayer that the Israelites be saved. In the first verse of chapter 11, Paul declares that God has not rejected his people. In verse 11, he continues to elaborate on this by suggesting that Israel did not stumble so as to fall beyond recovery. Their transgression permitted salvation to come to everyone else in order to make the Jews envious. Beginning with verse 25, Paul tells his readers that the Jews experienced a hardening of their hearts that would persist until the full number of the Gentiles had come in, and that it was in this way that all Israel would be saved. In its disobedience, Israel would also receive mercy (Romans 11:32). In sum, the general framework of the discussion of Israel in Romans 9–11 makes it abundantly clear that these chapters deal with the election of a faithful remnant within and beyond Israel, and that such an election had nothing whatsoever to do with salvation or damnation. This was confirmed by Revelation 7.

Nevertheless, the election by grace of a faithful remnant, first in Israel and then within the Christian community, raises some very difficult questions. Whoever was not elected in Israel was hardened and given a spirit of stupor, eyes that should not see, and ears that should not hear (Romans 11:8). The text appears to suggest that God did not merely pass them over, but that he created something contrary in them. This revelation is so offensive to our ways and sense of justice that Paul attempts to stem all counter-transference reactions by discussing the possibility that God is unjust (Romans 9:14–21). He tells us again that God is sovereign in his decision to have mercy or to harden someone, just as a potter can choose the kind of vessel she will make from a lump of clay. However, to deduce from this text that we are merely marionettes in the hand of God is to ignore not only the immediate context of the text but also the context of the entire revelation. Worse, it is to judge God by our own standards of justice and thus to break with him all over again. The text that immediately follows (Romans 9:22–9) makes this clear. Was not Jesus Christ the only one who bore God's wrath by becoming flesh and taking upon himself everything that humanity had made out of it? Did he not redeem humanity in this way by penetrating evil and death, thereby destroying them in their separation from the only Living One? Was this redeemed humanity therefore not headed for reconciliation and glory? Once again, it is not a question of salvation or damnation.

Nevertheless, God's election or rejection of some people to bear the good news for all people still bothers us because, judged by our ways and our sense of justice, it appears arbitrary. Once again we must take the context into account. Did God ever reveal himself as arbitrary in his dealings with humanity? Is the will of God arbitrary? Do we not pray for his will to be done on this earth, and does this not mean that we pray for life and the good? How do those who are hardened fit into all of this? It seems to me that what Jesus taught us regarding the Holy Spirit and the kingdom of heaven provides us with the key to these questions.

First, however, it is important to clear away the usual counter-transference reactions to these texts. It may well be that the interpretation of John Calvin was the most extreme, with his theory of predestination – a theory that turned the entire gospel upside down and inside out. His followers should have discovered that it was completely untenable in the context of writings such as Romans 9–11 and the entire book of Revelation.[9] However, a milder form of this theory is much more pervasive and dangerous. Much of Christianity divides humanity into the saved and the damned, with little or no compassion for the latter – a stark contrast with Paul's concerns for his fellow Jews who did not believe. Alternatively, humanity is divided into those who love their neighbours and those who do not regard their fellow human beings as equally loved by God. The only division of humanity that Romans 9–11 describes is the one between the faithful remnant elected by grace and everyone else.

To put this in terms of the metaphors used by Jesus, humanity is divided into bread dough with or without yeast, food with or without salt, bearers of light and prisoners of darkness, and participants in the kingdom of heaven and everyone else. From this we must not draw a doctrine of universal salvation. Such a doctrine is as foreign to the Bible as the one of predestination. The God of the Bible cannot be "programmed" according to our silly theological theories. He is free and will decide as he pleases. All we can go by is what the entire Bible reveals about what he loves (life and the good) and what he hates (evil and death). Returning to the only division of humanity of which the Bible speaks, the warning regarding damnation is always and only pronounced to those who have been elected to bear the good news. They must not take their election for granted, because acting as yeast, as salt, as bearers of light, or as workers in the kingdom of heaven, they have work to do. The only other division of which Jesus speaks is that of wheat and tares in the lives of those who belong to the faithful remnant.

Since the faithful remnant is to conduct itself as yeast, the remainder of humanity will act as the dough. Given our human finitude, what it is to be yeast is relative to what it is to be dough, and vice versa. No finite creature can be one or the other in the absolute. If the yeast and the dough were identical, nothing would happen. This would also be the case if the unique properties of yeast did not relate to the unique properties of dough in such a way that the entire mixture would rise and transform both of them in the process. Without yeast there is no dough, and without dough the yeast is without purpose. Both ingredients serve to make the dough rise in the process of producing the bread of life. The same is true for the metaphor of salt and food. Each plays its role in ensuring that food not only powers life as a kind of fuel but also sustains it as we enjoy our food in the company of our fellow human beings and our God. Similarly, light and dark each play their role.

Hence, if we are called to bring the good news to others, the faith that we have been granted in grace will be tested and possibly refined through them, because they will do everything possible not to give up their ways of life and thus will avoid coming face to face with the overwhelming insecurity of the freedom that comes with redemption. Is it perhaps the task of all those who have not yet received faith by grace – to refuse to call on God until they are completely stuck and have no way out? Does this kind of behaviour not compel the messengers to turn to God in order to do a better job, to the point that eventually there will be no one foolish enough to refuse the good news? Is this not what Paul is speaking of in Romans 9–11 when he says that eventually Israel will become jealous and their acceptance of the good news will mean "life from the dead" (Romans 11:11–16)? From this perspective, it is the role of the faithful remnant in Israel and in the Christian community, as well as the role of those who are "on the outside," in challenging them, to show the faithful remnant that the gospel is infinitely more beautiful than they claim it to be by their words and their lives. In other words, the faithful remnant must accept the "outsider," albeit one who shows its shortcomings, since God's love is without limits.

The implications are far reaching. There can be no boundaries between the faithful remnant and Israel or between this remnant and the Christian community. Nor can there be any clear boundary between these communities and the world (in the biblical sense). In its imperfections, the faithful remnant represents this world, as do the hardened remainders of Israel and the church. Even though a rapid reading of Romans 9–11 suggests a God whose ways are very harsh, hopefully it will now be more apparent why Paul marvels at God's plan to make all things new by turning everything towards the good of those who love him in order that more and more people will find his love irresistibly beautiful. This also sheds additional light on what it is to be our neighbour.

One of Jesus's parables and one of his most difficult actions both illustrate Paul's interpretation of the way in which God is busy reconciling himself with humanity in order to make all things new. In Jesus's parable of the prodigal son (Luke 15:11–32), the older and faithful son lived his whole life in the presence and love of his father, who shared everything with him. In contrast, his younger brother asked for his share of the inheritance, broke with his father, and departed to squander it in worldly living; he then recognized that his life was going nowhere, returned to his father to beg forgiveness, and asked for permission to stay on as a common servant. The father was so overjoyed to see his son return that he dressed him in fine clothing, organized a banquet, and killed the fatted calf. The older son was very put out by this treatment of his brother, which he regarded as something he himself deserved but had never received. The behaviour of his younger brother thus revealed something about his own love for his father. Although the older son had been in his father's presence and within his love during his entire life, he did not recognize that this love ought to have represented all the riches and joy a person could ever hope to have in life. He ought to have learned from this occasion that he had not fully reciprocated his father's love. If he had, his life would have been full to the brim without lack of any kind, and the very possibility of a grudge against his brother would have been unthinkable. His father would now have to teach him that he ought to learn something from what his younger brother had done to make his own life full and complete. The older son had been unable to fully reciprocate his father's love so as to make his own life rich, fulfilled, and complete and thus to also learn to forgive and love his younger brother. We are back to the intent of the law as the promise of a love for God and one's neighbour. It also teaches us something about the level of commitment and the quality of the relationships of love that God intended for his creation.

It is not difficult to imagine why Jesus was deeply troubled in announcing to his disciples that one of them would betray him. They were all shocked, looking at one another with consternation. Clearly, there was no obvious villain or any obvious exemptions. No one could be ruled out as being entirely incapable of doing the deed. Jesus asked Judas to get on with his business as quickly as possible. Much was to happen in that weekend of the Passover, during which Jesus knew he would be betrayed and executed. Judas went out into the night, thus separating himself from he who is the Light. In the gospel of John this event is immediately preceded by Jesus's declaration: "Amen, amen. Whoever welcomes the one I will send, it is I who will be welcomed, and the one who welcomes me will welcome the one who sent me" (John 13:20). Immediately following this assurance, Jesus dipped a piece of bread in a bowl, handed the bread to Judas, and sent him out to betray him. We must not arbitrarily separate these elements of the text.[10] Jesus had come to accomplish the will of his Father in all things, which thus included sending Judas to betray him.

It is next to impossible for us to make sense of this text without interposing significant counter-transference reactions. After humanity broke with God, it plunged itself into evil and death, but this altered nothing whatsoever on God's part. Humanity remained within his love, and its actions would remain within his will to reconcile himself with it and to make all things new. God's love and will could not be limited by anything done by humanity. He respected the freedom of humanity in his love for it and therefore adjusted his strategy around it. The entire first testament witnesses to this respect. He constantly held out his hands in one way or another to a disobedient and obstinate people (Romans 10:21). Even their disobedience would serve the larger purpose: to show the unlimited character of God's love for his creatures. The same holds for Christians today, who, as the second chosen witness, are busy repeating the same mistakes in appropriating what is "entirely other" to our moral, religious, cultural, and denominational ways.

It is also next to impossible for us to understand the radicality of God's love, which defines him in all his commitments and ways. Every time we believe that we can reciprocate his love, we discover that we have failed once again because we are constantly serving two masters. However, for God there is no middle ground: either you are in a relationship with him as the only Living One, which is life and the good, or you are separated from him and thus are in evil and death. In other words, we cannot sum up what is morally good in our lives and subtract what is morally evil in order to determine whether we are alive or dead. We are alive and in the good when the Living One establishes a relationship with us through Jesus Christ, and he with us through the Spirit. All our ways and criteria of justice, morality, religion, doctrine, and world-view have no bearing in this matter. We must not think that, if this is the case, then everything is predestined and there is nothing we can do, or that, regardless of what we do, grace will abound and God's love will be manifested to a greater extent. We must follow our Lord with the full knowledge that in the final analysis none of this is essential for God's will to be fulfilled. This is why Christians constantly receive the ultimate warning in the Bible if they fail to take their calling seriously. Nevertheless, in the end God's love will appear so complete and without limits that it is difficult to imagine that anyone would not accept it. In the meantime, it is, ironically, the two witnesses (Israel and the church) that are obscuring this limitless love from humanity.

If God is God, it follows that the consequences of humanity's breaking with him – the flesh, the principalities and powers, and thus the devil and Satan and everything else we bring forth in evil and death – operate within God's love and his will to reconcile himself with humanity. In the end, Satan and the devil will fulfil their roles and reveal themselves for what they are – powers destined for destruction.

It is within this broader context that we must interpret what Jesus said just prior to sending Judas to betray him. Judas was going to contribute to what the Bible refers to as the devil and Satan, but even these were within God's enveloping love and will. The principalities and powers rule from above, but above them God rules in his way of love and non-power.

Is this just another way of returning to the predestination – our playing the puppets' part in the Master's scheme? Not at all. We must remind ourselves that Jews and Christians who are possessed by faith in grace are themselves wheat and tares. They are not exclusively alive and in the good while everyone else is completely in evil and death. In other words, the execution of God's will to reconcile himself with humanity involves a battle between wheat and tares in the lives of believers as well as in the lives of everyone else. We are constantly warned not to attempt to separate the wheat and the tares within our own lives, in the lives of others, or in any community. In other words, God's work of making all things new largely escapes our comprehension because it has nothing to do with separating humanity into the saved and the damned. Moreover, following the death and resurrection of Jesus Christ, evil and death have been penetrated by him and thus destroyed in eternity.

Although it was a total victory over evil and death, their complete and total annihilation cannot occur in history until humanity has been disentangled from them, which involves the final judgment that will separate the wheat from the tares in everyone's lives. They remain only in so far as they are entangled in humanity. Their power is still terrible, but in so far as the faithful remnant within the church lives by the Spirit, that remnant is able to loosen the bonds of humanity's slavery to the flesh and the principalities and powers. Nevertheless, as Paul points out in referring to his own life, we usually do what we do not wish to do. Hopefully, this makes us long for our deliverance from this body of death (Romans 7:24).

In Paul's description of God's strategy for reconciling himself with humanity there is an important detail, which Christians are overlooking as much as our Jewish brothers and sisters did. Paul declares that Israel pursued the Law as the way of righteousness (Romans 9:30–3). This pursuit failed because it was not carried out in a way that was based on living by God's promise through faith; it was based on the way of human works. Jesus said that he was the way, the truth, and the life, and only through him could we be reconciled with the Father.

Salvation is by grace through the means of faith, that is, by living not through experience and culture but through the promises of God. It involves dwelling not in the collective identities and defining cultural or secular commitments of our societies but in Jesus Christ through the Spirit as he dwells in the Father.

In this regard, Christians have not sufficiently paid attention to the third promise and commandment of the Decalogue. The ease with which we use the name of Christ to name ourselves is deeply troubling, when we have paid little or no attention to the implications of humanity's attempting to name itself. Jesus warned us that among ourselves there would be those who would proudly remind him of all the wonderful things they had done in his name, and that he would have to disappoint them because he would not recognize them. There is no difference between them and those who will be saved "as through fire" because their lives turn out to be all tares and no wheat, or all impurities and no gold. As people who serve two masters, we cannot be anything but divided followers of Christ. As Christians, we have created all manner of traditions, named our spiritual fathers, and appropriated the revelation in cultural ways, much as the Jews have done.

We have also judged and divided humanity into the saved and the damned. This judgment has fallen back on ourselves because it has plagued many lives with preventable doubts about which side of this dividing line they will be on. Hence, it is important to be utterly clear that the only division of humanity we encounter in our Bibles is between a faithful remnant who bears the good news for all, and everyone else who cannot yet hear it. This division is likened to that between dough with and without yeast, food with and without salt. There are the bearers of light and those who are in the dark, the workers in the kingdom of heaven and those to be reached by them. Everything works in pairs, as is shown by Paul in Romans 9–11. In the process of making all things new, each element in each pair is transformed. The only other division of humanity that we encounter is the one compared to wheat and tares. This division runs through all our lives without any exceptions. It does not divide humanity into the saved and the damned but into what is unto life and the good and what is unto death and evil in all of our lives. The book of Revelation makes it very clear that in the final judgment God will retain whatever is unto life and the good, and will incorporate it into the new creation, while everything that is unto death will be destroyed.[11] In other words, God's reconciliation with humanity, and his will to make all things new, operate on a level that divides our lives but not humanity itself. It largely transcends our understanding, since only God can decide what he loves and thus what is unto life and the good. Any judgments we make amount to putting ourselves in his place, which is how the break with him began in the first place. In this context we must also remind ourselves of what we learned from the opening chapters of Genesis, namely, that humanity was created as one being in two persons and that we ought not to divide what God joined together. We have grown so accustomed to an individualistic understanding of ourselves and humanity – which is the consequence first of "technology changing people" and then of "technique changing people" – that we have largely banished this biblical teaching from our minds.[12]

In conclusion, the people of Israel remain God's people elected for all eternity as his first witness, but the faithful remnant now comes from all people and nations, including Israel. The Law has now become the law of liberty, but we are still far from understanding this. If we hold the first testament in our left hand, and the second testament in our right hand, we will read the Law and we will read about its complete fulfilment in Jesus Christ and how this Law teaches us a great deal about him. The Christian church appears to be repeating a great many of the mistakes that were made by Israel, and we ought not to be surprised if God continues to trim a great many branches from his olive tree because they have borne no fruit for the world (Romans 11:16–24). It appears to be impossible for most churches to believe that their confessions and traditions do not contribute at least something towards our salvation; this attitude legitimates a certain superiority over others, which is entirely contrary to the ways of the kingdom of heaven.

The Law of Freedom

As we have seen thus far, it is our human finitude in our separation from God that has transformed the created flesh into its opposite, thereby plunging it into an enslavement to the principalities and powers that it has brought forth. Humanity had to name itself, which led to the confusion of its language and the making of the false gods, by which each constituent group and society of humanity has made the finitude of its members liveable apart from God. Thus plunged into evil and death, not even God's chosen people were able to earn their own faith by means of good works. Faith is a gift that God grants to whom he wills, and his will is to reconcile himself with humanity and to make all things new. God thus separated Israel from the remainder of humanity, and a faithful remnant from the remainder of Israel; he separated Jesus Christ from all of humanity, and his followers from every people and nation – to be the yeast, the salt, the bearers of the light, and the workers in the kingdom of heaven until everything would be made new, including them.

Each and every group of Christians that has named itself as the body of believers or the true church has subjected itself to counter-transference reactions that permit its members to contribute something to their own salvation. This is understandable, but it is completely foreign to what the first and second testaments teach us regarding the Spirit and the law of freedom. We have confused the election of a faithful remnant with the question of salvation and damnation. Worse, we have convinced ourselves that it depends on our decision, as if we held the power to limit God's love and his plan to reconcile himself with humanity and to make all things new. Moreover, the making of such a decision would depend on our ability to discern life and the good, which is exactly what we lost in our break with God.

Again, our mistakes are similar to those made by the first witness elected by God. Paul warned us that even though the people of Israel were zealous in their pursuit of the Law as the way of righteousness, they failed because they did so not by faith but by their own works. The church as the second witness has essentially repeated these actions, either by accumulating good works or by creating a rigid morality, all based on God's law. In other words, by and large, the behaviour of the two witnesses has been little different from that of any society whose members strived to be virtuous by obeying its laws, even competing with each other for the favours of the king on the grounds of being one of his loyal subjects. No faith of any kind is required for such an endeavour, even if the law was originally received from God. It would appear that the law was used as a divine gift largely to satisfy the needs of societies, which can explain the universality of legal institutions among all cultures. Consequently, the difference between Israel and all other people was that Israel could boast of having the only true morality and a law received from the living God, while, from this perspective, other people had the cultural equivalent derived from naming themselves. Such an interpretation greatly benefits from the hindsight derived from the de-symbolization of all cultures as a consequence of the growing dominance of discipline-based approaches to knowing and doing. Nevertheless, the decisive difference stemmed from the Law of Israel being a revelation, thus requiring a discernment of faith.

As previously noted, such a discernment is evident from the opening chapters of the book of Genesis, which distinguish the revelation from the moralities and religions (and thus cultures) of the surrounding peoples. This discernment is also evident in the Law. If it had any common denominator with culture-based laws, it simply would not make sense. For example, in the part commonly referred to as the Decalogue, God identifies himself as the Liberator. Hence, it is unthinkable that he would immediately curtail the freedom he obtained for his people by commanding them how to behave. Moreover, why cast the form of this Law in the future tense and not the present tense? Why should the Law not have taken the form of "I (God) forbid my people to do the following list of things"? Another incomprehensible aspect of the Law is its claim that this list could be summed up in terms of a love for God and one's neighbour. Moreover, this love was commanded, thus transforming a list of "do not" into "do." Surely, the one thing that cannot be commanded is love itself because such a command would transform a relationship freely entered into by both parties into one of hierarchy and domination. Even in a democracy we are born into a legal system that exists with or without our freely given consent.

These difficulties disappear when we discern the Law as a revelation by means of faith. Israel received a Word from God that created something new and everlasting. Hence, this Word represented an intervention in the present that would play itself out and come to fruition in the future. Even if this Word is understood as a commandment in the present, it is a great deal more. Cast in the future tense, it promises that one day Israel will no longer have any need of these commandments because it will once again live out of love for God and neighbour. A communion of love will be re-established as a consequence of a complete reconciliation between God and humanity, of which Israel is to bear the good news to all.

The Law, understood in faith, thus guided Israel to live not by its experience and its culture-based ways and laws in order to satisfy the necessities that had risen from its break with God, but by the promise that the need of a morality, religion, and law would disappear as the kingdom of God approached. Doing so was made possible through faith in this promise: everything that is forbidden in the Law will become completely unthinkable and unliveable as the reconciliation takes place and a new communion of love is established in the kingdom of God. Choosing to live by this Law was to enter into life and the good; transgressing it amounted to once again stepping into evil and death. Consequently, there was no common denominator whatsoever between culture-based laws and God's Law. The differences soon engendered a growing clash between culture-based justice and God's justice. Israel thought it could satisfy the Law with its human approach to justice, and it found itself increasingly at odds with God's justice, which is fulfilled by love.

As noted in the previous chapter, the first commandment and promise of the Decalogue as discerned by faith is integral to God's promise to liberate his people and to reconcile himself with humanity as he makes all things new. Hence, when one day we again completely love our God, we will no longer have any need of other gods. We are able to accept this promise only through the gift of faith, which permits us to live, not by the experience and culture necessitated by our societies' having to name themselves, but by God's promise for a future that will be entirely secular without any morality or religion. We are thus liberated from these cultural necessities, transcending them as best as we can to obtain a taste of the life and the good that God offers.

The day will come when we will no longer have any need of images for the moral and religious purposes that correspond to the intuitions we have of those elements in our experience that appear to be god-like; they appear thus because their limits have not yet been experienced. We will know that these elements are integral to God's creation, and therefore we do not need to use religious images in order to have them do our bidding. We will not make such images, because the love for our God will be sufficient. The life and the good he offers will once again completely envelop our lives, as they did before we broke with him. It is in this manner that each and every commandment can be discerned through faith as a promise by which we can guide our lives. It is not because of some cultural necessity expressed through moral and religious standards that we must refrain from this or that action, but because it simply is not the kind of thing we would do out of love for God and our neighbour, whom he loves as much as he loves us.

For example, the prophet Amos was not angry with Israel because of what it had done to the poor and vulnerable members, as a social injustice according to some external standard. Instead, his anger was directed at Israel because their conduct showed that they did not love God, who loved these poor and vulnerable members as much as anyone else.[13] Similarly, coveting is always a test of whom or what we love more than Jesus Christ.[14] In sum, the Law was an integral part of God's work of reconciling himself with his people. The Law provided them with a set of promises that could orient their lives through faith as an alternative to serving the necessities resulting from their society's need to name itself apart from God.

This interpretation of the Law is confirmed throughout the first and second testaments, but especially in the prologue to the gospel of John. The Greek text of John 1:16 and 17 literally states that it is out of his fullness that we have all received grace upon grace because, although the law was given through Moses, grace and truth come from Jesus Christ. No one has ever seen God. God's only son, who is close to the Father's heart, has told us about him.[15] The Law was thus the first grace that God granted, but grace and truth came through the Word becoming flesh. Moreover, this second grace was granted to everyone, believers and unbelievers, whether they had died, were alive, or were yet to be born; this was a Word from God, valid for all times.

The two witnesses (Israel and the church) were to make this grace plain to all humanity by their words and deeds. Both the Law and Jesus Christ were thus integral to God's promise and his will to reconcile himself with humanity and to make all things new. Both are granted to those who have received the free gift of faith, without which they would be unable to understand what was happening. The total faithfulness of God is his truth, the way back to him through Jesus Christ. The two witnesses have generally failed to tell humanity that it has received this grace and truth.

The relationship between the first grace (the law) and the grace and truth in Jesus Christ is clearly revealed by Jesus himself in his Sermon on the Mount, in which he told everyone that he had come not to abolish the Law but to completely fulfil it. Once it has been fulfilled, humanity will be redeemed from the flesh and from the principalities and powers that have held it captive, and its debt will be forgiven by grace. We are free to go and to live our lives in freedom. We have now received God's law of freedom. The flesh and the principalities and powers that held us captive have been destroyed in eternity, although they have not yet been separated from human lives in our "bodies of death." This separation will have to wait until the final judgment.

According to our own experiences and ways of life, nothing appears to have changed, but if we live out of the promise that after a while the remnants of the principalities and powers in our lives will also disappear, we are able to live the law of freedom by means of faith freely granted to those who are set apart within Israel or the church. This is possible because Jesus has given a new meaning to the law by fully accomplishing it.

God knew that only his son, who became flesh but lived by the Spirit, could accomplish the Law, thereby penetrating what was separated from him. The Law was never intended to be an instrument of the kind of human justice that would find us guilty, and thus trigger our condemnation. It was God's first grace, which became total through the incarnated Word. We can now rely on this Law as a tutor to teach us the full and free life that God promises. It is a kind of minimum standard, to be surpassed by a love for God and one's neighbour if it is lived through faith. It is no longer a command but the full grace that we have all received.

Our relationship with God is thus marked by pure grace. God loves us as well as our fellow human beings because he is love – not for any reason, expectations, or anything that we might do or live by. This love is unchanged by our actions, and it expects nothing whatsoever in return. Consequently, we can have no claim on him when we fulfil this or that aspect of the law. He loves us without expecting anything, and he promises us that we will once again fully love him for no reason whatsoever and without any expectations. It is in this love, which expects nothing in return, that the glory of God appears.

If your neighbour asks you why you do the things you do for him or her, the answer ought to be: for no reason. Everything is grace since God has reconciled himself with humanity through Jesus Christ. There are no motives, reasons, incentives, expectations, or hidden agendas. There will only be relationships of love that show who God is and who we will be once again. This love will fully define and commit our lives to our God and our neighbours.

In the lives of the followers of Jesus Christ, the law becomes the law of freedom. A clear explanation of this occurs in the Epistle of James, where it is embedded in a description of the kind of Christian life that is possible through the Spirit sent by Jesus Christ. According to Jacques Ellul, James 1:16–21 deals with five themes: an introduction, a new birth through the Word, the creative Word, hearing the Word, and putting it into practice.[16] James declares that everything good that we can do comes from God. Literally translated, the Greek text speaks of "every excellent grace and every perfect gift" in our lives. The Greek word translated as "grace" simultaneously refers to the grace that we have received from God and which is saving us in this moment, and to every expression of happiness in our lives. In the same way, the Greek phrase literally translated as "every perfect gift" refers to the gifts that we have received in our person and to the moments in our lives that have been marked by our receiving something. It implies what will be confirmed later on, namely, that God does not test us and is not responsible for our being tempted by what we may love more than him. In so far as our lives "follow Jesus Christ," they are a gift from God and are not works for which we can take credit. All Christian works that we undertake as we follow our Lord thus begin with grace. Since this grace comes from the "Father of lights," there can be no change or shadow of variation in our receipt of it. God is a reliable Father who keeps his Word. We may count on his grace to create the possibility of a Christian life.

This text is polemical with regard to Greek culture, which regarded human life as being determined by the stars. By revealing that he is the Father of these lights, God liberates Greek culture from stoicism, which was dominated by astronomy. Whatever we do, God's grace, love, and promises will never change, making it possible for us to build our lives on them.

James 1:18 reveals that the Christian life begins with a new birth – a renewal of our entire being. By comparing the beginning of a Christian life to our first birth, we learn that it is lived by a new being that did not exist before. The first birth began our lives in the flesh separated from God, while the second birth begins a life in God. As with the first birth, we do not actively participate in it, because God brings about the second birth according to his will. He does this by planting the Word in us, according to James 1:21. It is an intervention of grace in our lives that is entirely independent of our wishes or orientations. God chooses those to whom he gives a second birth in order for them to become the first fruits of everything new he creates. As such, they signify a promise of what will follow as God makes all things new. Those who receive a new birth through grace are set apart to play a new role in the world. The remainder of the Epistle of James deals with the question of who these newborns might be and of how they must live in the world in order to be the first fruits of the new creation. In the most practical and concrete ways, they must bear light in that world, that is, in a manner that has also been compared to the functions of yeast or salt.

Since God's Word that has been implanted in these newborns is the same as the creative Word that we encounter in Genesis, it engenders something new in them. It is thus the beginning of recreating these people, and in the end it will bring forth the new creation. All of this began with Jesus Christ who was the incarnated Word – the totality of God's act of reconciliation with humanity, as described in the prologue to the gospel of John.[17]

In James 1:19–21 we learn that, following the second birth, people rely on listening to the Word, much like newborn babies depend on listening to a human language. It is by listening to the Word that we learn who we are, the situation in which we find ourselves, and the task to which we have been called: to serve in the kingdom of heaven. Since God's ways are not our ways, his Word is always surprising. We may encounter it wherever and through whoever he decides will speak to us. It means that we should always be on the alert for God's speaking, and, when it happens, we should listen very carefully. It always brings something new into our lives that we must not confuse with anything belonging to our ways and our culture. Doing so would amount to putting ourselves in God's place. This often happens when we substitute a theological or philosophical system or the teachings of our own denomination for God's Word. Hence, we must listen as carefully as we are able, reflect on what we hear, and be slow to speak about it.

We must be very careful in using biblical arguments when we have disagreements with someone, because we then turn these texts into "intellectual bullets" to gain our victory instead of God's victory. We must attempt to use God's Word to allow something new to be created in a situation, something that can transcend the dispute, something that can be a manifestation of God's love and reconciliation for us and thus for each other. We ought to remember that God's justice is for salvation and life, while our disputes are for division and death.

The reference to the justice of God in our text can be interpreted in three ways: what is just in the eyes of God; the rights that God has towards his creation as expressed in his covenants, which when obeyed express his justice; and the justice that is the power of the justification that God has through Jesus Christ.[18] There is no place for our judgments, whether they be based on our culture-based concepts of justice or on our philosophical and theological interpretations of the biblical revelation regarding God's justice.

Although God's Word is implanted in every newborn person, they must still receive it. In other words, a deliberate involvement is required to incorporate it into our lives. We must not impose on this text our Western, discipline-based approach to knowing. Here is yet another example of the kind of dialectical thinking found throughout our Bibles.

The Word is implanted in us, and yet we need to receive it. We must accept that the Word has been implanted in us and live accordingly. Once again in dialectical fashion, God does everything, but this everything also incorporates the little that we can do.

We now come to a third aspect of the Christian life. We have seen that it begins with a new birth and that growing up requires listening to the Word. We now arrive at putting that Word into practice. Of course, all three aspects are an integral part of the Christian life and thus cannot be separated from one another. We are born to live, and to live we must act. Conversely, if we do not act, we do not live. We are back to the relationship between faith and works. Generally speaking, the Christian church has encouraged an intellectualization of the Word by creating theologies, philosophies, doctrines, and ideologies. We do well to recall how Adam and Eve intellectualized the discernment of good and evil, because they acquired it by substituting themselves for God and by thus being disobedient to themselves and to their God. Similarly, the demonic has a purely intellectual knowledge of God that, according to our Bibles, causes it to tremble. In other words, the knowledge of God's Word cannot be purely intellectual. The results have been particularly disastrous when Christian theology and philosophy have uncritically adopted the discipline-based approach to knowing. Recall the parable about the building of a house on a rock or on the sand, as found in Matthew 7:24–7.[19] The common explanation of why the house built on the rock stands and the house built on the sand collapses is that the rock is Jesus Christ. However, a careful reading of the text makes it plain that the person who built the house on the rock is the one who put the Word into practice, while the one who built the house on the sand did not. The house built on the sand was built on an entirely intellectual understanding of the Word that was not put into practice. The situation is the same as the one following our first birth. If babies and toddlers did not put into practice what they metaconsciously discovered regarding their physical, social, and cultural selves, they would never develop into full human beings.[20] Our civilization suffers one crisis after another because our discipline-based approaches to knowing and doing, which are separated from experience and culture, make it impossible to put this knowing and doing into the various contexts of our individual and collective lives.[21]

In their slavish following of the world, Christian churches have organized their knowing and doing on the basis of discipline-based approaches in their institutions of learning and their seminaries, with the same disastrous results. On the one hand, we are treated to all manner of theological truisms that have no bearing on life and cannot be put into practice, and, on the other hand, the world presents a diversity of issues to which we cannot apply the practical wisdom that God gives for the asking. In conservative churches the members believe that they are saved by grace through the means of faith and that they only need to announce theological truisms to the world. In so-called liberal churches the members may be deeply concerned by the troubles of their neighbours but have no idea how to relate the gospel to them in a meaningful way. We have thus robbed the world of its yeast and salt, thereby transforming the gospel into its opposite.

Our text in James is particularly forceful on this point. It compares people who listen to the Word but do not put it into practice to people who look at their face in a mirror. After they have done so, they immediately forget what they look like. This mirror is the Word of God, which reveals to us that first and foremost we are loved by God, and we have been redeemed and set free because the ransom has been paid. We also learn how far we stray daily from the love, freedom, life, and the good that God offers us. Discerning this gap, we are able to repent and make changes to our relationships and our lives. Without God's Word acting as a mirror, we would have no alternative but to conduct our lives according to the way of life and the culture into which we are born. There would be no Christian life at all and thus no yeast, salt, or light in relation to a world whose societies must constantly rename themselves to survive apart from God. The Christian life cannot come from the world. It is born from God and is based on putting his Word into practice – a task in which the Christian community in the West appears to have entirely failed (I cannot speak about the other parts of the world).

Although in the context of any culture this would be entirely absurd, our text in James reveals that this putting of the Word into practice relates to our freedom. The Christian life is governed by the law of freedom. James 1:25 states that those who look deeply into the perfect law, the law of freedom, and who do not forget it but persevere in applying it, will be happy in what they do. This verse, in the form of a Jewish beatitude, is generally poorly translated because the Greek verb in the opening phrase occurs elsewhere only once, in Luke 24:12, where it refers to Peter bending down to regard the strips of linen that remained in the grave following Jesus's resurrection. Hence, to see the law of freedom involves a bending down, just as Peter had to do to see how Jesus had lowered himself, even to accepting his death at the hands of humanity. The law of freedom thus points to following Jesus Christ in lowering ourselves and accepting to be the least. This corresponds perfectly to Jesus's teachings regarding the kingdom of heaven, a topic to which we will return later on.

It is only when we humble ourselves and refuse to exercise any power over others that we can access the perfect law, the law of freedom. This freedom begins with God, the only one who is truly free, that is, obedient to nothing. It is in this freedom that he saves us through grace, because he is not subject to any kind of culture-based justice that is bound by the evidence of the good and the evil that we do. He cannot be subject to any criteria. When in his freedom God saves humanity by grace through the means of faith, he is reconciling himself with us, which includes the restoration of the freedom that humanity once had prior to its break with him, when there were no principalities and powers to hold us captive. Consequently, when we follow our Redeemer by lowering ourselves and refusing to exercise any authority over others, we encounter the law of freedom as a reflection of God's freedom. Clearly this has nothing in common with any human law; it is the exact opposite.

Anything contrary to the freedom that God is restoring to humanity is thus contrary to God's work of reconciliation. As he is restoring a communion of love and we are learning to live out of love for him and our neighbour, we cannot be obedient to anything, because relationships of love can be entered into only by people who are entirely free to give themselves to each other. If they are obedient to anything at all, this obedience will necessarily diminish the love relationship and thus trigger its destruction. The only way in which God and humanity can be reconciled and live together is in a relationship of love, as it was in Eden.

Our only response to God, who saves us from our bondage to the flesh and to the principalities and powers by means of grace, is to love him in return, because he is love. When the two witnesses show by their words and deeds what it means to be loved by this God, and how in our newfound freedom we will be able to love him in return, it is difficult to imagine how anyone would deny this love. However, these two witnesses have generally taken the place of God and have judged the world by turning the message of salvation, liberation, and love into one of moral and religious condemnation. It is based on a complete misunderstanding of the first grace as well as the second one. The fullness of the latter, extended to all, leaves us with the perfect law, the law of freedom.

Our freedom is thus a creation of God within us that results from our listening to the Word. When lived in relation to the world, the "law of freedom" is not a judgment and a condemnation but an offering of the fruit that results from listening to the Word and putting it into practice. Doing so involves learning to relate to the world as yeast relates to dough, and salt relates to food. It will surely put our faith to the test. Will we be able to follow our Redeemer in the way of life and non-power and maintain our freedom with regard to all the necessities and enslaving powers? Or will we harness our freedom and love to the ways of our culture in order to make them morally, religiously, and politically acceptable? In the latter case, we will love the ways of our culture, including our society's naming of itself, more than the kingdom of heaven and its law. For example, there cannot be a Protestant, Catholic, or Jewish form of the American way of life. Nor can there be a Christian form of democracy, and there certainly cannot be "one nation under God," because he is not in the business of backing our naming of ourselves. These are possible only if we love them more than the way of the kingdom of heaven. The law of freedom requires that we maintain this freedom that we have been granted in relation to our ways of life and cultures, whatever they may be. Anything else is a surrender of that freedom to the principalities and powers once again.

Our text tells us, regarding the Christian life, that those who lower themselves to find and practise the perfect law, the law of freedom, will be full of happiness in their actions. It is a life of freedom and joy that ought to make the world envious, at which point we can tell them that this is available to everyone. In grace no one is excluded, no matter who they are and how they have lived.

James 2:12–13 tells us that we must live the Christian life expecting to be judged by the law of freedom because the law of judgment is without mercy. In other words, under the law of freedom, if we disobey it we do not lose that freedom in order to be arrested and to stand accused before a judge. Instead, this law maintains our freedom by making us accountable for it to others and ourselves. Did we maintain it in our relationships with others and our God? From the perspective of the reconciliation and the coming of the kingdom of God as a communion of love, this is the all-important matter. The loss of our freedom would deprive us of our ability to love, thus jeopardizing the second grace extended to us. Consequently, the Christian life involves our constantly asking, Which word or deed will best express the freedom that God grants through his Word, and thus grow the kingdom of heaven in the world? How will this freedom open the door to loving more fully our God and our neighbour? It is in this manner that we will be judged by the law of freedom. Once again, this law has no moral or religious content of any kind and thus no common denominator with any culture-based way of life that is the result of a group's or society's naming of itself apart from God. The law of freedom places us within God's freedom to make our lives an expression of that freedom in order to open the door to a growing love through which the kingdom of heaven will be replaced by the kingdom of God.

Our text suggests that God will meet us according to our expectations of him. If we accept his freedom, knowing that God is love, we will encounter the judgment of his love. In contrast, if we expect God to behave like a human judge, applying moral and religious standards to our conduct and life, we can expect a kind of calculation of all the good and evil that we have done, and we will tremble in fear of condemnation. Freedom plays no role in this judgment and its consequences. Nevertheless, the text does not threaten us, because in God's freedom mercy will triumph over judgment.

Humanity, however, appears to prefer security and predictability over freedom. Putting the Word into practice is a scary business. We can no longer accept and take for granted our obligations, moral duties, religious principles, and legal obligations. We must seek to exercise our freedom in relation to this ensemble of constraints that holds us captive. We can no longer live according to the way of life of our society and its culture. All the stabilizing influences on our lives must be surrendered because in freedom nothing remains predictable. It is a terrifying prospect that can be faced only through the Christian life.[22]

The Spirit

The new birth, hearing the Word, and putting it into practice are impossible without the Holy Spirit. Once again, the biblical teaching regarding the Spirit has provoked numerous counter-transference reactions as a result of what some segments in the Christian community have done with it. We first encounter such problems in the writings of Paul, who is deeply concerned about the speaking in tongues when no one can interpret it. Nevertheless, with the benefit of what we have recently learned about our being a symbolic species dependent on cultures, we may be able to take another look at what Jesus taught us regarding the Spirit, as set out in the gospel of John beginning with chapter 13.

Once again, I will extensively rely on the interpretations of Jacques Ellul that were published previously.[23]

The principal teaching regarding the role of the Holy Spirit occurs in this passage of the gospel of John as an integral part of Jesus's last words to his disciples, just prior to his betrayal, arrest, trial, crucifixion, death, and resurrection. Jesus announced to his disciples that everything was about to change, and the book of Revelation shows that this included all of human history.[24] Without this context, the teachings regarding the Holy Spirit cannot be fully grasped.

Immediately after sending Judas away, Jesus told his disciples that now the Son of Man had been glorified and that God had been glorified in him. The events that had been set into motion would reveal who Jesus really was: the Lamb of God and the Redeemer of humanity. Next, Jesus told them that he was about to leave them and that they could not follow him where he was going. He gave them a new commandment, that they were to love one another as he had loved them, and said that in this way others would learn that they were his disciples. How could Jesus speak of a new commandment when this love had already been commanded in the book of Deuteronomy? What was new was not the commandment but the quality of the love, which Jesus was about to take to its limits as he laid down his life for them. The disciples were now to love each other to this extent. In this way they were to reveal Jesus's love to the world as he had revealed God's love, and others would be drawn into relationships of love as an incarnation of this "new" commandment. This is very far from the way in which the institutional church has reduced it to a proselytization of the world.

Next, our text reveals that the disciples were mostly confused about what Jesus was saying and what was about to happen. Up to that point he had led them by example, but this was about to end. Jesus consoled them with several promises. They would know that he was in the Father and that the Father was in him. Jesus was not speaking on his own authority, because it was the Father who was doing his work. They would continue to see him even though he would be absent, and they would continue to do his work and even more. All this would be possible because Jesus promised them the Holy Spirit.

Jesus also assured them that he was the way, the truth, and the life, which perfectly summed up his role in what was about to happen. He is the *way* back to the Father and makes possible a complete reconciliation between the Father and humanity. He is the *truth,* in the sense that a relationship with him is the way to life. There can be no greater truth than that. Consequently, it has nothing whatsoever to do with theological, philosophical, scientific, or religious truths. These are intellectualizations of aspects of life that can accomplish other things but not those that our text speaks about. Jesus is the *life* because of his relationship with the Father, who is the Living One. The way, the truth, and the life are completely inseparable from one another. Furthermore, Jesus was the way, the truth, and the life in the full sense, without any possible division between who he was bodily, socially, and culturally as well as spiritually. It is this Jesus who promised his disciples that he would send them the Holy Spirit.

We must deal with another common counter-transference reaction regarding this teaching about the Spirit. We appear to have convinced ourselves that, even though the early churches lived out of the promises made by Jesus to his disciples, this situation could not possibly endure. Our conviction may well rest on a misunderstanding of what happened after Christianity had spread throughout the Roman Empire. As noted, Christianity eventually became the empire's official religion, thus turning towards cultural ends. The resulting influx of new members could be managed only by means of organization, management, the setting of institutional standards and boundaries, and so on. It represented a disaster from which the Christian community has never recovered. The Reformation slavishly replicated these means by giving in to the same necessities. This is not a judgment on the people who did what was necessary under the circumstances in order to cope with the influx of new members as converts and of the people born into the new communities. Humanly, socially, and culturally speaking, there appeared to be nothing else that could be done, and yet I cannot avoid a strong sense that it was contrary to the revelation.

When Jesus was pursued by large crowds, he made no attempts to consolidate his ministry, as our churches did and continue to do. He did not invite people in the crowds to come forward to become members. He did not organize his disciples into a kind of management committee, nor did he attempt to create a physical infrastructure to house all the necessary activities that would have been involved.

Instead, just prior to his betrayal, Jesus instructed his disciples to love one another as he loved them and to open themselves to the guidance of the Holy Spirit. Hence, we need to look carefully at what Jesus taught them regarding the Spirit, while keeping in mind everything our Bibles teach regarding the Christian life. This life is to be based on loving one another because it will reveal to others who Jesus Christ is.

The Christian life needs to reflect the freedom of God; without it, the kind of love that Jesus commanded is impossible. No organizational and institutional constraints can thus be justified. They would decisively impair the freedom required for the love that is to win others. They would also restrict the openness of any fellowship with the Holy Spirit, who is free to come and go as he pleases. It may be time for us to reconsider what institutionalized Christianity has deemed to be self-evident and necessary for a very long time. If the Christian life is born from the free decision of God, how did we become convinced that we could organize people's conversion and the growing up of each new generation of Christians? We have simply extended our culture's way of life to reproduce our Christian fellowships, in much the same ways as the societies into which they are embedded have reproduced themselves. Again, there can therefore be no Protestant, Catholic, or Jewish forms of the American way of life – or of the Canadian way of life, for that matter. Nevertheless, this is essentially what has happened and continues to happen in North America.

What Jesus said regarding the role of the Holy Spirit is a Word of God and thus must be received through the means of faith. In other words, we must not repeat the mistakes of the first witness, who used cultural means to attempt to achieve justice through the Law. Similarly, we cannot achieve the Christian life by means of organization, management, catechism classes, doctrines, theologies, and statements of faith – all the means around which institutional churches are organized and propagate themselves. I recognize that this opens me up to charges of failing to deal with the hard realities of church life – "a dreamer," "an idealist," and possibly "a heretic." Nevertheless, I cannot abandon my conviction that Jesus is clearly telling us to go down a very different road, one that is based on the Spirit. This conviction has been reinforced by what I have learned regarding the role played by culture in the life of our symbolic species, which is now better understood as a result of desymbolization. I will therefore attempt to use these insights to sharpen the distinction between our first birth (and our subsequent life within the culture of our society) and what Jesus teaches regarding the second birth and the new life in him through the Spirit.

If we had been born into a traditional society, our growing up would amount to learning to dwell within its culture. As I have shown in a five-volume study of our civilization,[25] it would involve a great deal more than learning how to make sense of and live in the world according to this culture. Implicitly we would learn how to exclude anything that was radically other than this culture by symbolizing unknown elements in the world, and unknown possibilities for our lives, as more of what we already knew and had lived. Our indwelling in our culture would gradually become oriented by the greatest good experienced by our community or society, and this would turn into the absolute good because the unknown would have been symbolized as more of what had already been experienced and lived. In addition, entities in our lives of which we had not yet experienced any limits would be treated as myths, to use the terminology of cultural anthropology. In sum, this indwelling in our culture would have symbolically appropriated the entire universe for the collective life of our community. Everything would have been ordered according to those elements of experience to which we had not yet encountered any limits. We would have been incapable of understanding a revelation from a transcendent God other than in terms of our culture – unless this God intervened and created something new that permitted us to transcend this indwelling by means of what this culture referred to as faith. Our indwelling in our culture would have required us to make false gods; to make religious images of what we had intuited as having no limits, in order to render such god-like entities accessible and to force them to do our bidding; to name ourselves by a sacred and myths; and to exploit, dominate, and even kill others to make our way of life viable. From all these constraints the law of God's revelation promised to set us free.

By contrast, the indwelling in our cultures has taken on a somewhat different form for us, born into the so-called mass societies that emerged in the industrially advanced world following the Second World War. Discipline-based approaches increasingly took hold of our ways of life, thereby pushing the role of culture into the background. To compensate for this loss, the mass media now diffuse a bath of images that inform everyone of what used to be transmitted through customs and traditions: what to wear, what to eat and drink, what to own, what questions to ask one's doctors, what insurances are required for protection, what to think of complex events around the world, and a great deal more.[26] The media provide a complete guidance for our lives to ensure that what we desire and acquire add up to the kind of mass consumption that matches exactly what science and technique make possible in terms of mass production. We are possessed by public opinions rather than forming our own private opinions, and our behaviour is guided by what has been referred to as a statistical morality (as opposed to a traditional morality), which turns what most people do into what is normal and then into what is normative.[27] Consequently, growing up in these societies results in a dwelling in the integration propaganda constituted by the bath of images, supplemented by what remains of an increasingly de-symbolized culture.[28] This new form of indwelling requires the dominance of a different type of person than the one that was dominant in traditional societies. The latter functioned on the basis of a tradition-based orientation made possible by the brain-mind functioning as a mental map. In contrast, mass societies depend on other-directed people whose brain-minds function as a radar, scanning what everyone else is doing in order to establish what is normal, and then "going with the flow."[29] In sum, growing up in a mass society may be understood in terms of learning to dwell in its highly de-symbolized culture, complemented by its technical means for social integration. At the same time, these societies dwell in all their members through the organization of their brain-minds.

The form of this indwelling and the way in which mass societies dwell in their members are undergoing a fundamental change once again as the de-symbolization of language and culture continues, in part accelerated by a growing number of relationships being mediated by the new media and the internet.[30] This technical mediation is far from neutral. It substantially changes our embodiment, participation, commitment, and freedom in these relationships.[31] The shift to a growing reliance on images and discipline-based approaches to knowing and doing that are separated from experience and culture corresponds to a lesser reliance on language and culture, which, until now, had always been at the very centre of our being a symbolic species.[32] This shift appears to be accompanied by difficult adjustments that correlate with anxiety, depression, and other mental health issues. It also appears to give rise to a new set of mental illnesses.[33] Our social relations, groups, and societies are being diminished through disembodied relationships on the media and the internet.[34] These developments will have far-reaching implications for humanity as a symbolic species and for a Christian community that is entirely dependent on the Word.

What is almost entirely overlooked in relation to our current situation is that, in our all-out efforts to develop science, technique, and the economy, we are transforming ourselves through their vast influences on human lives, societies, and the biosphere. If our influence on our creations is much greater than the influence they have on us, we should be steadily able to realize our hopes and aspirations. If the contrary is the case, this will be impossible. Surely the last century provides all the evidence we need of which one of these two scenarios best describes what is happening to us.

Next, let us contrast our situation with what the revelation tells us about our second birth and our growing up in a Christian life, in which we listen to the Word and live according to how we can best put it into practice. In John 15, Jesus sets out the relationships that make this possible. God is the gardener, and Jesus is the true vine. The followers of Jesus are the branches that remain in him in order to bear fruit for the world. These new relationships will be established by the Holy Spirit. He will enable a complete relationship and communion between the Father, the Son, and his followers. In John 14:25–6, Jesus confirms this. The Spirit will dwell with the disciples and be within them. He will end their current confusion by reminding them of what Jesus had said, clarifying his words, and teaching them all things. It is by means of the Spirit that the wisdom of God will be comprehensible to them. There will be no other source of insight. In other words, the Spirit is the relationship between the gardener and the stalk and between the stalk and the branches. In the Christian life, only what comes from the stalk can bear fruit. The followers of Jesus are called to bear fruit for the world, which is made possible by their being grafted into the stalk. If they do not bear fruit, they will be cut off.

Once again, our text is speaking not of salvation or damnation but of being set apart to be the yeast or the salt for the world. If no fruit results, other shoots must be grafted into the stalk so that fruit will be produced for the world. Hence, being a shoot is not a mark of superiority. On the contrary, the shoots will be pruned so that they may bear more fruit. It is exactly as the letter of James explained regarding the purpose of the testing of our faith. If any of us are grafted into the stalk to bear fruit for the world, we can expect trials in order to bear more fruit and thus to become "perfect in all things."

Putting everything together, it is clear that, as people of our time, place, and universal technical order, we either dwell in our highly desymbolized cultures with their technical means of social integration, or we dwell in Jesus Christ through the Spirit. I cannot think of anything more radical than this revelation regarding the Holy Spirit. To reduce it to speaking in tongues and other manifestations is so bizarre that it is difficult to imagine how we have backed ourselves into a corner on this biblical revelation. Equally important, the disciples will dwell in the love of Jesus as he dwells in the love of his Father. The Father loves the Son, the Son loves his followers, and the followers are commanded to love one another without any limits. This love is the fruit held out towards the world.

How can we not be reminded of the original communion of love that God established in the Garden of Eden? How can we not be reminded of how, when this love was broken, humanity attempted to name itself, thus plunging the flesh into evil and unleashing the principalities and powers? Now that Jesus has gained the victory over the flesh and the principalities and powers, how can we not see that God created new kinds of relationships through the Holy Spirit? How can we fail to see that the fruits of these new relationships are turned to the world to share with others? I cannot give up my conviction that if the first and second witnesses had discharged the task for which they had been set apart, our situation would have been different. The second witness squandered God's work of making all things new by being distracted over institutional concerns and petty debates about the Holy Spirit. If we had followed the way, the truth, and the life through freedom, love, and non-power, Christianity would have developed in a radically different manner.

There is, of course, a great deal more to this deeply moving conversation between Jesus and his disciples, including the most comprehensive teaching regarding the Spirit in John 16. It is not found in the other gospels, and there is very little of it in the book of Acts. As a more detailed commentary on these passages in the gospel of John was published previously,[35] I will restrict myself to the following brief comments to show that a Christian life made possible by the relationships established through the Spirit would have steered the church in a very different direction, one that would have probably not been so different from the ways of the early churches. The second witness that God set apart for himself committed the same mistakes as did the first. God's ways are not our (cultural) ways. Living by his promises requires the means of faith, which is freely granted. When we come into the grip of faith, it has us; we cannot possess it.[36] Faith, reinforced by the Spirit, is the means that permits us to dwell, not in our cultures or in captivity to the flesh and the principalities and powers, but in Jesus Christ. In sum, the Spirit permits the Christian life to engage the struggle against everything in our ways of life and cultures that enslaves us – a struggle that is impeded only by our constantly loving something else more than our Liberator and the Christian life he offers. For example, in our age it means living in the recognition that the discipline-based approaches to science do not constitute a secular god in the domain of knowing, because they have spectacularly large lacunae. It means discerning that our technical means for increasing the power and efficiency of everything will only create an order of non-sense in which we as a symbolic species cannot live and thrive. It means realizing that economic growth will continue to reproduce the patterns that extract wealth through the destruction of human lives, societies, and the biosphere. It means that not everything is political, because the nation-state is impotent when it comes to the things that we really need and to which we aspire. It signifies that a disembodied life on the Web is no life at all. From the perspective of life, Christians ought to discern that the flesh and the principalities and powers have more powerful means than ever to reproduce evil and death because they are now reorganizing everything in the image of dead machines.

Before being written off as a hopeless pessimist, I must reiterate that in my five-volume study of our civilization I have carefully examined the limits of scientific knowing, technical doing, economic growing, and political organizing in order to develop other approaches that could go beyond these limits to accomplish what our current ways of life can never achieve. It is not a question of science, technique, the economy, and the nation-state being evil in themselves. What makes them evil is our living with them as if they have no limits and thus making them our contemporary secular gods. How can we fail to see that the kinds of issues faced by the second witness are not so different from those faced by the first witness? We have our own fertility cults of a secular kind. We are willing to sacrifice almost anything, including our entire planet, to our secular gods despite overwhelming evidence that they are not doing anything constructive for the overwhelming majority of humanity. I will gladly grant one point, namely, that the early church had one significant advantage over us. Many members were poor or were slaves, and they knew very well what it was like to be possessed by the system of that time, to have their humanity appropriated by it, and thus to not be able to be themselves. Hence, to be promised a way of life that would restore your freedom, your humanity, and your ability to live a meaningful life constituted a message of liberation and hope.

Nevertheless, we have also reconstructed this situation in order to legitimate ourselves. We ought to have paid more attention to Paul's letter to Philemon and other texts. By appealing to love, Paul asks Philemon to settle a social relationship that has been hindered by the institution of slavery. To appreciate what Paul is doing, one has to understand the historical context. As a historian well acquainted with the period, Jacques

Ellul has pointed out that, for practical reasons, the small groups of Christians could not have attempted any institutional reforms of slavery in the mighty Roman Empire.[37] Nor did they join the debates and ideologies regarding the legitimacy or non-legitimacy of slavery. Slavery had already posed a serious social, political, and philosophical problem, in part fuelled by the revolts of some slaves. The pressure on the institution had built up to the point that natural law had to be invoked in its defence (the usual sign of desperation). Under the circumstances, slaves were beginning to be granted more rights, and even ideas of abolition were entertained in some quarters.

Paul did not participate in any of this but instead addressed the immediate, concrete situation, thereby upsetting the institution from within – as opposed to forcing its reform from the outside through legal and political changes. Doing so enormously increased the responsibilities of the Christians involved. They could no longer hide behind a liberation movement, an ideology, philosophy, or theology. When a master and a slave are in Christ, it is their love for him, and not their cultural and social identities and commitments, that ought to shape their relationships with others. The fact that they are also master, slave, male, or female, or belong to any other social or economic category or ethnic identity, is secondary. A new communion becomes possible through the Spirit. In this particular case, the runaway slave Onesimus owed something to his master, Philemon, who in turn was indebted to Paul. Paul intervened by standing security for the slave if he ran away again. Paul referred to Philemon as a servant of Jesus Christ and to himself as a slave of Jesus Christ. Consequently, Philemon in effect became the servant of a slave, and Onesimus then became the apostle.[38] This letter shows how Paul went beyond his culture in order to dwell in Jesus and his love through the Spirit. It is a perfect example of what Jesus teaches regarding the law of the kingdom of heaven.

The Kingdom of Heaven

Following the resurrection of Jesus, his last words to his disciples, recorded in the previously discussed passages of the gospel of John, took on another dimension. To understand it, one must put them into the context of the entire revelation. Beginning in the opening chapters of the book of Genesis, we are told what we need to know regarding the relationship between the heavens and the earth. The former were created as the abode of God, which was entirely separate from his creation.

With the incarnation the heavens came to earth, as it were, because this earth was now the abode of Jesus, who, "although in the form of God, did not regard equality with God to be something to be exploited, but emptied himself, taking the form of a slave being born in human likeness. And being found in human form he humbled himself and became obedient to the point of death, even death on a cross" (Philippians 2:6–8). Consequently the relationship between the heavens and the earth was decisively transformed. After the resurrection this change would be for all of human history. Before the resurrection the only communication between the heavens and the earth had been mediated by angels. Jesus established a new connection that would be maintained by his body of believers. Its members would dwell in him as he dwelled in them through the Spirit. In Jesus Christ the reconciliation between God and humanity had been accomplished as he bridged the break between them.

The essential elements of this new relationship were promised by Jesus himself during his last words to his disciples.[39] He promised that the Spirit would comfort them by allowing them to go further into the truth through a more complete understanding of what was happening, and this would be their true consolation. Even though the disciples were clearly confused at the time, the Spirit would continue the conversation, as it were. Jesus made it clear that he was not speaking on his own authority but that he was telling them everything he had received from the Father. When he would no longer be with his disciples, the Spirit would transfer this truth to the disciples and to those who would come after them. The Spirit would thus reveal the only truth of the Word of God incarnated in Jesus Christ. As the Spirit would clarify everything, the disciples would come much closer to Jesus than they were when he was among them. Their faith would thus be strengthened, as would their maturing in the Christian life to which they had been called through their new birth. This life would bear fruit for the world, and thus they were to continue the work of Jesus. They would be joined by all those to whom God would grant a new birth and a new life through grace.

Something entirely new was introduced into human history by Jesus Christ and the body of his followers. It fulfilled exactly the prophecies regarding the kingship of Israel that had been announced in the first testament: a king would come who would rule the kingdom of heaven on this earth. Like the incarnation, the kingdom of heaven is hidden in this world and cannot be perceived other than by means of faith. The kingdom is found where the king is, and its subjects are those who do the works of Jesus after having received a new birth and a new life in him through the Spirit. They will dwell in Jesus as he dwells in them, they will be the fruits of God's love, and they are to pass this love on to the world. They will be in the world but not of the world and therefore will be able in their turn to bear fruit for the world. This has become possible because Jesus gained the victory over the flesh and the principalities and powers, and now God delivers the followers of Jesus from the darkness to transfer them to the kingdom of his beloved Son (Colossians 1:13). This kingdom will now contribute a new force to human history as a consequence of heaven being present on the earth. The kingdom of God, which will be established at the end of time, has now begun to move towards us within human history through the kingdom of heaven. The book of Revelation shows that the breaking of the seals on the scroll by the Lamb reveals the meaning of history, with the fifth seal representing the actions of the martyrs.[40]

Jacques Ellul summed up the differences between the kingdom of God and the kingdom of heaven in three ways.[41] First, the distinction between the kingdom of God and the kingdom of heaven appears only in the gospel of Matthew. In it Jesus speaks of the kingdom of God, but his teachings regarding the kingdom of heaven are exclusively transmitted through a set of parables. There is no mention of it in the first testament because there can be no such kingdom until the appearance of its king. The prophecies regarding the kingship in this first testament are now fulfilled. Usually we go no further than the explanation that the early church expected Jesus's return very soon, and when this did not happen, a rethinking had to take place, which led to the concept of the kingdom of heaven. Whether or not the concept developed in this manner, the explanation fails to grasp the fact that the kingdom of heaven is the exact fulfilment of the prophecies regarding the kingship of Israel and thus must be regarded as the result of an ongoing "conversation" between the Spirit and the believers who were being tested by the events of that time.

Second, the kingdom of God always refers to the end of time, when Jesus will return, the final judgment will take place, and the kingdom will be established. Its king is God the Father in the heavens on high and in eternity. In contrast, the kingdom of heaven always refers to the present, the here and now. Its king is the Son who was incarnated and came to us on earth, where his kingdom is now present. He has brought what was absolutely other and beyond the earth into this world. His reign began with his ascension and will last until his return to earth. Nevertheless, he continues to be present by dwelling in his followers through the Spirit, as promised. In other words, the kingdom of God is promised and will be fulfilled at the end of time, while the kingdom of heaven exists in the present for the purpose of bearing fruit to the world.

Both kingdoms thus play a role in the Christian life. Since the kingdom of God is coming, it is not we who are moving towards it, nor is it we who can bring it about. The kingdom of heaven may be understood as the movement of the kingdom of God towards us, with the result that its presence is the presence of the kingdom of God in so far as it has taken place and in so far as the end of time is already here.

Third, the kingdom of heaven has no organization and no limits or boundaries. What also characterizes this kingdom is the presence of Jesus Christ as its king. As such, there is a complete opposition between the kingdom of heaven and the church, which cannot escape its institutional character. The kingdom of heaven neither claims nor exercises any power whatsoever. It is the body of believers, of whom the greatest is the one who is the least and who stoops completely to the perfect law, the law of freedom. It is the way of humility and non-power in obedience to its king, who out of love humbled himself even unto death. His followers and members of the kingdom of heaven affirm this way of being in the world out of love for him and one another. There can be no restriction of freedom through the exercise of power of any kind, nor is there any way of limiting membership as the churches do.

In his study of the parables of the kingdom of heaven Jacques Ellul showed that this kingdom has the following characteristics.[42] It is a force that is active in the world and has neither place nor territory. It is a hidden power that, from the perspective of the world of power and domination, represents a certain weakness of non-power. This kingdom brings together in a complex relationship the actions of God and those of the followers of Jesus Christ. It establishes a new relationships between justice and love. Finally, the "laws" of this kingdom are the diametrical opposite of those of the world. Thus is characterized the role played by the kingdom in human history: that of the Word of God borne by Jesus's followers. The kingdom has no meaning other than in its relation to human history and the other forces that operate within it. This understanding can only be grasped through faith. Since these followers have been entrusted with much, more will be demanded of them than of those whom God did not call to the service of this kingdom; for this reason, in Revelation 1–3, the church goes through the judgment first.

While the first witness appropriated the law of God to achieve its own justice by its cultural means, the second witness has appropriated the body of believers and the kingdom of heaven by its institutional and cultural means in an attempt to legitimate itself. Once again, the results have been catastrophic. Having clothed itself in organizational, institutional, and cultural forms and necessities, the church has generally had very little to say to the world, and certainly it has not held out the love that Jesus commanded it to offer, to reveal who he is and why he came. Its role as yeast, salt, or light to the world appears to have diminished to the point that it recalls the conditions in Israel that led the prophet Elijah to ask God if he was the only one left.

What were these conditions that caused Elijah to despair? The usual answer, widespread in our churches, is that Israel loved its false gods more than the only Living One. It is another one of those theological truisms that get us off the hook because there is no need to put the Word of God into practice. With the benefit of what we have learned about the role of language and culture in individual and collective human life as a consequence of their de-symbolization, we are able to deepen our social and historical understanding of the situation. Israel, like any other society, faced the cultural necessities of having to name itself by means of a sacred and myths in order to make a life separate from God possible. Whenever it ceased to live the Law as the promise that its full love for God and neighbour would be restored, and instead elaborated that law to meet its institutional and cultural needs, it was pursuing false gods. This was not simply a question of erecting a few idols and running a variety of fertility or other cults, as if the remainder of the individual and collective life of the people remained largely unaffected. On the contrary, the creation of these idols was the sign that everything in the life of the people pointed in their direction, thus making the idols the confirmation of everything in their experience and their lives. Integral to these developments was the turning of the Law into a unique form of cultural morality and religion and thus a justification of all its institutions. This explanation can help us to appreciate the difficulty of living by the promise of the Law, which demanded a constant confrontation with cultural necessities by the means of the faith that was required to live out of this promise. Otherwise people would live by their experience and their culture, organized by the spiritual name it had given itself.

It is now clear that the struggle of Israel is our struggle as well. Jesus Christ has indeed gained the victory over the flesh and the principalities and powers. Everyone to whom God has granted a new birth and a new life has been transferred to the kingdom of his Son. This change can be discerned only through faith. It is not obvious from our experience and culture, other than from what has been lived as the new life through the Spirit.

Here we are confronted with the radical difference between the institutional churches and the kingdom of heaven. The need for our societies to name themselves to make possible a life separated from God has not yet disappeared. Those who within our societies have been granted a new birth and a new life have been promised that the day will come when they will no longer be the slaves of the flesh and the principalities and powers. If they live by this promise through the means of faith, they will be able to overcome their enslavement only to the point that they are able to love Jesus more than the principalities and powers that ruled their lives, even though obedience to this rule had made their lives liveable apart from God. It is a liveability either in pursuit of freedom and love or in resignation to slavery. To give up the latter is a very scary business because it will uproot us from everything that gives our society (and thus ourselves) a measure of having a grip on our lives in the world, a measure of security, a purpose for living, and much more. To remove that would instantly result in serious mental illness, if not suicide. From social and historical studies we know that when a society's naming itself becomes less effective as the society approaches the end of one of its historical epochs, the incidence of anomie, mental illness, and suicide increases.

The only one who was able to live by the Word through the Spirit was Jesus Christ. What was separated from God following humanity's break with him was penetrated and thus no longer separate. The flesh and the principalities and powers were defeated, but they continue to reign in everyone's lives until they can be removed in love. In this, God does not resort to any means of power, because doing so would destroy also our persons and our lives. Consequently, until we put the Word into practice and by faith discern concretely and specifically the forms of the principalities and powers that rule our age, we will be stuck in theological truisms that we are unable to relate to the world. Since the institutional churches (without any exceptions that I am aware of) have failed to do this, they have condemned themselves to serving the false gods of our age. They have attempted to superimpose either a spiritual gospel or a social gospel, neither of which is even a dimension of the revelation because the churches have completely and totally failed to put it into practice.

Simply put, our churches have no idea whatsoever of the way in which our knowing is ruled by science, because they have been unable to discern its limits (which can be done socially and historically) and therefore to transcend them with the practical wisdom that is free for the asking but which can only be lived by means of faith. There is absolutely nothing abstract about this. For example, discerning the limits of our discipline-based approaches to medical science transforms our attitudes towards health and disease and its treatment.

Similarly, our churches have no idea whatsoever of the limits of technical doing and the implications of treating this technical doing in the way that people treated their gods in the past. Discerning these limits has far-reaching practical implications, such as how we live with the new media and the threat of increasingly disembodied lives.

Our churches have no idea whatsoever that not everything is political. On the contrary, many conservative Christians do believe that everything is political and that they must mobilize the political means of power to impose their values on society for the supposed good of all. Unfortunately, there is not an ounce of love being held out to the world through these efforts. Matters have become out of control when political parties supported by a majority of conservative Christians have gained power. Have we not read in our Bibles that the only religion acceptable to God is that of taking care of the weakest and most vulnerable members of society? The Christian involvement in the debate over public health care in the United States is disturbing. So are the efforts of Conservative governments in Canada that almost entirely ignore the needs of the weakest and most vulnerable members of society. If it is power that Christians want, they will have it, but it has nothing whatsoever to do with the perfect law – the law of freedom and the kingdom of heaven.

In sum, I believe that in our time the difference between the institutional churches and the kingdom of heaven is once again a matter of putting or not putting God's Word into practice. Organizing and propagating themselves like any other institution in our societies, the institutional churches have assimilated the revelation to our social and cultural needs, thereby turning it into a morality and a religion. To join any of these churches is to put on the straitjacket of its theological, doctrinal, social, cultural, and historical tradition. It is more important to conform to the way in which things have always been done than for each generation to ask itself how it can best be a yeast, salt, or light for the world. We must discern the forms that the principalities and powers have taken in order to understand first our own enslavement and then our neighbours' enslavement. Not until then can we can speak of freedom, love, justice, and everything else that the revelation promises. Otherwise we will condemn ourselves to repeating theological truisms that neither we nor our neighbours can apply to anything in our lives in the world.

Does this mean that a faithful Christianity will turn itself into an economic, social, political, and environmental movement? If it did, it would not be a part of the kingdom of heaven, which avoids all ways of lording over others by the exercise of power and influence regardless of the means of persuasion used. The kingdom of heaven is following Jesus Christ, who was willing to humble himself in his way of freedom, love, and non-power.

We can now understand why, regarding the kingdom of heaven, Jesus taught exclusively through parables. He did so out of love in order to protect those people who had not yet been granted a new birth, a new life, and the means of faith to live it through the Spirit. To reject the kingdom of enslavement to the principalities and powers and to enter the kingdom of heaven is to be willing to forsake all security, false consolations, false hopes, false purposes, and anything that makes an enslaved life liveable, and thus to reject the secular, sacred, and myths by which our societies name themselves. No one can do this unless they know they are held in something much more secure and true: the love of the Father brought to us through Jesus Christ. Hence, by communicating the kingdom of heaven through parables, Jesus ensured that their radicality could only be understood by the means of faith. Everyone else was protected because they would hear only beautiful and moving little stories that would not put them in an existentially impossible situation of relativism, nihilism, and anomie.

The kingdom of heaven is the Word of God borne in the world by the body of Christ's followers, who have put this Word into practice and seek to incarnate it in their daily living through love. Doing so begins by confronting the flesh and the principalities and powers in their own lives. To the extent that they begin to gain a measure of freedom, love, and justice in relation to them, the Word incarnated in their lives becomes a yeast, salt, and light in the world. No theology, philosophy, morality, religion, or anything else that is not lived can accomplish this. Whether it is intellectually true or not makes no difference at all, because we are not intellectual machines programmed by ideas. Such intellectual systems operate on an entirely different level, which does not preclude their being useful for our lives from time to time. However, discipline-based approaches to theology, philosophy, and ethics belong to the kingdom of our secular god of knowing. Similarly, the practices for directing and counselling that are derived from our discipline-based approaches to helping people cope with their lives are in the service of our secular god that rules over human doing. Being present in our societies by throwing around our political weight is serving our secular god of the nation-state. It is resorting to means of power to have our ways imposed on others, in complete violation of the ways of Jesus Christ. We cannot use the pressure of the crowd on the individual to obtain conversions. We cannot use the power of the media (old or new) on behalf of the Christian life. We cannot rely on pedagogy and all the educational techniques of our society to help those who are born into Christian communities to move through the stages of "faith development." We can do this only if faith is an integral part of the cultural growing up of these children, in which case it is not faith but religion. Faith is a free gift from God that is granted to every person following a second birth into the Christian life. Once granted, faith can be nurtured, but that requires freedom, love, and fellowship – the diametrical opposite of organizing its transmission as if we had the power to grant and develop it.

We must devote ourselves to understanding the revelation regarding a second birth, the Christian life, its dependence on the means of faith granted by grace, the dependence on the Spirit to mature that faith, and the need to do all this in a community of freedom, love, and non-power. The Christian community acts as the body of Christ that is united in putting the revelation into practice, in its calling to serve in the kingdom of heaven as an active historical force in the world. We must then look around us to see where we can join a local manifestation of this body of our Lord. If we cannot find it in the institutional churches in our community, what are we to do? The answer is simple and yet difficult. We are called for service in the kingdom of heaven. We must be as clear as we can be that this is a matter of living the promise of freedom, love, and humility and the rejection of authority over others – and thus any means of power. If we are obliged to choose between the ways of a denomination and the way of the kingdom of heaven, we know the choice we must make. Above all, we must ask that the kingdom of God come, in the full knowledge that it *is* coming. Remember what Jesus Christ promised: in seeking his kingdom, we can ask for anything in his name, and it will be granted. It is a work of faith, hope, and love, and, with regard to the institutional church, an almost infinite patience appears to be required. We may well ask ourselves how the world of North America can come to know the Jesus of the revelation when the institutional churches appear to preoccupy themselves with everything other than what, to the best of my understanding, appears to be the revelation about the kingdom of heaven. Also in this context, we must hold on to the promise that, in the kingdom of God, God will be all in all.

In the meantime, institutional churches are doing an enormous amount of harm. I know a mother who said to her son that churches are men's clubs where women serve coffee. I have already told the story of the young preacher who was dismissed for failing to love the institution more than anything else. I recall a person who said that he was clearly predestined for hell, otherwise he would not be an alcoholic. How many people's lives have been thrown into turmoil because they were led to believe that having doubts was a sign of a lack of faith? These examples can be multiplied almost indefinitely. In response to the theological truism written on the wall of a university building, "Jesus is the answer," one person wrote: "What was the question?" It sums up the entire situation. The theological truism had not been put into practice, hence its author had no idea to what it corresponded. It is a sign that the yeast has lost its capacity to relate to the dough. In the same vein, institutional churches do not act as if they believed that the second birth, the Christian life, faith, and the Spirit are a gift from God. We believe we can organize the transmission of faith from generation to generation, and we design learning materials that are appropriate to the "stages" of its development. In so doing, churches put themselves in the place of God all over again. Once granted, faith can only be nurtured in a community of freedom, love, and non-power that is open to the Spirit. We appear to be very far removed from such a situation.

As noted, I have always been struck by accounts of the life reviews of people who have had near-death experiences. The accounts appear to indicate an insight into who the people were and the kind of lives they had lived. They remind me of situations in which people liberated from the principalities and powers could see themselves and the world without myths, as they truly are. These accounts are the best metaphors I know for imagining a secular life without myths. They also remind me of the revelation that, when our lives are passed through the fire so that all the impurities can be skimmed off and thrown away, little or nothing may remain, and yet we ourselves will be saved. What little does remain, God will incorporate into the new creation.[43]

Before we dismiss this thought as naive idealism, let us imagine what might be possible in faith in the context of our time. I cannot dismiss the possibility of living out of Jesus's promises that so characterized the early church. I will begin with human knowing. As a consequence of knowing being in the grip of discipline-based approaches, in which we participate as knowers, doers, supervisors, or managers, a body of believers could share their broken and de-symbolized experiences of what is happening to us in our work in order to transcend the limits of this discipline-based knowing. They could do this by creating an "ecology of knowledge" that integrates our divided and partial experience of what is happening into something more comprehensive in order that the revelation can address it. We need to create a dialogue between the Word of God and our practice of it, by more fully understanding our situation in terms of what each member of the body of believers knows and does not know. For example, one member may speak about what it is like to work on the "intellectual assembly line" of an enterprise-wide system; another on what it is like to work on a lean production assembly line; another on what it is like to be an engineer designing these systems; and still another on the kinds of health implications this has. I am referring not to a university-like intellectualization of these diverse experiences but to a collective attempt to discern what is happening. For such an ecology of knowledge (initially embedded in experience and culture) to work, its members must contribute their experiences for the others and, in love, respect differences of interpretation and even disagreements.

Once a better grip has been obtained on what is happening to human work and our workplaces, a dialogue must be established with the Word of God. The Bible has much to say regarding the business of hiring someone for a wage, and the risk of thus appropriating and dominating a significant part of someone's life and, via its influence on everything else, of that person's entire life. Many texts will cease to be theological truisms as they help us to understand what we are to be delivered from. This understanding does not necessarily have to remain entirely in the domain of human knowing. Opportunities may arise for some members to put it into practice. In any case, we will know better what holds us captive and what deliverance from this captivity involves. Each new generation needs to listen to the Word and come together to reach a better understanding and jointly put it into practice. In this way, they may avoid theological truisms and by grace nurture a living faith.

The effects of our work and the influences of our societies exercise an enormous control over our lives. Private opinions arrived at through experiences such as talking to others, further reading, and critical reflection have largely been replaced by public opinions. Since we are not quite sure where these have come from, they are a sign of our being possessed by the principalities and powers that rule our society. Similarly, a statistical morality that turns what most people do into what is normal, and what is normal into what is normative, is another sign of how we are possessed by these forces. Nevertheless, raising teenagers will bring us into direct contact with this kind of possession. As a parent, imagine objecting to something that your child requests, and being told that everyone in the child's class has done it, so why can't he or she do it as well? With the influence of the new media, do parents have any chance of convincing their children that a highly disembodied life is no life at all because it lacks participation, commitment, and freedom? If our children insist that this is "normal," what can we say and do?

In sum, if the members of a small body of believers could come together in a way that would make everyone more aware of how enslaved and reified they are that no one is exempt, and that no one can easily escape, would this not be the equivalent of confessing to one another how much we need what our Lord has promised us in terms of freedom, love, humility, and non-power? Could this not help us to break through status, gender, economic, and other differences, and slowly teach us to learn to live for each other in a love that is a fruit to the world? Could we realize that life does not have to be the way it is and that one day it will no longer be this way? It would involve each and every believer in a joint venture to understand the Word in relation to the world in which we live. It would facilitate putting this Word into practice, because without works there is no faith, and there is no faith without works. If this is a naive idealism, then our faith becomes a naive idealism. However, this is our Father's world. If he helps us to understand it by giving us faith, and strengthens it through the Spirit, then anything is possible.

In conclusion, the fellowship of the members of the body of believers cannot remain a theological truism. It must include the kinds of discussions and sharing that I have suggested, in order to discover the extent to which we dwell in our culture in an enslavement to the flesh and the principalities and powers. It involves looking in the mirror of God's Word in terms of the lived reality of our daily lives. When we put the Word into practice in this concrete way, we will be guided towards a Creator dwelling in Jesus as he dwells in us through the Spirit. Painful as this may be from time to time, it must be framed by an overwhelming sense of being loved and of having been pardoned and set free by grace without giving any consideration whatsoever to merit or circumstances.

If the members of the body of believers are to be able to act as yeast and salt in relation to the world, we cannot ever be satisfied with limiting ourselves to theological truisms. God has indeed transferred us from our darkness into the kingdom of his Son, but we must participate in it by doing our part in knowing how we dwell in our culture and how we together learn to dwell in Jesus.

The last and very important teaching that Jesus gave, in Matthew 18:1, regarding the kingdom of heaven, deals with finitude; it involves learning to live as creatures dependent on the only Living One. Jesus concluded his teachings by answering the question of his disciples as to who would be the greatest in his kingdom. Jesus took a child into their midst and told them that, unless they changed and became like children, they would never enter the kingdom of heaven. He went on to say that whoever became humble like this child would be the greatest in the kingdom of heaven, and whoever would welcome such a child in Jesus's name would welcome Jesus himself. He also warned them not to put a stumbling block before any of these little ones who believed in him. In other words, Jesus took a child, who could not even begin to dream of being the greatest, because children know very well that they are still growing up and developing every aspect of their person and life. The very condition of being a child thus precludes being the greatest. It is important to emphasize that Jesus was talking about the kingdom of heaven and not the kingdom of God, and therefore about the condition of the child in the present and not about what that child might become. When we enter the kingdom of heaven, God becomes our Father and we become his children.

This takes us back full circle to the opening chapters of Genesis. Being a creature of God implies accepting our human finitude. We can deal with this either by remaining within God's love or by attempting to refuse being his child, to break with him, and to go our own way, and thus finding ourselves in need of every means of power in order to compensate for our finitude as a creature. Nevertheless, a creature we shall remain, and this has resulted in our enslavement to the flesh and the principalities and powers. As God begins to make all things new through Jesus Christ, we must accept being his children, totally dependent on him; it is this subjective condition of a child that must mark our person and our life. Consequently, the best we can do as God's children is play at being a church, knowing that in our dependence it is all we as creatures can ever accomplish. Any claim that we can constitute a true church is to once again put ourselves in the place of God, acting as if we can bring his kingdom into being. A body of believers who dwell in Jesus through the Spirit and help to constitute the kingdom of heaven will never be anything more than children playing at being a church, with the promise that one day the kingdom of God will be established and this play will disappear. In the same vein, when we talk to one another about what is happening in our lives, when we look into the mirror of the Word of God, when we put what we have learned into practice, we are like children playing before our heavenly parent. If we accept our being children, we know we can turn to our Father in the way that our children turn to us when they are dependent on us. There is no room for pride, lording over others, judging others, and acting in ways that we now tolerate in our self-satisfaction, derived from taking ourselves much too seriously and refusing to accept our true condition.

There may well be another reason why Jesus summed up his teaching regarding the kingdom of heaven with the admonition that we must accept being God's children and thus learn to live with our human finitude in a relationship of loving dependence on him. Another characteristic of the condition of being a child is the absence of the metaconscious myths that come with spiritually naming ourselves. Although circumstances rarely permit it, children can from time to time be amazingly candid because they have not yet learned to dwell fully in the culture of their community; they are still somewhat open in a way that no adult can be open.

Now we are ready to consider the final chapter that deals with Ecclesiastes, where we learn that all is vanity. Yet, as children of our Maker, we can take joy in the simple pleasures of life and in the relationships that sustain us. In an age of de-symbolization, this biblical book is (in the opinion of Jacques Ellul) the closest in relevance to our time.

6 Christianity in the Grip of Vanity and Chasing after the Wind

Why Give the Last Word to Qohelet?

Why devote this last chapter to the last book that was accepted into the first testament? The importance of doing so, especially for our civilization, was inspired by Jacques Ellul and his commentary on Qohelet (Ecclesiastes).[1] He probed most, if not all, of the significant undertakings of our civilization, from a historical perspective as well as from the vantage point of faith. Unlike the theories of our civilization that have already mostly been forgotten, his work accurately foresaw most of the important events of the second half of the twentieth century – which amounts to the best possible scientific validation that any theory can receive. His correlation with subsequent events required a transcendence of reality by showing how our civilization is "newly possessed."[2] When someone with this kind of track record tells you that throughout his life he had struggled with the significance of Qohelet and that he received more from this work than from any other book of the Bible, I believe it is important to understand why this was the case and why he insisted on giving Qohelet the last words of his extensive writing (although a few works were finished and published after it).

The body of Ellul's writings is unique for the second half of the twentieth century because none of his books depends on the disciplines that are relevant to the subject at hand, although he makes use of them. The architecture of his many books and articles corresponds to his subject matter: what was happening to human life and society in the second half of the twentieth century, primarily as a consequence of technique. If we wish to examine this topic scientifically, it must be described in terms of a highly de-symbolized human and social world that nevertheless retains something of its dialectically enfolded character. Consequently, each book and article relates to the whole of his work, and this work in turn relates to what was happening. It may be compared to the architecture of a hologram in the sense that the entirety of his interpretation is present in each work, although its focus is on a particular aspect of human life at a particular time. I cannot sufficiently emphasize this point, because most works based on, or derived from, his insights are either a distortion through the discipline-based approaches of philosophy or theology, or an appropriation by an "-ism" such as environmentalism, feminism, anarchism, structuralism, or fundamentalism as a vantage point for interpretation.[3] Hence, we had better discover for ourselves why he regarded Qohelet as the summation of all his own work of scientifically examining and philosophically reflecting on a great many things under the sun during his lifetime and attempting to make sense of them through faith. Nevertheless, he knew that his attempts were no exception to the pronouncement of Qohelet. In his discussions at Bible studies he always sought out those who disagreed with him because he knew that in this way we evolve our knowing and doing in the world.

A great deal has changed in our world since Jacques Ellul stopped writing. For example, he described human life prior to the explosion of the internet and the social media, which are now so influential to our lives. Nevertheless, most of the new developments have reinforced and cumulatively expanded the kinds of patterns he described. It has become possible, however, to trace many of the characteristics of technique, and its evolution as a life milieu and system, to those of the discipline-based approaches at the heart of these developments.

Possibly one of the most decisive findings of Jacques Ellul's analysis relates to our dependence on language and culture and thus to our vulnerability to their de-symbolization by technique. If human words are a gift from God, if this gift was fundamentally redirected by our naming ourselves, and if technique has become the most powerful de-symbolizing force ever unleashed by humanity onto itself, then everything that has made us human until now is threatened by the development of technique. It is too early to conclude that the many changes in what it is to be human are a mutation to something else or that they represent a more or less irreversible decline. In any case, our growing dependence on images, discipline-based approaches, and intellectual approaches based on the principle of non-contradiction (including all branches of mathematics), are having a powerful de-symbolizing effect, which can probably be reversed only by a massive undertaking of re-symbolization. However, that window of opportunity may well be closing, as anything radically other still remains largely unthinkable and unliveable. To the faithful remnants of the Jewish and Christian communities, our present situation offers some serious difficulties because everything depends on a God who speaks and whose Word cannot be interpreted other than in relation to the human words of our cultures, whether or not they are highly de-symbolized. It is likely the reason that Jacques Ellul struggled so intensely with Qohelet for much of his life.

There could be a second reason. In contrast with many theologians, Jacques Ellul regarded the many contradictions in Qohelet as one of the keys to understanding it. He rejected the imposition of the principle of non-contradiction on this text, which holds that no person can possibly think two mutually exclusive thoughts at the same time. The usual conclusion is that the text must have been written by several authors to account for these contradictions. It is a strange argument because it cannot explain why, in the end, a single editor or group of editors integrated the contradictory fragments into a single text, and why this work became regarded as a Word from God to be incorporated into the canon of the first testament. Ellul argued, however, that we must discover the meaning of these contradictions and their contributions to the overall text. Discipline-based theological or philosophical approaches to biblical texts that explicitly or implicitly adhere as much as possible to the principle of non-contradiction are thus entirely incompatible with symbolization, language, and culture and thus inevitably lead to erroneous conclusions that bar our understanding and living the meaning of the text. If we are convinced that we have become rational, scientific, and secular (at least to some degree), we will be baffled by the multitude of contradictions in Qohelet and may have little choice but to dismiss this text as going in a direction where we cannot follow. I find this the summit of irony – contemporary human life is an endless sequence of contradictions, as I have attempted to show in my work.[4] Many of these contradictions derive from the kinds of developments briefly summarized previously and the de-symbolizing influence they have on the way we make sense of and live in the world. This further confirms why Jacques Ellul was so deeply affected by Qohelet.

A third reason for devoting my last chapter to Qohelet is related to its dependence on the opening chapters of Genesis, to which we devoted the beginning of this work. It is as if Qohelet were engaged in a retrospective of everything that had happened to humanity under the sun

– possibly triggered by a long period of silence during which God did not speak to his people; he did not speak to them again until the Messiah came as the Word incarnate. The material that follows is intended as a modest supplement to Jacques Ellul's commentary, arranged according to the three principal themes he identified, and it should be read as such.

Vanity and Myths

Having undertaken and observed what he could, Qohelet declared: "Vanity of vanities, all is vanity." Following the break between God and humanity, and the latter's attempt to make it complete by naming itself, each group and society became compelled to name itself by its works. These are the works "under the sun," as Qohelet refers to them, in the sense that they belong to a world that is no longer lived in as a creation but in rejection of its Creator. This must have been in Qohelet's mind, because the first word in his opening statement, commonly translated as "vanity," is the same word translated as "Abel" in Genesis 4. It also reminded Qohelet that everything does not end under the sun, since God heard the voice of Abel's blood crying out from the ground.

Nevertheless, Qohelet desired to probe everything under the sun in order to know how humanity was profiting from these works (including the idols, as we will see). In other words, all the ways of life and the cultures of every group and society are assembled under the sun – which takes us back to Genesis. The opening chapters of Genesis explicitly and implicitly differentiate the revelation received from the only Living One from the religions of the false gods of the surrounding peoples, and thus their cultures, which name themselves through these gods. Also following Genesis, Qohelet is not interested in creating a theology, a philosophy, or any other set of ideas. She (*Qohelet* is in the feminine in the Hebrew language) began with herself – the works that her hands had found to do, the things that she had undertaken, and the observations that she was able to make. It is all about our living under the sun and what it profits our lives, which can be probed only in terms of these lives – beginning with the life of Qohelet.

Much living had gone on since Genesis, and this permitted Qohelet to go further in a way that strikes me as so contemporary that it is as if this book had been directly addressed to us. It appears to anticipate our latest understandings of the roles played by symbolization, language, and culture in human history, including their trivialization by de-symbolization. I cannot help but be struck by the opening verse: "Vanity of vanities, all is vanity." In addition to summarizing everything that Qohelet is about to probe, this pronouncement includes the myths through which all groups and societies have named themselves. I am aware that this is a convenient interpretation for someone like myself. I have spent much of my life attempting to understand the roles played by science and technique in individual and collective human life and, via them, in the biosphere. Time and time again, I have been forced to conclude that, without a reference to myths, my own and everyone else's behaviour would be incomprehensible. I say this as someone who intellectually grew up as an engineer and thus has some insight, experience, and knowledge.

If humanity's break with God necessitated each group's and society's naming itself, and if this naming involved myths as the symbolic summation of its works – the ultimate expression of what the community was all about – then surely our understanding of myths contributes to our ability to grasp the relevance of Qohelet for our civilization. The sum of all the works of a group or society under the sun may be thought of as the total interpolation and extrapolation of everything known and lived by its members, with the result that the unknown, the past, and the future become extensions of this totality, and God is excluded from this myth world. Beginning with its opening statement, Qohelet pushes to the limit how the revelation is radically other than our ways.

In order to prevent this interpretation of myths from being imposed on the text, I will briefly summarize some of the translation issues that led Jacques Ellul to conclude that the translation of Qohelet's opening statement best renders the Hebrew text to which it corresponds.[5] As noted, in this expression, the first word, *hebel,* here translated as "vanity," occurs as the name of Abel in Genesis 4. At that time, it meant "mist, breath, or smoke," which dissipates and thus foreshadowed Abel's short and tragic life. Although Abel vanished without offspring, God heard the "voice" of his blood and remembered him. In Hebrews 11:4 Abel is referred to as righteous. It is possible therefore to translate the opening statement as "all is vanity" or as "all is Abel," and to equate the meaning of these translations in the sense that everything bears his name and is going to disappear, leaving nothing behind. Moreover, Abel's godliness, righteousness, and sacrifices were useless in preventing his death and disappearance. Hence, if everything is *hebel,* than nothing can avoid suffering and death. Worse, his godliness and sacrifices were the cause of his death. Even Cain did not escape being *hebel* and, despite his power and weapons, was also going to die and vanish. From the perspective of vanity, Cain and Abel were thus undistinguishable in their end as a breath or mist that is destined to disappear.[6]

Consequently, the assertion that all is Abel (*hebel*) thus includes all of us Abels because there are no exemptions. God's people work like everyone else, notwithstanding the Torah and the sacrifices, which even caused the deaths of many as a result of persecution. Did it require the long decline of the faithfulness of God's people's before Qohelet could have said such a thing? Is it possible for us as Christians, now very much in the same situation, to accept this of ourselves? Will our going to synagogues or churches, and will our religious services, rituals, and a great deal else, belong to *hebel*? Will everything else disappear like the playing of children? For Christians, will the need to organize our participation in the kingdom of heaven through institutions that are inseparable from a way of life and culture prove to be too difficult to overcome? Do we share this condition with our Jewish brothers and sisters?

Jacques Ellul goes on to explain that this interpretation of the name of Abel is confirmed in a number of subsequent biblical books of the first testament.[7] Since I know no Hebrew, I will closely paraphrase his explanations. In Isaiah, things that are closely associated with *hebel* (wind and breath) include illusions, idols, and death, as well as efforts that do not bear fruit. In Jeremiah, *hebel* is so closely associated with idols, idolatrous practices, and everything involving nothingness that we could possibly translate Qohelet's words as "vanity of idols," as well as "vanity of vanities," or say that "idols are wind." In addition, in Isaiah as well as in Qohelet, it has a strong implication of "uselessness": in the context of reality it refers to nothingness; in the context of truth it suggests a lie; in relation to effectiveness it points to uselessness; and with reference to security it suggest deceit. In Job, *hebel* designates something illusory as a consequence of its being fleeting, deceptive, or without result. This association also occurs in the Psalms, where we again find *hebel* related to *ruah*, meaning "faint breath, light wind, mist, or vapour."[8]

Qohelet knew all these meanings very well. They are clearly implied in his use of the word *hebel*, but he appears to assemble them into a bold new theme for meditation. From an etymological perspective, the meanings of words generally evolve from the more concrete to the more abstract, and Qohelet appears to follow this pattern. It is for this reason that Jacques Ellul preferred to give a greater weight to the more abstract meanings, while keeping in mind the more concrete earlier roots. The theme of vanity in Qohelet is generally used to relate the evil that a person can observe, speak about, or suffer, and includes the physical pain that may occur as a consequence of an activity such as hard work. It also suggests the illusory efforts to which all human activities are reduced, making them an evil. It is like a mist that rises from the ground in the morning and is dissipated by the sun without any results, but that does not make it into a nothingness. Furthermore, because everything is *hebel*, all is gathered into it as a kind of destiny and common death. The wise, the fool, the rich, the poor, and everyone else dies like the animals do. So also all human works have the same destiny, that of insignificance.

The above is a brief and inadequate overview of the analysis that led Jacques Ellul to prefer the translation "Vanity of vanities, all is vanity"; in the end, it refers to illusion that is lived as a reality. Qohelet strips away this vanity and invites us to take a good look at what remains of our self-satisfaction.

The phrase that is usually translated as "vanity of vanities" corresponds to the way in which the Hebrew language expresses a superlative. Hence, it means "all absolute vanity" or "vanity without exception." In examining everything under the sun, Qohelet can find only vanity, and this totality of vanities is itself a vanity among vanities.

This discussion suggests that the statement "Vanity of vanities, all is vanity" also describes everything under the sun that we are currently able to understand from a psychological, sociological, cultural, anthropological, religious, and historical perspective regarding the role played by myths in the collective lives of groups and societies. The myths rise out of a body of human experience as a group or society names itself, and for a period of time its members live as if the community were the only possible reality and had the only possible orientation for their way of life and reference points for their values. All too soon, radically other experiences under the sun begin to challenge these myths, and over time they jointly dissipate the reality, orientation, and reference points that were once the only liveable ones. This dissipation is so complete and radical that not only are future generations incapable of living by them, but they cannot imagine or believe that it was ever possible to do so. However, myths do not dissipate into a nothingness; something of them can live on in a mythology, and something of that group or society lives on as well.

It thus appears that the synonyms of *hebel* apply to every aspect of the role played by myths in individual and collective human life. For example, myths give rise to the metaconscious knowledge that can be intuited and expressed as the existence of false gods, to be elaborated and brought within conscious reach by the creation of idols.[9]

Despite this convergence between the foregoing explanation and our current understanding of the role played by myths, it is only our current understanding, and we must make nothing more of it. In other words, this convergence neither "proves" the revelation of Qohelet nor validates our current insights. "Vanity of vanities, all is vanity" has been discerned and received as a revelation from God, but our insights also fall under the judgment of vanity. Using the equivalent expression "sacred of myths, all is myths" only sums up our understanding of myths, but as de-symbolization continues, we may learn a great deal more about our being a symbolic species. This may turn out to be entirely other and thus may bring down our best understandings and force their replacement by others. We must remember that there is nothing more transitory than scientific knowledge. It is certainly more transitory than the tradition-based, culturally embedded knowledge of earlier civilizations.

Keeping all of this in mind, if individual and collective human life is suspended in myths, what do our meanings and values mean? If, by means of symbolization, we grasp the way in which everything is related to and evolves in relation to everything else and express this in terms of these meanings and values, then our understanding of everything being in its rightful place (or outside of it) is illusory. All the distinctions we make – which strike a delicate balance between overgeneralization and undergeneralization in order to maintain an intellectual grip on our lives and our world – may also be illusory. As I have pointed out elsewhere,[10] the process of differentiation is a dialectical one that establishes what something is relative to everything else that is known and lived, with the result that what something is directly depends on what everything else is not. The conclusion must not be drawn that this process is useless: during a historical epoch characterized by a unique set of myths, the members of a group or society thereby avoid relativism, nihilism, and anomie.

Myths are thus a shield that prevent a group or society from plunging into the hell of the impossibility of any relationships among people and between them and anything else in the world. What this means is that the shield endures only for that historical epoch, after which the myths dissipate and can never be lived again. Consequently, the distinctions made between what is useful and useless, meaningful and meaningless, and valuable or valueless share the judgment of Qohelet as belonging to vanity. However, we are now looking at myths, not by means of our culture but by means of faith. It also signifies that nothing in our lives is ultimately in its rightful place, that all relationships are distorted, and that something about it all is illusory. Yet the shield is a grace as well because it prevents us from descending into the hell of relativism, nihilism, and anomie. The Christian community is thus asked to play its role as yeast in relation to the dough, knowing that we ourselves are made of this dough except for what we have received from God as a free gift. It means that we can never brush aside the ways of life and cultures of other people as nothing more than simple idolatry; they shield them from an absolute hell.

Here we begin to uncover the radical, contradictory character of the revelation in Qohelet. Under the sun all is vanity, and all is vanity of vanities, but since this does not lead to the hell of relativism, nihilism, and anomie, there is another side to it (to which we will return later). We must not entertain the idea that Qohelet inserted God into his reflections as the "answer" to the "problem" of relativism, nihilism, and anomie. Individual and collective human life is not a "problem" to be solved by theologians and philosophers, who so often make use of God in a religious fashion, completely and totally negating everything he reveals about himself. God is busy creating something new in us, and by means of faith we will gain a perspective that is neither a theology nor a philosophy but a life.

Myths have given humanity the possibility of a non-life, one of enslavement to the flesh and the principalities and powers. It has allowed people to live as if they were no longer creatures named by their Creator and were living in a world of myths rather than in his creation. Living in this way has prevented humanity from dying immediately following the break with God by preventing a descent into an absolute hell of relativism, nihilism, and anomie. In other words, humanity's break with God occurred within his love, as manifested by the two trees in the centre of the Garden of Eden.

This interpretation – that the myths through which any group or society names itself are included in its vanities and its chasing after the wind – appears to be confirmed by what Qohelet does after she summarizes her findings. She poses the question of what people gain from their toil under the sun. This latter expression is reinforced by the constant reminder that we all must die. Given the traditional cultures of that time, it is significant that Qohelet restricts her observations to what is under the sun; this would exclude anything in the heavens (as Elohim's abode) or the places created by all cultures for the false gods that had been brought within their reach by corresponding religions.

In the case of the biblical heavens, Qohelet affirms what the opening chapters of Genesis tell us about Elohim as the hidden God who is inaccessible to us. Significantly, there is not a single reference to YHWH in this book. In other words, Qohelet is not speaking of the One who gave his unpronounceable name, who is present but hidden, and who reveals himself to us. It would appear, therefore, that from the very outset Qohelet informs us that she intends to be as truthful as possible by refusing the false reassurances that are derived from the absolutization of the orientation and reference points of a way of life; she states that her love for the only Living One does not permit her to make this God into something required by a culture in order for it to exist, or into a "solution" to its philosophical or theological problems. Hence, her constant insistence on dealing with what is "under the sun" differs from dealing with what is "under the heavens," by a refusal to be deceived by anything religious and cultural, including the use of the only Living One for these purposes. Qohelet's approach could be achieved only through the gift of faith because faith alone permits someone to refuse the way in which every group and society, including Israel, has named itself. As a member of God's people, Qohelet worked to discern everything under the sun and thus responded in faith to God's Word; her response was accepted as such by God and included in his Word.

The work of Qohelet questions the traditional hierarchy commonly created among the books of the first testament, that of the first, second, or third order of the Word: the direct Word of God (the Torah); the Word inspired by God and thus possibly affected by the persons receiving the inspiration (the prophets); and the words spoken by people, to which God himself bore witness by adopting them and adding them to the revelation (the writings). Such a hierarchy would appear to discount the role of the Word in the lives of his chosen people. This Word is the very same as that of the opening chapters of the book of Genesis, and thus, when it is addressed to a person, it creates something new in him or her. As Jacques Ellul has pointed out, Qohelet is a model of a person in God's grasp through the Word, which placed her in a new situation; in it, God's Word enabled her to show humbly everything that she had done to arrive at the conclusion that her life amounted to vanity.[11] In this way, Qohelet was able to see herself, others, and the world in their existence before God. This does not mean that the perspective of Qohelet is that of God. She knows very well that she is not God. She observes that, in terms of what is real under the sun, everything is vanity, but through the Word and thus according to what is true, everything is a gift from God.[12]

In regard to the same opening question regarding human toil, Qohelet tells us that she is interested not in ontological questions about what is, but in an existential concern for the person who toils and whose life is affected by this labour. Her perspective is not of how our means may benefit our lives, but of our ability to be more of a human being with a more enriched and deepened life. For example, can we add to our wisdom, escape from the vanities, or go beyond death? If everything in our lives under the sun amounts to a bundle of vanities, then we will no longer be able to make true distinctions between what is meaningful and what is meaningless, what is valuable and valueless, what is truthful and false, what is righteous and unrighteous, and what is wise and foolish. We may as well drop our existential distinctions, and the entire process of symbolization, experience, and culture by which we make sense of and live in the world would be cast adrift.

In this declaration that everything in our lives under the sun is vanity, does that include our myths? By these myths we master the past and the future as more of what we have come to know and live, thereby giving our lives and culture an absolute orientation and reference point in an ultimately unknowable universe. Qohelet appears to reject this way of naming ourselves when she declares, "The people of long ago are not remembered, nor will there be any remembrance of the people yet to come by those who come after them" (a literal translation of Ecclesiastes 1:11). In other words, the members of a society do not live the kinds of lives that were lived by those who went before them; nor will the members of future generations. Otherwise, people would at least be remembered to some extent through the way of life they have embodied. At the same time, Qohelet recognizes that under the sun there is nothing genuinely new in terms of human existence. All lives are stuck in vanities, with the result that "what has been is what will be, and what has been done will be done, and there is nothing new under the sun. Is there a thing of which it is said: 'See this is new'? It has already been in the ages before us" (Ecclesiastes 1:9–10). This appears to refute the idea that humanity is capable of bringing about any genuine existential progress – an issue to which we will return.

I am deeply struck by the opening chapters of Qohelet. From a historical and social perspective, what Qohelet said would probably have been shocking in a traditional society with a culture subjected to little de-symbolization. After all, did each new generation not inherit the way of making sense of and living in the world from those who went before, to the point that each generation participated in evolving a tradition that became the accumulation of what was regarded as making the most sense and was proved to have the best practices for dealing with life's situations?

Whatever may be the case for traditional societies, the opening chapters of Qohelet radically call into question our own civilization. Beginning with the so-called Industrial Revolution, have we not fundamentally changed human life, making it increasingly more rational, secular, and sophisticated? If Qohelet's assertions had not been included in the first testament, would we not have dismissed them as proof of how far we have progressed, and would this progress not have been completely unimaginable to those who went before us? What also may make us pause is that these opening chapters call into question three of the most important vanities in relation to which the members of the first generation of industrial societies lived their lives: the historically first secular myths of progress, work, and happiness. These myths enveloped the people in striving for limitless progress, for work that was capable of achieving everything they desired, and for a new kind of unlimited happiness that was just around the corner. According to these myths, Qohelet was simply mistaken regarding the beginning of industrial civilization. Once again, we must remind ourselves that Qohelet was talking about the lives of persons and not about the means by which these lives were sustained, or about a new ontology or foundation for human existence. As far as Qohelet is concerned, since all is vanity, the only thing new may be the forms taken on by these vanities. However, such changes make no real difference to people's lives. It is from this existential perspective that we will attempt to imagine human life created by these new vanities.

First, it may be helpful to reflect briefly on an event in Job's life. As in the life of Qohelet, God's Word had placed Job in an entirely new situation with a different perspective on his life and his world – one that produced many tensions with his friends. It also left many unanswered questions, and Job pleaded that God reveal himself to answer them. God did so, but many commentators have found his response rather puzzling, if not disappointing, given Job's situation and burning existential questions.[13] Consequently, it is difficult to understand how God's response to Job could have led to his conversion and a complete and total reconciliation between God, Job, and his friends.[14] This is much less surprising if we recognize that Job's life was also stuck in the vanities of his days, which included his culture and the myths by which Job's community had named itself. When God revealed his creation to Job, the revelation likely shattered these myths, along with the other vanities that must have been rooted in a blend of a natural and a social sacred. Job may even have had something equivalent to a life review associated with a near-death experience. In any case, God's response would have touched every aspect of his person and his life, with the result that God gained Job's heart and there was a complete reconciliation. I recognize very well that the text does not directly support such an explanation, but I believe that Qohelet sheds important light on how God reconciled himself with Job. Job had not yet confronted certain vanities in his life through the Word. Given the deeply symbolic character of the closing passage of the book of Job, this reconciliation may await everyone, including Jews and Christians.[15]

The first testament pays a great deal of attention to the presence of false gods, represented by the idols that brought them into the daily lives of the members of a cultural community. With the insights we have gained into our dependence on symbolization, language, and culture as a result of the weakening of their life-sustaining roles by desymbolization, we can sharpen our understanding of the revelation by contrasting it with our contemporary cultures – just as the authors of the first testament did in relation to the cultures of the people that surrounded them. The discipline-based approaches to human knowing and doing that have been imposed during the emergence of our civilization have indirectly given us a much greater insight into that human knowing and doing by rendering untenable our widespread notions of facts and theories, and their relationships to what they represent.

If, as Jews and Christians, we had regarded our situation with the eyes of faith, we might have recognized that the teachings regarding false gods were as applicable to our cultures and civilizations as were those of their predecessors. We are creatures who have a Maker. We have already noted that, before the break between God and humanity, our human finitude in the flesh presented no problems of any kind in a communion of love with him. Following the break, however, this flesh became an evil power that attempted to make our human finitude liveable apart from God. Our civilization is unique in that it has grappled with this finitude of our knowing and doing in a very different manner from that of its predecessors.

In order to avoid a variety of counter-transference reactions that could block our understanding of the revelation in Qohelet, we do well to reflect on how we participate in the myths of our civilization. We have been promised that one day we will no longer serve false gods, but in the meantime we had better be on the lookout for anything in our experience that takes a place in our lives as if it had no limits. Doing so is not first and foremost an intellectual undertaking but an existential one made possible through faith. Since myths operate on the level of metaconscious awareness, we cannot reach them directly. Hence, we will begin by existentially imagining the kinds of experiences that people had during the beginning of industrialization, which marks the origin of our present civilization.

The experiences of each new generation are different from those of their parents; their experiences in turn were very different from those of their grandparents; and all of their experiences were radically other than the experiences of the people living in the traditional societies that gave birth to industrialization. In this incredible turbulence some sets of experiences began to differentiate themselves from others, first in the higher socio-economic strata of society and later in the lower ones. Nevertheless, the more these developments took hold of human life, the less these differences mattered. As noted, every year people recognized that machines were becoming larger and faster, that every year their diversity and numbers increased, and that every year more factories full of these machines produced an ever greater output. By the differentiation of these experiences from all the others, it appeared certain that the struggle for survival would sooner or later come to an end, that poverty would be conquered, that the obvious scourges associated with this poverty would disappear along with it, that humanity would thus be able to increasingly divert its energy towards making social improvements, and that everyone could play their part to help bring about a much happier future for all. The miracles that could apparently be achieved with these industrial and economic inventions and innovations seemed almost limitless.

However, there were those who were told by their grandparents that they had once lived on the land, and, though they were very poor financially, they and others had many things that factory workers lacked. People were as tired as they used to be during planting and harvesting, but now that they worked in factories there was no relief in sight. The old people said that they once had time for each other, their children, and their neighbours, but that this was no longer the case. It was as if they had been robbed of almost everything in their lives. They told stories about people who just could not take it any more: some became violent, others started drinking to excess, and still others completely withdrew from society. There appeared to be no way out, and yet they were convinced that the door to the past had been slammed shut for those who worked in the factories.

For those who failed to find work, the situation was even worse. They could no longer feed and shelter themselves and were compelled to wander in a desperate search for handouts of food, sometimes in return for menial work of any kind. Such experiences dominated the lives of a great many people, who felt little or no hope. It made them very vulnerable and potentially open to the influences of those whose dominant set of experiences was positive.

For those who were less directly influenced by the industrial upheaval, it was tempting to hope that all this suffering and disorientation would be temporary, a necessary price to pay for a better future. For the majority of people, there was a great deal that no longer made sense. For example, if poor people stole as much as a loaf of bread to feed their children, they could be hanged or transported to penal camps in the colonies. For them, justice was a farce: through no fault of their own, they had been compelled to steal from others as their only possible source of daily bread other than acts of charity. To them, stealing seemed to be merely an act of relieving the rich of what they did not appear to need. What was the point of talking about the past or the future if you did not even know whether you could survive the present day? What did a commitment to a partner and parental responsibilities for children mean under these conditions?

How people lived their experiences and built their lives was thus deeply influenced by their circumstances. For the small minority who were in control of the new developments, their main preoccupation was the necessities imposed by these developments. For the vast majority of people, much depended on whether they could see any hope in what increasingly appeared to be inevitable. Was the financial and existential poverty of the factory workers a temporary phenomenon? Would the destitution and starvation of the many diminish quickly enough to avoid an uprising? Would the ever-increasing need for the state to intervene overcome the political traditions that had regarded such behaviour as completely unacceptable? What would happen as a result of the growing conflict between industrialization and the moral and religious traditions of the people? Would the industrial slums continue to grow in spite of widespread concerns?

With a great deal of hindsight, we can confidently affirm that all this constituted merely the obvious events on the "surface" of human experience. We are speaking of one of the greatest upheavals in human history, which penetrated deeply into individual and collective experience. A great deal of attention was given to the obvious conflicts between social classes; some even spoke of an inevitable war between them that would trigger a revolution. As noted, this first secular political religion legitimated the sacrifice of tens of millions of people. Ironically, it still does not get to the bottom of what was really happening in human experience.

Everything in human life was being turned upside down and inside out in a way that was deep and far reaching. Technology and the economy were being built up with the new architecture of reality and thus had to be separated from the remainder of society, which, for the time being, continued to be organized by means of symbolization, language, and culture. These had always created and evolved a symbolic universe with a dialectically enfolded architecture that had completely opposite characteristics to those of reality.[16] The backbone of the architecture of reality was the technology-based connectedness of human life and society, while the backbone of the traditional architecture was the culture-based connectedness of human life and society.[17] The former is ultimately an expression of the thermodynamic constraints, while the latter expresses the ultimate meanings and values turned into a sacred and myths.[18] Prior to industrialization, human history had been characterized by the culture-based connectedness generally dominating the technology-based connectedness, but this hierarchy was now being reversed.[19] Traditional societies enfolded their technology-based connectedness into their culture-based connectedness because the good life was believed to be found only by serving the false gods that made morality and religion uppermost in people's lives. The events marking the beginning of industrialization implied that living this way had been a terrible mistake. For a growing portion of the members of the industrializing societies, it became increasingly self-evident that the good life could not be found in this way. Rather, the priority had to be given to strengthening the technology-based connectedness of human life and society because everything else that people hoped for would follow in its wake. Eventually this led to the first secular sacred, that of capital, with its sustaining myths of progress, work, and happiness. Any radical alternative became unthinkable, unimaginable, and unliveable. This complete reversal of the role that materials, energy, and everything built up with them had always played in human life and society required all manner of philosophical, theological, and ideological reinterpretations. These reinterpretations achieved exactly what was necessary for society to be able to name itself through its first secular sacred and myths. What is so embarrassing is that it resulted in the complete transformation of not only the political and ideological spectra but also the theological spectrum in Christianity. It gave birth to the present conservative-liberal split that made it possible for almost all Christians to come to terms with this upheaval in human history.

Almost regardless of their socio-economic positions, political convictions, and religious beliefs, people lived as if an industrializing society was essentially a traditional society that had gained an incredibly new potential by adding industry to it and accommodating its economy, without having to give up anything essential. Even our contemporary literature on the history of technology and on economic history is virtually silent on the obvious reciprocal interactions that always take place between a symbolic species and its surroundings. As people change their surroundings, the new surroundings simultaneously change them as they build up their lives and as all their different experiences are symbolized by their brain-minds.[20] This means that as people changed their technology and economy during industrialization, the technology and economy simultaneously changed people through their vast influence on people's experiences. In turn, these experiences affected their brain-minds, which symbolized their lives and with which they continued to make sense of and live in the world.[21] I have shown that this "technology changing people" included language, behaviour, institutions, morality, religion, and art, and thus their entire culture as the symbolic basis for making sense of and living in the world.[22] In sum, industrialization turned out to be a complete remaking of what it was to be a human being and a community within local ecosystems and the biosphere. However, although everything designated by "technology changing people" did have a vast influence on human life and society, this influence lagged well behind that of everything designated by "people changing technology," with the result that it was not only excluded from the emerging secular sacred and myths but also made unthinkable by them.[23]

The upheavals included a decisive change in "human nature." The reigning ideologies of the last two centuries essentially have depicted human history as a struggle for survival, which was decisively transformed in favour of humanity by industrialization. In other words, human nature had actually always been materialistic, but it had never had an occasion to reveal itself throughout a society. By implication, no society had had the ability to develop industrial technology until the societies of Western Europe achieved it in the nineteenth century.

Many societies and civilizations had extraordinary technological developments, but, for reasons we find almost impossible to comprehend, not a single one systematically applied its technological know-how to the production of material things. With hindsight, the reasons are painfully obvious. We are the first civilization to live as if all human needs, with few exceptions, could be met by material goods and services. The advertisements following the Second World War made this point obvious in a way that, again with hindsight, appears to be more than a little naive. For example, the members of the "lonely crowd" should simply buy a particular brand of beer or alcohol and soon they would be surrounded by handsome young men and beautiful young women, and life would never be lonely again. The same claims were made for other products such as toothpaste, shampoo, and cars. This mythology was the conscious expression of the secular sacred and myths of the first generation of industrial societies.

Hence, the transformation of human nature, life, and society by means of industrialization made it possible for the post–Second World War consumer societies to emerge. It would be naive to believe that this occurred precisely when mass production became technically possible. We would still have to explain how mass advertising ensured that mass consumption always more or less matched mass production, and thus that human needs and wants evolved in lockstep with what became technically and economically possible.[24] This would be incomprehensible were it not for people living as if almost any need could be satisfied by material goods and services. With the exception of the very rich and powerful members of earlier civilizations, humanity had never been convinced of this possibility, and consequently traditional cultures placed a limited value on their technologies, to the point of placing outright restrictions on their use for certain purposes.[25]

From this brief overview and discussion of the development of the body of individual and collective human experience during the early phase of industrialization, it must not be concluded that there was an inevitability in it all, as summed up by the first secular sacred of capital and its sustaining myths of progress, work, and happiness. In the end, people had to metaconsciously commit themselves to one set of experiences or another, and doing so involved their entire being and lives through the way in which they lived each and every experience. For a time, everything remained relatively fluid, with the result that there was a window of opportunity for discerning where human experience was headed, in the knowledge that nothing in the world could have unlimited powers. Since we are speaking of societies over which the Jewish and Christian traditions had exercised an enormous influence, it might have been expected that, as in Israel, there would have been people (such as the prophets)[26] who had a sense of its direction. They could warn others that, if people did not intervene in the course of events, terrible consequences would follow. It must be remembered that the prophets were not people who foretold the future. Based on their discernment of the trends of their time, they had a clear and prophetic notion of where things were going, which God confirmed by calling them to render a service on his behalf.[27] Rarely did the Jewish people take notice. On the contrary, their theologians reinterpreted the Word in the new ways of the cultures of their societies, to once again bring God's ways much closer to theirs in order to make them acceptable and liveable. In the course of industrialization, Christian discernment of societal trends did not fare any better. Some put the focus on a person's individual salvation, faith, and relationship with God, which mimicked the growing individualistic tendencies in the cultures of those days and withdrew the active participation of Christians as yeast in the dough. Others put the focus on the social good that Christianity could offer during a time of upheaval and the breakdown of all traditions, including the moral and religious ones – the best that could be done within cultures that were increasingly becoming secular. Either way, Christians bowed down to the necessities of industrialization – including the new false gods that were emerging under their very noses. Despite two world wars, the Great Depression, the threat of nuclear war, the danger of an environmental collapse, and a host of related crises, the new religions took hold: the cult of the fact, the cult of efficiency, the cult of economic growth, and the cult of individual and collective disembodied life. Few voices expressed concern.[28] It is not unreasonable, therefore, to suggest that what we encounter here in the development of the body of individual and collective experience is a powerful element of the demonic and the satanic, to which almost all religious leaders and theologians appear to have been oblivious.

I hasten to point out that what we are speaking about is not "technology bashing." To raise a critical voice in warning of what awaits us if we permit an unlimited development of technology and technique is no different from the set point on the thermostat that regulates our furnace. It is constantly "criticizing" its performance, which is exactly what makes it possible for the furnace to keep us comfortable. To suggest that this thermostat "bashes" our furnace is absurd. It is a question of allowing nothing to become sacralized as a false god without limits. Technology is no more and no less than any other human work: good for certain things, harmful for some things, and simply irrelevant for other things. "Technology bashing" is the secular equivalent of warning people not to touch a sacred.[29]

In these discussions we should be mindful that the formation, reign, and decay of myths occur on the metaconscious level, where we are able to affect them only indirectly through the experiences we live, and not by philosophies, theologies, or ideologies. As a result, the Jewish or Christian communities can play a decisive role only if they live by faith and not by such intellectual creations. We have made faith into a kind of metaphysics rather than a gift of God that permits us to transcend our reality and to live according to his promises.

The set of experiences that had dominated all the others in the lives of the members of the first generation of industrial societies, as symbolized by their brain-minds, soon became exposed to a variety of experiences that decisively called it into question. I am not primarily referring to events such as the so-called Great War (a technological war), the Great Depression, the Second World War, and the explosions of the first atomic bombs. These events may have greatly shocked a number of intellectuals, philosophers, and theologians, but we are concerned here with something much more fundamental and far reaching. In building the new industrial technology and its matching economy, the industrializing societies became increasingly confronted with the limitations of symbolization, experience, language, and culture. In all its history, humanity had never encountered so many experiences that were radically other than what had made us human up to that point.[30] For example, in the chemical and electrical branches of industry, what was really happening in these technologies was almost entirely inaccessible to the human senses and thus not open to symbolization, experience, language, and culture in the usual manner.[31] The solution was soon found. Our relationships with technological processes, devices, and systems were to be mediated not symbolically through our cultures but through the appropriate disciplines.[32] Their domains could portray what was happening beyond the reach of human senses by using an architecture of reality for their internal consistency. Each domain was made externally consistent with the world via the "inputs" and "outputs" that represented it.[33] The importance of human words thus declined in favour of images of all kinds, especially mathematical images of what was happening in any domain.

This discovery opened the floodgates to radically other experiences, which first constituted the phenomenon that Max Weber referred to as rationality, and that some time later Jacques Ellul described as technique.[34] It can be shown to be the result of a growing reliance on discipline-based approaches to knowing and doing at the expense of their culture-based equivalents.[35] Entirely new kinds of experiences now began to dominate human thought and action. These in turn undermined people's lives as symbolized by their brain-minds, including the first secular sacred and its sustaining myths. New secular sacreds, those of technique and the nation-state, developed and were supported by the myths of science and history.[36] The discipline-based approaches that were first pioneered in industry, the military, and the state soon began to spread to all areas of human life in order to achieve the same efficiency and power in every human endeavour.[37] Any limits became increasingly unthinkable, unimaginable, and unliveable. These developments occurred at the expense of what had distinguished us from animals up to that point: symbolization, language, and culture. The upheavals of the twentieth century proved that technological and economic growth did not inevitably lead to progress but could deliver some major setbacks to humanity and possibly even a catastrophic end, such as an all-out nuclear war. Nevertheless, humanity had abandoned its confidence in symbolization, language, and culture in favour of discipline-based approaches, and there was no turning back. When difficulties arose, they had to be overcome through further scientific and technical developments involving discipline-based approaches. The latter could no longer be questioned in themselves. Whenever problems arose, they were always seen as the consequences of inappropriate or incompetent use or of fraud by vested interests but never because of the inherent limitations of discipline-based approaches. These have become untouchable in their rule over us, since we live with them as if they had no limits.[38]

Although it is possible to intellectually uncover the limitations of discipline-based approaches, any efforts to warn our societies and civilization that these limits are real and the source of many of our sufferings, failures, and difficulties are likely to fall on deaf ears. Intellectual arguments cannot directly dethrone secular myths unless they first provoke a conversion experience, that is, an awareness that we must develop a new intelligence for making sense of and living in the world – one that must include symbolization and everything built up with it, as well as discipline-based approaches, in such a way that the limits of one are overcome by the other. In other words, our false gods can be dethroned by a project of re-symbolization provided that our civilization engages in the secular equivalent of a conversion that will restore science and technique to their rightful places by desacralizing them. Even if such a scientific, technical, and professional conversion could take place, we would not enter into a liberal, socialist, anarchist, democratic, or environmentalist paradise. The entire process of re-sacralization would repeat itself all over again as we, through the flesh and the principalities and powers, would inevitably enthrone new false gods to reign over us from above.

In sum, for now, the Jewish and Christian communities are almost entirely enslaved to the secular Baals of our days by their participation in cults of scientific, technical, economic, and political fertility, which in secular terms we refer to as *growth* or as *moving forward*. It is very difficult to find a faithful remnant that has not yet bowed its knees to our false gods. I doubt very much that any of us could claim that we have never done this. We are flesh, ruled over by the principalities and powers that have their authority from the way in which our civilization has named itself through its works. Consequently, all our meanings and values are false, and this in turn pushes everything out of its rightful place in individual and collective human life. It would appear, therefore, that, if Qohelet had reflected on our experiences of today, she would have almost certainly arrived at the same conclusions: all is vanity and a striving after the wind. Moreover, living as if we can fill our spiritual backpacks with items that can protect us from this vanity is undoubtedly the vanity of all vanities.

In an attempt to interpret, as from "under the sun," the historical and social developments of our civilization, I have come to the conclusion that "underneath" them there appears to be a deeply disturbing proliferation of death. There are, of course, the many widely accepted symptoms of an apparent increase in anxiety, mental illness, suicide, the breakdown of relationships and groups, and the impairment of the life-sustaining capabilities of the biosphere. However, these are generally not associated with our efforts to understand life in terms of a non-life resulting from our discipline-based approaches to knowing, and a subsequent remaking of life in a reified form by means of discipline-based approaches to doing.[39] Qohelet constantly reminds us that we must all die and that death eliminates all distinctions and differences. We are now living in a civilization that appears to be hastening the process by remaking everything in the image of (dead) classical or information machines or, at least, remaking everything with the architecture of what we have referred to as reality. This architecture is the diametrical opposite of that of a community that names itself by means of a culture or the biosphere.

The remaking of all life into non-life began with the mechanization and industrialization of human work. Before any mechanization could take place, human work, as an activity carried out by a living human being, had to be decomposed into distinct and separate parts. Each part was assigned to a domain that contained the necessary production step to achieve the overall desired result. In each domain, the inputs that were received as the intermediary desired outputs from another domain were transformed into the next intermediary desired outputs on the way to the final result by an endlessly repeated process based on one part of a single category of phenomena. Any human activity, including work, had thus far derived its meaning and purpose from its participation in the way that everything was related to everything else, and had evolved in relation to everything else in human life and society. Given the complexity of this interrelatedness, the possibility of any situation ever repeating itself was virtually non-existent. Correspondingly, the human nervous system excels in its adaptation to changes and is damaged by repetition. Moreover, it is involved in and expresses itself through every human activity; and the effects of repetition can be suppressed only with a great deal of mental energy that produces nervous fatigue. Consequently, when human work is reorganized in the form of labour by means of the technical division of labour, nervous fatigue becomes its dominant characteristic. Human beings find it very difficult to "squeeze" their lives and persons out of any of their activities, with the result that they and classical or information machines have diametrically opposite strengths and weaknesses. Workplaces thus became subjected to an enduring tension between the almost non-life of technically divided labour and the life that could not be suppressed by the worker or by the discipline of the work organization.

As human work became increasingly reorganized to pave the way for mechanization and industrialization, the technology-based connectedness of human life and society was built up from domains that jointly exhibited all the characteristics of the architecture that we have referred to as reality. This new technology-based connectedness could not be effectively organized and adapted by symbolization, experience, and culture, with the result that it had to be organized by a market economy or by central planning. In the case of the former, the architecture built up with domains was extended by the *homo economicus* – people as wage earners, entrepreneurs, or owners of capital – and by the market mechanisms of supply and demand.[40]

With the separation of knowing and doing from experience and culture, and its restructuring by means of disciplines, the reorganization of life into non-life spread throughout society, building an order of what Jacques Ellul has referred to as non-sense;[41] in other words, within the cultural order of a society or group, its organization and adaptation make no reference to sense, i.e., symbolization, experience, and culture. It began the war that we are waging on ourselves, as well as the battle for the human spirit.[42]

We have now uncovered the changes in the forms that the vanities have taken on since the "genesis" of industrial civilization. The so-called industrializing societies and the industrially advanced societies have named themselves, not in the image of false gods with an imagined existence but in the images of non-life: capital (Mammon), progress, work, and happiness, followed by technique, the nation-state, and history.[43]

Before anything can participate in our civilization in general, and in its economies in particular, it must be commoditized. Doing so involves our behaving as if everything can be detached from human lives, communities, societies, ecosystems, and the biosphere in order to be made into a thing or commodity that can be traded in markets. As a prerequisite for commerce, this commoditization creates the well-known market "externalities" that combine into market forces, which give rise to our human, social, economic, and environmental crises. It is hardly surprising, therefore, that both the first and the second testament take a very dim view of a commerce that extends to the bodies and souls of people. The commoditization of all life is a kind of de-creation, transforming life into a kind of living death. What had been enslaved lives (slavery is always the model of sin in our Bibles) is now possessed by a system that continues this enslavement but superimposes reification upon it. There is nothing fundamentally new under the sun, but this system has the potential to expand human suffering enormously, as if the principalities and powers were flexing their muscles on the way to their own final destruction.

The negative experiences with classical machines have been forgotten with the rise of information machines. Following the Second World War, as the ways of life of the so-called industrially advanced nations began to be adapted and evolved on the basis of discipline-based approaches to knowing and doing, the result was an information explosion because less and less knowledge was embedded in experience and culture.[44] With hindsight, one can interpret these developments as societies' preparation for the computer, with more and more activities being reorganized by means of the technical division of labour. Nevertheless, we have learned little from previous experiences, and our expectations of the benefits of the so-called information and computer revolution have proved to be entirely unrealistic. We ought to have realized that the architecture of information machines and systems was no different from that of classical machines: it is built up from domains that are now occupied by rules, algorithms, subprograms, and so on. Artificial intelligence has never been able to divide human knowledge and expertise into what is referred to in the literature as frames, scripts, or microworlds – the equivalent of what we have referred to as domains. At first these new machines were incompatible with the large organizations that used them, compelling the so-called re-engineering of the corporation in the image of the computer.[45] It led to the large integrated database systems that are referred to as enterprise integration, whose peripheral devices that interface with the world are now the human beings who work with these systems.[46]

In addition, the explosion of the social media greatly multiplied the the number of relationships in our way of life that are now mediated by computers. It led to a flight towards disembodied individual and collective human life on the Web, whose architecture based on domains and a technical division of labour has put its stamp on everything.[47] In sum, the computer, the information systems, and the Web have contributed nothing new to human life under the sun, other than changing the forms of the vanities through which that life is lived.

Was this inevitable? Certainly not, if we had discerned the trends that our lives were helping to establish in terms of what really mattered – their true meaning and purpose for human life. I have spent almost my entire professional life showing engineering students that it is possible to do things very differently by taking an alternate approach to design and decision making.[48] Now that I am retired, Qohelet has helped me to see that it was all a vanity, but a vanity to which I had to put my hand nevertheless.

I will not attempt to summarize Jacques Ellul's commentary on what Qohelet teaches regarding the vanities under the sun.[49] I am simply extending this commentary to include the role that myths play– likely the most dominant vanity in human history as a consequence of groups and societies naming themselves in rebellion to their Creator. I believe that this dominance has come into sharper focus since Jacques Ellul wrote his commentary, as a consequence of the rapidly growing desymbolization of our lives, especially after his death in 1994. I will conclude this section by briefly commenting on the specific roles played by myths in some of the vanities.

Many vanities require the consent of our communities (what is left of them), which we extend through our myths. Monetary wealth is an obvious example. When people lose confidence in their financial system and withdraw their consent, there are runs on the banks, and a complete meltdown could result. There have been hundreds of these crises since the Second World War.[50] Similarly, a government can exercise power only as long as the people consent to it, usually by adhering to the myths through which they have collectively named themselves. When the legitimacy of the power of a government becomes widely questioned, people go out into the streets in defiance. At that point, the government can test their resolve by brutal suppression and intimidation, and even then it may fall, as we have seen a number of times in the immediate past. It is important to recognize that the increase in the de-symbolization of our cultures during the last two hundred years has required the state to step in, only to become the primary organizational locus to compensate for the loss of the self-regulating character of cultural communities. The result has been that everything has become political, which implies that no longer are there any limits to the scope of the state's role. The nation-state (or state-nation) constitutes one of our secular sacreds, served by the two remaining secular political religions, democracy and communism. In North America we constantly observe how the state seeks to be adored through a variety of democratic rituals.[51]

In sum, a variety of vanities have taken on the status of myths, thereby being legitimated. In our civilization these myths include capital, progress, work, happiness, and, later, technique, the nation-state, science, and history.[52]

There is an important relationship between what a community regards as good and just, and the myths through which it names itself. If the lives of its members constitute bundles of vanities, then their collective experience cannot possibly constitute the centre of their world as an absolute point of reference, nor can it embody the past and the future as an absolute orientation in that world. Nor is it possible for this collective experience to be the basis of discerning everything good and just. Nevertheless, this is what every community is compelled to do when it names itself. For example, as children grow up by acquiring the language and culture of their community, the organizations of their brain-minds begin to imply the metaconscious values by which individual and collective life is oriented.

Before extensive de-symbolization set in, the laws of a community were spontaneously obeyed as long as there was a correspondence between them and the metaconscious values. No individual person had any need to study these laws in order to acquire the ability to live by them as a good member of the community. Conversely, a law became inapplicable when the metaconscious values in the organizations of the brain-minds of these members were not sufficiently embodied in a law, with the result that the members could not identify with it and saw no reason to obey it. When such a law became spontaneously and massively disobeyed, a judge in a non-totalitarian society had no choice but to declare the law inapplicable.[53] It would appear that, given our sacralization of technique, our courts now act with some bias in relation to issues related to new technologies and undertakings.[54] Such a bias ought to come as no surprise, given that judges are as much influenced by technology and technique as everyone else.[55] For these and other reasons, we are a little better prepared for Qohelet's warning that there is no justice in our world. However, justice is not merely a vanity, since injustice is an evil. According to Qohelet, we treat some of the just according to the work of the wicked, and some of the wicked according to the work of the just. There will never be a just society. As Paul informs us in Romans 8:20, everything in creation is subjected either to vanity or to the power of nothingness, or situated between two voids. Once again, this is the experience of a believer who brings the world's vanity to God and also accepts responsibility for it. It is his experience and thus his person and his life, and that can never be made into a theology or philosophy of justice. The same applies to all other vanities. Since our lives and our world are distorted through our myths, it is impossible to make our experience or our life the centre of anything, or to make the collective way of life of our community a basis for spiritually naming ourselves. Hence, we must live differently, and that brings us to wisdom.

Wisdom and Myths

Humanity has always sought to overcome the relative character of its culture-based knowing and doing by creating absolute knowledge through science or universally valid wisdom. Our civilization is no exception. It has attempted to do so through discipline-based knowing and doing, and this makes it very difficult for us to understand Qohelet on the subjects of knowledge and wisdom.

There is an important difference between the human knowing and doing embedded in experience and culture and the human knowing and doing separated from experience and culture. In the case of physics, these two types have been referred to as *intuitive physics* and *school physics* respectively.[56] Babies and children acquire a great deal of metaconscious knowledge about the physical behaviour of their bodies and the world as they learn to sit, crawl, walk, run, throw balls, ride bikes, climb trees, and much more. However, this intuitive physics is ignored in high school when they are introduced to the domain of physics with the architecture of reality. They cannot enter this domain in the same way as they can enter a newly discovered part of their world. This approach gives rise to entirely new kinds of disembodied experiences, with foregrounds that are discontinuous from their backgrounds, because they have different architectures. The students acquire a different form of metaconscious knowledge that is discontinuous from the metaconscious knowledge derived from living in the world. However, those who go on in physics and eventually obtain a doctorate would not dream of applying their school physics to improve the physical dimension of their daily-life activities. The distinction between intuitive physics and school physics is paradigmatic of the relationships between the kind of knowing and doing related to life (of which Qohelet speaks) and the knowing and doing that has been organized by means of disciplines whose domains are separated from experience and culture and have an architecture that is diametrically opposite to that of symbolically mediated life in the world.

In the same vein, there are different forms of wisdom as well. There is the wisdom embedded in experience and culture and the wisdom separated from experience and culture, which largely began with the Greeks who built up philosophies with a growing use of the principle of non-contradiction. They thus created intellectually beautiful "domains" that had the most tenuous relationship to human life in the world – a subject to which we will return shortly. It is very important, therefore, to distinguish between, on the one hand, Qohelet's experience and life under the sun, including the knowing, the doing, and the pursuit of wisdom embedded in that experience and life, and, on the other hand, all knowing and doing organized by means of disciplines whose domains are separated from experience and life. If we confuse these two, it will be impossible to make sense of Qohelet.

What we have learned from the vast de-symbolizing influence of our discipline-based scientific knowing and technical doing on human lives and societies has shed a great deal of light on the way in which humanity was symbolically suspended in an ultimately unknowable universe prior to these developments. For example, Niels Bohr explained that we are so suspended in language that we do not even know what is up or what is down, and Albert Einstein was convinced that our theories limit what we are able to observe.[57] Based on my life's work, I will attempt a brief interpretive overview of what we may have learned regarding symbolization, experience, and culture as a consequence of their de-symbolization.[58]

What permits us to say that we live lives and that the reading or writing of this paragraph, for example, constitutes a moment of a life? We know very little about how the organizations of our brain-minds symbolically mediate each and every moment of our lives by working in the background as we make sense of each moment and express something of ourselves in our response to it. We also know little about how we are changed by each moment, because the organization of our brain-mind is modified by neural and synaptic changes that symbolize our experience of that moment, with the result that we can remember it. The emergence of the concept of brain plasticity was but a symptom of what largely remains an insufficient elaboration of the implication that each and every moment of our life modifies the organization of our brain-mind by symbolically "adding" the corresponding experiences to our life in the form of moments of that life. This plasticity of our brain-mind stops only as a result of the onset of terrible diseases such as short-term memory loss or a later stage of Alzheimer's disease, which in both cases makes it impossible to continue to live one's life. Each moment of life then becomes a separate instance that expresses the life lived before the onset of the disease but is separate from all other such instances.

It would appear, therefore, that when we speak of living our lives, and of our experiences being moments of those lives, we are referring to the metaconscious symbolic life that is made possible by the organization of our brain-minds. In other words, from the perspective of conscious experience, our lives are the sum total of everything we have genetically inherited and all the experiences that have modified that inheritance by building a life out of them. The opposite side of the coin is a complementary perspective of the life we live, which is made possible by the organization of our brain-mind always working in the background and (usually) instantly recognizing a situation for what it is in terms of where it symbolically fits into our life; our brain-mind then makes the appropriate neural and synaptic modifications to its organization to symbolize it. At this point, the organization of our brain-mind symbolically relates the experience of a situation to all other experiences of our life, permitting us to metaconsciously deal with a situation according to its meaning and value relative to those of all other experiences symbolized by the organization of the brain-mind; this enables a response that embodies the corresponding meaning and value for our life as a whole. Simply put, the organization of our brain-mind symbolically represents the interpolation and extrapolation of all our experiences into a life, which simultaneously and symbolically turns each experience into an expression of that life.[59]

In the case of babies and children, the extraordinarily great plasticity of their brain-mind permits them to discover almost everything about their lives, because very little has been genetically inherited. For example, they learn how to focus their eyes once they discover that there are meaningful things "out there" on which to focus. The experiences of moving their limbs lead them to discover that they have a physical body distinct from the world. As they learn to metaconsciously externalize these kinds of discoveries, they begin to respond to other people as a social self, at first by means of non-verbal communication. As the sounds of language spoken by others become distinguished from all other sounds, they learn to use vocal signs. Eventually they learn (metaconsciously) that such signs constitute a language by which they can transcend their immediate experiences. They then begin to enter as a cultural self into the symbolic universe of their community. This symbolic universe interposes between such immediate experiences and the ultimately unknowable universe. The need for this brain-mind plasticity becomes readily apparent when we try to imagine living in the world without any awareness of being a physical self, a social self, or a cultural self.

Initially, the high levels of plasticity of the brain-mind of babies and toddlers can be attributed to their experiences forming a limited context that shields them from being overwhelmed by new discoveries. Only the few experiences that can take their symbolic place in the limited context of their lives can take on a meaning and value and be lived as a moment of a young child's life. As the organization of the brain-mind becomes more complex, it becomes open to an ever-greater diversity of new experiences being lived, but a child's metaconscious awareness of all of this continues to express itself in a highly playful attitude to the child's life and the world. Since children's ability to supplement this symbolization by means of reasoning remains extremely limited, there is a growing convergence between the organizations of the brain-minds of their community members and that of their own brain-mind. Long before the threats of relativism, nihilism, and anomie can materialize in the lives of children, their organization of the brain-mind, participating as the deepest metaconscious knowledge they have acquired, symbolizes the sacred and myths of the culture of their community. In other words, the organization of their brain-mind begins to perform the equivalent function, on the level of their cultural life, that the DNA performs on the level of their biological existence. Simply put, each experience becomes an expression of this "cultural DNA" and the embodiment of it. Their lives are thus not so much suspended in language as they are in the sacred and myths of their culture; these lives themselves are constituted by this sacred and myths, with the children's experiences being the individually unique and culturally typical expressions of them. Without this cultural unity acting as "DNA," there would be no lives at all and thus no community.

This is a brief and thus inadequate overview of how babies and children learn to deal with the ways in which everything is related to and evolves in relation to everything else in their lives in the world. It is within this interrelatedness that we need to understand all human activities involving knowing and doing.

It is impossible to know anything in human life absolutely, as if it could be understood in itself and on its own terms. What something is involves its relationships with other entities, and this in turn involves the relationships between those entities and still other entities, and so on. Consequently, this knowing is necessarily open ended and is thus affected by this complete interconnectedness, of which whatever we desire to know is a participating entity.

Moreover, this looking outward from what we seek to know must be complemented by a looking inward, where we encounter the same kind of interconnectedness. The characteristics of the whole must be understood in terms of the relationships and interactions between the smaller wholes that constitute it. Each of these smaller wholes must in turn be known in terms of those even smaller wholes that contribute to its make-up, and so on. Once again, we encounter a potentially open-ended search for knowledge because we have never discovered the so-called definitive building blocks of our universe. In turn, these outwardly and inwardly oriented searches for knowing something are a great deal more complex in living entities that are biologically enfolded and, in the case of human life, culturally and dialectically enfolded.

The aforementioned search for knowledge is embedded in the activities that are integral to our lives and thus to our education, experience, intelligence, creativity, and culture. Understanding the influence we may have on what we are attempting to know, and the reciprocal influence on us of what we are examining, involves our being a member of a symbolic species and a member of a particular society and civilization, which enormously affect all our symbolic activities.[60] An understanding of these dependencies is entirely open ended and dialectically enfolded.

This pathway to knowledge is so dependent on our backgrounds and the sequence of activities we undertake that it would be completely subjected to relativism were it not for the grafting of these activities into our lives and thus into the cultural unity that holds life together. It would appear that many great thinkers in the past had some inkling of this, which would explain the many different attempts to escape the relativity of knowledge gathering to find more robust methods and approaches. Many societies and civilizations invented their own unique forms of science. At times, this need for science was greatly stimulated by a culture's going into a decline, with the result that its weakening cultural unity was less able to sustain what the members had come to know and live, and the threat of relativism was more acutely experienced. Whenever the members of a culture believe that they have achieved absolute knowledge in a form equivalent to our facts, we can be certain that this belief has been made possible by means of myths. Apart from myths, everything we can know is relative. We can have only a partial understanding of what something is and how it adapts within everything else in human life in the world. Babies and children learn everything they know by listening to the words of their parents and others, because only language has the architecture capable of symbolically mapping the previously mentioned interconnectedness. Doing so by means of images is radically impossible because images only have the architecture of what is real. Moreover, such knowledge acquisition (as in science) is not cumulative. In the case of babies and children, noncumulative transformations occur when they begin to live as a physical self in the world, when they do so as a social self, and finally when they do so as a cultural self.

There is thus an openness in our human knowing that is apparent in children and that ought to be apparent in scientists, but it is entirely absent in the daily lives of adults. As adults, we can only know more of what we already know because anything that is radically different has been excluded by the way we have learned to make sense of and live in the world through our culture anchored in myths. Anything that is radically different will necessarily be interpreted in terms of what we already know, and when this becomes less and less successful, our culture is either in the process of a mutation that occurs during the transition from one historical epoch to another, or it is approaching a decline and its possible collapse. Hence, any non-cumulative organization of a culture involves a number of generations, each departing more and more from the culture's way and unity and moving in the direction of making the new radically different experiences normal. Such a reorganization gradually develops new points of reference and a different orientation through a new sacred and myths. These slowly reduce the relative character of people's lives (including their knowing) and turn restore what is true for them in order to once again protect them from the threats of relativism, nihilism, and anomie.

This overview of the symbolic character of our living and knowing also applies to our doing. If we act on something, we act on its integrality with the way in which everything is related to and evolves in relation to everything else. Again, we are unable to do anything absolutely, with the result that we cannot truly know what we are doing. Moreover, in our doing we are sustained by a variety of relationships, we are threatened by other relationships, and we are focusing on still others that we are attempting to affect. Once again, this precludes our doing anything on its own, that is, self-contained and absolute. We can only do something relative to certain entities, knowing that these are relative to still other entities, and so on. Children know this very well, which is why they do things playfully. For adults, this is impossible. They are essentially limited to doing more of the same because anything that is radically different has been made unliveable and unthinkable. After all, the organization of the brain-minds of adults has symbolized the unknown as being more of what they have known and lived, by interpolating and extrapolating all their experiences of a life lived in a community and sustained by a local ecosystem. The body of collective experiences has been absolutized and symbolically put at the centre of all human history and the universe as the measure of all things.

It must not be imagined that human life was secure during any historical epoch. There were ongoing contradictions between the life lived in a symbolic universe by means of a culture and the way in which a variety of events manifested themselves as being radically different. When the influx of such events became too great, the threat of relativism, nihilism, and anomie increased until a cultural mutation ushered in a new historical epoch; failing this, a society or civilization collapsed because of its inability to give meaning, direction, and purpose to the lives of its members by means of a viable culture.

The vulnerability of human life anchored in myths helps to explain why many communities set out on a search for wisdom. The search that has marked our current situation the most began in Greece when it was the centre of Western civilization. The eventual decline of Greek culture was partly due to its many contacts with other cultures, which often had very different practices that, in some cases, were more successful than those of the Greeks. For example, in one such culture, women played a key role in trade. They negotiated deals and managed the financial affairs, while the men took care of sailing and navigating the commercial vessels. One wonders why the Greeks did not educate their women. The resulting relativization of Greek culture led Socrates to engage in the equivalent of modern knowledge engineering, by which people who had a recognized mastery were interviewed to discover the rules that underlay their expertise. In the end, no such rules could be found, and this failure undoubtedly contributed to the decline of Greek culture and the shift of the centre of Western civilization from Greece to Rome.

Socrates and his students, Plato and Aristotle, benefited from the invention of universal knowledge built up with the principle of non-contradiction. It was part of a search for the foundations of human knowledge that marked Western philosophy for a very long time. Consequently, Greek philosophy was the forerunner of the kind of domain that much later became associated with all discipline-based approaches to knowing and doing. Thus, the relationship of Greek philosophy with human life became increasingly tenuous. The principle of non-contradiction makes it impossible to understand anything about human communication, relationships, groups, and societies. In the first chapter I pointed out that no communication between persons can occur when each is totally different or completely similar. Human communication is suspended between these two poles of anomie, requiring that a dialectical tension between persons be similar enough that they can understand one another, and different enough that they can enrich each other's lives with something genuinely new and interesting. In the same way, viable relationships, groups, and societies are suspended between the same two poles of anomie – requiring a dialectical tension between individual diversity and a shared cultural unity. This became painfully evident by the later development of Greek philosophy.

The far-reaching implications may be illustrated by the history of Western logic.[61] It began as Aristotelian logic, which was embedded in experience and culture and had as its goal the sharpening of human thought through debates between different points of view. It eventually became eclipsed by the development of discipline-based science in general and Boolean algebra (developed in 1847) in particular. The latter was based on the premise that algebra could represent ideas as well as numbers or quantities. The complete separation of this logic from daily-life thinking and culture came with the claims of Gottlob Frege, who became the founder of modern logic. He decisively argued that if logic were an inborn engine of the brain (as Plato and many others had argued), or if human thinking ultimately depended on rules and algorithms manipulated by the brain, then logic should have evolved along with the human brain. This evolution was impossible because the laws of logic could not evolve as expressions of "eternal" mathematical truths – with the result that reason based on culture had to be a mixture of the logical and the psychological. Consequently, logic had to decontaminate itself from its cultural elements based on the principles of non-contradiction and internal consistency. Bertrand Russell initially thought that the domain of logic constructed with these principles was ultimately grounded in common sense. The consistency of non-Euclidian spaces could be guaranteed if Euclidian space was consistent, and this could be ensured by the consistency of arithmetic. The latter was ultimately founded on set theory, which in turn was founded on a number of actions that at first appeared to be grounded in common sense and thus in culture. However, Russell discovered an inconsistency that necessitated the abandonment of all common sense and thus any connection with culture and the world. Logic became a non-cultural domain built up without any reference to sense or culture. In other words, its elements have neither meaning nor value. Instead, they are connected by the principle of non-contradiction, making logic incommensurate with any culture. It is important to distinguish *non-sense*, designating something that does not belong to the world of sense, from *nonsense*, which does belong to the world of sense but is incompatible with it. In the case of discipline-based approaches to knowing and doing, a domain corresponding to a particular discipline is preferably built up with the principles of mathematics and thus with the principle of non-contradiction. Such a domain must be externally consistent with the "experience" of an experiment or a result to be obtained in the world. Nevertheless, its internal architecture is incompatible with the world it represents or on which it acts. The same conclusion applies to any human actions based on computer simulations, which have a mathematical architecture.

In our civilization, the forms of knowing, doing, and living based on symbolization and culture have been brushed aside as remnants of a religious and superstitious past that we have outgrown thanks to new forms of human life. Consequently, any wisdom that earlier societies had to offer has joined the relics of our dark past, and we have a hard time convincing ourselves that Qohelet might be different.

Compared to the culture-based approaches to human knowing and doing, the discipline-based approaches are characterized by the autonomy of the domain of each and every discipline, which means that the category of phenomena it studies is separate from all others.[62] It amounts to a complete negation of the way in which everything is related to and evolves in relation to everything else, by limiting the context to only one category of phenomena. The autonomy of these domains in turn creates the autonomy of their corresponding disciplines. All this autonomy would have been impossible to achieve were it not for technique (as the system of all discipline-based approaches to doing) taking on the status of a secular sacred, and for science (as the system of all discipline-based approaches to knowing) taking on the status of a myth. This point is significant because this autonomy is a vanity behind which hides the relative character of these forms of human knowing and doing.

We now live as if we had gained the capacity of absolute knowing and doing. One of the most obvious examples is the creation of "facts," which are no longer open to evaluation and criticism. A fact is an autonomous element of our knowledge or a justification for our actions that is regarded as valid in itself, having lost its relative character. Forgotten are its dependence on the body of knowledge of a discipline and its theories, the experimental design in relation to which a fact is established, and the vantage point of the scientific or technical specialists involved in these activities – which vantage point includes the specialists' ongoing dependence on their highly de-symbolized culture. When a fact thus loses its relative character, it becomes an autonomous and absolute element of the knowledge of something or of the justification for an action. Consequently, we treat our facts in exactly the same way that earlier cultures treated their false gods – as being absolute and unlimited. We receive these facts either from the secular sacred of technique or from the myth of science, both of which we treat as if they also had no limits. Again, nowhere in our universities is there any research that attempts to discover the limitations of discipline-based approaches to knowing and doing in order to transcend them by creating other approaches. We have essentially enthroned science as the secular god of knowing, and technique as the secular god of doing. We are completely in the grip of secular religious attitudes towards these human creations, which is why we are not searching for their limits even though almost all our crises are related to these attitudes. All life is suffering in its being re-engineered to take on the architecture of non-life. Hence, our secular false gods may well be even more destructive and dangerous than the traditional gods of the past.[63]

As an example, the autonomy of engineering disciplines was confirmed through a research project that attempted to answer the following two questions: What do future engineers learn about the way in which technology influences human life, society, and the biosphere? To what extent do they learn to use this understanding to adjust design and decision making in order to achieve the desired results and at the same time prevent or greatly minimize the harmful effects to human lives, societies, and the biosphere? The findings showed that they learned almost nothing that might have challenged the autonomy of the engineering disciplines.[64] Engineering ethics has suffered the same fate at the hands of autonomous disciplines. It has been unable to affect engineering design and decision making in any way whatsoever. It has become an end-of-pipe ethics that is typical of professional ethics today, despite the ritual incantations to the contrary expressed by professional bodies.

In sum, naming ourselves in terms of our scientific and technical works means that anything that is radically different from our discipline-based organizations cannot be taken seriously. Past civilizations and their accomplishments have thus been symbolically eliminated, and radically different futures, such as a more socially viable and environmentally sustainable one, have been excluded. We have sprinkled the term *sustainable development* over our curricula, but it has had no decisive effect on their structure or their ongoing reorganization. Hence, knowing and doing based on symbolization, experience, and culture, which have a radically different approach and architecture, have been degraded to the status of being too subjective to be able to offer us any help. Nevertheless, an alternative approach to engineering design (which the profession acknowledges it has had difficulty teaching for some time) has been proposed, one that aims to complement the strengths and weaknesses of approaches based on symbolization, experience, and culture with those of approaches based on disciplines.[65] Moreover, such a perspective is applicable well beyond engineering, as I have shown elsewhere.[66] This is as close as I have been able to come in injecting some practical wisdom into the technology-related professions.

What appears to dominate our daily lives is a constant adaptation to everything being made more efficient and powerful thanks to technique. At the same time, we are being confronted by a barrage of collisions between these more efficient and powerful elements and our lives, our communities, and the biosphere – to which these elements are entirely inadapted. Hence, practical wisdom would dictate that we rebalance the efficiency and power of everything that is technically modified with its ability to participate in and contribute to the interconnectedness of all life on the planet. For now, there is no chance of such a practical wisdom being developed, and, if it were, it would be ignored because of the way we live with our discipline-based approaches as if they had no limits and thus did not need critical evaluation, modification, and more context-compatible application. We look back at other civilizations and wonder why they engaged in (frequently bloody) rituals in order to convince the gods to bring rain, instead of taking direct and practical steps to deal with a drought. Are we really very different when we hope for a more viable and sustainable future for our children and grandchildren but "worship" efficiency, power, and economic growth?

Is there anything new under the sun in our civilization? It would be very helpful if we were more mindful that our lives, including our knowing and doing, take place in an interconnected world that ultimately we did not create. Throughout history every nomadic group, society, and civilization has made something new by reorganizing something of the connectedness that was already there and then reconnecting it differently. Everything we do involves a loss and a gain of possibilities. Humanity simply cannot create something new out of nothing. By organizing human knowing and doing into disciplines, our civilization has exchanged the possibility of the slow and incremental developments of earlier civilizations, which were aimed at making a contribution to the connectedness within which they functioned, for the possibility of endless increases in the efficiency and power of everything. For example, our children may ask us how we ever managed to live without cell phones. The answer is that the social patterns of life were such that no cell phones were required.

Another difference between our civilization and previous civilizations is that we have implicitly decided that the connectedness of all life is to be re-engineered into that of non-life. We begin with one kind of architecture and reorganize it as much as possible into another one. Again, there are gains and losses that are impossible to add up to a net gain or loss. Not long ago our civilization decided that slavery was an unacceptable form of life, but we appear to sense little conflict between our values and the re-engineering of ourselves in the image of information machines and systems.

For example, the discipline of cognitive psychology proceeds as if all of human life could ultimately be understood in terms of information: its acquisition, transmission, and processing, and its application to human activities. Consequently, the domain of cognitive psychology can be limited to such information processes as if they occurred in a computer of some kind or in a neural network simulated by it. Cognitive psychology thus rejects the study of the human brain-mind prior to de-symbolization and instead examines the degree to which these brain-minds have come to resemble information-processing devices. If cognitive psychology recognized the limit that it has imposed on itself, its findings would be very interesting and surely alarming. Instead, this discipline considers the highly de-symbolized brain-minds that are unique to our civilization to be "normal." This shows the degree to which technique has taken hold of our lives in a completely uncritical and thus unscientific manner. The self-evident character of technique is becoming part of our human nature.

Another example is the rise of scientism: an unlimited belief in the powers of science. It is entirely based on what we know to be false. As Thomas S. Kuhn has shown for the history of several disciplines, knowing more is not synonymous with knowing better, because of the occurrence of what he referred to as scientific revolutions, which disconnect facts from theories to rearrange them into new theories.[67]

There is both a gain and a loss of understanding. Moreover, the absence of a "science of the sciences" makes it impossible to arrive at a comprehensive scientific understanding of human life and the world by integrating the findings of the multitude of disciplines. Without some kind of scientism, we would have to acknowledge that discipline-based science presents us with the most fragmented and piecemeal knowledge base that any civilization has ever possessed.

Any contemporary search for wisdom is thus blocked by our myths. The meanings and values by which we live cannot be communicated directly, because we acquired them metaconsciously in the organization of our brain-mind, to which we have no direct access. Such meanings and values symbolize the ways in which our activities are integrated into our lives and thus "clothe" them. The deepest of these meanings and values constitute the secular sacred and myths. Hence, by attempting to uncover our contemporary secular sacred and myths, by searching for entities in our lives that appear to have no limits, we have essentially spoken only of the symptoms of such myths in our lives. The myths themselves cannot be communicated as such until they cease to be "living" myths, that is, when they no longer constitute the deepest metaconscious knowledge of living human beings. At that point, they have been pushed out by new emerging myths, which reduces their metaconscious depth and brings them within range of our intuitions. They can then be expressed in the form of an explicit mythology.

Living myths also express themselves through the unresolvable contradictions in individual and collective human life. For example, we have shown that discipline-based science has obvious limits, with the result that living as if it had no such limits will produce all manner of contradictions in our lives. The same is true for technique. As we have shown, contradictions will manifest themselves between what we expect of our life and what we actually experience. It is also true for our living with the nation-state as if it had no limits and thus as if everything had become political. Elsewhere,[68] I have examined some of these contradictions in the American and Canadian ways of life.

Contradictions inflict an even greater existential toll on human life when the influx of experiences that are radically different from our lived cultural unity becomes too great. These situations make us realize that human life is always hovering over a chaos ruled by relativism and nihilism or suspended between two poles of anomie: one characterized by individual differences having overwhelmed a cultural unity; the other by a cultural unity having crushed individual differences. Even when our society is temporarily able to hold out against such a situation, it is impossible to live a life, to know something, or to carry out an activity without at least some level of distortion. Whether this is small or total, we can never accept ourselves, others, and the world for what they truly are. It would require the kind of playful attitude that we lost as adults when our lives became constituted by a cultural unity – we cannot regain this attitude through science. We are suspended in an ultimately unknowable universe by means of a cultural unity, and we cannot deal with anything other than by making it into something that more or less conforms to this cultural unity. We cannot be ourselves, we cannot allow others to be themselves, and we cannot deal with the world as it is. Whether our relationships are mediated by a culture or by disciplines makes no real difference in the end.

These statements may appear to be very abstract, but we live their meanings concretely in our daily lives. Everything we live and everything we know and do is relative and thus open ended. We deal with this situation by absolutizing it through our cultural unity who we are, who the other is, and what the world is. The open-endedness is thus removed, along with the fundamental dependencies that come with it, leading to an endless stream of contradictions. These are arranged in such a way that they veil the fact that I am alienated from myself, from others, and from my world. The mode of this alienation will eventually pass, as future experiences will unmask all of this in the process of "re-masking" human lives differently.

Within this contradictory interconnectedness of our lives and the world, what do our means truly accomplish? If they are created through a cultural approach, they will seek to improve the way in which an activity contributes to at least the local connectedness that is anchored in a cultural unity. If, however, the means are arrived at through a discipline-based technical approach, they will reify whatever is improved, by first intellectually severing all connections and retaining only those that can make a contribution to the increase of efficiency and power. Once determined, such increases are then imposed on the pre-existing connectedness, causing its fundamental distortion as some relationships are affected and others are completely ignored as if they did not exist. Hence, these technical means will increasingly create the kind of connectedness that will reify everything that lives within it and evolves in relation to it. The greater the efficiency and power of technical means, the greater their capability of causing this distortion and reification. In any case, technical means cannot respect the internal integrality, and the external compatibility with everything else, of anything they touch.

Since we inherit a certain interconnectedness of our communities and the world from previous generations, we cannot create anything genuinely new but can only replace one form of this connectedness with another. No net benefit or harm can be determined. We can do nothing but rearrange what is already there, whether it be matter, energy, biological life (governed by a DNA pool), or cultural life.

Can any culturally mediated or discipline-mediated means create genuine progress in our lives? If these means can only rearrange the connectedness of everything, and if the net benefit or harm of such rearrangements cannot be determined, a genuine scientific evaluation of progress or of a lack thereof in human history is impossible. We are left with the impression that sometimes human existence appears to improve a little and at other times it suffers setbacks, and the net benefit or net harm of the sequences of such improvements and relapses cannot be determined. Human life remains alienated or both alienated and reified. In other words, on the level of our existence we cannot liberate ourselves from this alienation and reification, even though humanity has now declared slavery to be an unacceptable form of human life. Our ability to see this more clearly is hampered by the impossibility of fully experiencing what the rearrangements of the patterns of connectedness mean in relation to human life. For example, today we still do not connect our spectacular successes at improving the efficiency and power of everything to our equally spectacular failures at ensuring the viability and sustainability of the new forms of interconnectedness. There is thus nothing new under the sun.

We are back to our inability to say "I am." Everything we live, know, and do is integral to an open-ended connectedness that we cannot fully live, know, or act on. In other words, we can only say "I am" in relation to these patterns of interconnectedness, which I have experienced, understood, and acted on in a limited way that will always remain unfulfilled and incomplete. Everything I know is relative to everything else I know, and thus what something is, is what everything else is not. The same is true for any of my activities and certainly for my life as a whole. Simply put, all I can possibly say is that I am in relation to the connectedness of my time, place, and culture, and of whatever non-cultural elements have been introduced into it. I am thus a relative being who has made this life liveable by symbolizing the unknown as everything I could possibly know and live if I could do so forever; in that sense I have absolutized my "I am." I express this in my daily-life behaviour when I say things like "this is ..." and so on. What this "something" is can only refer to how I have fitted it into my life relative to everything else in that life, how I have fitted my life into the lives of others, and how we have all fitted our collective life into our surroundings.

We now come to the greatest contradiction. How can I write these paragraphs stating what I did? Should I not have become silent, in recognizing that I am simply adding more contradictions, presumably in the hope that my reader will be convinced by them? What I have attempted to do is to bring to the surface some of the most important contradictions of our contemporary societies. In so doing, I have uncovered something of the ways in which these contradictions play out in my own life and writing. I recognize that all this will be swept away by new experiences that are to come. Not even the contradictions of my own life will endure. When these contradictions are swept away, my life could become unliveable, but my death will likely intervene before this can happen. This is as far as I can go with my life under the sun, but it is hardly the end of my story. Consequently, my statements will not become a symptom of pessimism, depression, or mental illness or a pathway towards suicide. On the contrary, they will turn out to be the complete opposite. It is here that I return to Qohelet.

We now face a major obstacle that also takes the form of a contradiction. It is lived by the Jewish and Christian communities alike. None of us has been able to live with the knowledge that the societies of which we are members have named themselves and us along with them. Even when we did not know exactly how they did it, we ought to have taken seriously what Genesis reveals in this regard. It might have prevented us from making matters even worse by also naming ourselves. What is necessary for a society also applies to a religious tradition and the institutions that take charge of it. Such institutions went one step further and named their particular brand of Judaism or Christianity, which then had to be legitimated in relation to the other brands. We forget that such naming constituted the break with God, as revealed in the opening chapters of Genesis, and that we are incapable of naming anything, other than by giving it a place in the cultural unity of our society. We cannot know or practically do anything else. In sum, we do not live as people who have been named by God. For example, in Protestant Christianity, such naming began by placing our salvation, our faith, and our sins at the centre of everything. To varying degrees, it is all about our personal lives and how we individually participate in God's work of salvation. Tragically, this reflects exactly the cultural unity of the first generation of the industrial societies that gave birth to our civilization. The increasingly individualistic orientation of our civilization was reflected in a corresponding individualistic orientation within Judaism and Christianity. It made less individualistic forms of life increasingly unthinkable and unliveable, and our theologians obliged by casting them in either a liberal or a conservative form, not recognizing that either form could be readily assimilated into the cultural unity of our societies. The details were then poured into these forms according to their cultural contexts, religious traditions, and intellectual fashions. Of course, Jews or Christians are a people of a time, place, and culture – and this they cannot escape. What we must seek to escape is the making of these circumstances into our defining commitment, because this would fly in the face of the entire first and second testaments. All we can hope for is that God will name us as faithful Jewish or Christian servants, but we have neither the ability nor the responsibility to take this upon ourselves. All we can do is to live as best we can out of his revelation, but we can never say that this is or is not Jewish or Christian.

We appear to have forgotten that faith is a gift from God, granted in grace to permit a people to do the exact opposite of all of this. Christians are called to labour in the kingdom of heaven, to serve by not centring anything on one's own life or on one's religious institution. We are called to live, not according to the myths by which our society has named itself but by doing the exact opposite of what our culture guides us to do, which is to put our collective body of experience at the centre of everything. Instead, the entry into the kingdom of heaven comes about when we give up that centring and attempt to live out of a love for our God and for others. Doing so precludes any attempt to gain power over others or to dominate them by imposing Christianity on them, for example, through a morality. The incredible convergence of the North American political and religious maps tells us that, by and large, we have attempted to increase the power of a political party of our choice so that it can dominate through morality. This could only be the result of bowing to our secular Baals of scientific, technical, and economic "fertility."

Our commitments are obviously to an institution, a tradition, and the ways in which they interpret the Bible, define its application to our lives, and legitimate their authority. No institution or tradition can legitimate itself without inserting itself into the institutional framework of our society and thus into the way in which this institutional framework is legitimated by our society's naming itself. The moment that Christianity becomes institutionalized it is lost. I know very well that we are cultural and historical beings and that we cannot live without institutions. I also know that this makes it next to impossible for the Spirit to play the role in our lives of which Jesus spoke.

This preparation for reading Qohelet is not intended to be a foundation for yet another philosophy or theology, nor does it constitute a preliminary sketch for a sociology of knowledge. It is simply a summary of my interpretation of what we can learn about the way in which we are culturally suspended in an ultimately unknowable universe as a consequence of the de-symbolizing effects of our discipline-based approaches to knowing and doing.

Hopefully, we are now better prepared to understand Qohelet. I believe that a solid argument can be made that she has developed the implications of the opening chapters of Genesis more than any other book of the first testament has done. Moreover, she has done so with a great deal of hindsight into much of the history of the Jewish people. Qohelet appears to insist upon everything being a vanity that plunges human lives into deep structural and unresolvable contradictions that stem from our refusal to accept being God's creatures living in his creation – a life that is made possible by a communion of love. Perhaps we can understand this better by seeing ourselves as being suspended in a symbolic culture anchored in myths. The opening chapters of Genesis set out the fundamental relationships between the Creator and humanity within his creation, with the constant implication that this is completely and incomparably different from what the cultures surrounding Israel lived and believed. Once again, I am not claiming that our current understanding of our being a symbolic species is confirmed by Qohelet or vice versa. It may well be a coincidence, one that will vanish like a mist under the sun. However, I must confess that I am deeply struck by the fact that Qohelet puts all the contradictions of our lives centre stage and weaves them into her message.

If all human activities under the sun were experienced and lived as a vanity, as Qohelet says, what does this imply for the search for human wisdom? Is it the one activity that can escape being yet another vanity? If our lives under the sun are subjected to vanity, then our lives and our world comprise false meanings, values, and relationships, with the result that everything is in the wrong place and falsely connected. It amounts to a complete distortion of the way in which everything in this creation was created and designed so that its potential would evolve in relation to everything else. Instead, everything became subjected to vanity. Can we then draw some intellectual wisdom from our knowledge gathered by science or philosophy? Can we gather some wisdom from examining our works, to constitute a kind of practical wisdom? Qohelet appears to find that search also marked by contradictions.

What about a wisdom for our lives? On the first two levels wisdom was related to what we know and what we do, but now it shifts to a third level, that of who we are: our lives and our being under the sun.[69] Qohelet finds that, on this level, wisdom collapses completely; it is the sum of all vanities. In other words, the wiser we become, the more we become aware that all is vanity and a striving after the wind.

Consequently, the more we pursue wisdom, the more we plunge ourselves into vanity by means of a flood of words.

God and Our Myths

We now turn to the third important theme in Qohelet, which reveals God. Qohelet reopens her examination of everything under the sun by declaring that all is vanity and concludes with an admonition both to fear God and to observe his precepts, for that is the entire human being (a close translation included in the original French text but omitted in the English translation).[70] If everything under the sun is a vanity, including our person, experience, and life, what remains that we could do in truth? How would it be possible to fear God? Can a bundle of vanities fear God, and, if it could, would it be acceptable to him? Is a life filled with vanities still a life, and, if so, what kind of person can live such a life? Once again, Qohelet plunges us into all manner of existential contradictions, with her closing admonition possibly being the greatest of them all.

Of course, we could escape this impasse by asserting that piety had to be added somewhere, but this would constitute an injustice to Qohelet, whose criticism of everything she has lived and experienced under the sun has been razor sharp. Moreover, her word has been discerned as a Word of God and accepted into the first testament as such. Her examination of everything under the sun included the history of Israel up to that point, and, with the benefit of that hindsight, Qohelet appears to be sending us back to the opening chapters of Genesis once more.

As noted, following its break with God, humanity found it necessary to name itself in order to secure a spiritual being, orientation, and reference points. As a symbolic species under the threat of de-symbolization, we can perhaps add a little to our understanding. Each and every group and society made itself and its world through its myths, which it was constantly compelled to mutate into other myths as incompatibly different experiences made them vanish like a mist under the sun.

The implications reach so deep and so far that they call into question almost every contemporary form of Judaism and Christianity. Simply put, if we name ourselves by placing our individual and collective life at the centre of everything, by symbolizing anything incompatibly different as being more of what that individual and collective life has come to know and live, we are building our individual lives and the life of our community on a bundle of vanities that envelop and turn everything else into vanities. This process masks who and what we have become in our separation from the only Living One, to make our situation existentially bearable in our struggle against relativism, nihilism, and anomie. These conditions exclude any possibility of human relationships, and thus of human life itself, and confirm what our Bibles teach us about hell (which, by the way, has nothing in common with the Dante-like images that are so dear to some Christian circles).

We do well to remember that the first testament reveals that only God can say "I am." The implications of this are so far reaching that the first and second testaments may be interpreted as explanations of what this means for human life. As noted, we can never say "I am." We can at best say, "I am an individually unique manifestation of a time, place, and culture." Our persons thus participate in a make-believe living that symbolically arranges our experiences by means of the cultural unity through which our society names itself. When this symbolic organization is weakened by incompatibly different experiences, it vanishes, and so do all the experiences that it kept in their places. Consequently, all metaconscious meanings, values, and knowledge, including those of our social self and the social selves of others, vanish with it. It is through our relationships with others that we become aware of our socio-cultural selves as individually unique expressions of our society. Consequently, when the secular sacred and myths of our society vanish under the sun, our social and cultural selves and our lives vanish with them.

Our persons and our lives, being relative to a time, place, and culture, are thus not nearly an affirmation of our relative character but a declaration that they have no existence apart from this context. When our time, place, and culture disappear, we disappear with them, and we cannot be remembered other than in the most trivial and superficial manner. Much as our biological selves cannot grow, adapt, and live without our DNA, so also our cultural selves cannot grow, adapt, and live without our "cultural DNA," which is made up of our secular sacred and myths.

Qohelet appears to provide us with a further illumination of the consequences of humanity's break with God and of the decisions then taken by God. As the communion of love broke apart, humanity imposed on itself the need to accomplish with its words what God had provided through his Word. Humanity thus began to hover over a void resulting from the disillusion of all relationships and lives. Each group and society became a kind of cultural womb within which the members of each new generation became people of a time, place, and culture by listening to human words. The liveability of this womb could be ensured only by absolutizing it, which introduced into the creation all manner of sacred elements; each group and society related to them as false gods and physically brought them into its world as idols. This turned everything into a vanity, including its members as persons and the lives they lived. All this would disappear in death.

Jews and Christians cannot escape the situation created by the break with God. We cannot assume that we are persons and have lives like everyone else and that the revelation has added something all-important to our persons and our lives. Qohelet sweeps away this kind of belief as more vanity. No compromise of any kind is possible. The only way that remains open for our being persons with lives is to place ourselves between the two poles of fearing God and listening to his Word and to do so by accepting the gift of faith. It is our relationship with the only Living One that makes us creatures and constitutes our persons and our lives.

How are we to understand what Qohelet means by fearing God? How can we possibly live out of fear? Such fear must be understood in the context of the revelation, with the result that the answer immediately follows: there is no better way of fearing God than to love him with all our heart, mind, and strength. It opens up the possibility of learning how we can live as his creatures within our finitude by listening to his Word, which traces the boundary between life and death, and between good and evil. All this is enveloped in grace. Qohelet informs us in the closing verse that God will bring all our works to judgment in order to make what is just appear. In other words, we are not headed for a trial but for a removal from our works of everything that is evil and unto death. Even though the second testament borrowed the concepts of redemption and a witness from a trial-centred Roman law, we ought not to extrapolate this to Christianity and put the judgment of people and nations at its core, as has been done since the third century. Recall that the first grace was the Torah, and the second grace was Jesus Christ. Nor must we conclude that we can immortalize ourselves by our works that remain after God has brought them to justice. Qohelet tells us clearly enough that we and our works are included in the declaration that everything under the sun is vanity and a chasing after the wind.

Qohelet thus leads us to discover the only true wisdom, which is also announced in Psalm 111:10, that the beginning of wisdom is fearing God.

This wisdom confirms that everything depends on our relationship with our Maker. Everything flows from that relationship. Qohelet shows us that by severing this relationship we plunge our whole person, experience, and life into vanity. Nothing will remain other than what God will remember. We have attempted to sustain ourselves by constituting our cultural selves and our lives out of a bundle of vanities. Through the gift of faith, God offers us the possibility of recognizing the situation, of transforming our lives by engaging in an all-encompassing struggle against what enslaves us (summed up in the principalities and powers that reign over us), and of beginning to gain a taste of freedom.

Jesus also confirms this possibility when he compares the people who build their house upon a rock to those who build it on sand. If we pay careful attention to the context, we may avoid the usual misinterpretation. Building a house on a rock represents listening to God's Word and putting it into practice. Building a house on sand designates neglecting to put it into practice.

In declaring that everything she has undertaken, experienced, and examined in her life is vanity, Qohelet shows how fearing God and listening to his Word has actually set her free from these vanities. They have been unmasked and shown for what they are: a striving after the wind. As such, Qohelet is prophetic of Jesus Christ as the one who was truly free from the vanities that surrounded him while he lived by the Spirit in relation to his time, place, and culture. It is essential not to make this into a theological abstraction by imagining, as best we can, the conditions in which Jesus lived his complete freedom. He was dealing with a culture that had turned the Torah into a legitimation of the social, political, legal, moral, religious, and aesthetic necessities of his days. The same is true for Qohelet and her days – an insight that she could only have through the gift of faith.

Jesus told us that he is *the way* back to the Father, *the truth* that will be restored to our lives as creatures, and *the life* that flows from that relationship with the only Living One. Jesus thus became the second Adam, who completely and totally lived by fulfilling the beginning of all wisdom. Jesus revealed a true person, experience, and life. His love for and obedience to the Father, even unto death, allowed him to escape the vanities of his days. Recall all the religious factions with their own interpretations of the Torah, all the political divisions over what to do about the Roman occupation, all the expectations people sought to impose on Jesus according to their culture, and a great deal more. His escape from all these vanities upsets everything in our theological traditions. It helps us to understand that God offered freedom to his people, urging them to respond to his love by listening to his commandments. Jesus clearly showed God's law to be the true source of wisdom and freedom, which the people of that time had mostly turned into a source of enslavement. He showed freedom in relation to the Law and what it taught about the Sabbath, alcohol, adultery, sickness, disability, money, taxes, prostitution, social status, and every other cultural necessity. I do not know a single Catholic or Protestant congregation that would let him get away with this today.

As the way, the truth, and the life, Jesus made it possible for his followers to dwell in him as he dwelled in the Father through the Spirit. This possibility permits us to respond to the questions posed by God to Adam (following Adam's break with him), and to do so without hiding behind our vanities. We cannot name ourselves through Peter or any of the reformers. We cannot adopt and live by whatever our time, place, and culture regards as progressive, such as the environmentalism, feminism, socialism, and pacifism of our time. We are doing this in one way or another to justify ourselves.

We must be as clear as we can be on these issues. Qohelet has found everything under the sun to be a vanity and a chasing after the wind. In other words, her faith set her free from them, as she unmasked everything and stripped it of any pretence. By means of this freedom she concludes that, beyond the vanities, we can fear God and listen to his Word. Hence, loving our Maker and listening to him as his creatures with a finitude that needs to be respected is what constitutes an entire human being.

There is absolutely nothing moral or religious in this. It is the very condition of our being creatures loved by our Maker. The moral and religious virtues dispensed by our churches make no difference whatsoever because they all amount to vanities. In chapter 9, Qohelet makes this exceedingly clear when she tells us that the same fate comes to all, including the good and the evil, the clean and the unclean, and those who sacrifice and do not sacrifice. No Christian community can tolerate this knowledge, as each faction names itself as different from all the others by essentially boasting of its superior moral and religious works. The conservatives have their long lists of "do nots" and regard the liberals as having too short a list or no list at all. In turn, the liberals regard the conservatives as people they cannot even begin to understand. Nevertheless, Qohelet pronounces our hierarchies, pecking orders, and self-justifications to be vanities. Our divisions are based on vanities and prevent us from being liberated by listening to the Word. We are like Nicodemus; Jesus had to show him gently what truly mattered for Israel. With the gift of faith, we need to learn that our religious institutions and the necessities they impose on us are nothing but vanities.

Is it tenable for us to believe that what happens in the Christian community today is much different from what Qohelet faced in Israel in her days or from what Jesus faced in his days? The faithful remnant was always small, and sometimes a faithful person wondered if he or she were the only one left. No, all is vanity then and now, and we amount to nothing more than the "breath" of Abel. However, we are not merely walking around in a mist of our vanities, unable to experience and live what is true. Our cultural selves and our lives are constitutive of this mist. Until God creates something new in us, we only imagine that we can worship God, there is light, we can act as yeast, and we can live a Christian life. According to Qohelet, this is yet another vanity. As a bundle of vanities we do not constitute a true person able to live a true life. We must first be born to a true life through the Spirit. Not until then can we attempt to penetrate the mist and begin to experience and live what lies beyond: the fear of God and living in his ways. The pathway from "all is vanity" to this is the recognition of our persons and our lives as being vanities, and then a birth and growth in a new life. It enables us to humbly walk before our God, since it is a gift from him that we must learn to put to work at the margins of our vanities.

What we have learned from our examination of Qohelet and our understanding of what it is to be a symbolic species endangered by desymbolization is that our persons, experiences, and lives are enslaved to a time, place, and culture. By putting our enslaved persons and lives at the centre of everything, and symbolizing this by our secular sacred and myths, we are being guided into ever more vanities. We must abandon all this in faith and learn to live out of a love for God and the other. In this way, we abandon ourselves by surrendering to the One who seeks to bring us back into life and the good – for which he has put everything on the line, including himself. In this abandonment of ourselves we will find the way to truly being a person and living a life. If this surrender only takes the form of a flood of words, we have understood nothing. We must begin with who we are concretely as a person of a time, place, and culture in order to discover the vanities in ourselves, unmask them, and take up the offer of freedom – all of which is made possible by the gift of faith.

From this exploration of Qohelet, we may conclude that there is no way in which we as creatures can begin with the the knowledge that all is vanity and arrive at the conclusion that life is the fear of God and listening to his Word. There is no possibility of imposing a kind of evangelical or neo-Calvinist theology. Our historical and cultural beings and lives amount to a bundle of vanities, and these will disappear under the sun. There can be no question of converting vanities into a true person and a true life. The entire history of Israel suggests this. Using all the cultural resources at its disposal, Israel had done everything possible to organize and institutionalize the propagation of the fear of God and of living in his ways from one generation to another. The people of Israel had not understood that they could not do this on their own without the intervention of the Spirit, with the result that only the spiritual descendants of Abraham bore the promise, and these people constituted a small faithful remnant. Sometimes this remnant was so small that a faithful person would ask God if they were the only one remaining.

Perhaps we ought to read Qohelet backwards, beginning with "Fear God and walk in his ways; and you will discover that anything else is vanity." This reversal would sum up a reading of Qohelet that begins with the end and works back towards the beginning of her book.[71] Doing so might resolve some intellectual, theological, and philosophical difficulties, but get us no closer to what concerns Qohelet: our existence under the sun. There must therefore be a reason why Qohelet did not reverse her opening and closing statements.

One possible explanation is that Qohelet desired to make her testimony comprehensible to herself and her fellow creatures. In order to achieve this she had no choice but to begin incognito. Her own life, the lives of others, and her world were marked by an enslavement to a time, place, and culture or the surrounding cultures. She found that, without exception, communities had named themselves as a consequence of their break with God in order to establish a spiritual point of reference for making sense of and living in the world. Out of respect for other people, it simply would not do to approach them with the admonition to fear God and to walk in his ways. This approach had characterized Israel, and today it characterizes the Christian community. Proceeding in this manner would amount to casting pearls before swine because the latter would quickly discover that they could not eat the pearls or in any way sustain their lives with them. Similarly, there is no point whatsoever to tell the members of a community that they must do the exact opposite of what is preventing them from having their individual and collective human life be swallowed up by relativism, nihilism, and anomie.

Qohelet presents us with a model of people who have received a new life from God by being born anew of the Spirit, which enables them to grow and begin to experience and understand how their former self and life had been nothing but vanities. Everything beyond these vanities is now experienced as a gift from God, who once again names such people.[72] Consequently, they have begun the task of penetrating in depth their culture and the cultures of others by not permitting anything sacred into their lives. Anything that falls short of this task will quickly be transformed into a vanity, to be ruled over by the principalities and powers. The entire history of Israel and the church testify to this. An escape is possible only by people who put themselves entirely in the hands of their Maker. He holds out to them a new relationship, first through the prophecies of the Messiah to come and then through Jesus Christ. Qohelet had to find a way to communicate this and remain on the level of her person and her life, and not on the level of intellectual, theological, or philosophical abstractions about that life. Doing so was possible only by adopting the role of a witness. I use this word with extreme caution, given the false meaning it has in the Christian community.

The model of a witness was adopted from Roman law, just as was the previously discussed concept of redemption. Witnesses were people who had *experienced* something in their lives in the world and, as a result, were summoned to participate in a tribunal by giving an account of what they had experienced and lived, following which they no longer played any role in the proceedings. In other words, they testified to what they believed were the true relationships that had constituted an event of interest to the trial. Such an intervention is in sharp contrast to the testimonies of contemporary expert witnesses, who speak of scientific and technical facts entirely separated from any lived experience; the prosecution and the defence then place these facts in a context to give them meaning and value through a legal narrative. During the time in which the second testament was written, everyone in the Roman Empire likely knew exactly what was expected of a witness at a trial. Moreover, from a historical perspective, Roman law was unique and departed from all prior legal systems.[73] Once again, the second testament borrowed the cultural and legal concepts of redemption and a witness in order to insert them into an entirely different context than a trial. Much of contemporary Christianity has mistakenly centred the Christian message around a final trial that will acquit or damn people – which is completely antithetical to the gospel. It has turned Christianity into the ultimate morality by which humanity will be judged. The "fruits" of this interpretation are plain to see: highly insular "communities" with attitudes of superiority and entitlement to judge everyone else.

To us, Qohelet speaks as such a witness and not as an intellectual, theologian, or philosopher. She has no overriding commitment to a methodology, a principle of non-contradiction, detached objective observations, or any other scientism. Those are vanities. For example, as a consequence of being a member of a symbolic species, a human observer is dialectically enfolded into what is being observed. Countertransference reactions can never be ruled out, although they can be minimized through a critical awareness of their possible occurrence – but this awareness has been ruled out by our current scientisms.

Qohelet proceeds as an incognito believer, observing her life and the lives of others under the sun. Nevertheless, her implicit vantage point is that of a creature who fears God and seeks to walk in his ways. Proceeding in this manner has important practical consequences. For example, placing the Decalogue in the context of the opening chapters of Genesis means that, when she encounters in her life and the world religious gods, sacred entities, idols, usages of God's name for religious purposes or explanations, or any declarations regarding good and evil, she can be confident that what she is observing cannot be true.

She knows that we are all creatures living in God's creation, whether or not we acknowledge this. Consequently, anything sacred, and everything religious built on it, represents a distortion of an entity in this creation into something that has no limits. Similarly, any moral declarations are untrue. God began the Decalogue by telling his people that he had set them free and that the following of his ways ensured that this freedom would not be sacrificed by a distortion of the creation; this distortion came about when some of the creation's entities were turned into the sacreds that they could not possibly be, and then was furthered when many other entities and actions were made religious or moral. Similarly, it was not immoral to work on the Sabbath, to dishonour one's parents, to kill, to commit adultery, to steal, to lie, or to covet. These activities were, first and foremost, a passage from God's willingly granted freedom, life, and the good into enslavement, evil, and death. In other words, what every culture did was to create its own world within the creation by distorting all relationships and entities and by anchoring this activity in a sacred and myths. Consequently, whatever was true for human life in this world was untrue in terms of the relationships revealed in the opening chapters of Genesis. It plunged individual and collective human life into vanity, to the very depth of each historical person and his or her life.

Everything thus became utterly contradictory under the sun. Qohelet sought to put the backs of the people of Israel to the wall but did this in such a way that it also applied to all other members of humanity. Simply put, with a knowledge of the architecture of the relationships of God with his creation, Qohelet observes that the architecture of her culture and the cultures of others amounts to a complete distortion of this architecture, resulting in an explosion of vanities. Everything remains ultimately dependent on taking created elements or human works as being sacred, which they can never be in the architecture revealed in God's Word. With this approach, Qohelet could move incognito among others, as if her life continued to be named like theirs.

Qohelet was thus able to engage in a dialogue with others, which slowly revealed that everything rooted in their spiritual name was nothing but a vanity. Her dialogue had nothing in common with the usual attempts to convert people by convincing them of their sins, in the expectation that this would bring repentance and a conversion. Qohelet did not ask others to repent in order to send them on the way with the advice to fear God and to walk in his ways. Qohelet was incognito and therefore was able to observe without being overcome by the despair or suicide that might have been triggered by the knowledge that nothing in her life or the lives of others made any sense whatsoever. Qohelet begins as a person to whom God has extended grace and a new life. We encounter this same situation in the Decalogue: the people have been liberated, and now it is a question of maintaining this freedom by respecting their finitude as creatures dependent on their Maker, as set out in the (so-called) commandments. God does everything, but it permits her to proceed as she does. She can now see herself and others in the mirror of God's Word in order to understand who she and her fellow human beings truly are. It is not a question of attempting to add the fear of God and his ways to our lives. This is impossible because these are all vanities, to which nothing can be added without its also being turned into a vanity. Any recognition of sin and a subsequent repentance do not constitute the beginning of a new life. They can at best be the symptoms of a new life having been granted from above.[74]

We now begin to approach the radicality of Qohelet's testimony. By committing ourselves to fearing God and walking in his ways, we become truly free. We will learn that, being created in the image of God, we no longer need to name ourselves or to depend on the name our community gives itself. Once again, we may use as a metaphor what we have learned about ourselves as a symbolic species that is endangered by de-symbolization. Qohelet is guiding us towards learning to live without again enslaving ourselves to our secular sacred and myths, which have turned our so-called secular societies into houses of vanity.

Even if this metaphor turned out to be yet another vanity, we would discover this in the process. Nothing I have attempted to explain ultimately depends on this metaphor, but, given our illusions of being secular and free from a sacred and myths, I trust that it will be helpful. However, we must never confuse the metaphor with God's Word.

We are back to the opening statement of Qohelet: everything in our lives and the world is vanity. We are able to discover this and to share it with others incognito. In this way, we share with them where our lives began; we have inherited from those who went before us a rearrangement of the creation, which constitutes our "house of vanities." We make this house into our home by our spiritual commitments to it. Generation after generation of people dedicate their lives to endless "renovations" of their home. A substantial portion of the Christian community in North America now desires to make its own "home renovations" and to use political power to achieve it. Hopefully a faithful remnant remains – a remnant that recognizes that all of this is yet another vanity. We have no choice but to live in the house that we have inherited from previous generations, but we may not dedicate our persons and our lives to it. We thus become sojourners in this house, people who have committed their persons and their lives to the architecture of God's creation and to living in it by his ways. Nevertheless, we remain surrounded by the architectures of the world that our secular societies make for themselves.

Jacques Ellul summed up Qohelet's position as follows: "In reality, all is vanity. In truth, everything is a gift of God."[75] This summation is based on a fundamental distinction found in both the first and the second testament between what is real and what is true in human life.[76] This is poorly understood, as is evidenced by our scientists confusing reality with truth and by our theologians doing the reverse.[77] Jacques Ellul has attempted to clarify this important biblical distinction,[78] and I will seek to explain it by drawing in part on my own work.[79] The distinction is based on lived truth and lived reality. It is impossible to communicate these directly. They are "clothed" in our relationships, our lives, and our persons. We can certainly not communicate directly our secular sacred and myths, either to ourselves or to others. As the deepest metaconscious meanings and values of our lives, they cannot be communicated directly any more than can all the other meanings and values by which we live. We can only discuss the implications of our being symbolically suspended in our secular sacred and myths, but doing so cannot change our lives. If it did, we might experience something equivalent to a life review described by people who have survived so-called near-death experiences. Such accounts typically speak of how these people became aware of what truly happened during the events of their lives, including the effects on others and themselves. Their ability to gain such insights is usually accompanied by the presence of a reassuring light. Once again, I am simply drawing on these accounts as no more and no less than a metaphor for imagining what none of us is able to experience and live.

The usual behaviour of the members of the Christian community shows that we are not exempt from naming ourselves as Christian members of our culture by putting our experiences and our lives centre stage; we do this by reading our Bibles in order to learn more about our salvation, our faith, our sins, and our eventual passage to heaven. Such an approach will almost certainly entirely distort the biblical message. Our persons and our lives have no more permanence than do the secular sacred and myths of our society; therefore, we cannot make them the centre of anything – certainly not of our understanding of the revelation as our "truth."

Simply put, we cannot take our persons and our lives and "add" a true conversion by listening to God's Word, putting that Word into practice, engaging in prayer, and participating in a gathering of Christians, as a superposition of the elements of a spiritual life on our cultural life. It amounts to living as if we could serve two masters. Implicit in our daily lives is a commitment to a secular sacred and myths: the equivalent of the false gods of the past. These cultural masters always appear to win when the gospel becomes trivialized as a kind of spiritual veneer over our persons and our lives, which are still constituted of vanities. In this way we cannot be a light, yeast, or salt to the world, because our daily-life commitments are to that world. This situation can be rationalized and justified only if we live the American or Canadian ways of life as if they were mostly Christian except for whatever we may disagree with – which we then feel called to "Christianize," even with the use of political power. The course of events in North America would be incomprehensible without the enormous influence exercised over it by the Christian community by using a great deal of political force. This action alone manifests a complete lack of respect for our neighbours, who are loved by God as much as we are, with the result that we show a lack of love for our God when we attempt to impose our values on our neighbours. Does our God not make the rain fall on everyone in order to sustain all of us?

Consider the issues of abortion and gay marriage. Surely we cannot discuss these issues apart from the kind of society we have, and the kinds of relationships it sustains or weakens, which all of us, by our daily lives and our commitments to its cultural masters, help to maintain and evolve. We live under the illusion that we essentially still live in genuine societies, to which we have added the new possibilities created by our science, technique, and democracy. We forget that we had to surrender almost everything for this life. Socially speaking, we have become other-directed persons living in anti-societies, in the sense that they have the diametrically opposite characteristics of traditional pre-industrial societies.[80] One of the things that we have had to give up is the long and stable friendships and intimate relationships sustained through stable social groups. I recognize that traditional families have been able to moderate somewhat the prevailing social influences, but most studies suggest that their ability to do so is steadily weakening. Hence, if we regard abortion as a common symptom in social entities that are no longer capable of adequately sustaining human relationships and the groups they help to constitute, we need to deal with those issues as the primary cause and regard abortion as a symptom of broken-down relationships. Doing so opens up the possibility of showing compassion for those who find themselves in the difficult position of having to make a choice, because either way there will be deeply troubling and long-lasting consequences for these people and those who support them.

As another example, consider the so-called war on drugs. It represents one more instance of dealing with the symptoms rather than the underlying causes. The inability of our contemporary mass societies to sustain the lives of their members drives these people to escape into drugs, even though they know full well how detrimental this can be for their lives. There are a great many ways in which we can reduce the "production" of anxiety, depression, mental illness, violence, and anomie if we choose to do so.[81] We are not questioning our commitments to our secular sacred and myths that justify the conditions that cause all manner of dislocations in the relationships constituting the fabric of individual and collective human life. What is incomprehensible is that the majority of the members of the Christian community in North America show by their behaviour that they are serving their cultural masters. They have not understood the message of Qohelet, and certainly not her strategy of being incognito with others in order not to push them closer to relativism, nihilism, and anomie. Loving God, and loving these people because of that love, means not to undermine what holds their persons and lives together until they are ready to hear and understand that they have been liberated from that enslavement.

A similar argument can be made for homosexuality. The biological functioning of our sexual and reproductive systems is under attack, of which the significant drop in sperm count is perhaps the best known symptom. Superimposed on this malfunctioning are significant cultural factors because in our societies the secular sacred transgression of technique is sexual intercourse.[82] Simply put, technique has had such a major de-symbolizing effect on culture and our being a symbolic species that we attempt to escape from its enslaving influence by asserting our biological selves through sexual intercourse dominated by technique.[83]

In these examples I am attempting not to settle the many controversies but simply to point to the fact that the positions of most people are based on their confusing of symptoms with root causes and thus legitimating a self-justifying and judgmental attitude towards others. In addition, it is deeply disturbing how American Christians have politicized these issues as if they were the business of the state and as if Christians were obliged to use political force to impose a religious morality on their society. It constitutes a double error. They have also turned a blind eye to the manipulation by unscrupulous politicians and corporate America, which has been well documented.[84] Many of these Christians have also supported the politicization of the withdrawal of health care from millions of Americans. It is as if they had never read about God's judgment of the nations according to their treatment of their weakest and most vulnerable members. As the letter of James says, the only religion acceptable to God is the care of such people. Ironically, nearly half a century of Christian political muscle flexing has contributed to America's becoming the most unequal of all industrially advanced nations, with well-documented and serious consequences.[85] Christians have thus helped to create a nation under our secular gods, which blatantly disregards its weakest and most vulnerable members. Caring for such people is dismissed as socialism. I am also looking into the future of Canada, whose Christians are not far behind. All this helps to produce Christian forms of the American and Canadian ways of life, as if we could take our "cultural DNA" and splice in the equivalent of religious genes that are named "Christian" and "faith based."

We live in a time under the sun when it is extremely difficulty for us to discern that we have named ourselves through a secular sacred and myths. Our powerful counter-transference reactions tend to make us forget that the lives of believing Jewish and Christian members of our societies are deeply rooted in this naming. During such times it becomes much easier to forget that, in the rare cases that babies and children are raised by animals, for example, or in other ways are deprived of listening to human words, they do not become members of our symbolic species and they exhibit few human characteristics other than a mere physical resemblance to human beings. When children do become members of our symbolic species by listening to human words, they also learn to suspend their lives above the void of potential relativism, nihilism, and anomie by implicitly learning to serve the cultural masters of their society.

All this appears to correspond rather well to what, in the first and second testaments, is referred to as sin: a condition of enslavement to cultural masters to the point that it becomes impossible to live as free creatures, which in turn makes it impossible to love God and our neighbour. Any preoccupation with particular "sins" represents a counter-transference reaction that assimilates the Word into something with which we can deal, but it amounts to our substituting the symptoms for our true condition before God. It becomes possible for these sins to take on a religious and moral character, thereby transforming them into the reality and highly de-symbolized cultural truths that our societies create for themselves. They are thus brought within our cultural control and our ability to do morally good works and to avoid morally evil ones. At this point, it ought to become clear that something fundamental has gone missing. Since sin is the condition of our enslavement to cultural masters that resulted from humanity's break with God, we cannot do anything about it: the path back to the Garden of Eden is blocked. Hence, our condition of enslavement cannot be reduced to our actions as slaves, whether or not they are moral or religious. It thus obliterates what we can do nothing about and leaves us with what we can potentially bring under our moral and religious (and thus institutional) control. It veils our bowing to our cultural masters and unveils the possibility of self-justification and the judgment of others one sin at a time. As we are slaves to our cultural masters, our "sins" have no moral or religious content whatsoever; they represent particular instances of our not loving God and of our walking in cultural ways. When we "sin" against others, we fail to recognize them as fellow creatures loved by God. For this reason, everything in the Torah can be summed up in terms of love and of our failure in this love by loving something else, something that is associated with naming ourselves as members of a society. Anything other than love is an assimilation into the moral and religious necessities of the way in which our community has named itself in its separation from God. It is not a question, therefore, of believers living more moral and religious lives than non-believers do, or of believers being better human beings than everyone else is. There is no reason that God chose them over others. Their assumed superiority amounts to an even greater vanity than that of their fellow human beings.

It is thus essential, for the living of a Christian life, that we discern the times in terms of our relationships with our cultural masters. This discernment cannot be replaced by using our new-found understanding – of being symbolically suspended in an ultimately unknowable creation by means of our secular sacred and myths – to construct a theology or philosophy aimed at showing how the relative and open-ended character of our knowing, doing, and living can be "solved" by God's presence. Following Qohelet, we need to remain on the level of our lives and not escape into intellectual constructs about these lives. What Qohelet has done in her analysis of human life under the sun is entirely existential, drawing on the architecture of creation revealed in the opening chapters of Genesis to detect how the architecture established by the cultures of her time distorted it to produce a life of vanities. It once again reminds me of a life review, as well as of the biblical distinction between what is real (seeing) and what is true (listening to the Word) in our lives.

Prior to the emergence of our present civilization, the traditional pre-industrial societies were ordered by a culture that was anchored in a traditional sacred and myths with low levels of de-symbolization; these societies constituted what was true for human life by means of the only available point of reference, namely, the collected body of experience and life of a community. What was true for such a community thus became an absolutized false truth. What was real for such a community was mostly subjected to this false truth, except for the incorporation of idols. These communities were thus able to avoid the high levels of de-symbolization that we encounter today.

These developments occurred under the sun as well as under the heavens, that is, in the presence of God. By his presence and his communication to his people, God introduced something new into Israel's culture that was not created by it and that did not belong to it– something radically other than its cultural morality and religion. Qohelet shows that this revelation constituted what was true in the lives of the members of the Jewish people and beyond, thanks to the means of faith and the link established by the Spirit. Following the resurrection and ascension of Jesus Christ and the granting of the Spirit, what is true in human life was permanently and decisively established in a new way, one that was based on people's indwelling in Jesus as he dwelt in his Father.[86] Much of this point has been greatly trivialized by the so-called neo-Pentecostalists, as well as by their opponents.

In our contemporary so-called secular mass societies characterized by high levels of de-symbolization, what is real in the lives of their members has grown enormously at the expense of what is "true"; but what we hold to be true is untrue because it was established by the absolutization of everything derived from symbolization, language, and culture. The mass media has built an increasingly dominant reality, one based on images, within the symbolic universes of these societies, and this reality gradually all but replaced them. It resulted in a growing reliance on images, the domains of disciplines, and computer simulations, to the detriment of everything that had been built up with language. The former became associated with an unlimited knowing, doing, and organizing, and the latter with highly de-symbolized human lives. Although these developments represented a threat to us as a symbolic species, the new secular sacred and myths legitimated the reversal of what is real and what is true in individual and collective human life.[87] Everything received from God that is radically other than what is real, and what remains of what is untrue in human life, has largely been assimilated by the ruling cultural masters. Hopefully, a faithful remnant remains that has not bowed its knees to them. In this respect there is also nothing new under the sun. From a social perspective it is clear that the majority of the Jewish and Christian communities live in ways that appear not to have penetrated their highly de-symbolized cultures, which are dominated by the reality of images. Doing so would have enabled them to exclude anything sacred and religious from the lives of their members. It has made these lives vulnerable to being swallowed up by the vanities that are ruled over by the principalities and powers. The message of Qohelet is thus even more important today than ever before.

If the faithful remnant are to grow within these communities, we must place ourselves entirely in the hands of our Maker, who holds out to us a relationship that creates in us the beginning of a new life, one that must grow and mature through this relationship. Qohelet provides us with the model of a person who, by the means of faith and the Spirit, has been able to see her existence and the collective existence of her people, as well as those of other people under the sun, as they truly are before God. As a creature totally dependent on her Maker, she went as far as a human being can go in terms of what is true. Qohelet thus discovered the contradiction between this lived truth and the lived reality that includes the false truth and the vanities of human existence. The interplay between what is true and what is real in Qohelet's life is central because what is real keeps the truth grounded in what is happening in human life and the world, while what is true prevents reality from turning into something that is so harsh and cold that it might drive people to despair.[88] This fundamental tension will be removed at the end of human history in the new creation, in which listening to the Word and seeing reality will be reconciled. It is symbolized in the last section of the book of Revelation, which is organized around a sevenfold proclamation of what John saw in this new creation.[89]

When Qohelet had journeyed incognito as far as she was able with her fellow human beings by sharing the vanities of their lives and cultural homes under the sun, she announced that, beyond all these vanities, there was true life and hope. The true life is based on the fear of God and on walking in his ways because it, and it alone, permits humanity to be named by God and thus not suspended in its own eternity. It brings us back to the opening chapters of Genesis, with their attack on religion, morality, and magic.[90] This put Qohelet entirely at odds with the Jewish religious establishment of her days requiring her to withdraw within herself in terrible solitude; such is frequently the experience of the members of a faithful remnant under threat by the religious establishment. It prepared her for giving us her testimony when she was called on to be a witness to her own life and everything she had observed under the sun.

Many members of the Christian community may find Qohelet's last remark reassuring. As noted, Christianity has put the final judgment at its centre under the influence of Roman law. Simply put, after all this talk about vanity, Qohelet returns to familiar ground. Hence, we need not concern ourselves too much about the opening remark that all is vanity under the sun. It would be a disastrous but understandable counter-transference reaction. God will bring into the open everything that is hidden, including everything unconscious and subconscious in ourselves. He will reveal to us what is in our hearts in terms of who we truly serve by naming ourselves. For the first time we will truly know who we are and what our life is before God. For the first time we will truly know his love, pardon, and grace. I am personally unable to conceive that anyone would turn him down.

Once again, we must remain on the level of our existence and not escape into theology. Any doctrine of universalism or of judgment and hell are equally false. God will sovereignly decide. Based on everything he has told us, I would wager that everyone will be in for a beautiful surprise. When he accomplishes his work of reconciliation with humanity in the new creation, nothing will ever be able to disturb it, because everything that is not within life and the good will have been separated out and destroyed. God will then be all in all. It fulfils Qohelet's penultimate remark: the vanities of our persons and our lives will fall away, and we will discover the fear of God and will walk in his ways. Once again, it would be a terrible mistake to transform this into a theological doctrine amounting to a kind of insurance policy for heaven. We are liberated from our vanities right here and now and are invited to play our parts in working for this reconciliation, beginning in our own lives so that we can share it with others. It involves the constant testing of our fear of God and our walking in his ways, which involves living the new life that we have been granted and excludes reducing it to abstract doctrines and theologies about this new life. It includes confronting our cultural masters in our own lives. Only when we do so will we have any true experience to which we can testify if an occasion arises that someone may hear and understand us.

When we struggle with our new life, we remain creatures created within time, space, and the life-sustaining land. We must resist any attempt at transcending this finitude by the greatest vanity of them all: the supposed eternity of our secular sacred and myths. We must live our finitude by fearing God and illuminating our path with his Light.

All this has become a great deal more difficult because we live in societies that see themselves as being more and more secular. The Torah in general, and the Decalogue in particular, show what such societies ought to look like: there would be nothing of a secular sacred character or any God-like entities that have no limits and thus are unlike anything else that has been created. There would be no religious use of God's name. Nor would there be any "factual" images of any kind. No members of such societies could declare what is good and evil because there would be no ultimate reference points for such declarations. However, in our societies we experience the exact opposite. The architecture of our so-called secular societies, as well as the places that it assigns to everything within them, has distorted everything and disrupted their created potential in relation to everything else. Nothing is in its rightful place and thus is unable to unfold its created potential in harmony with everything else in creation. Hence, we are once again confronted with individual and collective human life pieced together out of vanities. We must follow Qohelet and journey incognito to help our fellow human beings understand how their cultural selves and lives have become a bundle of vanities. It is only beyond these vanities that a truly secular life begins and where enslavement to anything sacred and religious ends.

We are now back to where we began. Hopefully, we can now understand more clearly why God warned humanity of the danger of putting itself in his place. It would trigger humanity's descent into a non-life of vanities resulting from a servitude of everything sacred and religious, which would come from the need to name ourselves as a group or society. Of course, biologically, life has continued, and a cultural substitute for life was created and has evolved throughout the ages. Qohelet revealed that this amounted to vanities under the sun. We cannot escape them, but we can discern them for what they are and entrust ourselves to our Maker and his ways. It is a scary business because our lives continue to be suspended above a chaos of a potential relativism, nihilism, and anomie. We must learn to discern that everything in reality is vanity, but that everything in truth is a gift from God.[91] During our time under the sun, it appears that the Christian community has failed in this discernment and has been unable to act as a true presence in North America; we have blocked the light with our darkness, turned our yeast into dough, and spoiled the salt. We have created an "I-Christianity," concerned only with *my* conversion, *my* faith, and *my* going to heaven. We have thus added more vanities under the sun. We have failed to reach out to a humanity that cannot live without God; when it attempts to do this, it becomes trapped in a life in the world that is nothing but vanities. We simply added some Christian vanities to the scene as we became lost in the labyrinth of our vanities. Perhaps we have now gained some new insights, thanks to the "metaphor" of our current knowledge that we are a symbolic species endangered by de-symbolization. If we all begin to struggle with these issues and live out our total dependence on our Maker, God may again create something new in us. Only then can our false presence in North America come to an end.

Epilogue

Qohelet's approach to human life in the world (including her own) provides us with a key to understanding the organization of the work of Jacques Ellul. It ought to come as no surprise, given his lifelong struggle to understand the meaning and significance of Qohelet for our time. Before explaining this interpretation of the body of his work, I will begin with what it cannot mean in the North American context.

The work of Jacques Ellul does not hold out a model for Christian scholarship. Such a concept is highly problematic for several reasons. Observing ourselves and our world in a manner that is as faithful as possible to God requires standards of scholarship that cannot be found in the first and second testaments, and I am not aware that anyone has ever been able to derive such standards from these sources. Does this mean that, when a faithful Christian seeks to understand our life and our world, this activity can be designated as Christian? Only if we claim to possess the ability to separate the wheat from the tares in our activities by judging them. We can do this only by putting ourselves in the place of God, as I have attempted to show.

Nevertheless, in North America, Christian scholarship has become big business, given the proliferation of Christian schools, colleges, and universities that in one way or another claim to be "Christ centred" and "faith based." Collectively these institutions produce an enormous number of "Christian" books, magazines, and journals, which are published by "Christian" publishers. All this is rather astonishing given the endless contradictions between these "Christian" endeavours. It is as embarrassing as when Christian clergy of all kinds prayed to the same God for victory on both sides of the conflict during the Second World War. Doing so reveals a god who is certainly not the God of the first and second testaments. What it does reveal is the extent to which the Christian community is in the grip of its time and place and a technical order with a highly de-symbolized culture. The technical order has profoundly de-symbolized human language and harnessed it to the integration propaganda that is diffused by the old and new media, and to public relations in particular, which use words to create particular effects.[1] If the Christian community had discerned what was happening to human life, it would have been a great deal more careful with how it named its activities, especially since this naming tends to be rooted in the way our contemporary secular societies have named themselves. For example, when in a discussion one Christian tells another that what he or she has just explained is the consequence of a faith-based decision or of prayerful consideration, it becomes impossible for the other party to disagree. Consequently, such qualifications exclude both parties from a true communion – with far-reaching consequences, as we will see.

I believe that the work of Jacques Ellul is the diametrical opposite of Christian scholarship. He essentially followed the approach of Qohelet. In his social works he examined individual and collective human life in the twentieth century as he also experienced and lived it, and interpreted it in the historical context of Western civilization, which gave birth to the world he described. In his interpretation he refused anything sacred or religious, thus unmasking (among other things) the limitless character of discipline-based contemporary science. Consequently he could not subscribe to the scientisms of an objective and detached observer who was free from all the counter-transference reactions that result from clashes between what is being observed and the deeply held values of the observer. He also unmasked the unlimited character of technique, of the nation-state now served by secular political religions, and of a history in the grip of these endeavours.[2] Without using the language of Qohelet, Jacques Ellul showed how these three constitute our ultimate vanities, by arguing that these human works cannot deliver what they claim and that, individually and jointly, they are incapable of changing human life in any fundamental manner. This is clear if such observations are made in the context of the architecture of God's creation, but no one is excluded, especially in a so-called secular society. If we, via our contemporary societies, name ourselves as being secular, let us look at this seriously and confront our complete failure to live the spiritual direction by which we mistakenly believe we live.

We would thus jointly discover the multitude of contradictions that hold our lives together.

Ellul's work was widely read in the United States during the 1960s and 1970s, a brief period during which the most technically advanced society on the planet changed the way in which it named itself through its secular scared and myths. Ellul appealed to a great many people who felt that something was going wrong with the way we lived together and dealt with life in the biosphere. This feeling was short lived as a new secular eternity took hold of human life. Generally speaking, the large Christian and Jewish communities paid little attention to Ellul's testimony, and, if they did, it was not understood. The reviews of Christian commentators mostly missed the point.

In his attempt to include everyone in his analysis of human life in the twentieth century, Jacques Ellul not only exposed the many contradictions out of which this life was constituted, but he could not avoid intellectually nudging people towards the void of a potential relativism, nihilism, and anomie. However, the risk was diminished by his refusal to provide a total explanation. In addition, he was keenly aware of what people had done with Karl Marx's full explanation of human history, and how it had been used to justify some of the most totalitarian regimes of our history as well as the first secular political religion.[3]

An existential approach can never be total. It can show how science, as a human activity, cannot possibly be limitless and that, if we wish to behave responsibly in a secular fashion, we ought to discover its limits and find other forms of knowing that are able to transcend them in order not to put all our (knowledge) eggs in one basket. The same can be shown for technique, the nation-state, and history. Despite these precautions, Jacques Ellul told me that occasionally he would receive a letter to the effect that the writer could not understand why he had not committed suicide when the implications of his analysis of human life became apparent. It is here where his reflections on his reading of the Bible, which he accepted as the Word of God, join his socio-historical works.

The relationship between these two parts of his work can easily be misunderstood. The social and historical part was undertaken in his refusal of anything sacred and religious and was based on the opening chapters of Genesis. Everything was created and was thus dependent on the Creator, which excluded the possibility of anything being autonomous or limitless. These opening chapters amount to a harsh critique of religion, morality, and magic,[4] which are, individually and jointly, incompatible with freedom and thus with the love that requires it.[5]

From the perspective of Qohelet, the analysis of human life under the sun was undertaken incognito by Jacques Ellul as a believer. In the other part of his work, he deals with his reflections on his reading of God's Word and its practical implications for life. He takes the perspective of reading Qohelet "backwards," in the sense that the closing verses provide the point of departure and a committed vantage point for observing human life under the sun in the twentieth century.

The two perspectives are inseparable. This becomes a great deal more understandable from what we have learned about ourselves being a symbolic species threatened by the de-symbolization that results from technique. Our relationships with others and our surroundings are always reciprocal in character. The same applies to our reading of the first and second testaments. When we read them in a translation corresponding to our mother tongue, our interpretation cannot avoid imposing something of our time, place, and culture on the words of the text. At the same time, this reading may create something new in us through the Spirit. The two components involved in this reading are inseparable – another human activity constituted of both wheat and tares. Nevertheless, the deeper a reader's understanding of a time, place, and culture, the greater is the possibility of the reader having a critical awareness of what he or she may be imposing on the reading, which we cannot but interpret through our human words.

It is this reciprocal relationship between the socio-historical works undertaken incognito, and the reflections on the revelation made as a believer, that gives Jacques Ellul's work the existential depth that has struck a chord with a number of us. His work is in sharp contrast with the historical, sociological, theological, and philosophical works carried out in the servitude of discipline-based approaches, which many regard as being the most objective, detached, and value free, and thus liberated from any or all cultural moorings. But this scientism also amounts to a vanity. In the same vein, how can a theological or philosophical treatise speak of freedom, love, vocation, work, government, institutions, or anything else in human life under the sun without acknowledging that these words take on very different meanings depending on their time, place, and culture? Owing to their asocial and ahistorical character, these treatises accept the secular eternity (which we have created by naming ourselves) as the only possible way of making sense of and living in the world. In this way, they implicitly speak of this eternity, which provides them with a religious spirit that is then confused with the revelation. This is particularly true when such works speak of technology, science, the state, democracy, politics, and history. Once again, I make these comments as someone who has attempted to go beyond discipline-based approaches throughout my entire life in order to develop alternatives that can transcend their limits.

Once again, Jacques Ellul followed the example of Qohelet. If everything under the sun is vanity, and if our going beyond these vanities reveals the fear of God and the possibility of walking in his ways, then our lives must remain unbroken. It is impossible to have some parts subjected to this revelation, while others escape it. Hence, there can be no autonomous disciplines equivalent to secular mini-gods. When Qohelet focused her attention on anything under the sun, it became the momentary foreground of her intellectual life, which expressed the orientations of her life as a whole. I encounter this same kind of unity in all the works of Jacques Ellul, which accounts for its deeply existential character.

Living our lives in this way has made the recent preoccupation of the Christian community with intense debates over creationism or evolutionism appear a strange diversion. It was an embarrassing situation. Until Darwin's theory appeared, such a topic could not have been considered as the subject of the opening chapters of Genesis; Jews and Christians once read these passages in a very different way. Moreover, these opening chapters have a vastly deeper and more important significance than do the petty debates. I am tempted to say that they were triggered by counter-transference reactions that completely obliterated the true message: to help us understand that the architecture of our world *under the sun* has nothing in common with the architecture of the world *under the heavens*. By imposing the former on the latter, humanity was able to name itself and put itself in the place of God. Since science has no limits, these chapters had to have a scientific content, and thus evolutionism or creationism was imposed on their texts.

Unmasking the secular myth of science requires an intellectual life that avoids an escape into discipline-based approaches, with far-reaching consequences. For example, none of the works of Jacques Ellul can be understood exclusively in terms of the primary subject of the work. It is as if each of his works represented a piece cut out from a hologram-like interpretation of human life in the world, in the sense that the entirety of this life and the world is present in each work. Such a relationship is necessary because of the dialectically enfolded character of human language. As noted, what a word means is what all the other words in the vocabulary of the language do not mean, as embedded in lived relationships through experience and culture. Consequently a word, phrase, or sentence that we read, whether it be in the first or second testament, is first of all interpreted in this way. Only to the extent that we have learned to recognize that our person and our life are constituted of vanities, and that we have begun to live differently, can language begin to take on entirely different meanings. In our North American setting, this often does not go much further than our personal devotions and our participation in the life of a congregation. If this is the case, then our interpretation of what we read in the first and second testaments will be extremely limited and robbed of its true meaning. In contrast, to the extent that in our daily lives we are able to let go of our cultural ways and to humbly walk before our God and practise his ways, we will begin to experience more of a lived truth and correspondingly less of the world's reality and our cultural false truth. All this will nevertheless remain intertwined as both wheat and tares.

For example, if we believe that we live in free democratic societies, we will have a great deal of difficulty comprehending the use of the word *freedom* whenever it occurs in the first and second testaments. If, however, we begin to understand how our civilization possesses us through the way in which our society has named itself, we will understand that we do not live in free and democratic societies and that what our Bibles offer us is something incomparably different. As our appreciation of the radically other character of the first and second testaments deepens, we will develop a keener awareness of the extent to which our lives are trapped in vanities. It is by means of such a *lived* dialogue that we grow what is true in our lives at the expense of what is real. We can also develop in the opposite direction, where we impose more and more of our cultural ways on our understanding of the first and second testaments. This would necessitate a kind of lived dualism between our daily lives and our so-called spiritual lives, which according to our Bibles is an impossibility. We have only one heart, and it loves either our cultural masters or the God who reveals himself. In the former case, the tares gain ground over the wheat, while in the latter case the reverse occurs.

All this constitutes a microcosm of the dialectical tension between the two parts of the work of Jacques Ellul. The more deeply we learn to comprehend our cultural ways, the more clearly we can differentiate them from walking humbly before our Maker, following his ways. The more deeply we comprehend how these cultural ways are the ways of false gods (traditional or secular), the more we are able to differentiate them from the only true living God. The more deeply we understand what we are involved in and contribute to during the week, the more we will be ready to hear something entirely different on Sunday. For this reason the metaphors of yeast, salt, and light are fundamental; they have no significance whatsoever other than in direct relation to dough, food, and darkness. If we keep our yeast and salt in the cupboard, they might as well be anything else, and it would make no difference whatsoever. If we hide the light of understanding under a bushel, there might as well not be any understanding. Consequently the conservative-liberal split continues to be a disaster; both forms of Christianity fall equally short in this regard. For the same reason neither branch has a true influence other than by using the ways of the world and by flexing a political, religious, or moral muscle. When we look at the churches, we are reminded that they have all become victims of the conservative-liberal split and thus incapable of discharging their calling in the world. It is in the midst of this tragedy that the work of Jacques Ellul calls us to an entirely different way of relating to and being in the world, a way that could reunite the conservative and liberal dimensions of Christianity in being a yeast in the world. I believe that this is the true significance of his work in our times.

For further illustration, let us take a look at how we interpret the Word. Clearly, what this means to us depends on what we have understood regarding human words. As in the case of freedom, it is very important to understand how our time, place, and culture and the associated naming of ourselves have affected human languages. Rationalization in general, and industrialization in particular, made humanity aware that symbolization, language, and culture were not well suited to anything that had the architecture of reality. To overcome these limitations, the domains of disciplines were substituted wherever the approaches based on symbolization, language, and culture could not reach. These domains were separated from any cultural world by means of a triple abstraction.[6] In order to deal with them, language also had to be separated from experience and culture by the kinds of developments that I described in the introduction. Gradually discipline-based approaches to knowing and doing became all important in any society that was evolving its way of life by means of technique rather than culture.[7] These developments could not occur other than at the expense of symbolization, language, and culture.[8] What we are left with in our daily lives is a highly desymbolized language and culture. The pronouncements in the first and second testaments regarding our use of language and its relationship to our hearts and lives cannot be understood in terms of our experiences of language in our present societies. We need to imagine the essential role that language played in traditional societies, a role that it continues to play in a highly de-symbolized form in some daily-life relationships. Our failure to make this subtle distinction will limit our ability to understand a great many texts.[9]

We can extend these kinds of arguments to the entire vocabulary of our Bibles. We will not understand the term *redemption* if we do not know what, in our specific context, we are being redeemed from. The same is true for concepts such as *the flesh* and *the principalities and powers*. If we fail to experience the forms that these take during our own time, our understanding will remain superficial. At the same time, if we reduce their meaning entirely to the forms that they take today, we will equally fail to understand their deeper biblical meanings. In sum, these words require that the conservative and liberal dimensions of Christianity be reunited by our walk with the Light, to allow it to illuminate everything we do and think as unique individual expressions of our time, place, and culture.

What I have always found so interesting is that many of the people I have encountered who have a deep and rich understanding of the work of Jacques Ellul have tended to be agnostics. They frequently are touched by the existential character of his Christian reflections, but they cannot follow him because of the counter-transference reactions that stem from their experiences with organized Christianity. It is in discussions with such people that I have often learned the most, and experienced what the metaphors of Christianity, such as yeast and salt, could become if churches had not transformed it into a religion and morality. This is particularly catastrophic in so-called secular mass societies. For many people, Christianity as an anti-religion, anti-morality, and anti-magic (as revealed in the opening chapters of Genesis) could be the good news of liberation, were it not for churches sending the opposite message.

Reading the work of Jacques Ellul as that of a historian, sociologist, theologian, environmentalist, anti-nuclear activist, advocate for delinquent youth, pacifist, or Christian anarchist amounts to the taking of major and significant activities in his life and turning them into constructs that are reigned over by discipline-based approaches, worldviews, or ideologies with all their values and beliefs embedded in our secular sacred and myths.[10] It is the worst possible betrayal of the work that sought to be existential in character by avoiding an escape into intellectual constructs of any kind about our lives.

This existential quality of the work of Jacques Ellul strongly struck a number of prominent people whom we interviewed for a five-hour program of the Canadian Broadcasting Corporation (CBC) to introduce him to the Canadian public.[11] Their experiences were very similar to my own, which makes it possible for me to comment. I first encountered this existential quality by reading the opening chapters of his work *The Technological Society* (the literal translation of the French title is "Technique – the wager of the twentieth century").[12] What I read struck me deeply because it implied exactly the way in which my mindset worked. I was close to finishing my doctorate in mechanical engineering and had already decided that what the world needed was not another professor of fluid mechanics. Instead, it was urgent to discover exactly how engineering design and decision making contributed to the kinds of human, social, economic, and environmental issues discussed in the social sciences and on the media. Reading Jacques Ellul made me realize that the root problem went much deeper. My mindset was clearly in the grip of technique, and thus I was more a part of the problem than I was a part of the solution. This realization was rather disturbing for someone who had been recognized by academic bureaucrats as forward thinking in such matters.

Hence, I could not just "add" some new methods and approaches to my engineering tool-box. What was required was nothing short of an intellectual conversion and a complete rebuilding of my mindset, which could only be done through very different experiences. It was clear that Jacques Ellul would be the best person to help me, but he initially turned me down because he was already overextended. Fortunately he changed his mind when I received a NATO postdoctoral fellowship from the Committee for Challenges to Democratic Societies, and I promised not to bother him for more than the equivalent of one day a year! When I arrived in France, I quickly realized that the intellectual conversion of my engineering mindset was impossible without a conversion of my mindset as a whole. It required a rethinking of almost everything I had learned regarding Christianity in the churches I had attended as I grew up.

Given its existential character, the applicability of the work of Jacques Ellul cannot be limited to that of intellectuals and scholars. I believe the contrary is the case, precisely because his work is first and foremost existential in character by its focus on our lives under the sun. It concerns everyone: believes and unbelievers, professors and people with little education, adults and children, and so on. Qohelet addresses all of us who have some intuition that there is a great deal about our lives that makes little sense and that we are being trapped in all kinds of contradictions. Even the people who believe that in their persons and lives they are doing well enough are invited to take a second, hard look.

Is the way in which we and our fellow members of society have named ourselves truly able to make sense of our daily life's thoughts and actions? I am not speaking of anything metaphysical but of the meanings and values established by living all our relationships as integral to life. Is it possible to believe that we may have absolutized our experiences and thus suspended ourselves in a secular sacred and myths, as manifested by our person and our life being constituted of vanities? If we are at all able to journey down this road, it will soon reveal that Qohelet has put most, if not all, of contemporary Christianity in the light of disobedience. Christians appear quite content to serve two masters in order to have it all. On the one hand, we live as if we are constantly adding new abilities and possibilities to our lives thanks to science and technique; and we are convinced that this will bear the greatest fruit for our society when the political party of our choice leads the nation. We do not dwell on everything that we have had to give up for this, because, even on this level, we believe that we can have it all. On the other hand, we imagine that we as Christians have the ability to make faith-based decisions or that, after prayerful consideration, we will make the right decisions. In this way we are able to expand the kingdom of heaven – as if there were no vanities, principalities and powers, and a kneeling to the secular sacred and myths of our society. Spiritually we can have it all as well.

Of course, we recognize full well that our world is plagued by crises of all kinds, and the media keep bringing them to our attention. Nevertheless, we are confident that on balance we are moving forward. Besides, were we not warned that there would be plenty of turmoil until the end of time? By thus dissociating our persons and our lives from any possibility that we may be contributing to and sustaining these crises, we can once more have it all. We are thus back to the opening chapters of Genesis, where the expression translated as "good and evil" can also mean "everything under the sun" in the Hebrew language. It is in this way that the serving of two masters limps along as the greatest vanity of them all.

Our servitude of two masters limps along because, on many levels, we are also becoming aware that something may be going fundamentally wrong. Many of our neighbours are losing their jobs, and our children are facing the constant threat of unemployment and underemployment.

We allow corporations to externalize all social responsibilities to the point of not even paying people a living wage, thereby indirectly starving them. They would indeed be starving were it not for the intervention of community organizations and the public purse. Moreover, many people suffer from anxiety, depression, a sense of being adrift, a need to escape with drugs or alcohol, a desire to lash out at others in violence, and much more. Our political masters attribute much of this to the failure of these people to meet the demands for full participation that are ultimately rooted in our secular sacred and myths. The more these kinds of difficulties become acute, the more we tend to follow extreme politicians who have identified plausible scapegoats but have no idea of what is really happening. There is an upsurge of intolerance and even neo-fascistic tendencies –in the Christian community as well. In sum, it would not take Qohelet very long to show the depth and breadth of the contradictions that have engulfed our lives.

Jacques Ellul began his work by speaking out about our "presence in the world" (the literal translation of the French title of his first book).[13] It prompted one of the leading theologians of that time to inquire as to what he meant by technique, implying that the questioner lacked an intuitive awareness of its being a secular false god. The question confirmed the non-theological character of the work. Nevertheless, especially in North America, it was welcomed by those who liked it as an interesting theological study. Next, Ellul warned us of civilization's wager that technique could solve all the problems with which the cultures of traditional societies had been unable to deal – a wager that would put all of us at risk. In North America his warning was widely read but little understood. Technique amounted to a new architecture for a human world that our civilization was busy constructing for itself within creation. Its orientation was the diametrical opposite of the human worlds that earlier societies had constructed for themselves as members of a symbolic species totally relying on symbolization, experience, and culture. As noted, technique orients each human thought and action in relation to itself by choosing its most efficient form. Doing so involves severing that form from the interrelatedness of everything it is related to, and evolves in relation to, everything else in a creation where nothing can be absolute or autonomous. In contrast, all earlier civilizations relied on our being a symbolic species by symbolically respecting the interconnectedness of creation, but anchoring it in an eternity of their own making.

Consequently, technique plays its role as if it were an alternative to symbolization, experience, and culture. As such it presents the most fundamental threat to our symbolic species. Babies and toddlers develop by listening to human words – a function that technique cannot perform unless there is a fundamental mutation of our being a symbolic species, one that substitutes images for language. In addition, technique threatens life by re-engineering it in the image of non-life with the architecture of reality. Owing to the widespread misunderstanding of what Jacques Ellul meant by technique, my first book dealt with the culture-based architectures that all traditional pre-industrial societies built for themselves as belonging to a symbolic species and thus fully relying on symbolization, experience, and culture.[14] The book was the outcome of the intellectual intersection of my own mindset reflecting the architecture of technique and then encountering the works and lectures of Jacques Ellul. Following his reading of my manuscript, he alerted me to the possibility that he had already said what I was saying in it. I asked him for the references in his own works. A few days later he acknowledged that he had not done so, but we agreed that it was implicit in his writings and lectures. The engineering disciplines may be regarded as the model disciplines of technique, much as physics is the model discipline of the sciences. As such, technique is the paradigm for re-engineering the creation in the image of technical and information processes. I had hoped that differentiating culture from technique would help people to understand the writing of Jacques Ellul, but I was sadly mistaken.

In a later work, Jacques Ellul showed how technique had evolved into a life milieu and system.[15] The implications were also widely misunderstood, yet it goes to the very heart of his work. How is it possible that technique as a human creation can become a system in which its elements interact much more directly with one another than with everything else, and do this by means of its own internal mechanisms of development that can be described in terms of the "laws" it obeys? How can such a system gain an autonomy with regard to our species? Ellul showed that two historical and social conditions must be met before a human creation such as technique can begin to function as an autonomous system. First, the phenomenon of technique that we have created must be equipped with its own internal mechanisms of development in which human beings participate on the terms of the system, with the result that they essentially function as its "cogs." For this to be possible, a second condition must be met. Human beings must devote themselves to the system as the "creator" of everything good for human life and society, to the point that they can no longer imagine how they would live, who they would be, and what the world would be without it. People are willing to serve this ultimate good with all their hearts and minds. Hence, no human creation can possibly function as a system without taking on the status of a secular sacred; when a society bestows its highest value on something it has created and absolutizes itthe creation and absolutizes it, this creation becomes the greatest good humanity can ever know. In such a case, a system has a much more decisive influence on human life and society than they have on it. This situation ends when people no longer give their hearts and minds to the system, and treat it as a mere human work with unique strengths, weaknesses, and limitations.

With my engineering mindset I sought to understand how this worked and how, historically, it had come into being. It gradually became clear that at the very core of the system of technique was a reorganization of all human knowing and doing by means of disciplines. The domains of these disciplines were separated from experience and culture, which created their potential autonomy provided that human beings had an unshakeable trust in the objectivity, factuality, and reality of the disciplines. It thus required both a scientism and a technicism. How had humanity backed itself into this re-engineering of itself and the creation? A further study was needed to confirm the architecture that humanity was building through technique.[16]

Jacques Ellul also examined how the de-symbolization of all cultures by technique required a complement to permit humanity to make sense of and live in the world. He called this complement *integration propaganda*.[17] Furthermore, if the system of technique was now autonomous because of its secular sacred status, politics could have no decisive influence over it, thus creating what Jacques Ellul referred to as the political illusion.[18]

A further analysis examined how the members of the societies that were dominated by the system of technique became possessed by technique and the nation-state as the new secular sacred as well as by science and history as their sustaining secular myths.[19] Ellul made it clear that, although Christians could not escape the life milieu and system of technique, they need not relate to them as such, by simply withdrawing their secular religious servitude and thereby reducing technique to the status of any other human work. By refusing the vanities that shroud technique and the nation-state, and treating them as no more and no less than what they are in the course of human events, Christians would identify their limits and transcend them by means of other approaches to knowing and doing.[20]

Within these developments the de-symbolization of human language has far-reaching implications for humanity as a symbolic species, and for Christianity in particular. Consequently, Jacques Ellul examined the humiliated Word and our false presence in the world.[21] The former helped to clarify the fundamental biblical distinction between listening to the Word and seeing the world, thus further illuminating the significance of integration propaganda. In this manner, all his work fits together in the knowledge that there can be nothing sacred in God's creation. It eliminates any basis for the creation of false gods, religions, moralities, and secular magic. It unmasks the most fundamental vanities in our lives, and, to the extent that we can bear this without counter-transference reactions, we can begin to comprehend a little of what God is holding out to us through his Word. It mirrors the approach by Qohelet in which everything in reality is vanity, but everything in truth is a gift from God.[22]

There is another aspect that needs to be emphasized. By describing technique and its development as a life milieu and system, Jacques Ellul was able to warn us of what could happen unless humanity withdrew its worship of its own work. In this manner he exercised the prophetic dimension of being a believer capable of identifying anything sacred by the means of faith and thus being able to strip bare all our illusions. It was a call for humanity to awake and to change course by intervening in technique as one of its own works, one that we were perfectly capable of controlling as soon as we refused to be its slaves. Since humanity did not assert its freedom, these developments are now so entrenched in our state as a considerably re-engineered symbolic species and in our reorganization of creation into our world that – even if we now recognize that we have made a dreadful mistake because technique can never deliver the limitless good that we believed it was capable of bestowing – we would have to disorganize and then reorganize all the structures and systems that we have been building for over two hundred years. This is not about to happen, because in North America the Christian community continues to provide us with evidence that it has understood very little of the relevance of the first few commandments of the Decalogue for our so-called secular mass societies. Our lamps appear to have gone out.

For those readers who believe that all this is a little extreme, we do well to remind ourselves of a fundamental biblical teaching that is at the very core of Jacques Ellul's understanding of the principalities and powers. In the first and second testaments there are entities that humanity has introduced into the creation that appear to be able to expand without limits and thus appear to acquire a spiritual power over humanity. Three obvious examples are money, which became Mammon; towns and cities that collectively became Babylon the Great, capable of trading in the bodies and souls of people; and the state as the centre of political power that globally became the Rome of the apocalypse. He examined these developments in several works.[23]

The principalities and powers are illustrative of what happens to human words when they are detached from God's Word. Humanity also "creates" a world by its words, beginning with the city and its tower called Babel, which symbolized humanity's desire to name itself and decide its own eternity. As discussed earlier, when God confused human language, each group and society symbolically appropriated everything it had experienced by naming it. Doing so anchored it in its own eternity of a sacred and myths. This was accomplished by symbolizing the "beyond" of present individual and collective human life as more of what a group or society already knew and lived. The symbolic cultural approach to human life in creation could not respect the relativity of the fabric of relationships constituting human life, because something sacred had to be introduced into the creation. Consequently, this enterprise could not tolerate any limits. Whatever was sacralized was under a kind of internal compulsion to expand and become all in all in taking the place of God. When it involved money to facilitate trade, a town, village, shelter, or centre of power (commercial, military, political, and religious), it expanded without limits and thus played a fundamental role in human history as designated by the second, third, and fourth horsemen in the apocalypse.[24] Each culture attempted to establish its own eternity. Now technique, in collaboration with the nation-state, is attempting to surpass that eternity. As Jacques Ellul has shown, technique recognizes no limits as the efficiency of everything continues to be increased, and this can go on almost indefinitely. Similarly, the nation-state must be adored by demanding our love, as many dictators have shown. At one point in the United States, political heretics were told to "love it or leave it." Why should allegiance be pledged to a flag by the placing of a hand over one's heart? A non-religious attitude would recognize that almost everyone likes certain things about their country, dislikes others, and is left indifferent by still others. Instead, we have turned democracy into a secular political religion that performs the exact same social functions as all traditional religions. In a similar vein, from a biblical perspective, the city represents our attempt at creating an exclusively human world that shuts God out in order to permit us to name ourselves. In sum, naming ourselves and creating our own eternity has unleashed a variety of powers that respect no limits, and this is associated with the denial of our status as creatures and of the finitude that comes with it. We need to recognize the architecture of the relationships between God, humanity, and the creation as set out in the opening chapters of Genesis and apply it to our own civilization.

A considerable portion of the Christian community in North America has created a Christian version of this situation. As noted, when Christians, during a discussion on significant issues, declare that their position is faith based or reached after prayerful consideration, they endow themselves with the capacity to discern between wheat and tares; when they judge and eliminate the tares, their decisions cannot be disagreed with – as if God were on their side. Their brothers and sisters, who may have also wrestled with these issues but have come to a different conclusion, are thus implicitly condemned as having permitted the tares to overcome the wheat in this particular incidence. This judgment divides the parties to such a discussion in an ultimate manner, which is nothing but a demonic act that contributes to and sustains the demonic in human history. If everything Christians do could be summed up by the two great commandments, then these totalitarian tactics would be considered their very antithesis. It becomes particularly embarrassing when self-declared Christian members of the Republican, Conservative, and former Reform parties in the United States and Canada legitimate their decisions in the aforementioned manner. I find these developments to be increasingly disturbing because they are symptomatic of a kind of Christian neo-fascism. It adds even greater urgency to an attempt to reunite the conservative and liberal dimensions of Christianity. The best model for doing so that I know is the work of Jacques Ellul as inspired by Qohelet.

As things stand, North American Christianity has been assimilated largely by our new secular eternity, while it vainly attempts to provide society with a religious establishment to serve its false gods. We have already suggested that this began when Christianity became the official religion of the Roman Empire and continued when it justified the medieval order. When the corruption of the order became unbearable, Christianity reformed itself in a manner that plunged much of Western Europe into religious wars and barbaric treatments of so-called heretics. Finally, Christianity became a relatively faithful servant, first of the industrial order and then of the technical order. It conveniently split itself into a conservative and a liberal branch that, each in its own way, greatly facilitated the serving of two masters. There is little question that on the fringes of this organized and institutionalized Christianity there remained a faithful remnant. However, as in Israel, it was unable to transform Christianity from a morality and religion serving cultural necessities into the anti-morality and anti-religion revealed in the opening chapters of Genesis. There was thus a stupendous lack of effectiveness in terms of official Christianity's being a yeast or a salt for the benefit of its host societies. Just as the religious establishment in Israel generally bowed to the sacred and myths expressed in false gods and idols, so also the Christian establishment became assimilated by the need of its host societies to name themselves. The religious establishments thus drew their members into the service of two masters. I readily acknowledge that none of us can avoid doing so, but living it as a normal state of affairs is a different matter altogether.

We have entered an age of biotechnology, nanotechnology, and information technology and are beginning to take the next steps in re-engineering human life and this creation. It involves re-engineering everything in the image of the architecture of non-life (and thus of death). It will greatly intensify the enormous pressures that are already being exerted on all human relationships, as well as on the groups and communities that these relationships help to constitute. We appear to be inching towards what the first and second testaments refer to as hell. This statement is hardly speculative. These new ventures represent the extension of discipline-based approaches into critical areas where they will undoubtedly produce the same diversity of collisions with everything living that has been documented during the last two hundred years. Hence, the urgency for Christianity to recover its true role for the benefit of its host societies is greater than ever. The wager of the twentieth century has been lost, and we may be well on the way to losing the wager of the twenty-first century as well. An institutionalized Christianity that is unable or unwilling to listen to a faithful remnant will bear much of the responsibility for what is happening and what will continue to happen in North America if it does not withdraw its religious adherence to secular false gods. It is time for sleepers to awake and relight their lamps.

In this work I have argued that the relighting of our lamps involves repenting and following the path of Qohelet. If we do not discover how our sociocultural selves and our lives are nothing but a bundle of vanities, then much of what we read in our Bibles will be an abstraction. We will have no idea of how the flesh and the principalities and powers in our time, place, and de-symbolized cultures have robbed us of our freedom and thus of our ability to love. We will thus be incapable of understanding what God meant when he declared that he had set us free and that we had his permission to live by his ways and not by the ways of our culture. We will also be unable to understand the magnitude of the task that God is undertaking to reconcile himself with us and with the making of all things new. We will have no idea whatsoever of what sin is, other than as moral and religious misrepresentations of it. It makes the biblical message so trivial and superficial that we will have no choice but to make the message into a kind of spiritual veneer to cover our vanities, rather than something that calls us into question to the very depth and breadth of our persons and our lives. Until we discern that in reality all is vanity, we will have insurmountable difficulties in fearing God and walking in his ways, and we will fail to benefit humanity. Nevertheless, the work of reconciliation will continue.

How different our future in North America might be if the Christian community understood and discharged the task to which it is been called! It would refuse anything sacred and religious and thus shake the very foundations of technique and the nation-state.

It is not possible to describe what a true presence of Christianity in North America might look like, for the simple reason that such a presence would be an expression of the freedom we have been granted. What we can know is that this freedom cannot once again be expressed in the form of a religion and morality in the service of secular false gods that have been derived from our need to spiritually name ourselves in our separation from God. Every society is under the necessity of confronting the risk of relativism, nihilism, and anomie summed up in the biblical images of hell.

If Christians repent and once again take up the promise of freedom, we will have to confront what constitutes everything that endangers that freedom, according to the architecture of the relationships between God, humanity, and the creation that was set out in the opening chapters of Genesis and decisively restored once and for all by the work of Jesus Christ and the Spirit. With an eye on these texts, Qohelet has shown us how we may begin this journey incognito as creatures entirely dependent on our Maker. Since God loves us unconditionally and freely grants us the means to live within life and the good, our dependence, instead of enslaving us, frees us from everything that can fundamentally threaten our freedom, thus making it possible for us to love him in return. By giving us his unpronounceable name and by willing life and the good for us, he enables us to start a new life. We learn this by listening to his Word, which involves abandoning both the life that we began by listening to human words, and our suspension in nothing but vanities because everything in our old life was anchored by a sacred and myths. Qohelet shows us that there is nothing abstract, philosophical, or theological about this. The moment we accept to live by what the Epistle of James refers to as the law of freedom,[25] we begin to unmask the vanities in which our life is suspended. They will lose their hold on our life because we cannot go back and live as if they were true. It is as if we had lived through a financial crisis that was both the cause and the effect of people losing their trust in Mammon, thereby precipitating a run on the banks. The reference points provided by Mammon, as the value of values through which everything that has been reified and commoditized can take on a monetary value, have momentarily disappeared. Similarly, we will be like people who have lost the reference points of our culture by which we make sense of and live in the world. It will become impossible to judge anything or anyone, and this is exactly how Jesus instructed his followers to live. Without such reference points, Christians will be unaffected by our secular political religions, statistical moralities, and public opinions. All this and more will lose their ultimate hold on our lives, to be reduced to influences with which we can struggle. We do not need any ultimate reference points if we live for God and others instead of for ourselves. It is the law of freedom expressed in the two great commandments.

According to the approach set out by Qohelet, we are called to be a new people of the Word. We first became human by listening to a symbolic language. We now enter a new life by listening to the Word as a new way of making sense of and living in the world, a way that requires no secular sacred and myths as ultimate reference points. Again, there is nothing abstract about this. We watch our children grow and develop into human beings, and we can see how their lives are threatened by the de-symbolizing influences of screen-based toys and devices, followed by a completely uncritical education that has no concept whatsoever of what is truly happening to them. Our schools behave as if the development of a triple reference system were all that really mattered. These schools are cheered on by an array of false prophets who insist that this is the path to becoming trans-human or post-human. They are not bothered by the meaninglessness of these terms within the broader architecture of our lives and our world. Are we so mesmerized by science and technique that we have forgotten the outrageous claims made by their predecessors about a general artificial intelligence – of which not a single goal has ever been realized? Have we forgotten the experts who promised us that nuclear power would soon bring electricity that was "too cheap to meter"? Have we forgotten how the gurus of automated manufacturing promised us a work week of less than fifteen hours, and a leisure society? Have we forgotten the promises of fifth-generation computers, to which we should all be talking at this moment? Have we forgotten the promise of ultimate security through star wars? Have we forgotten the new economy based on limitless hydrogen? Why would we now believe the latest generation of false prophets who are essentially telling us to forget about human life being lived from the vantage point that is constituted by our bodies and that our humanity acquired by listening to human words, in order to retain only that portion of our lives that undermines and destroys this by de-symbolization? They appear to forget that the triple referencing system – required for human knowing and doing without embodiment, participation, commitment, and freedom – cannot be reached without the very developments that they deny and threaten.[26] What kind of public good and common future does this represent? Can anything be more sociopathic than technique?[27]

The social sciences and humanities appear to be in the grip of examining our statistical differences under categories such as social class, ethnicity, and gender as if these differences were primary instead of being increasingly derived from the differences in the way we develop our humanity in our time of de-symbolization. If we are truly concerned about what is happening to human life, we need to re-symbolize all of this by putting it in the context of the architecture of our life in this creation. We will discover that what we are facing is yet another generation of contradictions rooted in an architecture of a civilization in which its member societies have to name themselves through a secular sacred and myths.

Would it not be existentially more fruitful if we began by examining how the development of ourselves and our children is being affected by de-symbolization, how our society reinforces this de-symbolization through the schools, and how we are thus creating a self-fulfilling prophecy based on our contradictions? How can we protect the growth and development of our children from de-symbolization, from scientism, from technicism, from everything being political, and from the peculiar idea that this is the only future that history can possibly hold for us? How can we live together in relationships, families, and groups that are not enslaved to the dictates of the contradictions of our time, place, and technical order? How do we live our freedom and thus contribute to a Christianity that bears fruit that this world can appreciate because it comes from love and not from an enslavement to false reference points served by our religious and moral creations?

We can sum up what the current generation of false prophets is promising us as follows. Whenever we are told of another success of the new artificial intelligence and big data, what has truly happened is that a human activity has been reified and represented in a mathematical domain built up with the principle of non-contradiction. Thus severed from a human life, its architecture has nothing in common with the original activity. This "model" is constituted by sophisticated statistical and computational techniques that obtain a more efficient result than what a human activity could achieve, but at the expense of the skill level in a human life. However, the model is achievable only in this domain and not in a human life, because its adaptation and evolution are ultimately rule based and thus autonomous from a human life functioning in the background. It can thus strengthen all manner of information systems, to the exclusion of human life. The improvements achieved with neural nets do not fundamentally alter the situation. Now suppose that all human activities of a life will thus one day be replaced by such ingenious achievements in mathematical domains. It would be impossible to assemble them into a life because each one of them is a reification of an expression of such a life. What kind of future does this leave for our children and grandchildren? The same is true for all the achievements of nanotechnology and biotechnology, which can never be assembled into a living biosphere that can sustain our lives and every other life form. Our future is likely to be dominated by increasingly disembodied lives, corresponding to declining levels of participation in and commitment to our activities. We will be separated more and more from our works – a kind of psychological, social, and spiritual dying to these works.

Once we go down the path of Qohelet and begin to discern all the contradictions in our lives, thus opening up our promised freedom, many of us will likely discover that there are no others with whom we can share this interpretation of a lived Christianity that cannot be reduced to an ontology, philosophy, theology, world-view, morality, or religion. We may have to turn inward, incognito, in a profound solitude, in the conviction that we must hold ourselves ready for the new possibilities that will open up when our God creates them by ending his silence and addressing us again. His Word will be borne by his people through the intervention of the Spirit. Under these conditions, the faithful remnant will grow and may begin to play a more public role if the world is ready to listen. In the meantime, the members of the faithful remnant must keep their lamps burning as they wait for God. They must not be troubled by the myriad of lamps lit by the institutionalized Christian establishment that reflect the bewildering set of contradictions exposed by Qohelet, incognito, exposed in her fear of God and of living in his ways. As we wait for God, it is our responsibility to make our lamps burn as brightly as possible with the best understanding of our situation. That is why Qohelet speaks in a way that is contemporary and applicable to our lives, our societies, and our civilization.

Notes

As noted in the preface, my references point to descriptions of "sub-maps" and patterns of connections. When these descriptions are entirely contained within one chapter, I indicate this, but in most cases the context of the entire reference is indispensable.

Preface

1 These connections will be more fully developed in a completed but as yet unpublished volume entitled *In the Days of Our Youth.*
2 Unfortunately, I have relied mostly on French biblical translations rendering the Hebrew as accurately as possible, which I then translated into English. In most cases, I know of no equivalent attempts in English.

Introduction

1 Willem H. Vanderburg, *The Growth of Minds and Cultures: A Unified Interpretation of the Structure of Human Experience*, 2nd ed. (Toronto: University of Toronto Press, 2016); Vanderburg, *The Labyrinth of Technology* (Toronto: University of Toronto Press, 2000); Vanderburg, *Living in the Labyrinth of Technology* (Toronto: University of Toronto Press, 2005); Vanderburg, *Our War on Ourselves: Rethinking Science, Technology and Economic Growth* (Toronto: University of Toronto Press, 2011); Vanderburg, *Our Battle for the Human Spirit: Scientific Knowing, Technical Doing and Daily Living* (Toronto: University of Toronto Press, 2016).
2 Uwe Poerksen, *Plastic Words: The Tyranny of a Modular Language*, trans. Jutta Mason and David Cayley (University Park: Pennsylvania State University Press, 1995).

3 Jacques Ellul, *The Humiliation of the Word*, trans. Joyce Main Hanks (Grand Rapids, MI: Eerdmans, 1985).
4 Jacques Ellul, *Propaganda: The Formation of Men's Attitudes*, trans. Konrad Kellen and Jean Lerner (New York: Vintage, 1965).
5 Ellul, *The Humiliation of the Word*.
6 Ellul, *The Humiliation of the Word*.
7 Vanderburg, *The Growth of Minds and Cultures*; Vanderburg, *Our War on Ourselves*, ch. 1.
8 Jacques Ellul, *The New Demons*, trans. C. Edward Hopkin (New York: Seabury, 1975); Vanderburg, *The Growth of Minds and Cultures*.
9 Vanderburg, *The Growth of Minds and Cultures*.
10 Vanderburg, *The Growth of Minds and Cultures*.
11 Vanderburg, *Our War on Ourselves*, chap. 1; T.W. Deacon, *The Symbolic Species: The Co-evolution of Language and the Brain* (New York: W.W. Norton, 1998).
12 Helen Keller, *The Story of My Life* (New York: W.W. Norton, 2003).
13 L. Wittgenstein, *Philosophical Investigations*, trans. G.E.M. Anscombe (Oxford: Blackwell Publishing, 1953).
14 Vanderburg, *Our Battle for the Human Spirit*.
15 Vanderburg, *Living in the Labyrinth of Technology*; Vanderburg, *Our War on Ourselves*; Vanderburg, *Our Battle for the Human Spirit*.
16 Ibid.
17 Vanderburg, *Our War on Ourselves*.
18 Vanderburg, *Living in the Labyrinth of Technology*, part 2.
19 Vanderburg, *Living in the Labyrinth of Technology*, part 2.
20 Vanderburg, *Our War on Ourselves*.
21 Vanderburg, *Our War on Ourselves*.
22 Vanderburg, *Our Battle for the Human Spirit*.
23 David Bohm, *Wholeness and the Implicate Order* (New York: Routledge, 2002); Bernard d'Espagnat, *In Search of Reality* (New York: Springer-Verlag, 1983).
24 Jack P. Manno, *Privileged Goods: Commoditization and Its Impact on Environment and Society* (Boca Raton, FL: Lewis, 2000).
25 Vanderburg, *Living in the Labyrinth of Technology*.
26 Vanderburg, *Living in the Labyrinth of Technology*.
27 Vanderburg, *Living in the Labyrinth of Technology*.
28 Vanderburg, *Our War on Ourselves*.
29 Vanderburg, *Our War on Ourselves*.
30 Jacques Ellul, *Métamorphose du bourgeois* (Paris: Calmann-Lévy, 1967); Vanderburg, *Our War on Ourselves*.
31 Jacques Ellul, *La pensée marxiste*, comp. and ed. Michel Hourcade, Jean-Pierre Jézéquel, and Gérard Paul (Paris: La Table Ronde, 2003).

32 Vanderburg, *Living in the Labyrinth of Technology.*
33 Vanderburg, *The Growth of Minds and Cultures;* Ellul, *The New Demons.*
34 Ellul, *Métamorphose du bourgeois;* Vanderburg, *Living in the Labyrinth of Technology.*
35 Adam Smith, *An Inquiry into the Nature and Causes of the Wealth of Nations,* 2 vols. (Chicago: University of Chicago Press, 1976).
36 Will Herberg, *Protestant, Catholic, Jew: An Essay in American Religious Sociology* (Garden City, NY: Anchor Books, Doubleday, 1960); Kevin M. Kruse, *One Nation under God: How Corporate America Invented Christian America* (New York: Basic Books, 2015).
37 Jacques Ellul, *The Subversion of Christianity,* trans. Geoffrey W. Bromiley (Grand Rapids, MI: Eerdmans, 1986); Ellul, *Métamorphose du bourgeois;* Vanderburg, *Living in the Labyrinth of Technology.*
38 Vanderburg, *Living in the Labyrinth of Technology.*
39 Vanderburg, *Living in the Labyrinth of Technology.*
40 Vanderburg, *Our War on Ourselves.*
41 H.H. Gerth and C. Wright Mills, eds., *From Max Weber: Essays in Sociology* (New York: Oxford University Press, 1963); Rogers Brubaker, *The Limits of Rationality: An Essay on the Social and Moral Thought of Max Weber* (London: Allen & Unwin, 1984).
42 Vanderburg, *Living in the Labyrinth of Technology,* part 2.
43 Jacques Ellul, *The Technological Society,* trans. John Wilkinson (New York: Knopf, 1964); Ellul, *The Technological System,* trans. Joachim Neugroschel (New York: Continuum, 1980).
44 Vanderburg, *Living in the Labyrinth of Technology.*
45 Michael Hammer and James Champy, *Reengineering the Corporation: A Manifesto for Business Revolution* (New York: Harper Collins, 1993); Thomas H. Davenport, *Process Innovation: Reengineering Work through Information Technology* (Boston: Harvard Business School Press, 1993).
46 Vanderburg, *Living in the Labyrinth of Technology;* Vanderburg, *Our War on Ourselves.*
47 Simon Head, *Mindless: Why Smarter Machines Are Making Dumber Humans* (New York: Basic Books, 2014).
48 Ellul, *The Technological Society;* Ellul, *The Technological System;* Jean-Luc Porquet, *Jacques Ellul: L'homme qui avait (presque) tout prévu* (Paris: Cherche Midi, 2003).
49 Vanderburg, *The Labyrinth of Technology.*
50 Thomas Kuhn, *The Structure of Scientific Revolutions,* 2nd ed. (Chicago: University of Chicago Press, 1970).
51 Ellul, *The Technological Society;* Ellul, *The Technological System.*

52 Ellul, *Propaganda*.
53 Jacques Ellul, *Les relations publiques* (Paris: l'Année Sociologique, Presses Universitaires de France, 1965).
54 Ellul, *Propaganda*.
55 Vanderburg, *Our War on Ourselves*.
56 Jeffrey Freed and Laurie Parsons, *Right-Brained Children in a Left-Brained World: Unlocking the Potential of Your ADD Child* (New York: Simon & Schuster, 1997).
57 Sherry Turkle, *The Second Self: Computers and the Human Spirit* (New York: Simon & Schuster, 1984); Turkle, *Living on the Screen: Identity in the Age of the Internet* (New York: Simon & Schuster, 1995).
58 Vanderburg, *Our Battle for the Human Spirit*.
59 Vanderburg, *Our Battle for the Human Spirit*.
60 Vanderburg, *Our Battle for the Human Spirit*.
61 Vanderburg, *Our Battle for the Human Spirit*.
62 Vanderburg, *Our Battle for the Human Spirit*.
63 Max Weber, *The Protestant Ethic and the Rise of Capitalism*, trans. Talcott Parsons (London: G. Allen & Unwin, 1930).
64 Herberg, *Protestant, Catholic, Jew*.
65 Kruse, *One Nation under God*.

1 The Possibility and Impossibility of Living a Secular Life

1 Jacques Ellul, *The New Demons*, trans. C. Edward Hopkin (New York: Seabury, 1975).
2 Jacques Ellul, *La pensée marxiste*, comp. and ed. Michel Hourcade, Jean-Pierre Jézéquel, and Gérard Paul (Paris: La Table Ronde, 2003).
3 A. Petersen, *Quantum Physics and the Philosophical Tradition* (Cambridge, MA: MIT Press, 1968), 188.
4 "Autobiographical Note," in *Albert Einstein: Philosopher-Scientist*, ed. P.A. Schlipp (Evanston, IL: Library of Living Philosophers, 1949).
5 Thomas S. Kuhn, *The Structure of Scientific Revolutions*, 2nd ed. (Chicago: University of Chicago Press, 1970).
6 Bernard D'Espagnat, *In Search of Reality* (New York: Springer-Verlag, 1983).
7 Paul Ricoeur, *Freud and Philosophy: An Essay on Interpretation*, trans. Denis Savage (New Haven, CT: Yale University Press, 1970).
8 Willem H. Vanderburg, ed., *Perspectives on Our Age: Jacques Ellul Speaks on His Life and Work*, 2nd ed. (Toronto: Anansi, 2004); Jacques Ellul, *The Technological System*, trans. Joachim Neugroschel (New York: Continuum, 1980); Richard Stivers, *Evil in Modern Myth and Ritual* (Athens: University

of Georgia Press, 1982); "The Festival in Light of the Theory of the Three Milieus: A Critique of Girard's Theory of Ritual Scapegoating," *Journal of the American Academy of Religion* 61, no. 3: 505–38.

9 Willem H. Vanderburg, *Our Battle for the Human Spirit: Scientific Knowing, Technical Doing, and Daily Living* (Toronto: University of Toronto Press, 2016).

10 Ellul, *The New Demons*; Stivers, *Evil in Modern Myth and Ritual*; Willem H. Vanderburg, *Our War on Ourselves: Rethinking Science, Technology, and Economic Growth* (Toronto: University of Toronto Press, 2011).

11 Jacques Ellul, *The Subversion of Christianity*, trans. Geoffrey W. Bromiley (Grand Rapids, MI: William B. Eerdmans, 1986).

12 Ibid.

13 Ellul, *The New Demons*.

14 Willem H. Vanderburg, *Living in the Labyrinth of Technology* (Toronto: University of Toronto Press, 2005).

15 Georges Devereux, *From Anxiety to Method in the Behavioral Sciences* (New York: Humanities Press, 1967).

16 Willem H. Vanderburg, *The Growth of Minds and Cultures: A Unified Interpretation of the Structure of Human Experience*, 2nd ed. (Toronto, University of Toronto Press, 2016).

17 Raymond Williams, *Key Words: A Vocabulary of Culture and Society* (London: Fontana, 1983).

18 Uwe Poerksen, *Plastic Words: The Tyranny of a Modular Language*, trans. Jutta Mason and David Cayley (University Park: Pennsylvania State University Press, 1995).

19 J.H. Van den Berg, *The Changing Nature of Man* (New York: Delta, 1961).

20 Hubert L. Dreyfus, "Christianity without Onto-theology: Kierkegaard's Account of the Self's Movement from Despair to Bliss," in *Religion after Metaphysics*, ed. Mark A. Wrathall (Cambridge: Cambridge University Press, 2003).

21 Jacques Ellul, *On Freedom, Love, and Power* (expanded ed.), comp., ed., and trans. Willem H. Vanderburg (Toronto: University of Toronto Press, 2015).

22 Vanderburg, *Our Battle for the Human Spirit*.

23 Vanderburg, *Our War on Ourselves*, chap. 2.

24 Vanderburg, *Our Battle for the Human Spirit*.

25 Jacques Ellul, *On Being Rich and Poor: Christianity in a Time of Economic Globalization*, comp., ed., and trans. Willem H. Vanderburg (Toronto: University of Toronto Press, 2014), part 2.

26 Jacques Ellul, *Propaganda: The Formation of Men's Attitudes*, trans. Konrad Kellen and Jean Lerner (New York: Vintage Books, 1973); Ellul, *Les relations publiques* (Paris: L'Année Sociologique, Presses Universitaires de France, 1965).

27 Ellul, *On Freedom, Love, and Power*, part 1.
28 Ellul, *On Freedom, Love, and Power*, part 1.
29 Ellul, *On Freedom, Love, and Power*, part 1.
30 Jacques Ellul, *The Humiliation of the Word*, trans. Joyce Main Hanks (Grand Rapids, MI: William B. Eerdmans, 1985), chap. 2.
31 Ellul, *The Humiliation of the Word*, chap. 2.
32 Ellul, *On Freedom, Love, and Power*, part 1.
33 Ellul, *On Freedom, Love, and Power*, part 1.
34 Ellul, *On Freedom, Love, and Power*, part 1.
35 Ellul, *On Freedom, Love, and Power*, part 1.
36 Ellul, *On Freedom, Love, and Power*, part 2.
37 Jacques Ellul, *Apocalypse: The Book of Revelation*, trans. George W. Schreiner (New York: Seabury, 1977).
38 Ellul, *On Freedom, Love, and Power*, part 1.
39 Ellul, *On Freedom, Love, and Power*, part 1.
40 Ellul, *On Freedom, Love, and Power*, part 1.
41 Vanderburg, *The Growth of Minds and Cultures*.
42 Vanderburg, *The Growth of Minds and Cultures*; Vanderburg, *The Labyrinth of Technology* (Toronto: University of Toronto Press, 2000); Vanderburg, *Living in the Labyrinth of Technology*; Vanderburg, *Our War on Ourselves*; Vanderburg, *Our Battle for the Human Spirit*.
43 Ellul, *On Freedom, Love, and Power*, part 1.
44 Ellul, *On Freedom, Love, and Power*, part 4.
45 Ellul, *On Freedom, Love, and Power*, part 1.
46 Vanderburg, *Our Battle for the Human Spirit*.
47 Vanderburg, *Our Battle for the Human Spirit*.
48 Vanderburg, *Our War on Ourselves*.
49 Vanderburg, *Our Battle for the Human Spirit*.
50 Vanderburg, *Our Battle for the Human Spirit*.
51 Ellul, *On Freedom, Love, and Power*, part 1.
52 Ellul, *Apocalypse*.
53 Ellul, *On Freedom, Love, and Power*, part 3.
54 Vanderburg, *The Growth of Minds and Cultures*.
55 Vanderburg, *Our War on Ourselves*; Vanderburg, *Our Battle for the Human Spirit*.
56 Ellul, *On Freedom, Love, and Power*, part 1.
57 Ellul, *On Freedom, Love, and Power*, part 1.
58 André Chouraqui, *Entête (La Genèse)*, (Paris: Jean-Claude Lattès, 1992).
59 Ellul, *On Freedom, Love, and Power*, part 1.
60 Ellul, *On Freedom, Love, and Power*, part 1.

61 Ellul, *The New Demons*.
62 Vanderburg, *Our Battle for the Human Spirit*.

2 The Roots of a Non-secular Life

1 Dante Alighieri, *The Divine Comedy*, trans. A.S. Kline (Luxembourg City: Poetry in Translation, 2000).
2 Jacques Ellul, *On Freedom, Love, and Power* (expanded ed.), comp., ed., and trans. Willem H. Vanderburg (Toronto: University of Toronto Press, 2015), part 3.
3 Jacques Ellul, *The Ethics of Freedom*, trans. Geoffrey W. Bromiley (Grand Rapids, MI: Eerdmans, 1976).
4 Ellul, *On Freedom, Love, and Power*, part 3.
5 Jacques Ellul, *Apocalypse: The Book of Revelation*, trans. George W. Schreiner (New York: Seabury, 1977). For an overview see the epilogue in Ellul, *On Freedom, Love, and Power*.
6 Ellul, *On Freedom, Love, and Power*, part 4.
7 Ellul, *On Freedom, Love, and Power*, part 4.
8 Ellul, *On Freedom, Love, and Power*, part 1.
9 Willem H. Vanderburg, *Our Battle for the Human Spirit: Scientific Knowing, Technical Doing and Daily Living* (Toronto: University of Toronto Press, 2016).
10 Ellul, *On Freedom, Love, and Power*, part 1.
11 Ellul, *On Freedom, Love, and Power*, part 1.
12 Jacques Ellul, *The Humiliation of the Word*, trans. Joyce Main Hanks (Grand Rapids, MI: Eerdmans, 1985).
13 Willem H. Vanderburg, *Our War on Ourselves: Rethinking Science, Technology, and Economic Growth* (Toronto: University of Toronto Press, 2011); Vanderburg, *Our Battle for the Human Spirit*.
14 Vanderburg, *Our Battle for the Human Spirit*.
15 Vanderburg, *Our Battle for the Human Spirit*.
16 Vanderburg, *Our Battle for the Human Spirit*.
17 Jacques Ellul, *On Being Rich and Poor: Christianity in a Time of Economic Globalization*, comp., ed., and trans. Willem H. Vanderburg (Toronto: University of Toronto Press, 2014), part 2.
18 Jacques Ellul, *The Meaning of the City*, trans. Dennis Pardee (Grand Rapids, MI: Eerdmans, 1970).
19 Ellul, *The Meaning of the City*.
20 Ellul, *Apocalypse*.
21 Ellul, *Apocalypse*.

22 Ellul, *Apocalypse.*
23 Ellul, *On Freedom, Love, and Power*, part 1.
24 Ellul, *Apocalypse.*
25 Ellul, *On Freedom, Love, and Power*; Ellul, *The Humiliation of the Word.*
26 Ellul, *On Freedom, Love, and Power*, part 1.
27 See also Ellul, *Apocalypse.*
28 Vanderburg, *Our Battle for the Human Spirit.*
29 Vanderburg, *Our War on Ourselves.*
30 Willem H. Vanderburg, *The Growth of Minds and Cultures: A Unified Interpretation of the Structure of Human Experience*, 2nd ed. (Toronto: University of Toronto Press, 2016); Arnold Toynbee, *A Study of History* (abridged version), ed. D.C. Somervell (New York: Dell, 1978).
31 Vanderburg, *Our Battle for the Human Spirit.*
32 Vanderburg, *Our War on Ourselves.*
33 Vanderburg, *Our Battle for the Human Spirit.*
34 Vanderburg, *Our Battle for the Human Spirit.*
35 Ellul, *On Freedom, Love, and Power*, part 3.
36 Ellul, *On Freedom, Love, and Power*, part 3.
37 Ellul, *Apocalypse.*
38 Jacques Ellul, *An Unjust God? A Christian Theology of Israel in Light of Romans 9–11*, trans. Anne-Marie Andreasson-Hogg (Eugene, OR: Wipf & Stock, 2012). For an overview, see the postscript in Jacques Ellul, *On Being Rich and Poor.*
39 Ibid.
40 Ibid.
41 Ellul, *On Freedom, Love, and Power*, part 2.
42 Ellul, *On Freedom, Love, and Power*, part 4.
43 Vanderburg, *Our War on Ourselves.*
44 Vanderburg, *Our Battle for the Human Spirit.*
45 Jacques Ellul, *Si tu es le fils de Dieu* (Paris: Editions du Centurion, 1991).
46 Ellul, *Si tu es le fils de Dieu.*
47 Ellul, *Apocalypse.*
48 Ellul, *The Meaning of the City.*
49 Ellul, *Si tu es le fils de Dieu.*
50 Ellul, *Si tu es le fils de Dieu.*
51 Ellul, *Si tu es le fils de Dieu.*
52 Vanderburg, *The Growth of Minds and Cultures*, 2nd ed.
53 Willem H. Vanderburg, *Living in the Labyrinth of Technology* (Toronto: University of Toronto Press, 2005).
54 Vanderburg, *Our Battle for the Human Spirit.*
55 Vanderburg, *Our Battle for the Human Spirit.*

56 Vanderburg, *Our Battle for the Human Spirit.*
57 Vanderburg, *Our War on Ourselves.*
58 Kevin M. Kruse, *One Nation under God: How Corporate America Invented Christian America* (New York: Basic Books, 2015).
59 Jacques Ellul, *Hope in Time of Abandonment*, trans. C. Edward Hopkin (New York: Seabury, 1973).
60 Ellul, *Si tu es le fils de Dieu.*
61 Ellul, *Si tu es le fils de Dieu.*
62 Ellul, *Si tu es le fils de Dieu.*
63 André Chouraqui, *Entête (La Genèse)*, (Paris: Jean-Claude Lattès, 1992).
64 Chouraqui, *Entête.*
65 Chouraqui, *Entête.*
66 Chouraqui, *Entête.*
67 Ellul, *The Meaning of the City.*
68 Ellul, *The Meaning of the City.*
69 Ellul, *The Meaning of the City.*
70 Ellul, *The Meaning of the City.*
71 Chouraqui, *Entête.*
72 Chouraqui, *Entête.*
73 Chouraqui, *Entête.*
74 Chouraqui, *Entête.*
75 Chouraqui, *Entête.*
76 Chouraqui, *Entête.*
77 Ellul, *Apocalypse.*
78 Ellul, *Apocalypse.*

3 Language, Myth, and History

1 Jacques Ellul, *The Meaning of the City*, trans. Dennis Pardee (Grand Rapids, MI: Eerdmans, 1970).
2 Ellul, *The Meaning of the City.*
3 Ellul, *The Meaning of the City.*
4 Jacques Ellul, *Apocalypse: The Book of Revelation*, trans. George W. Schreiner (New York: Seabury, 1977).
5 Willem H. Vanderburg, *The Labyrinth of Technology* (Toronto: University of Toronto Press, 2000), chap. 10.
6 Ellul, *The Meaning of the City.*
7 Ellul, *The Meaning of the City.*
8 Ellul, *The Meaning of the City.*
9 André Chouraqui, *Entête (La Genèse)*, (Paris: Jean-Claude Lattès, 1992).

10 Jacques Ellul, *The Humiliation of the Word*, trans. Joyce Main Hanks (Grand Rapids, MI: Eerdmans, 1985).
11 Willem H. Vanderburg, *The Growth of Minds and Cultures: A Unified Interpretation of the Structure of Human Experience*, 2nd ed. (Toronto: University of Toronto Press, 2016).
12 Jacques Ellul, *Reason for Being: A Meditation on Ecclesiastes*, trans. Joyce Main Hanks (Grand Rapids, MI: Eerdmans, 1990).
13 Willem H. Vanderburg, *Our Battle for the Human Spirit: Scientific Knowing, Technical Doing, and Daily Living* (Toronto: University of Toronto Press, 2016).
14 Vanderburg, *Our Battle for the Human Spirit.*
15 Ellul, *Reason for Being.*
16 Jacques Ellul, *On Freedom, Love, and Power* (expanded ed.), comp., ed., and trans. Willem H. Vanderburg (Toronto: University of Toronto Press, 2015), part 3.
17 Ellul, *Reason for Being.*
18 Ellul, *The Humiliation of the Word.*
19 Lucien Malson, *Les Enfants sauvages* (Paris: Union Générale d'Editions, 1964); Roger Shattuck, *The Forbidden Experiment* (New York: Washington Square, 1981).
20 Ellul, *Apocalypse: The Book of Revelation.*
21 Ellul, *Apocalypse.*
22 Ellul, *Reason for Being.*
23 Ellul, *On Freedom, Love, and Power*, part 4.
24 T.W. Deacon, *The Symbolic Species: The Co-evolution of Language and the Brain* (New York: W.W. Norton, 1997).
25 Sherry Turkle, *The Second Self: Computers and the Human Spirit* (New York: Simon & Schuster, 1984); Sherry Turkle, *Alone Together: Why We Expect More from Technology and Less from Each Other* (New York: Basic Books, 2011); Hubert Dreyfus, *On the Internet* (New York: Routledge, 2001) (although the second edition brings this book up to date regarding advances made in the design of search engines, the first edition has a more comprehensive discussion of the relevance problem, which is fundamental for understanding this work); Vanderburg, *Our Battle for the Human Spirit.*
26 Vanderburg, *Our Battle for the Human Spirit.*
27 Vanderburg, *The Growth of Minds and Cultures.*
28 Vanderburg, *The Growth of Minds and Cultures.*
29 Vanderburg, *The Growth of Minds and Cultures.*
30 Vanderburg, *Our Battle for the Human Spirit*, chap. 1.
31 Willem H. Vanderburg, *Our War on Ourselves* (Toronto: University of Toronto Press, 2011).

32 Vanderburg, *Our War on Ourselves*.
33 Vanderburg, *Our Battle for the Human Spirit*.
34 Vanderburg, *Our Battle for the Human Spirit*.
35 Vanderburg, *Our War on Ourselves*, chap. 2.
36 Vanderburg, *Our Battle for the Human Spirit*.
37 Vanderburg, *The Growth of Minds and Cultures*.
38 Jacques Ellul, *The New Demons*, trans. C. Edward Hopkin (New York: Seabury, 1975); Willem H. Vanderburg, *Living in the Labyrinth of Technology* (Toronto: University of Toronto Press, 2005).
39 Jacques Ellul, *On Being Rich and Poor: Christianity in a Time of Economic Globalization*, comp., ed., and trans. Willem H. Vanderburg (Toronto: University of Toronto Press, 2014), part 2.
40 Barbara Kingsolver, *The Poisonwood Bible* (New York: HarperPerennial, 1998); Geraldine Brooks, *Caleb's Crossing* (New York: Viking Penguin, 2011).
41 Ellul, *On Freedom, Love, and Power*, part 3.
42 Ellul, *On Being Rich and Poor*, part 1.
43 Ellul, *The Humiliation of the Word*, chap. 2, part 4.
44 Ellul, *The Humiliation of the Word*, chap. 2, part 4.
45 Ellul, *On Freedom, Love, and Power*, part 4.
46 Ellul, *The Humiliation of the Word*.
47 Ellul, *On Being Rich and Poor*, part 2.
48 Ellul, *On Being Rich and Poor*, part 2.
49 Vanderburg, *Our Battle for the Human Spirit*.
50 Ellul, *On Being Rich and Poor*, part 1.
51 Malson, *Les Enfants sauvages*.
52 Ellul, *On Being Rich and Poor*, part 2.
53 Ellul, *On Being Rich and Poor*, part 2.
54 Ellul, *On Being Rich and Poor*, part 2.
55 Ellul, *On Being Rich and Poor*, part 2.
56 Ellul, *On Being Rich and Poor*, part 2.
57 Ellul, *On Being Rich and Poor*, part 2.
58 Ellul, *On Being Rich and Poor*, part 2.
59 Ellul, *On Being Rich and Poor*, part 2.

4 Born Neither Free nor Equal, but Loved

1 Jacques Ellul, *Apocalypse: The Book of Revelation*, trans. George W. Schreiner (New York: Seabury, 1977).
2 Jacques Ellul, *Money and Power*, trans. LaVonne Neff (Downers Grove, IL: Inter-Varsity Press, 1984).

3 Jacques Ellul, *On Freedom, Love, and Power* (expanded ed.), comp., ed., and trans. Willem H. Vanderburg (Toronto: University of Toronto Press, 2015), part 4.
4 Jacques Ellul, *The Ethics of Freedom*, trans. Geoffrey W. Bromiley (Grand Rapids, MI: Eerdmans, 1976).
5 Willem H. Vanderburg, *The Growth of Minds and Cultures: A Unified Interpretation of the Structure of Human Experience*, 2nd ed. (Toronto: University of Toronto Press, 2016).
6 Jacques Ellul, *On Being Rich and Poor: Christianity in a Time of Economic Globalization*, comp., ed., and trans. Willem H. Vanderburg (Toronto: University of Toronto Press, 2014), part 2.
7 Ellul, *The Ethics of Freedom.*
8 Willem H. Vanderburg, *Our Battle for the Human Spirit: Scientific Knowing, Technical Doing and Daily Living* (Toronto: University of Toronto Press, 2016).
9 Ellul, *On Being Rich and Poor*, postscript.
10 Ellul, *On Being Rich and Poor*, part 2.
11 Ellul, *On Being Rich and Poor.*
12 Willem H. Vanderburg, *Living in the Labyrinth of Technology* (Toronto: University of Toronto Press, 2005).
13 Vanderburg, *Living in the Labyrinth of Technology.*
14 Vanderburg, *Living in the Labyrinth of Technology.*
15 Jacques Ellul, *Perspectives on Our Age*, ed. Willem H. Vanderburg, rev. ed. (Toronto: House of Anansi Press, 2004), chap. 4.
16 Jacques Ellul, *On Freedom, Love, and Power* (expanded ed.), comp., ed., and trans. Willem H. Vanderburg (Toronto: University of Toronto Press, 2015).
17 Vanderburg, *The Growth of Minds and Cultures.*
18 Vanderburg, *Our War on Ourselves* (Toronto: University of Toronto Press, 2011), chap. 2.
19 Vanderburg, *Living in the Labyrinth of Technology*, part 2.
20 Vanderburg, *Our Battle for the Human Spirit.*
21 Vanderburg, *Our War on Ourselves*, chap. 2.
22 Vanderburg, *Our Battle for the Human Spirit.*
23 Henry Mintzberg, *The Rise and Fall of Strategic Planning: Reconceiving Roles for Planning, Plans, Planners* (Toronto: Maxwell Macmillan Canada, 1994).
24 Joel Bakan, *The Corporation: The Pathological Pursuit of Profit and Power* (Toronto: Penguin Canada, 2004).
25 Willem H. Vanderburg, *The Labyrinth of Technology* (Toronto: University of Toronto Press, 2002).
26 Jacques Ellul, *Propaganda: The Formation of Men's Attitudes*, trans. Konrad Kellen and Jean Lerner (New York: Vintage, 1965).

27 Vanderburg, *Our Battle for the Human Spirit.*
28 Jacques Ellul, "Dieu," *Études théologiques et religieuses,* année 52, no. 4, 1997.
29 Vanderburg, *The Growth of Minds and Cultures,* 2nd ed.
30 Vanderburg, *Our Battle for the Human Spirit.*
31 Vanderburg, *The Labyrinth of Technology.*
32 Vanderburg, *Our War on Ourselves.*
33 Vanderburg, *Our Battle for the Human Spirit.*
34 Jacques Ellul, *An Unjust God? A Christian Theology of Israel in Light of Romans 9–11,* trans. Anne-Marie Andreasson-Hogg (Eugene, OR: Wipf & Stock, 2012).
35 Jacques Ellul, *Living Faith: Belief and Doubt in a Perilous World,* trans. Peter Heinegg (San Francisco, CA: Harper & Row, 1983).
36 Ellul, *Propaganda.*
37 David Riesman, Nathan Glazer, and Reuel Denney, *The Lonely Crowd: A Study of the Changing American Character* (Garden City, NY: Doubleday Anchor, 1950).
38 Vanderburg, *Our Battle for the Human Spirit.*
39 Kevin M. Kruse, *One Nation under God: How Corporate America Invented Christian America* (New York: Basic Books, 2015).
40 Will Herberg, *Protestant, Catholic, Jew: An Essay in American Religious Sociology* (Garden City, NY: Anchor Books, Doubleday, 1960).
41 Jacques Ellul, *The New Demons,* trans. C. Edward Hopkin (New York: Seabury, 1975).
42 Ellul, *The New Demons.*
43 Herberg, *Protestant, Catholic, Jew.*
44 Herberg, *Protestant, Catholic, Jew.*
45 Richard Stivers, *Evil in Modern Myth and Ritual* (Athens: University of Georgia Press, 1982).
46 Vanderburg, *Our Battle for the Human Spirit.*
47 Jacques Ellul, *False Presence of the Kingdom,* trans. C. Edward Hopkin (New York: Seabury, 1972).
48 Jennifer Chandler, "The Autonomy of Technology: Do Courts Control Technology or Do They Just Legitimize Its Social Acceptance?" *Bulletin of Science, Technology and Society* 27, no. 5 (Oct. 2007): 339–48.
49 Vanderburg, *Living in the Labyrinth of Technology.*
50 Bakan, *The Corporation.*
51 Vanderburg, *Living in the Labyrinth of Technology.*
52 Ellul, "Dieu."
53 Ellul, *Apocalypse.*
54 Vanderburg, *Living in the Labyrinth of Technology.*

55 Vanderburg, *Living in the Labyrinth of Technology.*
56 Vanderburg, *Living in the Labyrinth of Technology.*
57 Vanderburg, *Our War on Ourselves.*
58 Vanderburg, *Our War on Ourselves.*
59 B. Lietaer, *The Future of Money: A New Way to Create Wealth, Work and a Wiser World* (New York: Random House, 2001).
60 Vanderburg, *Our Battle for the Human Spirit.*
61 Lietaer, *The Future of Money.*
62 Vanderburg, *Our Battle for the Human Spirit.*
63 Lietaer, *The Future of Money.*
64 Ellul, *On Being Rich and Poor*, part 2.
65 Vanderburg, *Our Battle for the Human Spirit.*
66 Ellul, *False Presence of the Kingdom.*
67 Jacques Ellul, *The Meaning of the City*, trans. Dennis Pardee (Grand Rapids, MI: Eerdmans, 1970).
68 Ellul, *Apocalypse.*
69 Ellul, *Apocalypse.*
70 Ellul, *Apocalypse.*
71 Ellul, *Apocalypse.*
72 Ellul, *Apocalypse.*

5 The Law, the Spirit, and the Kingdom of Heaven

1 Jacques Ellul, *The Humiliation of the Word*, trans. Joyce Main Hanks (Grand Rapids, MI: Eerdmans, 1985).
2 Jacques Ellul, *Histoire des institutions: L'antiquité* (Paris: Presses Universitaires de France, 1961).
3 Willem H. Vanderburg, *The Growth of Minds and Cultures: A Unified Interpretation of the Structure of Human Experience*, 2nd ed. (Toronto: University of Toronto Press, 2016), chap. 8.
4 Vanderburg, *The Growth of Minds and Cultures*, chap 8.
5 Jacques Ellul, *Si tu es le fils de Dieu* (Paris: Editions du Centurion, 1991).
6 Jacques Ellul, *On Being Rich and Poor: Christianity in a Time of Economic Globalization*, comp., ed., and trans. Willem H. Vanderburg (Toronto: University of Toronto Press, 2014), part 1.
7 Jacques Ellul, *An Unjust God? A Christian Theology of Israel in Light of Romans 9-11*, trans. Anne-Marie Andreasson-Hogg (Eugene, OR: Wipf & Stock, 2012).
8 Jacques Ellul, *Apocalypse: The Book of Revelation*, trans. George W. Schreiner (New York: Seabury, 1977).

9 Ellul, *An Unjust God?*; Ellul, *Apocalypse*.
10 Jacques Ellul, *On Freedom, Love and Power* (expanded ed.), comp., ed., and trans. Willem H. Vanderburg (Toronto: University of Toronto Press, 2015), part 4.
11 Ellul, *Apocalypse*.
12 Willem H. Vanderburg, *Our Battle for the Human Spirit: Scientific Knowing, Technical Doing and Daily Living* (Toronto: University of Toronto Press, 2016).
13 Ellul, *On Being Rich and Poor*, part 1.
14 Ellul, *On Being Rich and Poor*, part 2.
15 Ellul, *On Freedom, Love, and Power*, part 4.
16 Ellul, *On Being Rich and Poor*, part 2.
17 Ellul, *On Freedom, Love, and Power*, part 4.
18 Ellul, *On Being Rich and Poor*, part 2.
19 I continue to rely on Jacque Ellul's exegesis of the previously cited text in James regarding the Christian life.
20 Vanderburg, *The Growth of Minds and Cultures*.
21 Willem H. Vanderburg, *Our War on Ourselves* (Toronto: University of Toronto Press, 2011); Vanderburg, *Our Battle for the Human Spirit*.
22 Jacques Ellul, *The Ethics of Freedom*, trans. Geoffrey W. Bromiley (Grand Rapids, MI: Eerdmans, 1976).
23 Ellul, *On Freedom, Love, and Power*, part 4.
24 Ellul, *Apocalypse*.
25 Vanderburg, *The Growth of Minds and Cultures*; Willem H. Vanderburg, *The Labyrinth of Technology* (Toronto: University of Toronto Press, 2000); Willem H. Vanderburg, *Living in the Labyrinth of Technology* (Toronto: University of Toronto Press, 2005); Vanderburg, *Our War on Ourselves*; Vanderburg, *Our Battle for the Human Spirit*.
26 Jacques Ellul, *Propaganda: The Formation of Men's Attitudes*, trans. Konrad Kellen and Jean Lerner (New York: Vintage, 1965).
27 Vanderburg, *Living in the Labyrinth of Technology*
28 Vanderburg, *Our War on Ourselves*.
29 Vanderburg, *Our Battle for the Human Spirit*.
30 Vanderburg, *Our Battle for the Human Spirit*.
31 Vanderburg, *Our War on Ourselves*.
32 Vanderburg, *Our War on Ourselves*.
33 Vanderburg, *Our Battle for the Human Spirit*.
34 Vanderburg, *Our Battle for the Human Spirit*.
35 Ellul, *On Freedom, Love, and Power*, part 4.
36 Jacques Ellul, *Living Faith: Belief and Doubt in a Perilous World*, trans. Peter Heinegg (San Francisco: Harper & Row, 1983).

37 See Jacques Ellul's discussion of this letter in his *Ethics of Freedom.*
38 Ellul, *The Ethics of Freedom*, 477.
39 Ellul, *On Freedom, Love, and Power*, part 4.
40 Ellul, *Apocalypse.*
41 Ellul, *On Freedom, Love, and Power*, part 3.
42 Ellul, *On Freedom, Love, and Power*, part 3.
43 Ellul, *Apocalypse.*

6 Christianity in the Grip of Vanity and Chasing after the Wind

1 Jacques Ellul, *Reason for Being: A Meditation on Ecclesiastes*, trans. Joyce Main Hanks (Grand Rapids, MI: Eerdmans, 1990). In this work Jacques Ellul gives a convincing explanation of why *Qohelet* was so titled: to reflect its ironic content with a Hebrew name that is a feminine pronoun.
2 Jacques Ellul, *The New Demons*, trans. C. Edward Hopkin (New York: Seabury, 1975). The literal translation of the original French title is "the newly possessed."
3 Frédéric Rognon, *Générations Ellul: Soixante héritiers de la pensée de Jacques Ellul* (Geneva: Labor & Fides, 2012).
4 Willem H. Vanderburg, *Our Battle for the Human Spirit: Scientific Knowing, Technical Doing, and Daily Living* (Toronto: University of Toronto Press, 2016).
5 Ellul, *Reason for Being.*
6 Ellul, *Reason for Being.*
7 Ellul, *Reason for Being.*
8 Ellul, *Reason for Being.*
9 Willem H. Vanderburg, *The Growth of Minds and Cultures: A Unified Interpretation of the Structure of Human Experience*, 2nd ed. (Toronto: University of Toronto Press, 2016).
10 Vanderburg, *The Growth of Minds and Cultures.*
11 Ellul, *Reason for Being.*
12 Ellul, *Reason for Being.*
13 Jacques Ellul, *On Freedom, Love, and Power*, expanded edition, comp., ed., and trans. Willem H. Vanderburg (Toronto: University of Toronto Press, 2015), part 2.
14 Ellul, *On Freedom, Love, and Power*, part 2.
15 Ellul, *On Freedom, Love, and Power*, part 2.
16 Willem H. Vanderburg, *Our War on Ourselves: Rethinking Science, Technology, and Economic Growth* (Toronto: University of Toronto Press, 2011).

17 Willem H. Vanderburg, *Living in the Labyrinth of Technology* (Toronto: University of Toronto Press, 2005).
18 Vanderburg, *Living in the Labyrinth of Technology*.
19 Vanderburg, *Living in the Labyrinth of Technology*.
20 Vanderburg, *Living in the Labyrinth of Technology*.
21 Vanderburg, *Living in the Labyrinth of Technology*.
22 Vanderburg, *Living in the Labyrinth of Technology*.
23 Vanderburg, *Our War on Ourselves*; Vanderburg, *Our Battle for the Human Spirit*.
24 Ibid.
25 Jacques Ellul, *The Technological Society*, trans. John Wilkinson (New York: A.A. Knopf, 1964).
26 Jacques Ellul, *On Being Rich and Poor: Christianity in a Time of Economic Globalization*, comp., ed., and trans. Willem H. Vanderburg (Toronto: University of Toronto Press, 2014), part 1.
27 Ellul, *On Being Rich and Poor*, part 1.
28 In this context, the voice of Jacques Ellul after the Second World War was truly prophetic in warning us of almost all the major difficulties that humanity was beginning to encounter as a consequence of the unfolding of the course of events.
29 Willem H. Vanderburg, *The Labyrinth of Technology* (Toronto: University of Toronto Press, 2000).
30 Vanderburg, *Our War on Ourselves*.
31 Vanderburg, *Living in the Labyrinth of Technology*, part 2.
32 Vanderburg, *Living in the Labyrinth of Technology*, part 2.
33 Vanderburg, *Living in the Labyrinth of Technology*, part 2.
34 Vanderburg, *Living in the Labyrinth of Technology*, part 2, chap. 7.
35 Vanderburg, *Our War on Ourselves*.
36 Ellul, *The New Demons*; Richard Stivers, *Evil in Modern Myth and Ritual* (Athens: University of Georgia Press, 1982).
37 Ellul, *The Technological Society*.
38 Vanderburg, *Our Battle for the Human Spirit*.
39 Vanderburg, *Our Battle for the Human Spirit*.
40 Vanderburg, *Our War on Ourselves*.
41 Jacques Ellul, *L'Empire du non-sens: L'art et la société technicienne* (Paris: Presses Universitaires de France, 1980). For a further elaboration see Vanderburg, *Living in the Labyrinth of Technology*.
42 Vanderburg, *Our War on Ourselves*; Vanderburg, *Our Battle for the Human Spirit*.
43 Ellul, *The New Demons*.

44 Vanderburg, *Living in the Labyrinth of Technology*.
45 Vanderburg, *Living in the Labyrinth of Technology*.
46 Vanderburg, *Living in the Labyrinth of Technology*.
47 Vanderburg, *Our War on Ourselves*.
48 Vanderburg, *Our War on Ourselves*.
49 Ellul, *Reason for Being*.
50 Bernard Litaer, *The Future of Money: A New Way to Create Wealth, Work, and a Wiser World* (New York: Random House, 2001).
51 Stivers, *Evil in Modern Myth and Ritual*.
52 Ellul, *The New Demons*.
53 Vanderburg, *The Growth of Minds and Cultures*.
54 Jennifer Chandler, "The Autonomy of Technology: Do Courts Control Technology or Do They Just Legitimize Its Social Acceptance?" *Bulletin of Science, Technology and Society* 27, no. 5 (Oct. 2007): 339–48.
55 Chandler, "The Autonomy of Technology."
56 M. McCloskey, "Intuitive Physics," *Scientific American* 248 (April 1983): 122–30.
57 W. Heisenberg, *Physics and Beyond: Encounters and Conversations* (New York: Harper & Row, 1971), 63; P.A. Schilp, ed., "Autobiographical Note," in *Albert Einstein: Philosopher-Scientist* (Evanston, IL: Library of Living Philosophers, 1949), 63.
58 See especially Vanderburg, *The Growth of Minds and Cultures*; Vanderburg, *Our War on Ourselves*; Vanderburg, *Our Battle for the Human Spirit*.
59 Ibid.
60 Ibid.
61 Jeremy Campbell, *The Improbable Machine: What the Upheavals in Artificial Intelligence Research Reveal about How the Mind Really Works* (New York: Simon & Schuster, 1989).
62 Vanderburg, *Our War on Ourselves*.
63 Vanderburg, *Our War on Ourselves*.
64 Vanderburg, *The Labyrinth of Technology*.
65 Vanderburg, *Our Battle for the Human Spirit*.
66 Vanderburg, *Our War on Ourselves*.
67 Thomas S. Kuhn, *The Structure of Scientific Revolutions*, 2nd ed. (Chicago: University of Chicago Press, 1970).
68 Vanderburg, *Our Battle for the Human Spirit*.
69 Ellul, *Reason for Being*.
70 Ellul, *Reason for Being*.
71 Ellul, *Reason for Being*.
72 Ellul, *Reason for Being*.

73 Jacques Ellul, *Histoire des institutions: L'Antiquité* (Paris: Presses Universitaires de France, 1961).
74 Ellul, *On Being Rich and Poor*, part 2.
75 Ellul, *Reason for Being*, 31.
76 Jacques Ellul, *The Humiliation of the Word*, trans. Joyce Main Hanks (Grand Rapids, MI: Eerdmans, 1985).
77 Ellul, *The Humiliation of the Word.*
78 Ellul, *The Humiliation of the Word.*
79 Vanderburg, *Our Battle for the Human Spirit.*
80 Vanderburg, *Our Battle for the Human Spirit.*
81 Vanderburg, *Our Battle for the Human Spirit.*
82 Ellul, *The New Demons*; Stivers, *Evil in Modern Myth and Ritual.*
83 Ellul, *The New Demons*; Stivers, *Evil in Modern Myth and Ritual.*
84 Kevin M. Kruse, *One Nation under God: How Corporate America Invented Christian America* (New York, Basic Books, 2015); Will Herberg, *Protestant, Catholic, Jew: An Essay in American Religious Sociology* (Garden City, NY: Anchor Books, Doubleday, 1960).
85 Vanderburg, *Our Battle for the Human Spirit.*
86 Ellul, *On Freedom, Love, and Power*, part 4.
87 Vanderburg, *Our Battle for the Human Spirit.*
88 Ellul, *Reason for Being.*
89 Jacques Ellul, *Apocalypse: The Book of Revelation*, trans. George W. Schreiner (New York: Seabury, 1977).
90 Ellul, *On Freedom, Love, and Power*, part 1.
91 Ellul, *Reason for Being.*

Epilogue

1 Willem H. Vanderburg, *Our Battle for the Human Spirit: Scientific Knowing, Technical Doing, and Daily Living* (Toronto: University of Toronto Press, 2016).
2 Jacques Ellul, *The New Demons*, trans. C. Edward Hopkin (New York: Seabury, 1975).
3 Jacques Ellul, *La pensée marxiste*, comp. and ed. Michel Hourcade, Jean-Pierre Jézéquel, and Gérard Paul (Paris: La Table Ronde, 2003); Ellul, *The New Demons.*
4 Jacques Ellul, *On Freedom, Love, Power*, expanded edition, comp., ed., and trans. Willem H. Vanderburg (Toronto: University of Toronto Press, 2015), part 1.
5 Ellul, *On Freedom, Love, Power*, part 1.

6 Willem H. Vanderburg, *Our War on Ourselves: Rethinking Science, Technology, and Economic Growth* (Toronto: University of Toronto Press, 2011).
7 Vanderburg, *Our War on Ourselves.*
8 Jacques Ellul, *The Humiliation of the Word,* trans. Joyce Main Hanks (Grand Rapids, MI: Eerdmans, 1985).
9 Ellul, *The Humiliation of the Word.*
10 Frédéric Rognon, *Générations Ellul: Soixante héritiers de la pensée de Jacques Ellul* (Geneva: Labor & Fides, 2012).
11 Willem H. Vanderburg, ed., *Perspectives on Our Age: Jacques Ellul Speaks on His Life and Work,* 2nd ed. (Toronto: Anansi, 2004).
12 Jacques Ellul, *The Technological Society,* trans. John Wilkinson (New York: A.A. Knopf, 1964).
13 Jacques Ellul, *The Presence of the Kingdom,* trans. Olive Wyon (New York: Seabury, 1967).
14 Willem H. Vanderburg, *The Growth of Minds and Cultures: A Unified Interpretation of the Structure of Human Experience,* 2nd ed. (Toronto: University of Toronto Press, 2016).
15 Jacques Ellul, *The Technological System,* trans. Joachim Neugroschel (New York: Continuum, 1980).
16 Vanderburg, *Our War on Ourselves*; Vanderburg, *Our Battle for the Human Spirit.*
17 Jacques Ellul, *Propaganda: The Formation of Men's Attitudes,* trans. Konrad Kellen and Jean Lerner (New York: Vintage, 1965).
18 Jacques Ellul, *The Political Illlusion,* trans. Konrad Kellen (New York: Knopf, 1967).
19 Ellul, *The New Demons.*
20 Vanderburg, *Our Battle for the Human Spirit.*
21 Ellul, *The Humiliation of the Word;* Jacques Ellul, *False Presence of the Kingdom,* trans. C. Edward Hopkin (New York: Seabury, 1972).
22 Jacques Ellul, *Reason for Being: A Meditation on Ecclesiastes,* trans. Joyce Main Hanks (Grand Rapids, MI: Eerdmans, 1990), preface.
23 Jacques Ellul, *Money and Power,* trans. LaVonne Neff (Downers Grove, IL: Inter-Varsity Press, 1984); Jacques Ellul, *The Meaning of the City,* trans. Dennis Pardee (Grand Rapids, MI: Eerdmans, 1970); Jacques Ellul, *Apocalypse: The Book of Revelation,* trans. George W. Schreiner (New York: Seabury, 1977).
24 Ellul, *Apocalypse.*
25 Jacques Ellul, *On Being Rich and Poor: Christianity in a Time of Economic Globalization,* comp., ed., and trans. Willem H. Vanderburg (Toronto: University of Toronto Press, 2014), part 2.

26 Vanderburg, *Our War on Ourselves*, chap. 2.
27 Willem H. Vanderburg, *Living in the Labyrinth of Technology* (Toronto: University of Toronto Press, 2005).

Index

www.ingramcontent.com/pod-product-compliance
Lightning Source LLC
LaVergne TN
LVHW090759070826
844660LV00022B/1030

* 9 7 8 1 4 8 7 5 2 3 0 3 9 *